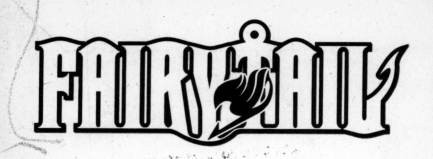

10

Hiro Mashima

Translated and adapted by William Flanagan
Lettered by North Market Street Graphics

Ballantine Books · New York

A Del Rey Manga/Kodansha Trade Paperback Original

Fairy Tail volume 10 copyright © 2008 Hiro Mashima
English translation copyright © 2010 Hiro Mashima

Published in the United States by Del Rey, an imprint of The Random House Publishing Group, a division of Random House, Inc., New York.

DEL REY is a registered trademark and the Del Rey colophon is a trademark of Random House, Inc.

Publication rights arranged through Kodansha Ltd.

First published in Japan in 2008 by Kodansha Ltd., Tokyo

ISBN 978-0-345-51457-8

Printed in the United States of America

www.delreymanga.com

9   8   7   6   5   4   3

Translator/Adapter: William Flanagan
Lettering: North Market Street Graphics

Contents

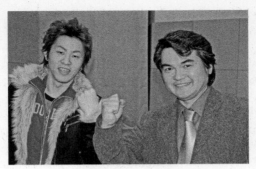

With Kase-sensei!

Weekly Shônen Magazine is celebrating its fiftieth birthday!!! And as part of the festivities, I get to draw a manga that is a tribute to Kase-sensei's manga, *Chameleon*. This is a picture of when I conferred with him. I think it's pretty incredible to be able to be in the same photo as a manga-ka that I've admired ever since my student days! And that thought was keenly felt throughout the entire interview. Even so, Kase-sensei is a fun guy! But that's only natural since the most interesting manga come from interesting people, huh?

—Hiro Mashima

Honorifics Explained

Throughout the Del Rey Manga books, you will find Japanese honorifics left intact in the translations. For those not familiar with how the Japanese use honorifics and, more important, how they differ from American honorifics, we present this brief overview.

Politeness has always been a critical facet of Japanese culture. Ever since the feudal era, when Japan was a highly stratified society, use of honorifics—which can be defined as polite speech that indicates relationship or status—has played an essential role in the Japanese language. When addressing someone in Japanese, an honorific usually takes the form of a suffix attached to one's name (example: "Asuna-san"), is used as a title at the end of one's name, or appears in place of the name itself (example: "Negi-sensei," or simply "Sensei").

Honorifics can be expressions of respect or endearment. In the context of manga and anime, honorifics give insight into the nature of the relationship between characters. Many English translations leave out these important honorifics and therefore distort the feel of the original Japanese. Because Japanese honorifics contain nuances that English honorifics lack, it is our policy at Del Rey not to translate them. Here, instead, is a guide to some of the honorifics you may encounter in Del Rey Manga.

-**san**: This is the most common honorific and is equivalent to Mr., Miss, Ms., or Mrs. It is the all-purpose honorific and can be used in any situation where politeness is required.

-**sama**: This is one level higher than "-san" and is used to confer great respect.

-**dono**: This comes from the word "tono," which means "lord." It is an even higher level than "-sama" and confers utmost respect.

-kun: This suffix is used at the end of boys' names to express familiarity or endearment. It is also sometimes used by men among friends, or when addressing someone younger or of a lower station.

-chan: This is used to express endearment, mostly toward girls. It is also used for little boys, pets, and even between lovers. It gives a sense of childish cuteness.

Bozu: This is an informal way to refer to a boy, similar to the English terms "kid" and "squirt."

Sempai/ Senpai: This title suggests that the addressee is one's senior in a group or organization. It is most often used in a school setting, where underclassmen refer to their upperclassmen as "sempai." It can also be used in the workplace, such as when a newer employee addresses an employee who has seniority in the company.

Kohai: This is the opposite of "sempai" and is used toward underclassmen in school or newcomers in the workplace. It connotes that the addressee is of a lower station.

Sensei: Literally meaning "one who has come before," this title is used for teachers, doctors, or masters of any profession or art.

-[blank]: This is usually forgotten in these lists, but it is perhaps the most significant difference between Japanese and English. The lack of honorific means that the speaker has permission to address the person in a very intimate way. Usually, only family, spouses, or very close friends have this kind of permission. Known as *yobisute*, it can be gratifying when someone who has earned the intimacy starts to call one by one's name without an honorific. But when that intimacy hasn't been earned, it can be very insulting.

FAIRY TAIL

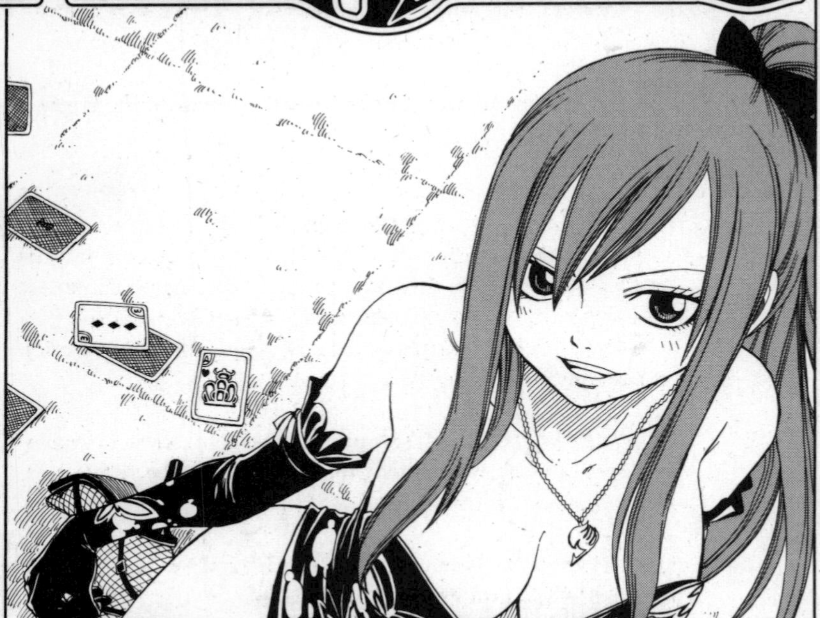

10

HIRO MASHIMA

Listen up, guys! This is the table of contents for *Fairy Tail 10!*

FAIRY TAIL

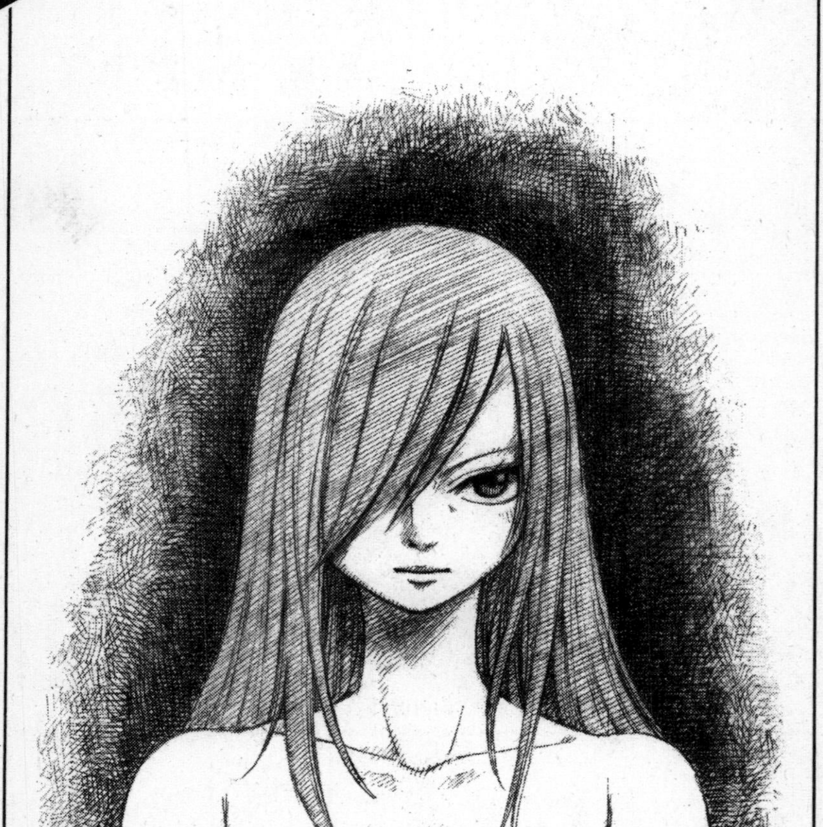

Chapter 75:
Dream of a Butterfly

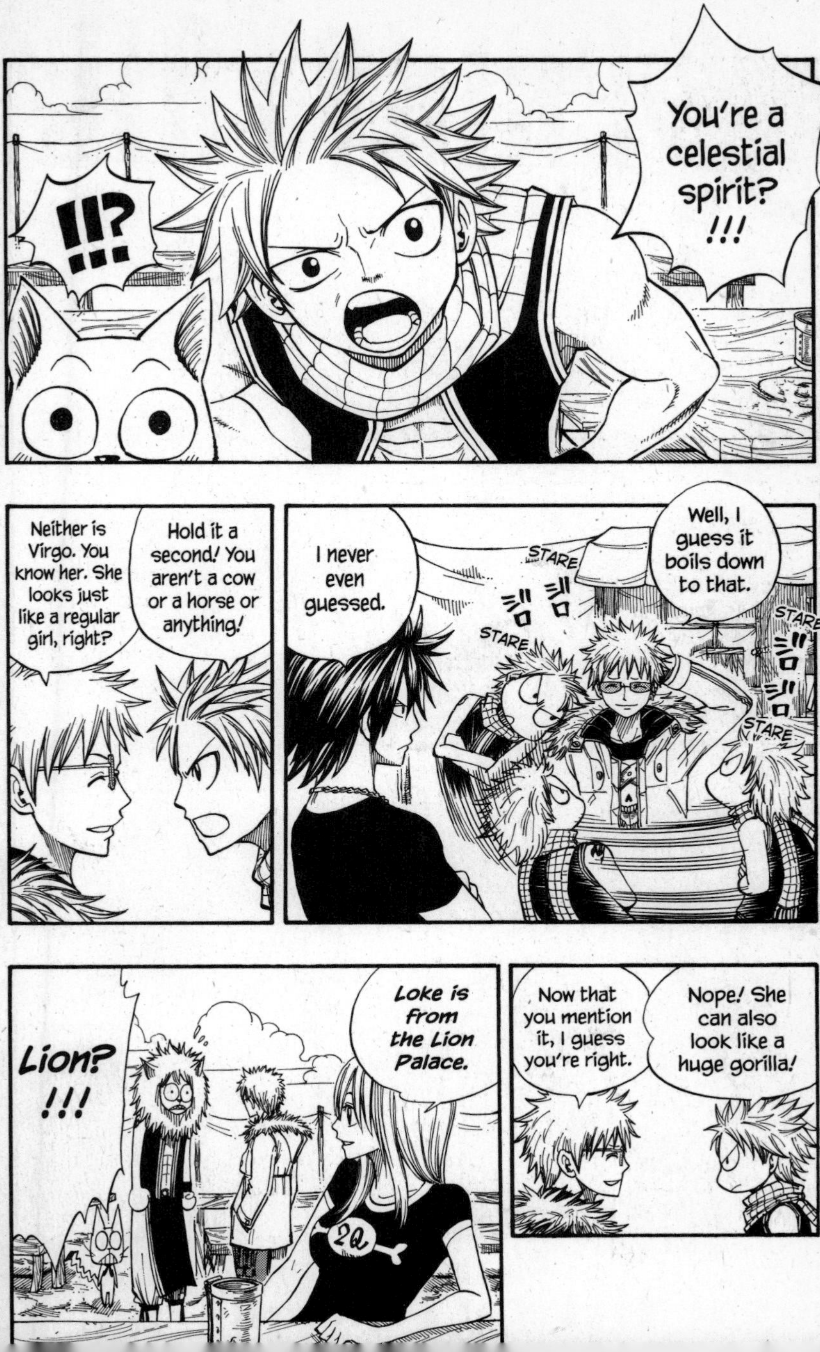
You're a celestial spirit? !!!
!!?
Well, I guess it boils down to that.
STARE
ジロ
STARE
ジロ
STARE
ジロ
STARE
ジロ
I never even guessed.
Hold it a second! You aren't a cow or a horse or anything!
Neither is Virgo. You know her. She looks just like a regular girl, right?
Nope! She can also look like a huge gorilla!
Now that you mention it, I guess you're right.
Loke is from the Lion Palace.
Lion? !!!

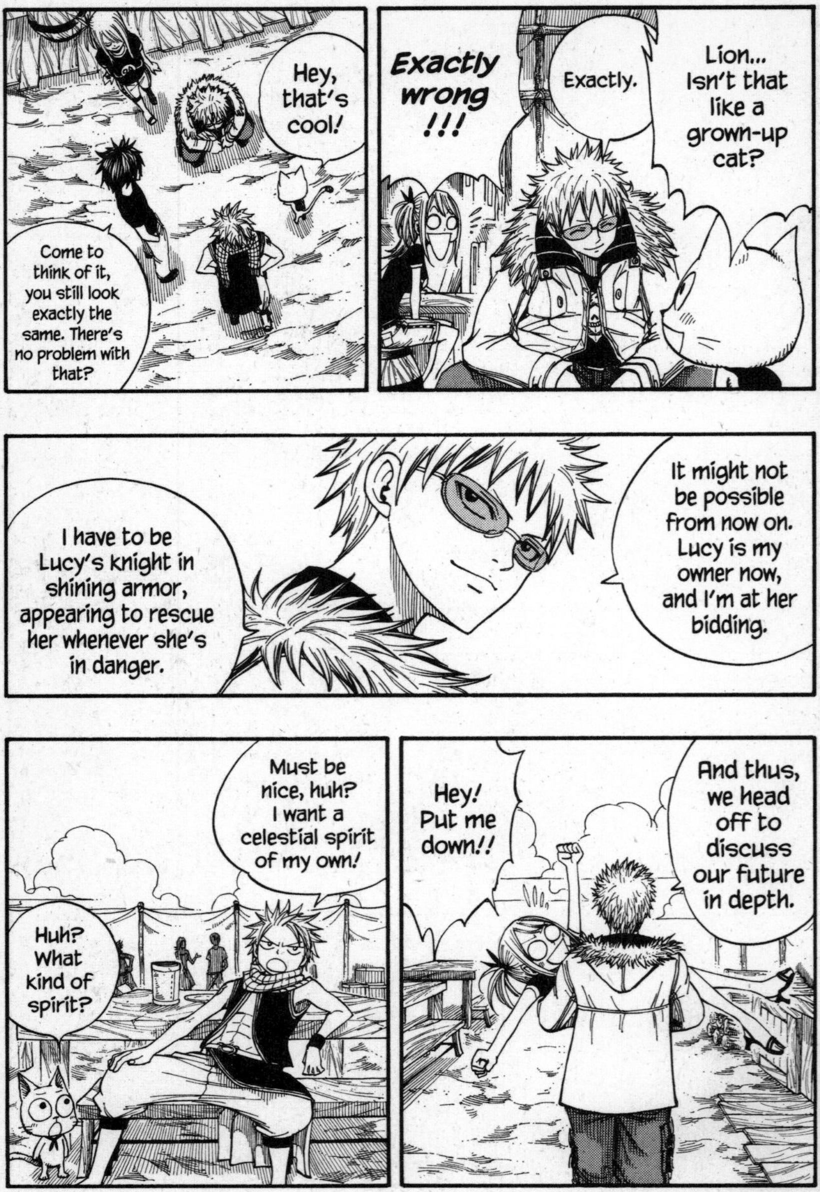
Lion... Isn't that like a grown-up cat?
Exactly.
Exactly wrong!!!
Hey, that's cool!
Come to think of it, you still look exactly the same. There's no problem with that?
It might not be possible from now on. Lucy is my owner now, and I'm at her bidding.
I have to be Lucy's knight in shining armor, appearing to rescue her whenever she's in danger.
And thus, we head off to discuss our future in depth.
Hey! Put me down!!
Must be nice, huh? I want a celestial spirit of my own!
Huh? What kind of spirit?

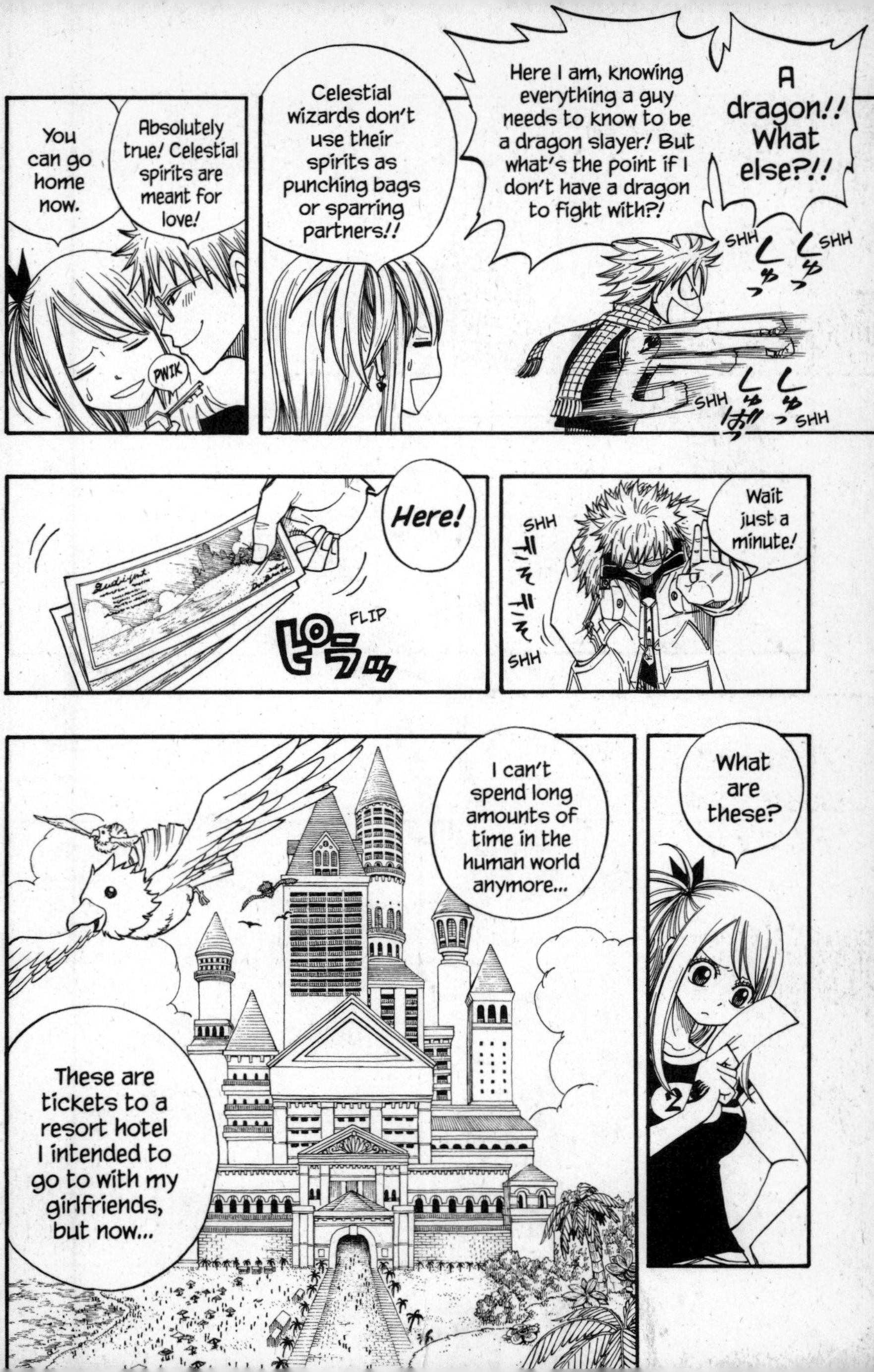
A dragon!! What else?!!
Here I am, knowing everything a guy needs to know to be a dragon slayer! But what's the point if I don't have a dragon to fight with?!
SHH
SHH
SHH
SHH
Celestial wizards don't use their spirits as punching bags or sparring partners!!
Absolutely true! Celestial spirits are meant for love!
You can go home now.
PWIK
Wait just a minute!
SHH
SHH
Here!
FLIP
What are these?
I can't spend long amounts of time in the human world anymore...
These are tickets to a resort hotel I intended to go to with my girlfriends, but now...

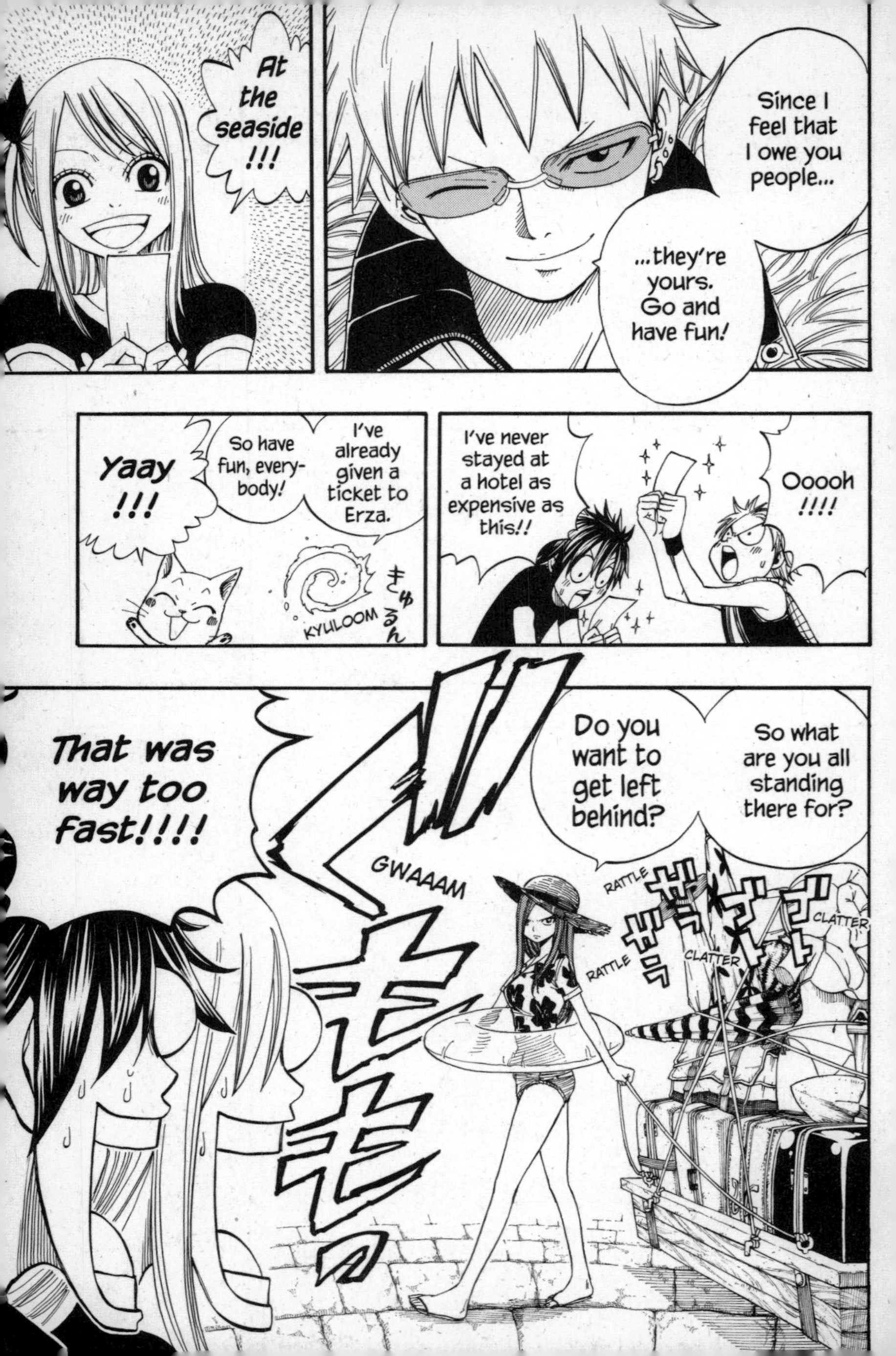
Since I feel that I owe you people...
...they're yours. Go and have fun!
At the seaside!!!
Ooooh!!!!
I've never stayed at a hotel as expensive as this!!
I've already given a ticket to Erza.
So have fun, everybody!
Yaay!!!
KYULOOM
きゅるん
So what are you all standing there for?
Do you want to get left behind?
RATTLE
CLATTER
CLATTER
RATTLE
GWAAAM
That was way too fast!!!!

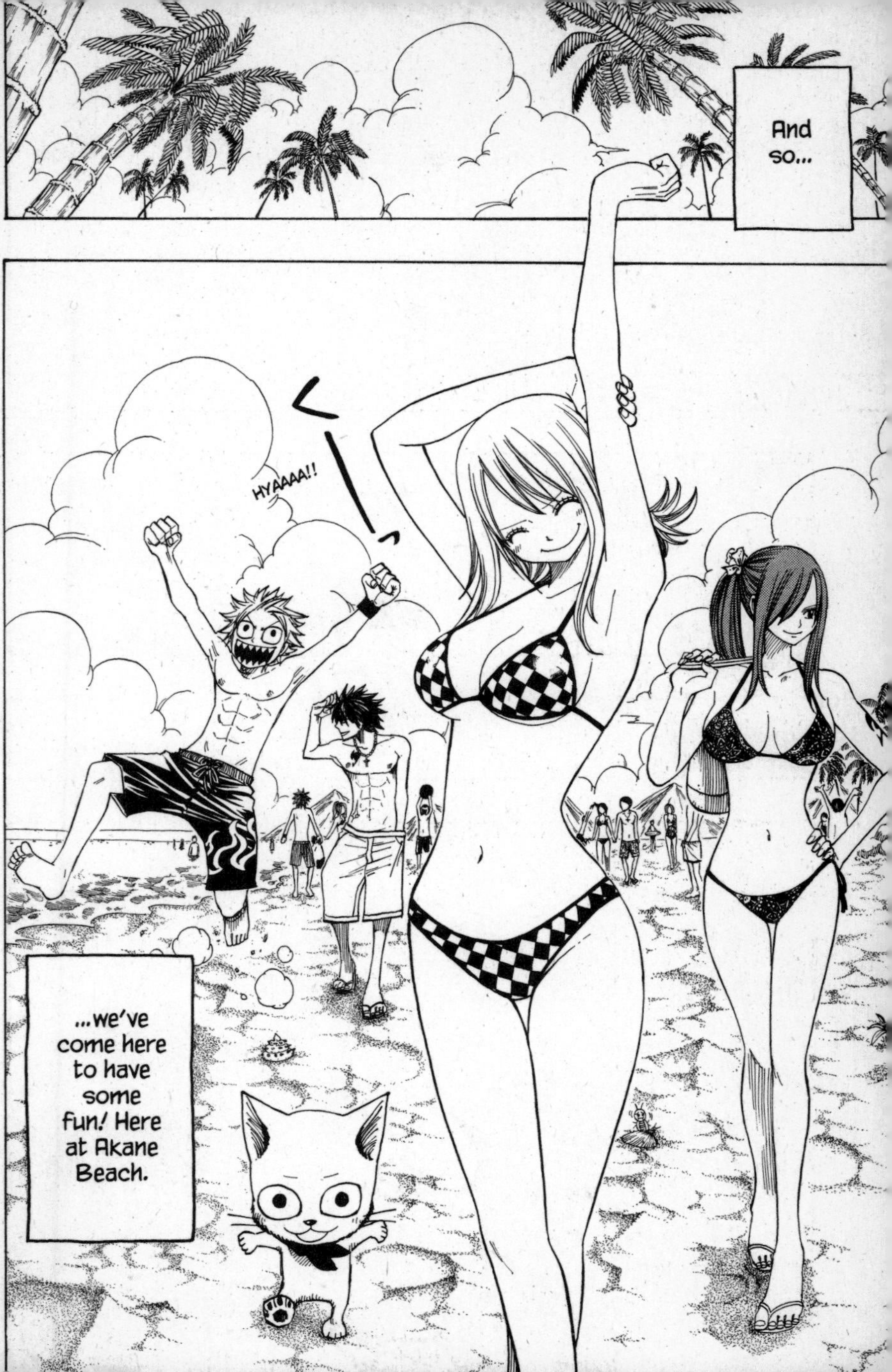
And so...
HYAAAA!!
...we've come here to have some fun! Here at Akane Beach.

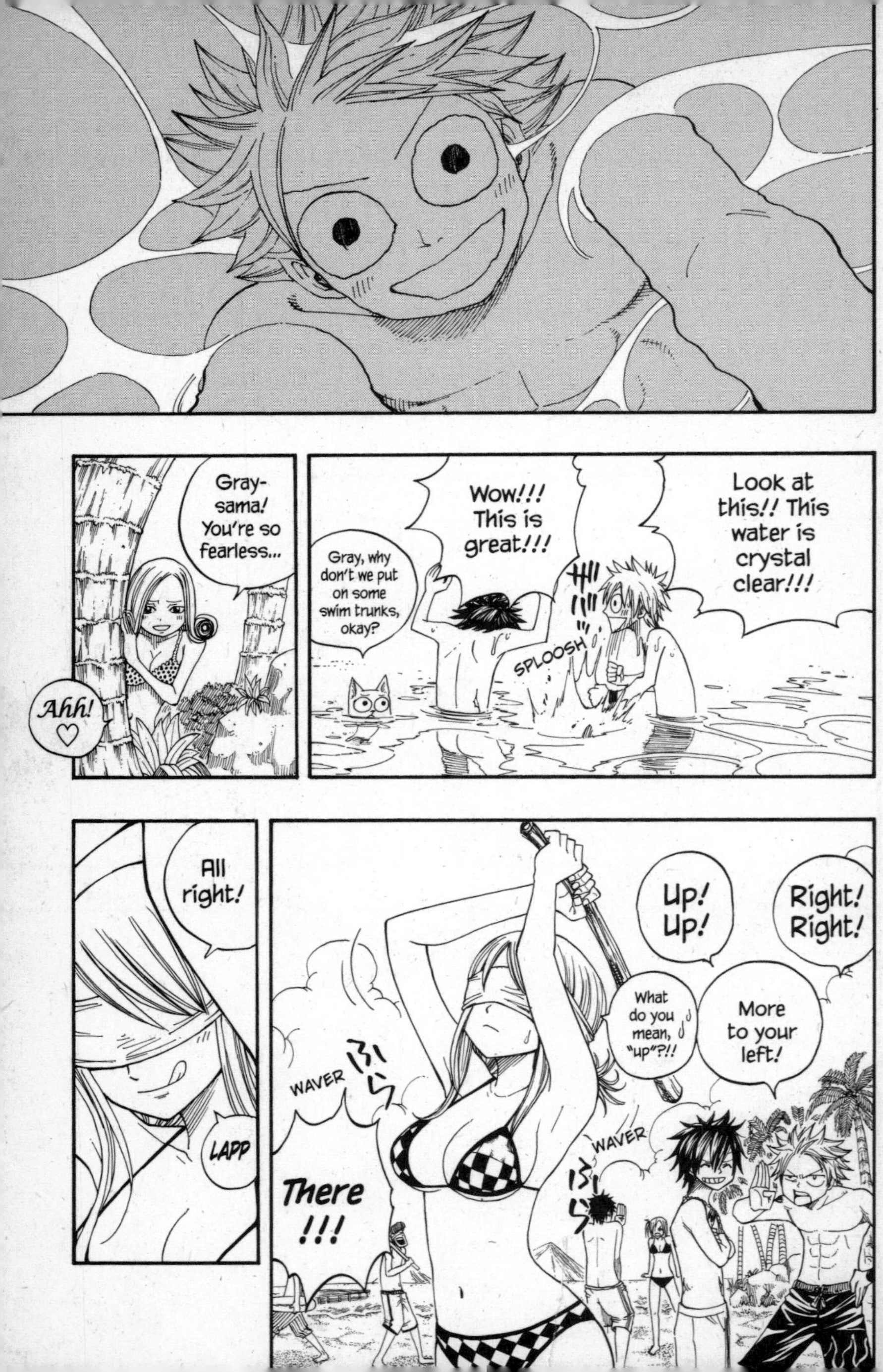
Look at this!! This water is crystal clear!!!
Wow!!! This is great!!!
Gray, why don't we put on some swim trunks, okay?
SPLOOSH
Gray-sama! You're so fearless...
Ahh! ♡
Right! Right!
Up! Up!
More to your left!
What do you mean, "up"?!!
WAVER
WAVER
There !!!
All right!
LAPP

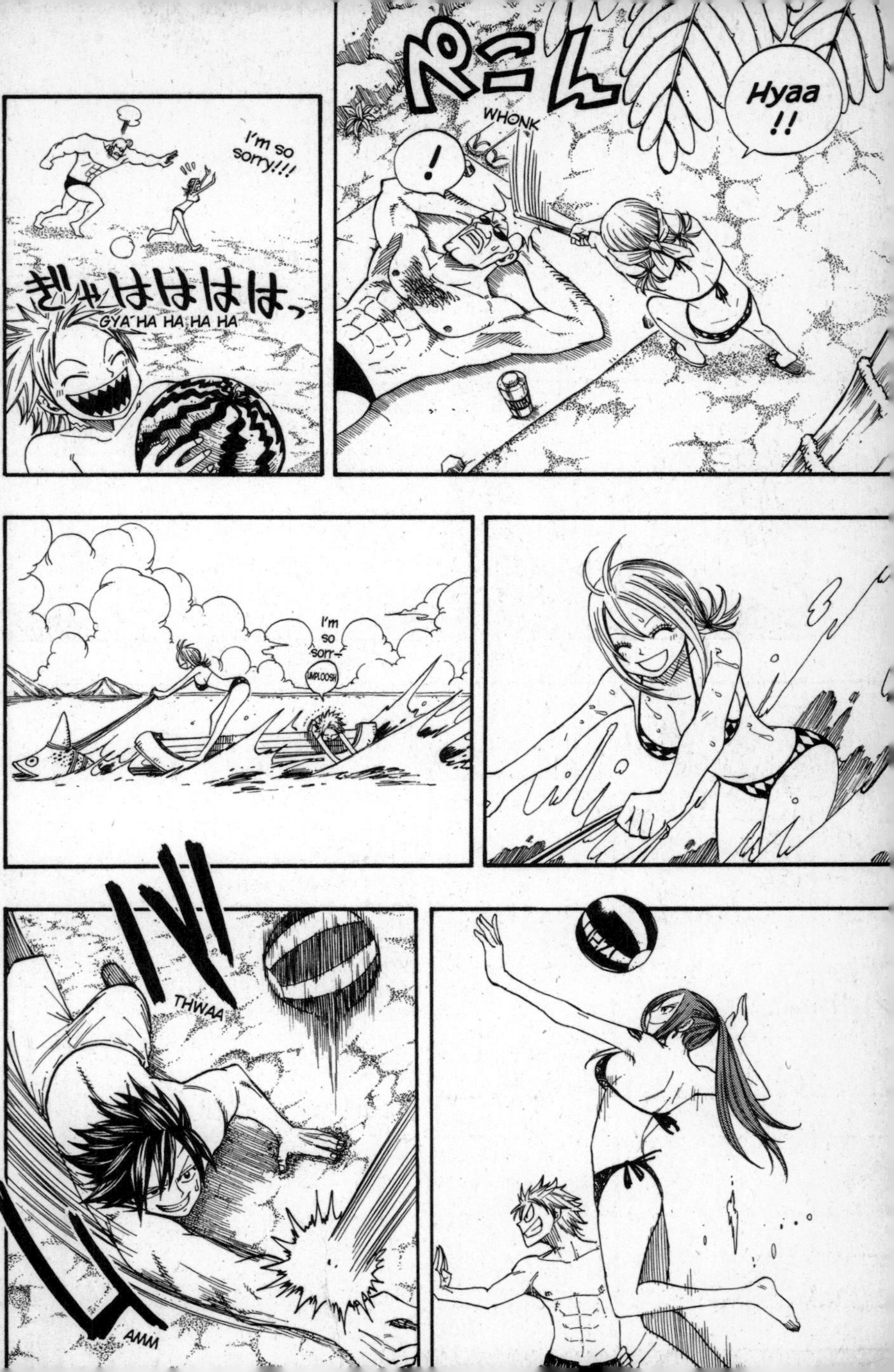

ぺこん
WHONK
!
Hyaa !!
I'm so sorry!!!
ぎゃははははっ
GYA HA HA HA HA
I'm so sorr—
UMPLOOSH
THWAA
AMM

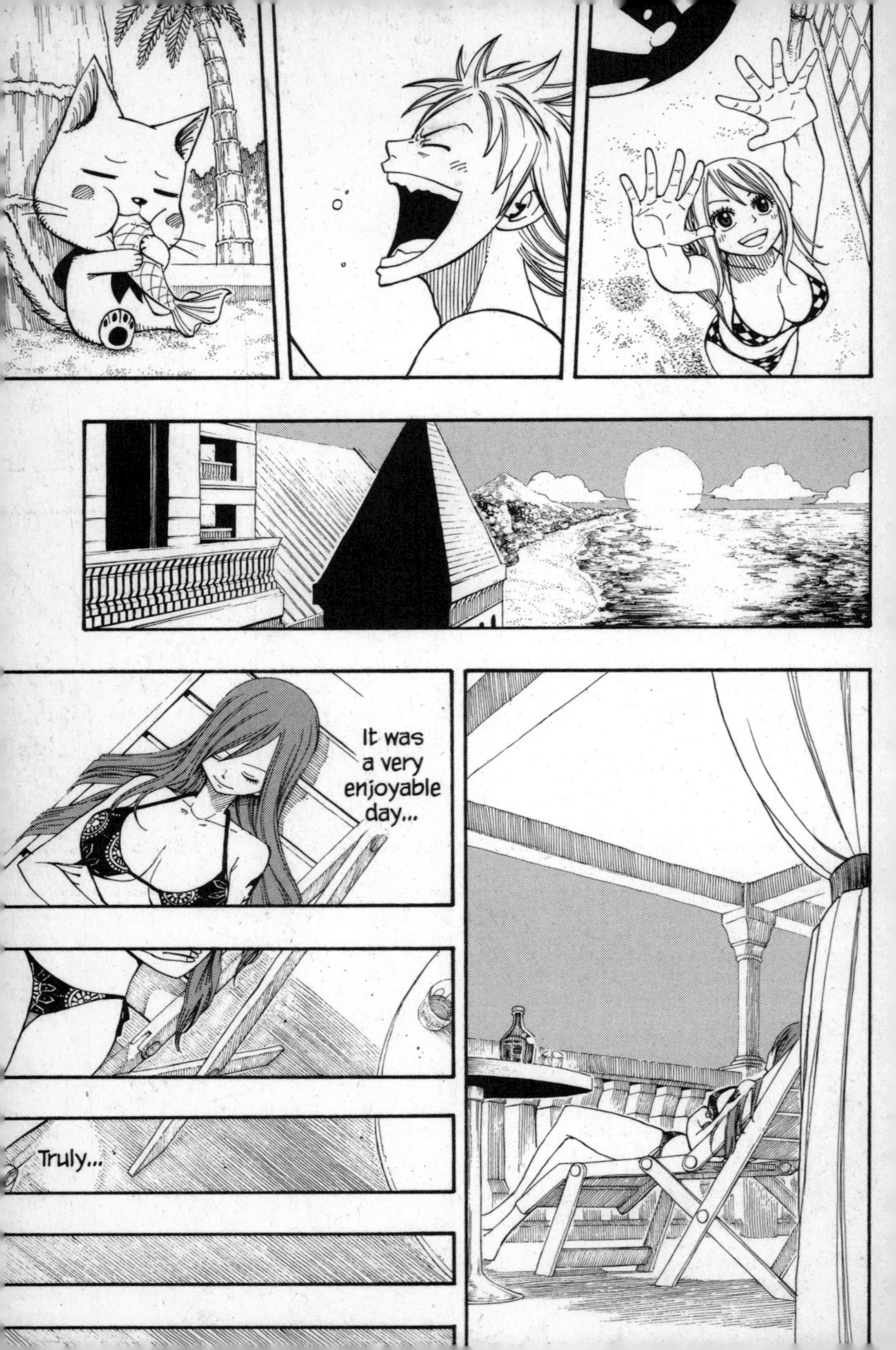
It was a very enjoyable day...
Truly...

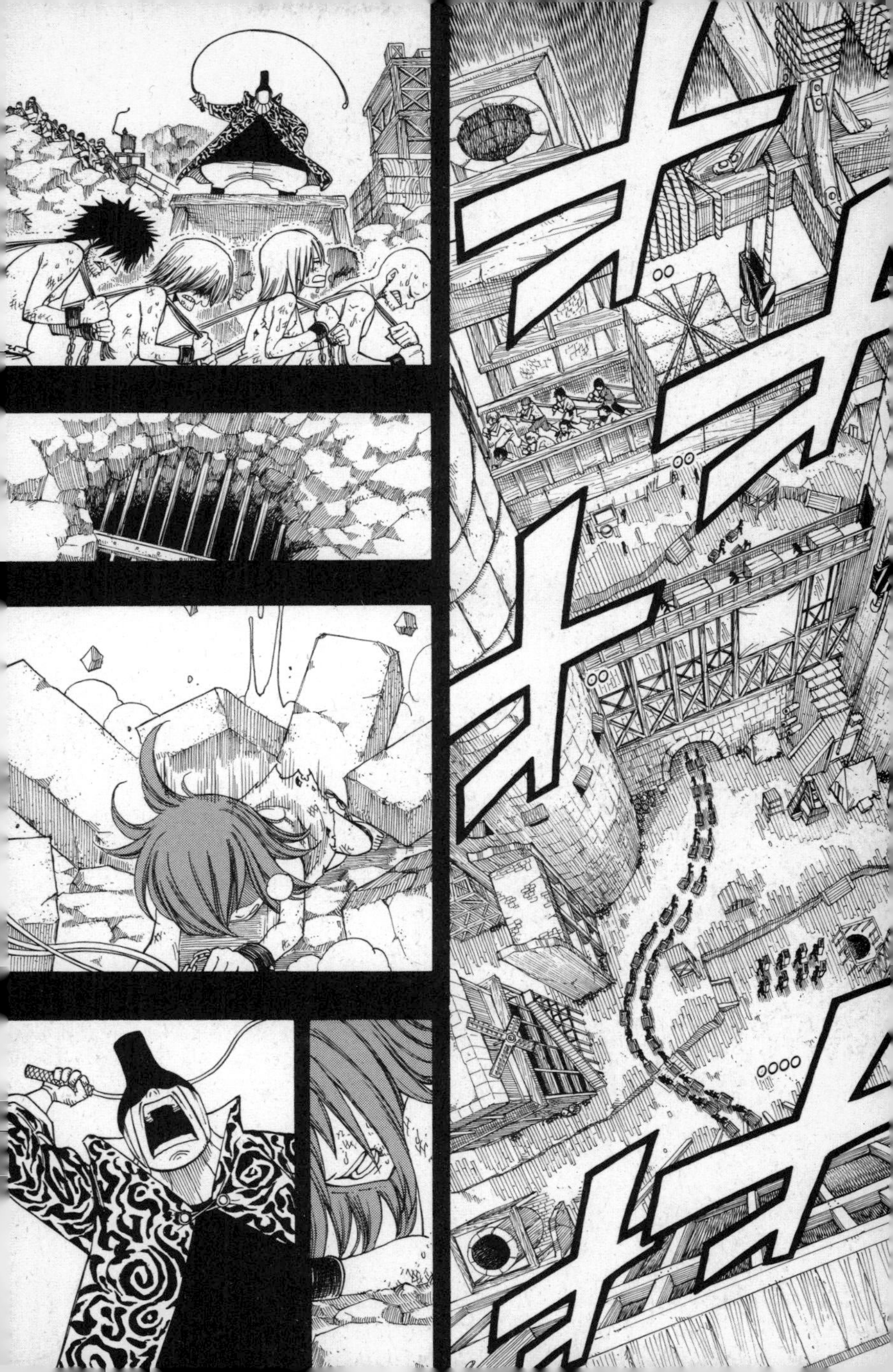

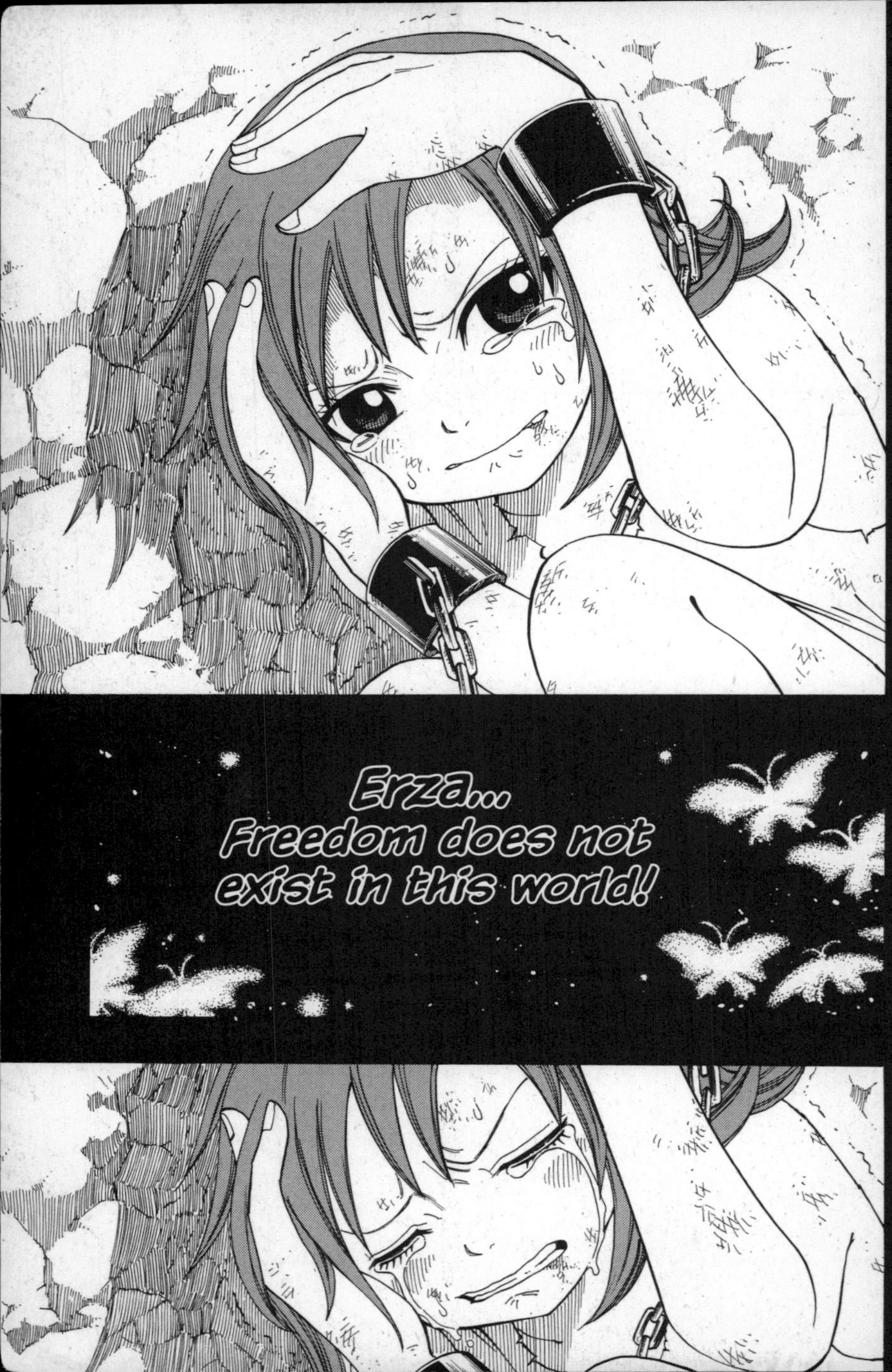
Erza... Freedom does not exist in this world!

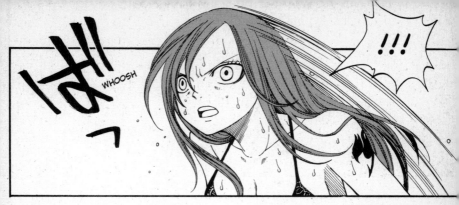

WHOOSH

!!!

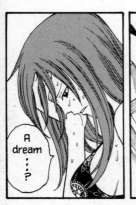

A dream ...?

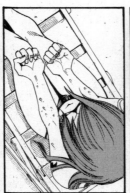

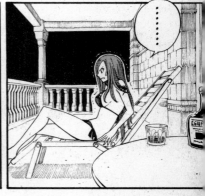

....

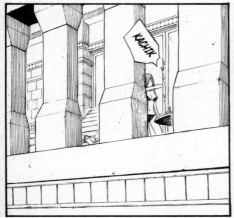

KACHIK

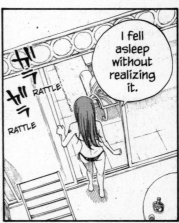

RATTLE

RATTLE

I fell asleep without realizing it.

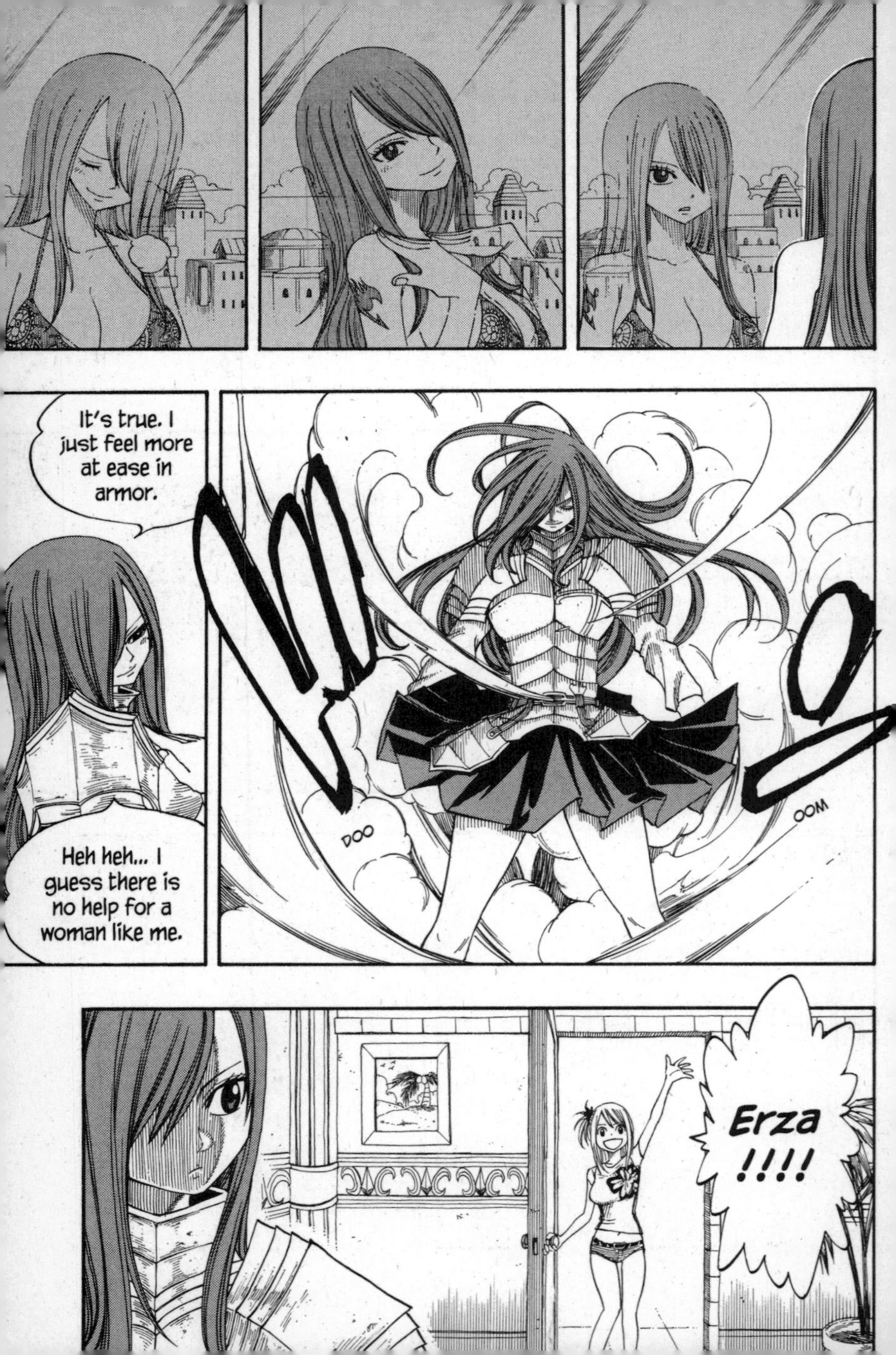
DOO
OOM
It's true. I just feel more at ease in armor.
Heh heh... I guess there is no help for a woman like me.
Erza !!!!

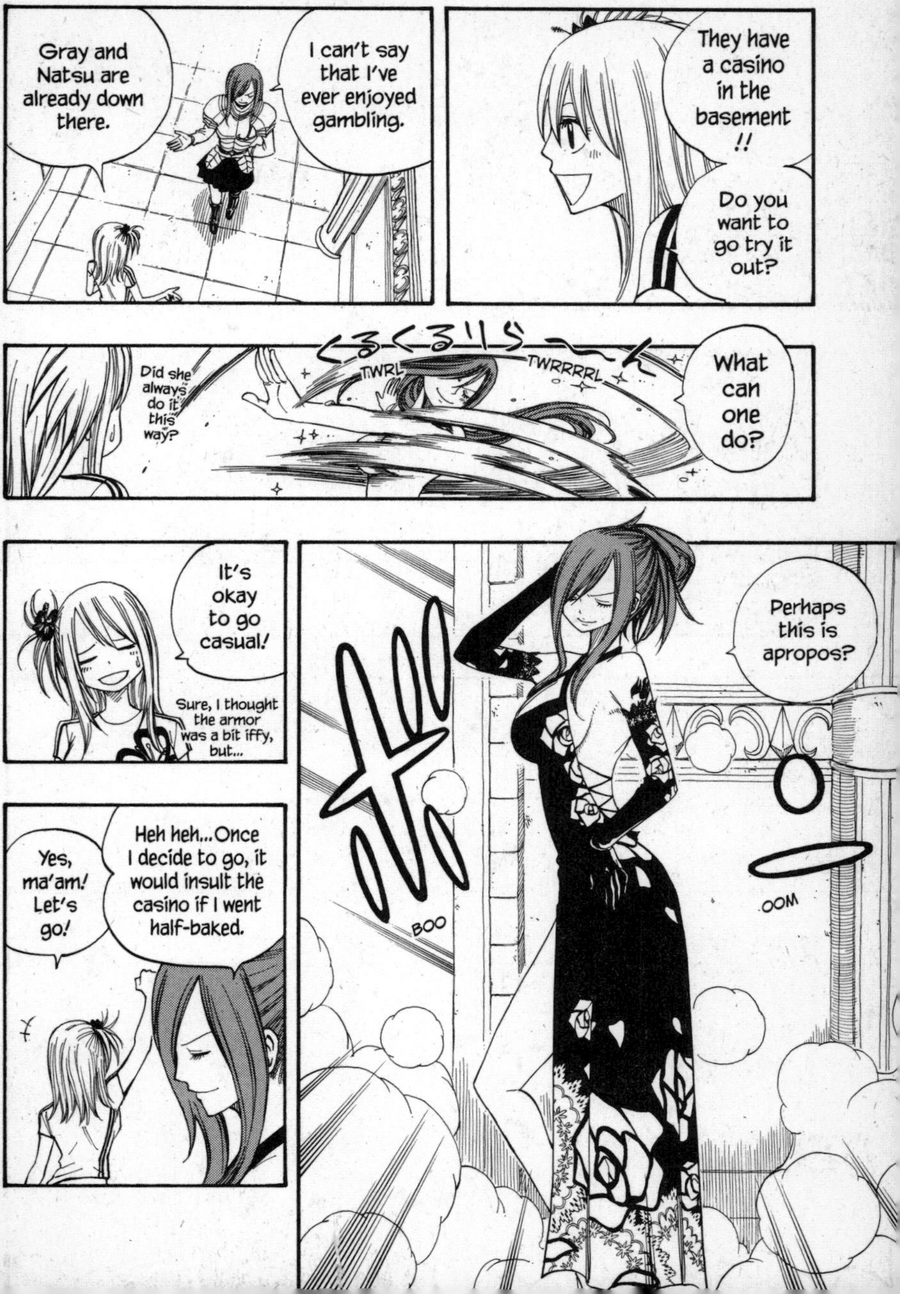
They have a casino in the basement!!
Do you want to go try it out?
I can't say that I've ever enjoyed gambling.
Gray and Natsu are already down there.
What can one do?
くるくるりら～～ん
TWRRRRL
TWRL
Did she always do it this way?
Perhaps this is apropos?
BOO
OOM
It's okay to go casual!
Sure, I thought the armor was a bit iffy, but...
Heh heh...Once I decide to go, it would insult the casino if I went half-baked.
Yes, ma'am! Let's go!

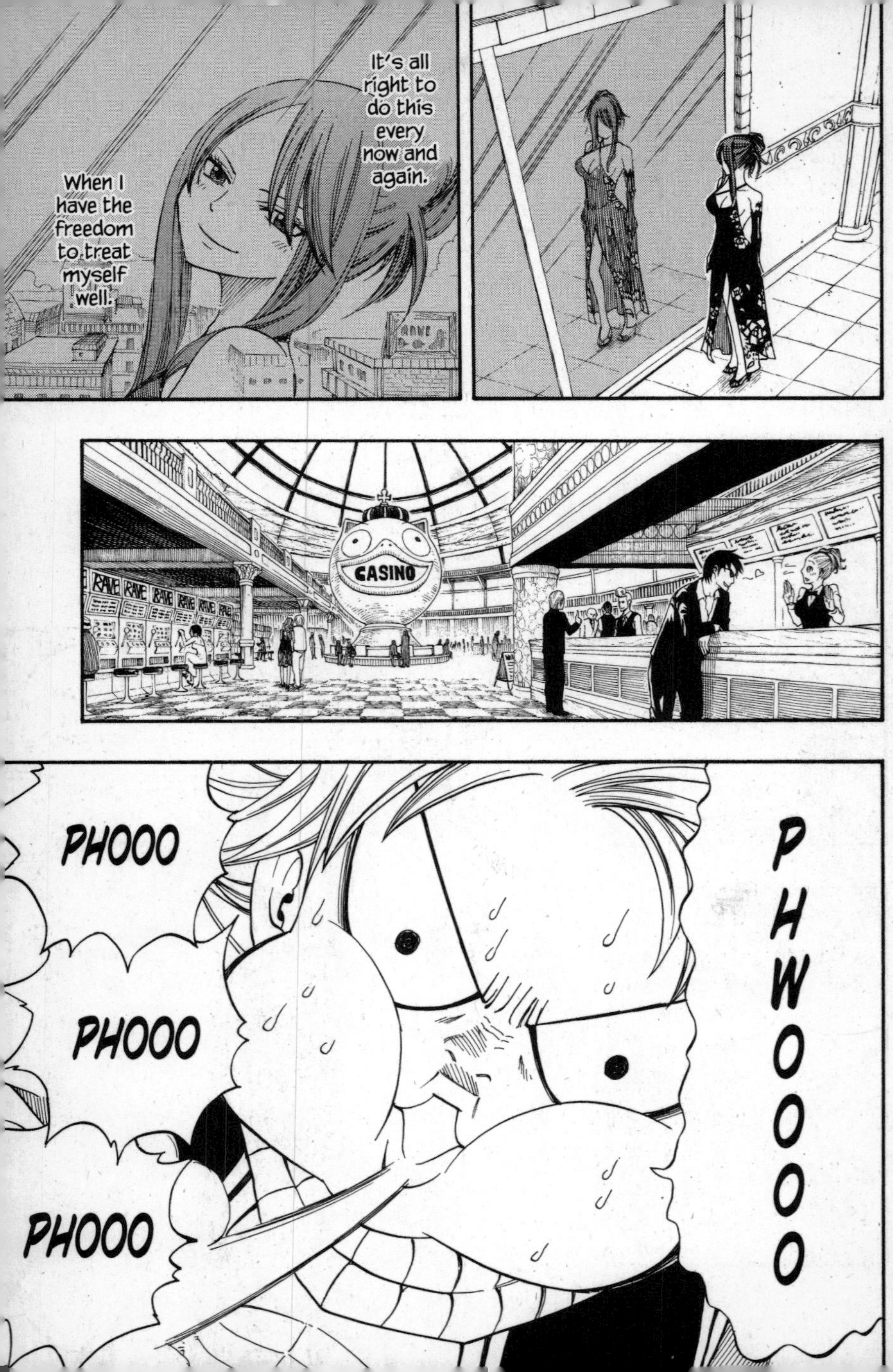
It's all right to do this every now and again.
When I have the freedom to treat myself well.
CASINO
RAVE
PHWOOOOO
PHOOO
PHOOO
PHOOO

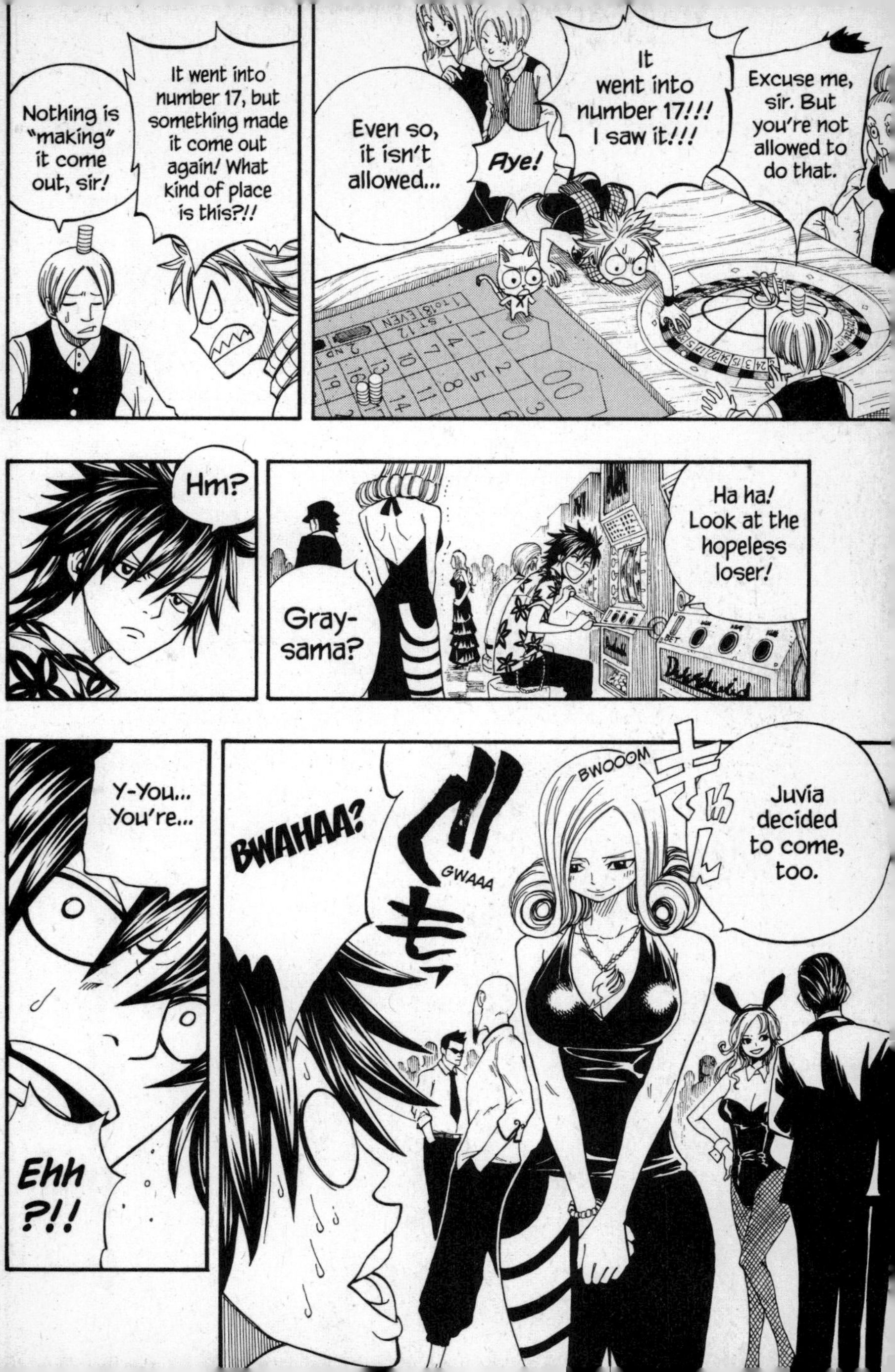
Excuse me, sir. But you're not allowed to do that.
It went into number 17!!! I saw it!!!
Aye!
Even so, it isn't allowed...
It went into number 17, but something made it come out again! What kind of place is this?!!
Nothing is "making" it come out, sir!
Ha ha! Look at the hopeless loser!
Gray-sama?
Hm?
Juvia decided to come, too.
BWOOOM
BWAHAA?
GWAAA
Y-You... You're...
Ehh ?!!

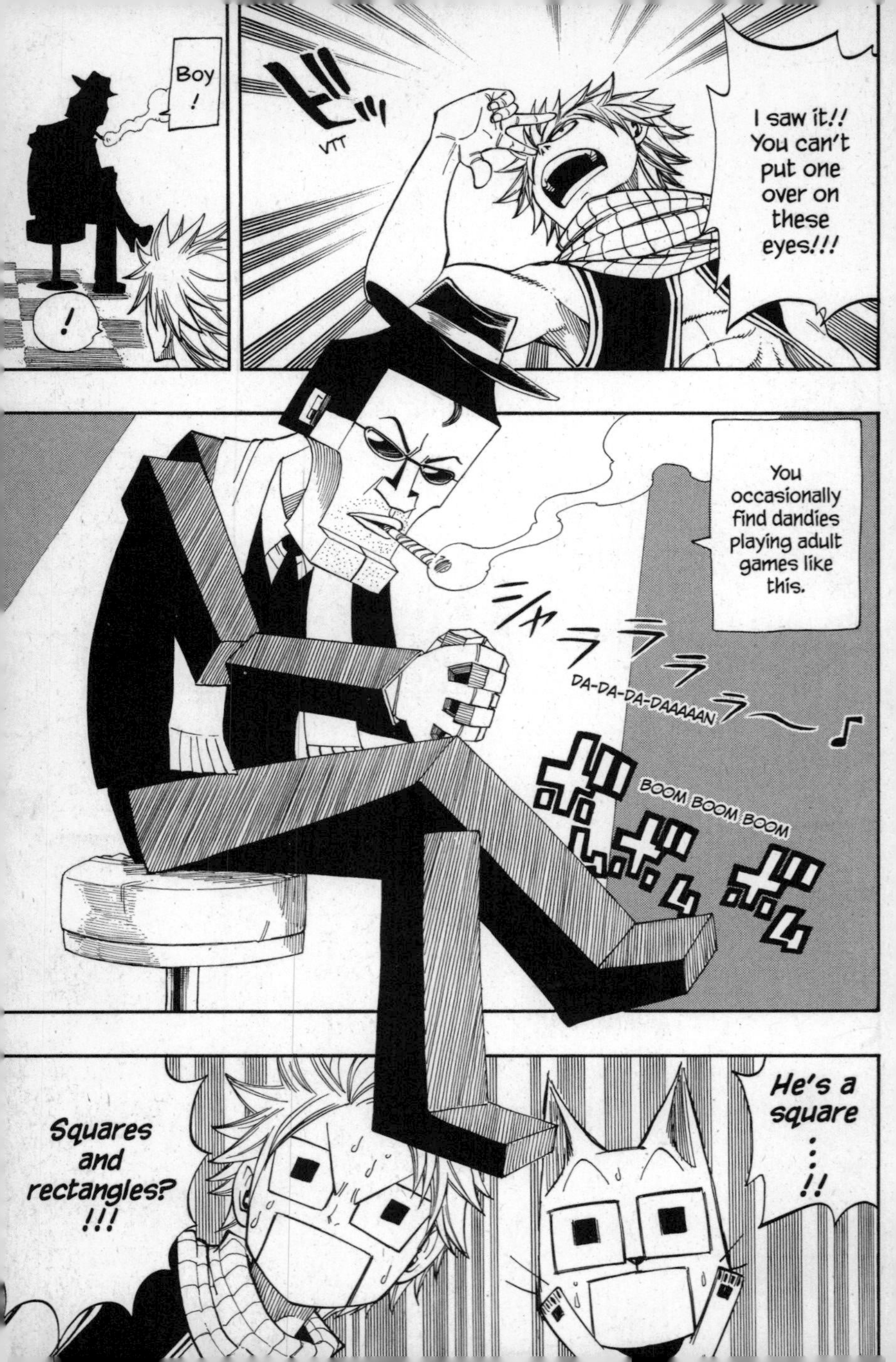
VTT
I saw it!! You can't put one over on these eyes!!!
Boy!
!
You occasionally find dandies playing adult games like this.
DA-DA-DA-DAAAAAN
BOOM BOOM BOOM
He's a square...!!
Squares and rectangles?!!!

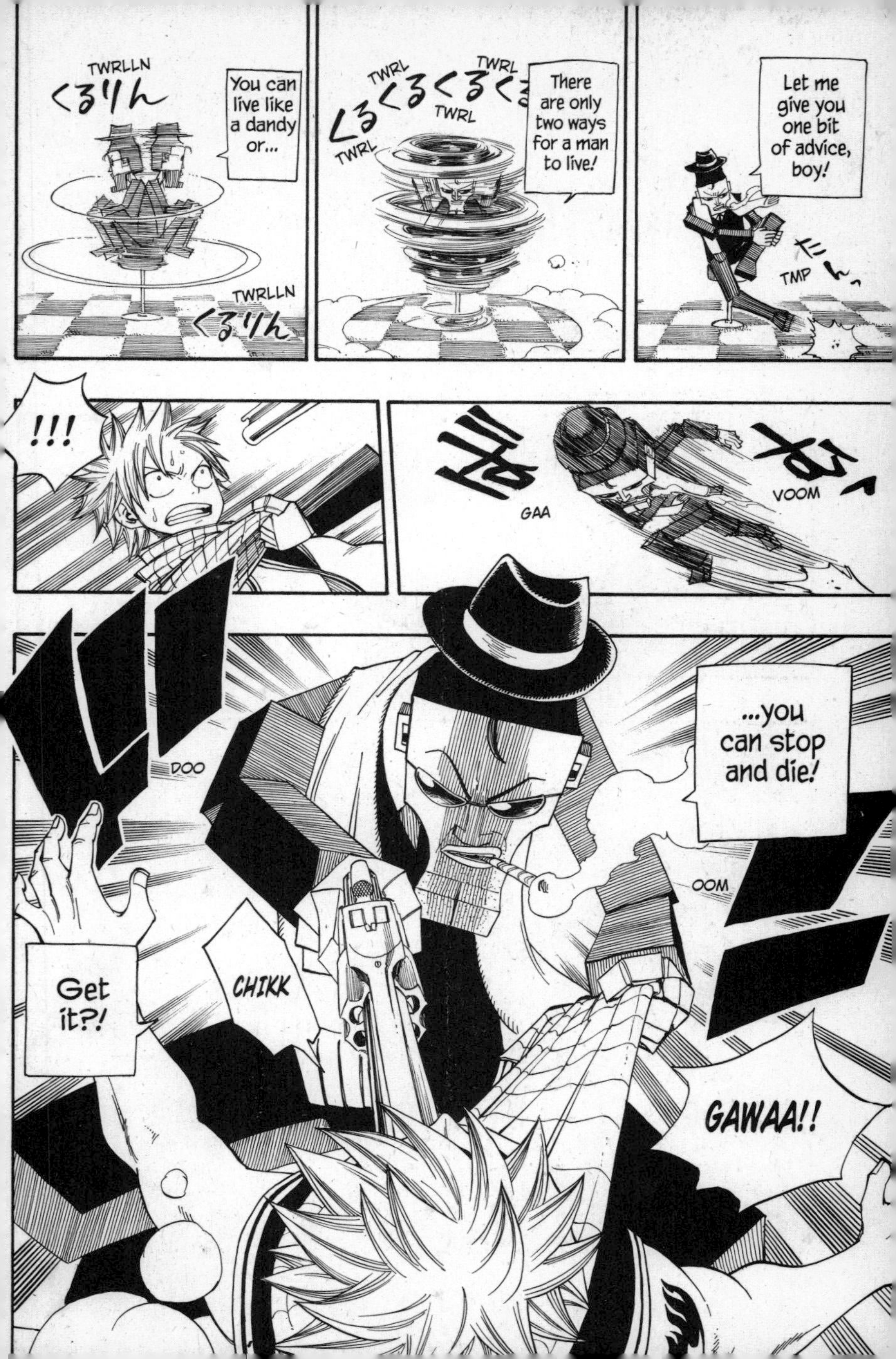
Let me give you one bit of advice, boy!
TMP
TWRL
TWRL
TWRL
TWRL
There are only two ways for a man to live!
TWRLLN
You can live like a dandy or...
TWRLLN
VOOM
GAA
!!!
...you can stop and die!
DOO
OOM
CHIKK
Get it?!
GAWAA!!

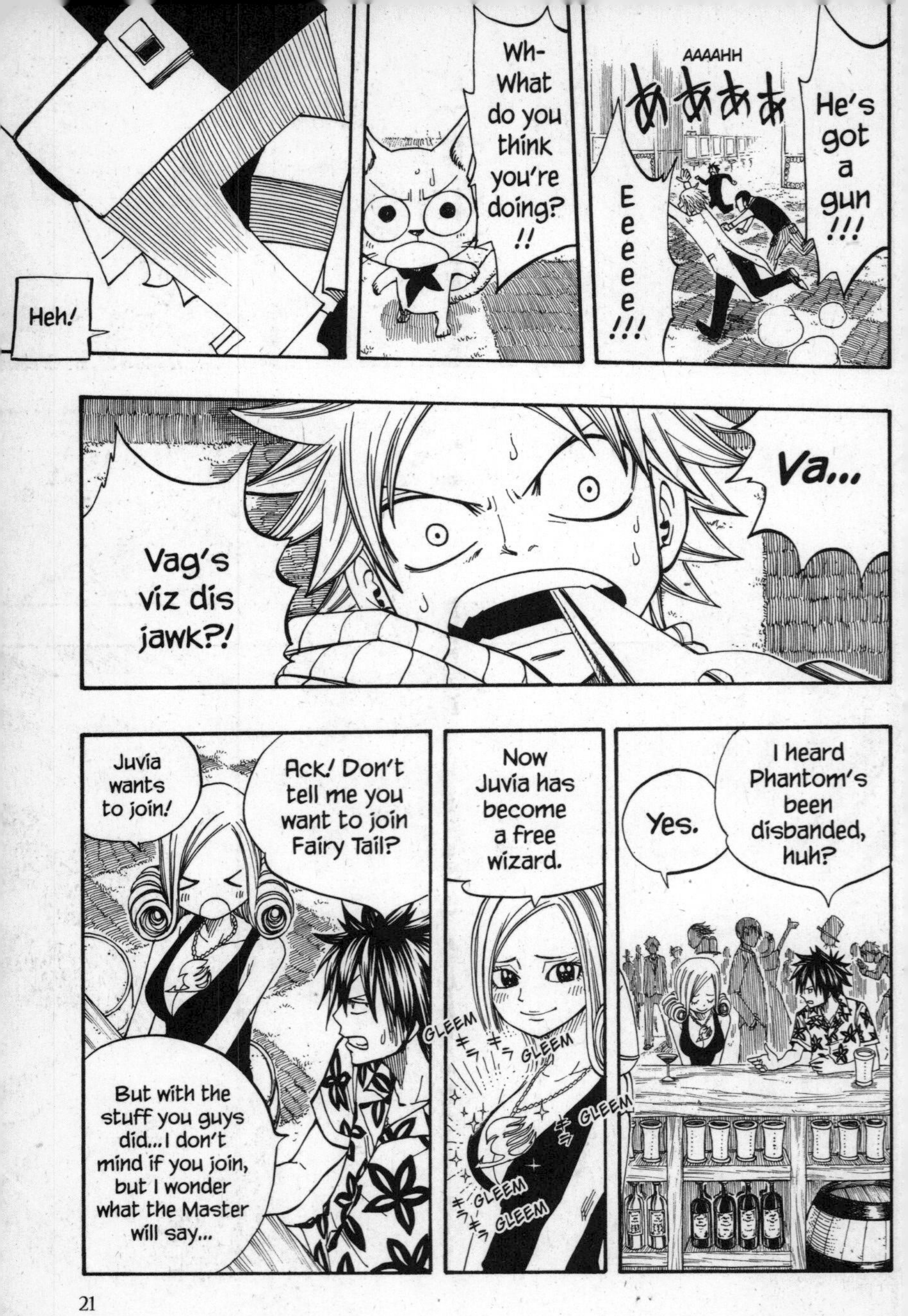
He's got a gun!!!
AAAAHH
ああああ
Eeeee!!!
Wh- What do you think you're doing?!!
Heh!
Va...
Vag's viz dis jawk?!
I heard Phantom's been disbanded, huh?
Yes.
Now Juvia has become a free wizard.
GLEEM
GLEEM
GLEEM
GLEEM
GLEEM
Ack! Don't tell me you want to join Fairy Tail?
Juvia wants to join!
But with the stuff you guys did...I don't mind if you join, but I wonder what the Master will say...

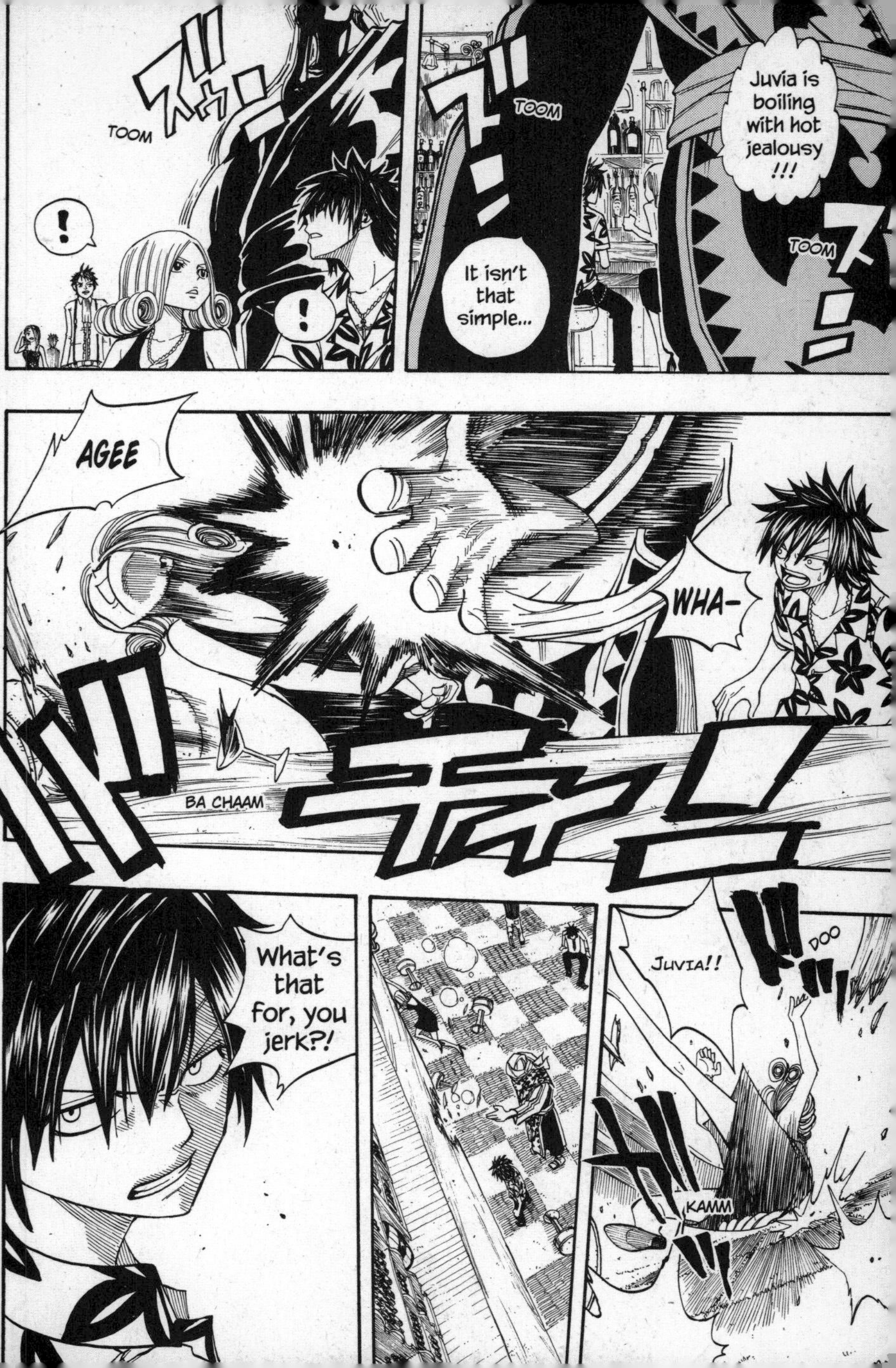
Juvia is boiling with hot jealousy!!!
TOOM
It isn't that simple...
TOOM
TOOM
!
!
AGEE
WHA-
BA CHAAM
Juvia!!
DOO
KAMM
What's that for, you jerk?!

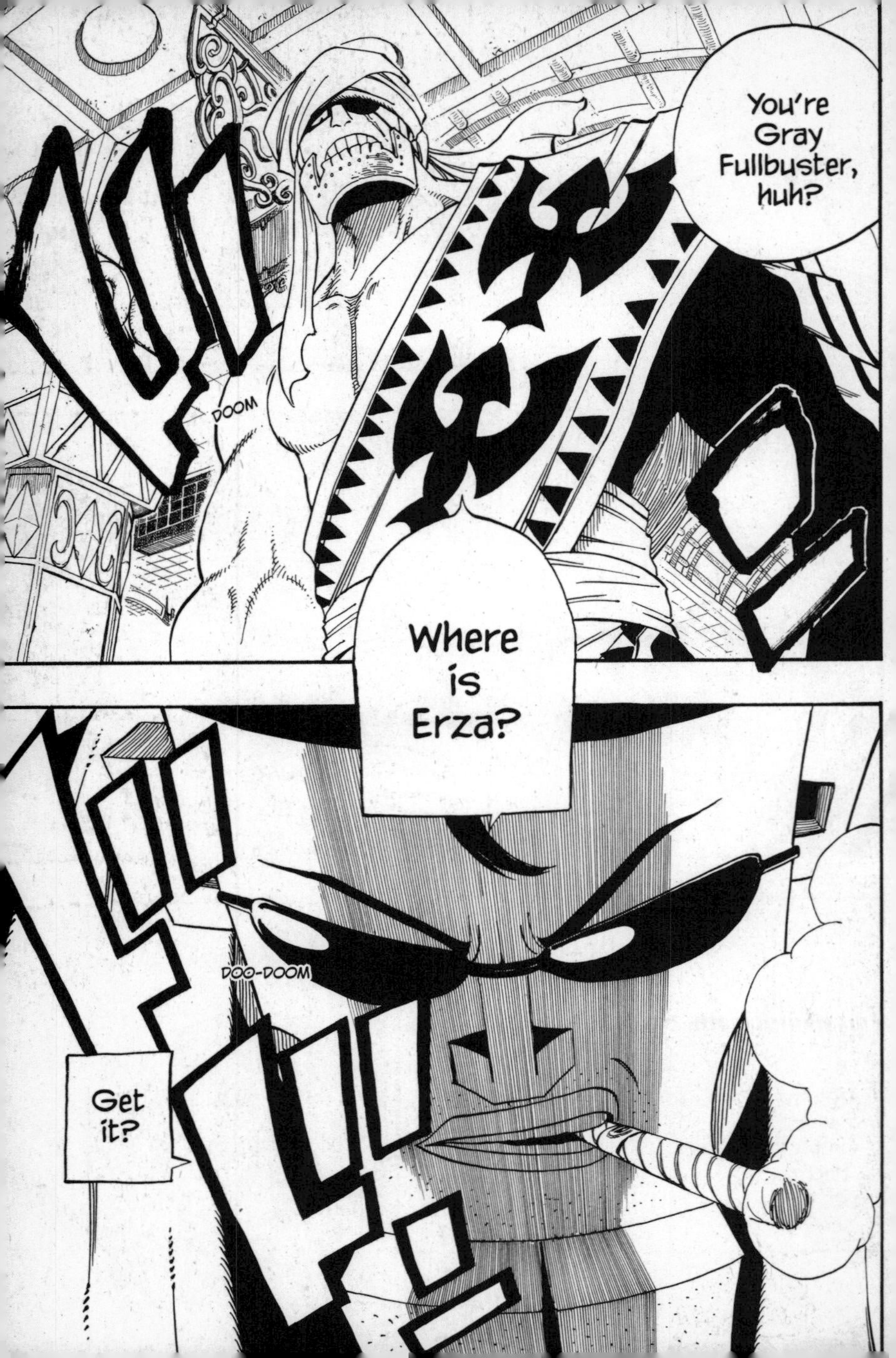
You're Gray Fullbuster, huh?
DOOM
Where is Erza?
DOO-DOOM
Get it?

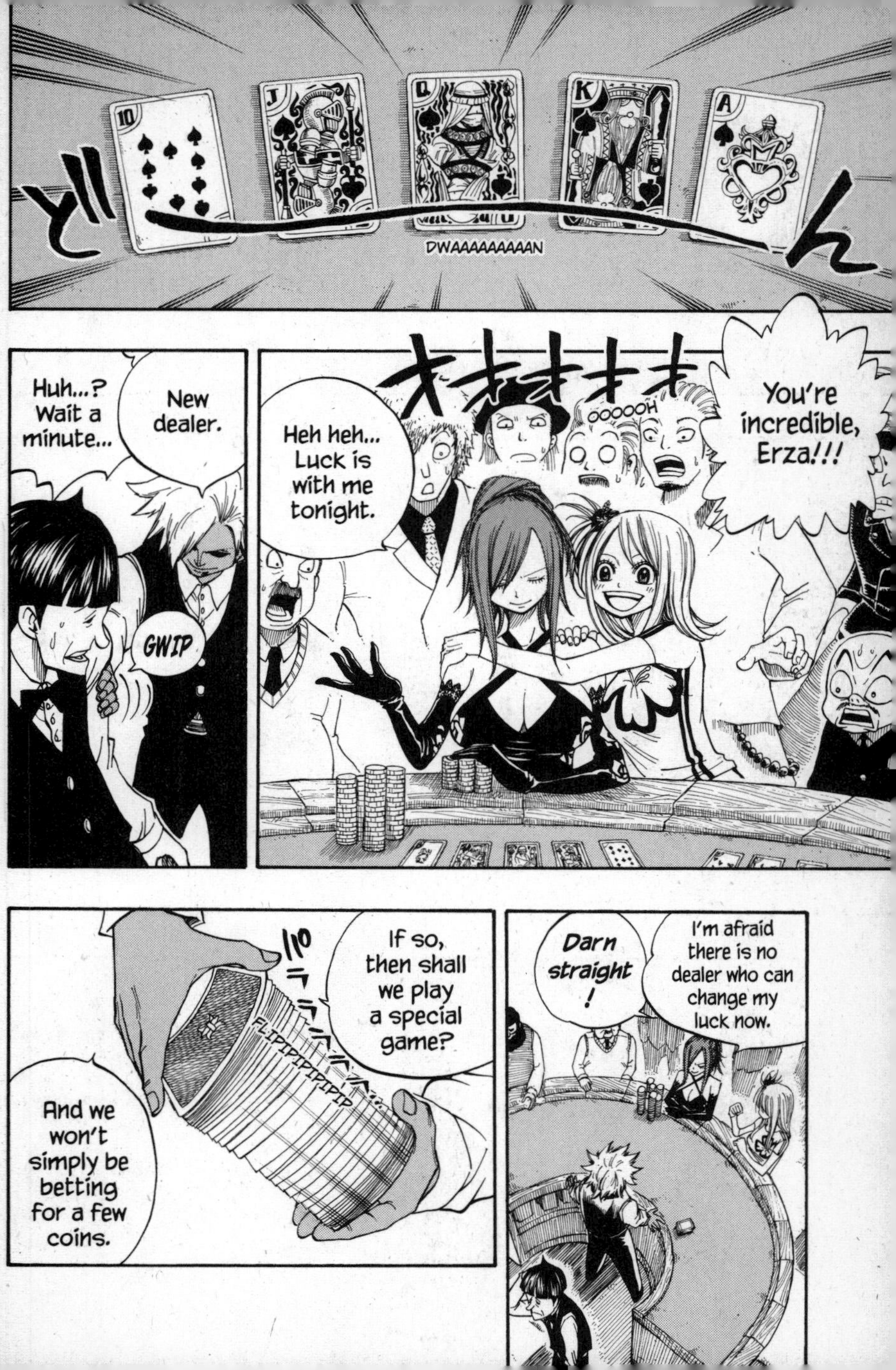
DWAAAAAAAAAN
You're incredible, Erza!!!
OOOOOH
Heh heh... Luck is with me tonight.
New dealer.
Huh...? Wait a minute...
GWIP
I'm afraid there is no dealer who can change my luck now.
Darn straight!
If so, then shall we play a special game?
FLIPIPIPIPIPIP
And we won't simply be betting for a few coins.

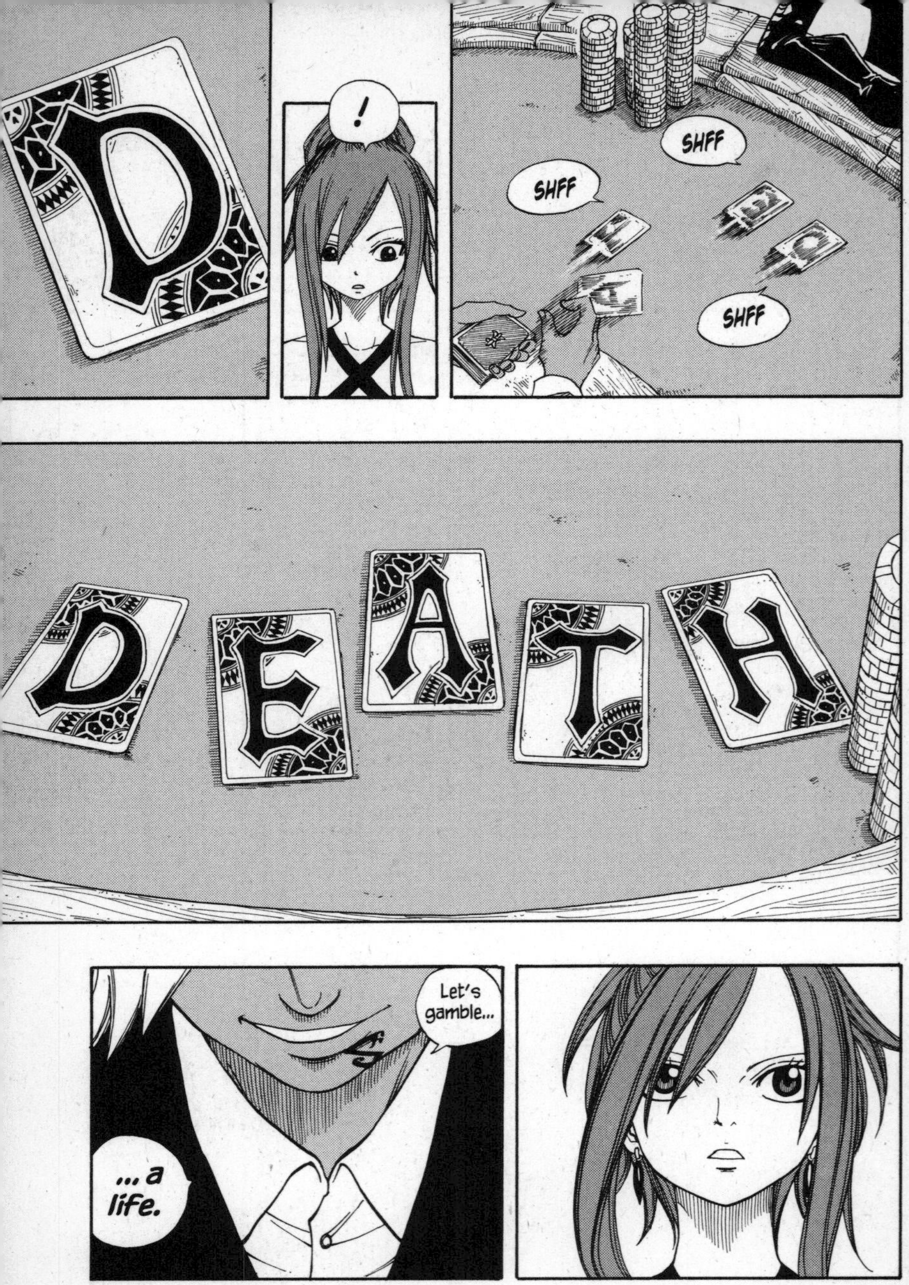
SHFF
SHFF
SHFF
!
D
DEATH
Let's gamble...
... a life.

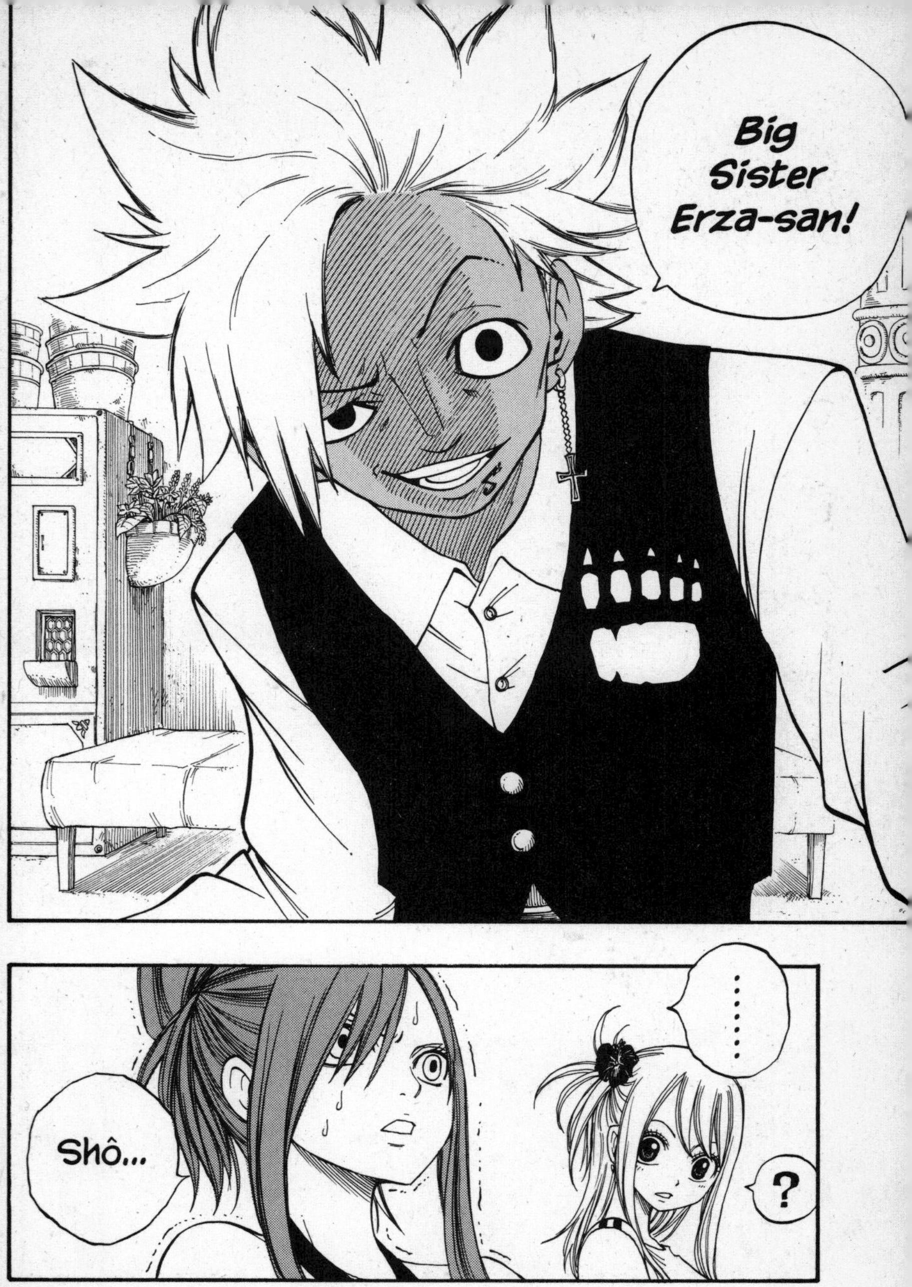
Big Sister Erza-san!
......
?
Shô...

FAIRY TAIL

Chapter 76:
The Tower of Heaven

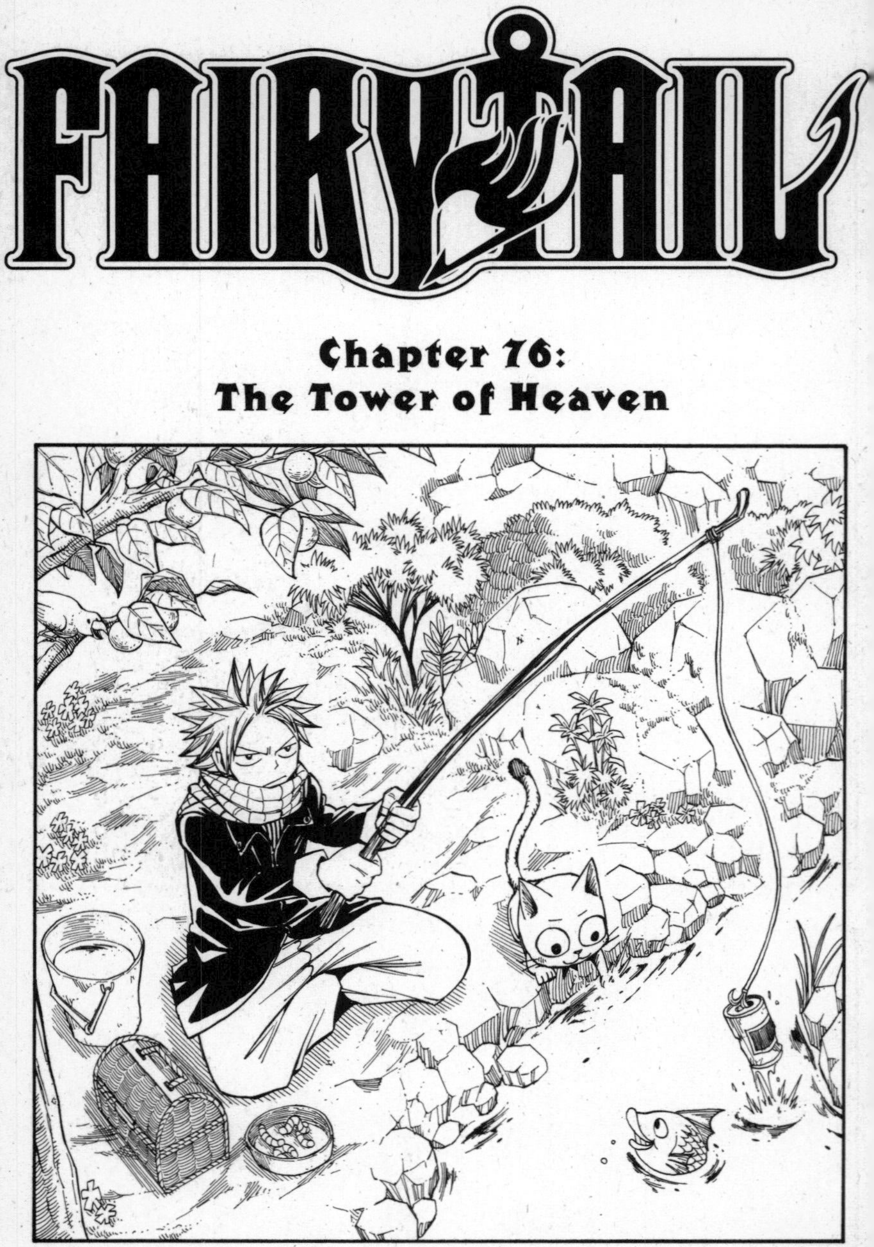

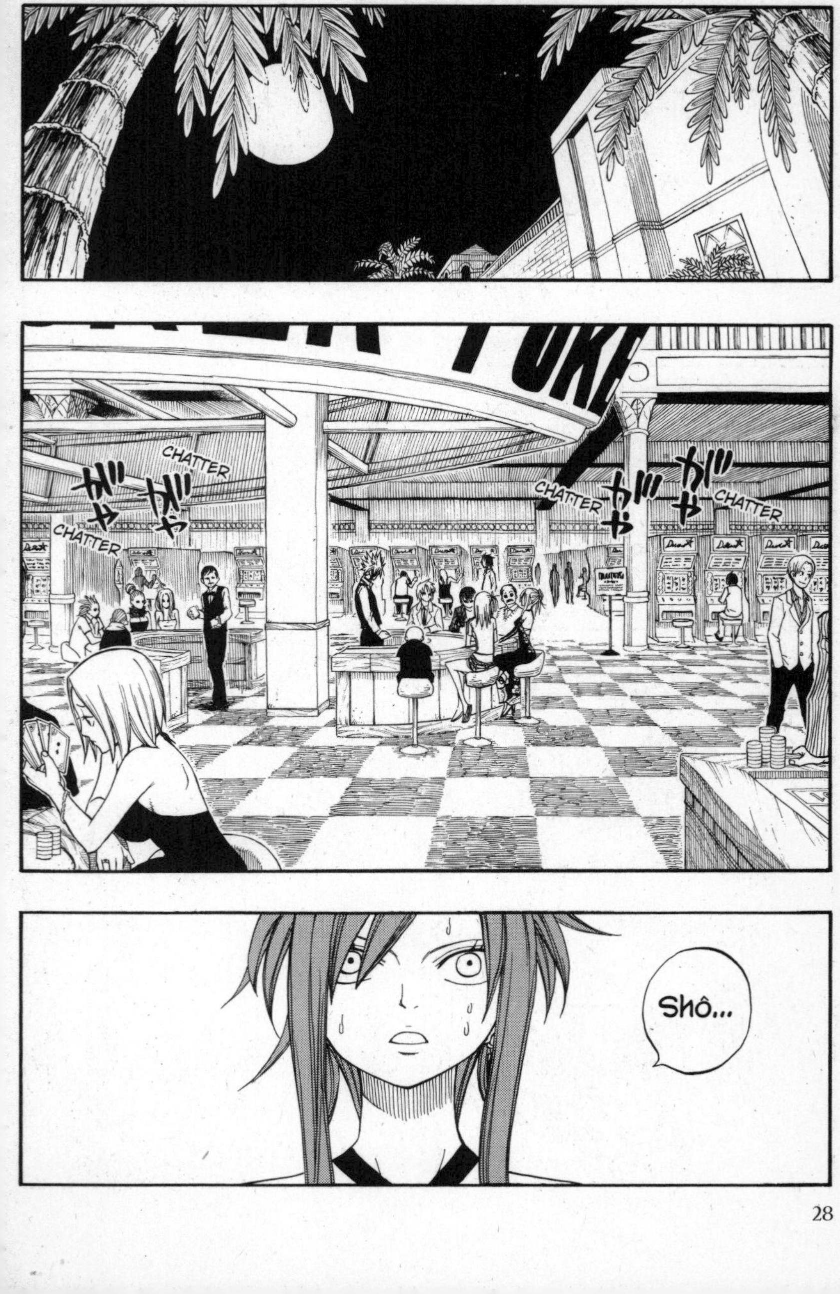
ガヤ
CHATTER
ガヤ
CHATTER
ガヤ
CHATTER
ガヤ
CHATTER
Shô...

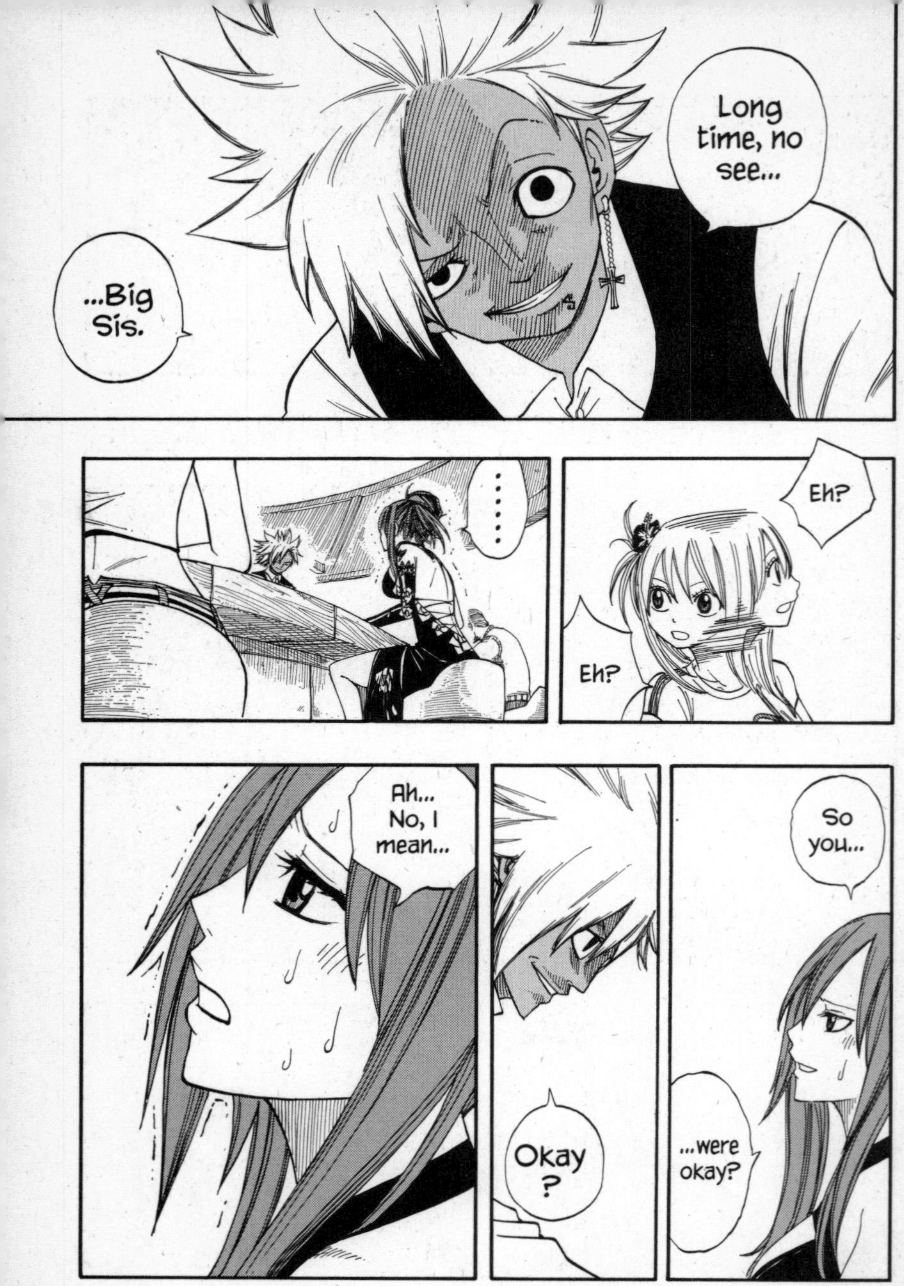
Long time, no see...
...Big Sis.
Eh?
Eh?
......
So you...
...were okay?
Okay ?
Ah... No, I mean...

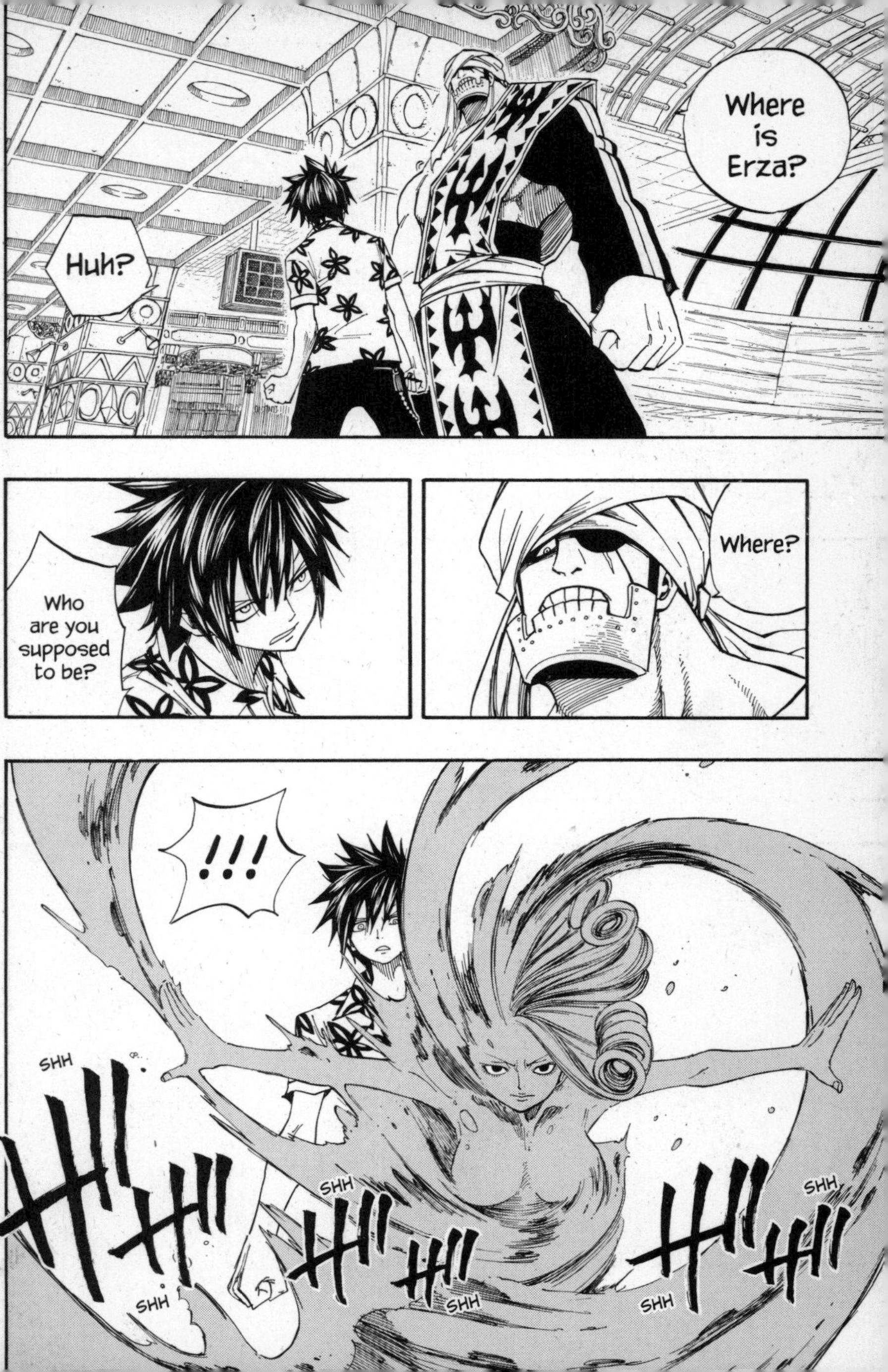
Where is Erza?
Huh?
Where?
Who are you supposed to be?
!!!
SHH
SHH
SHH
SHH
SHH
SHH

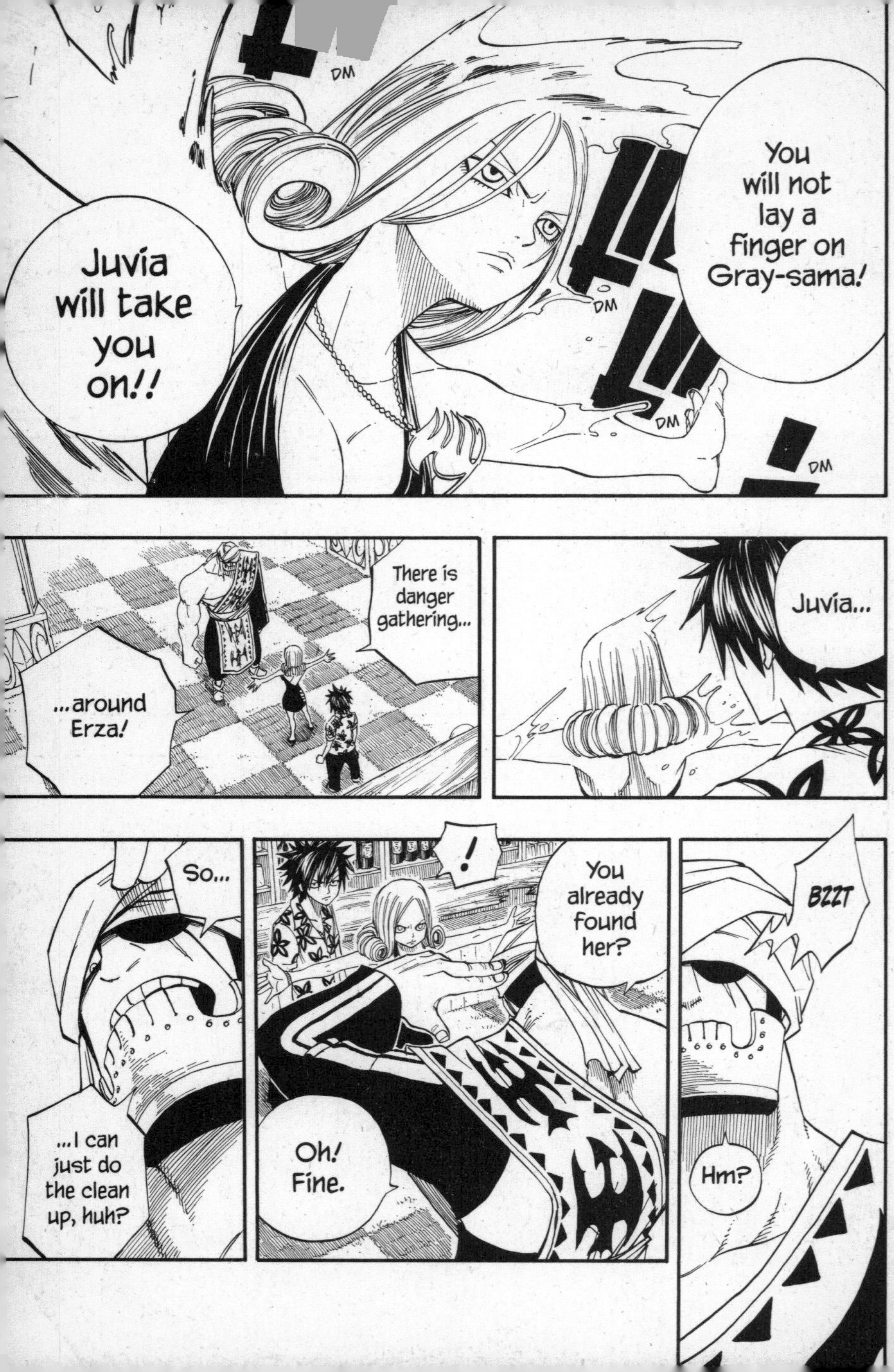
DM
DM
You will not lay a finger on Gray-sama!
DM
DM
Juvia will take you on!!
Juvia...
There is danger gathering...
...around Erza!
BZZT
Hm?
!
You already found her?
Oh! Fine.
So...
...I can just do the clean up, huh?

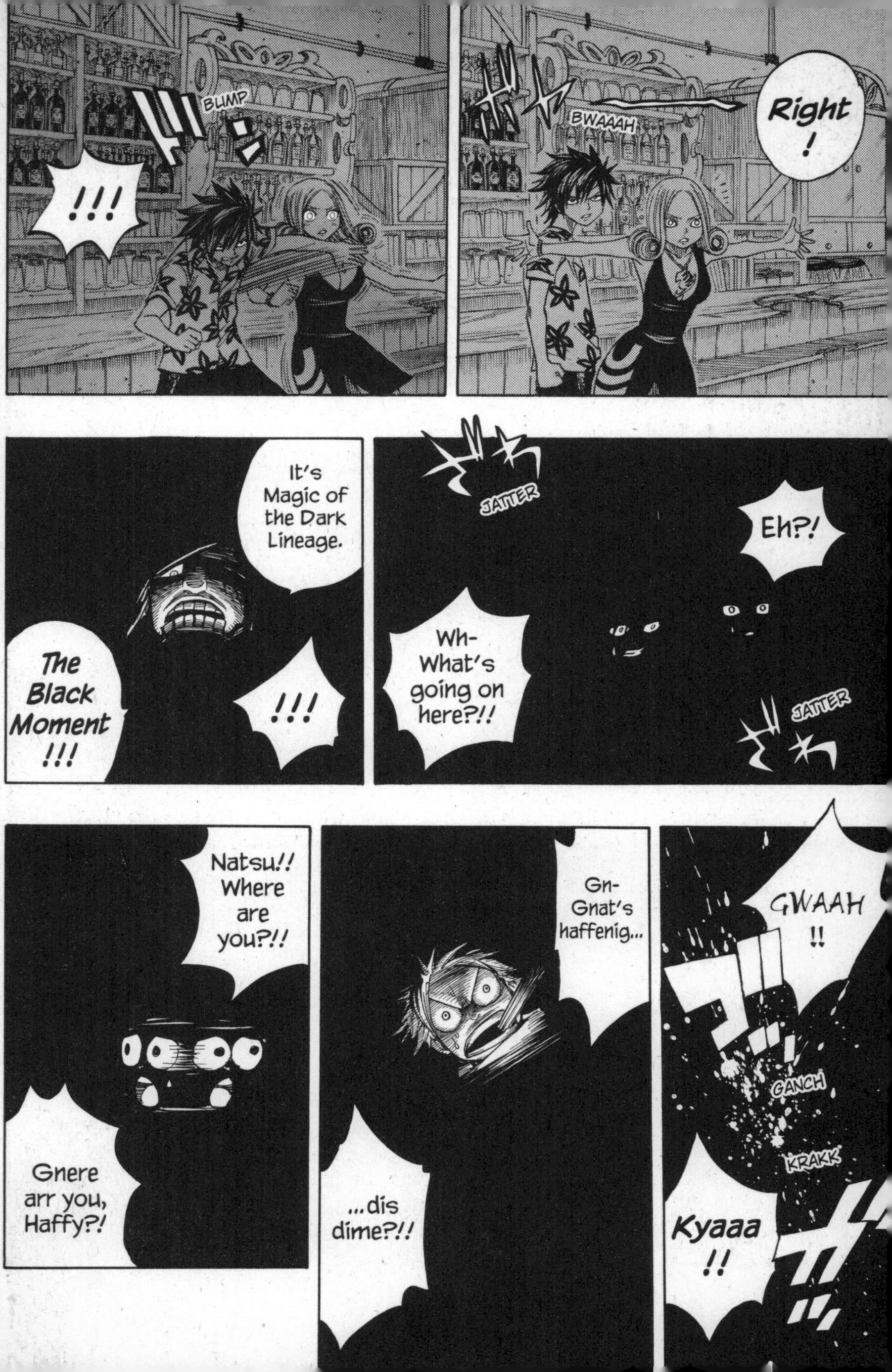

Right!
BWAAAH
BUMP
!!!
Eh?!
JATTER
Wh- What's going on here?!!
JATTER
It's Magic of the Dark Lineage.
The Black Moment!!!
!!!
GWAAH!!
GANCH
KRAKK
Kyaaa!!
Gn- Gnat's haffenig...
...dis dime?!!
Natsu!! Where are you?!!
Gnere arr you, Haffy?!

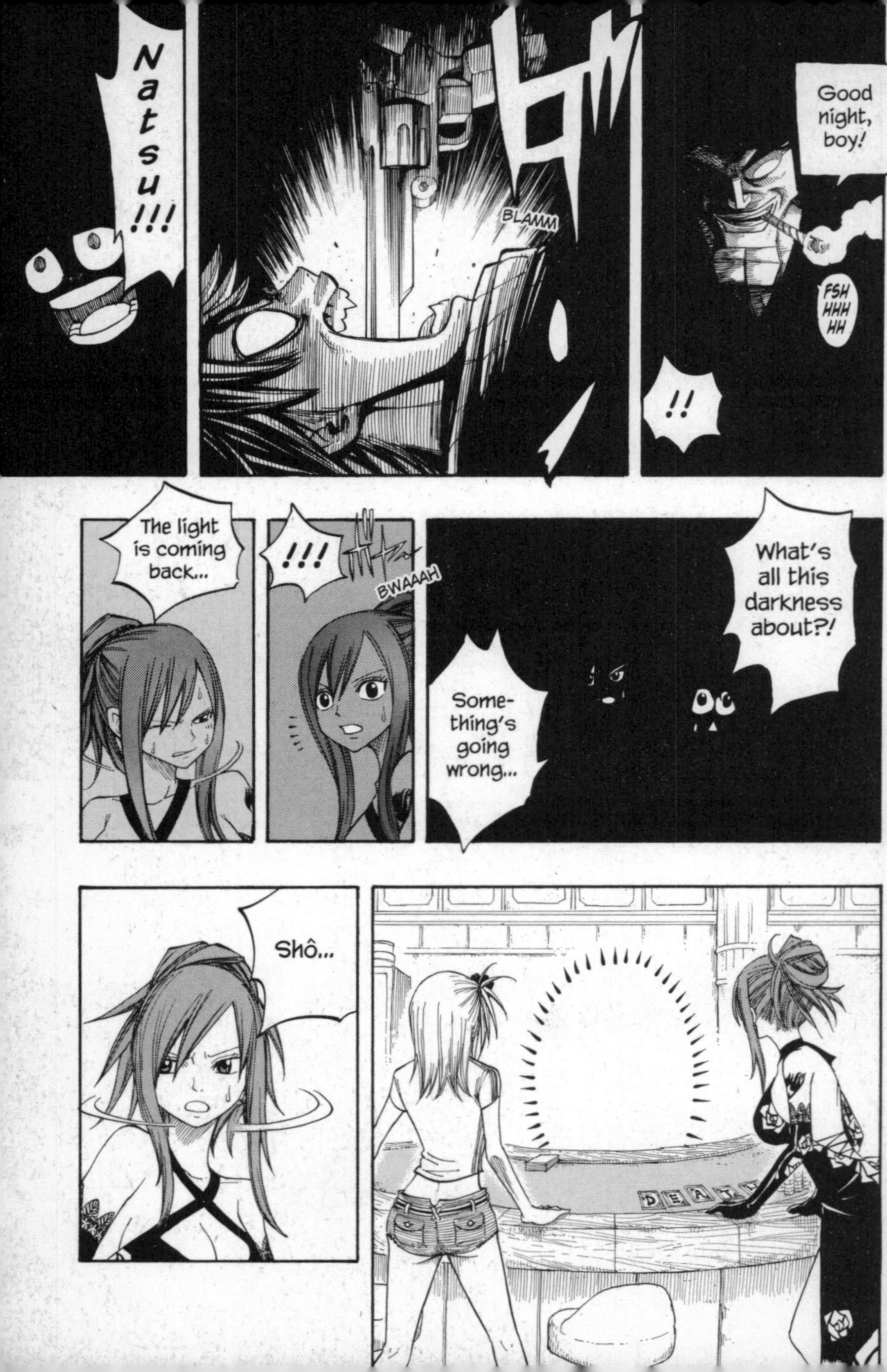
Good night, boy!
FSH HHHHH
!!
BLAMM
Natsu!!!
What's all this darkness about?!
Something's going wrong...
!!!
BWAAAH
The light is coming back...
Shô...

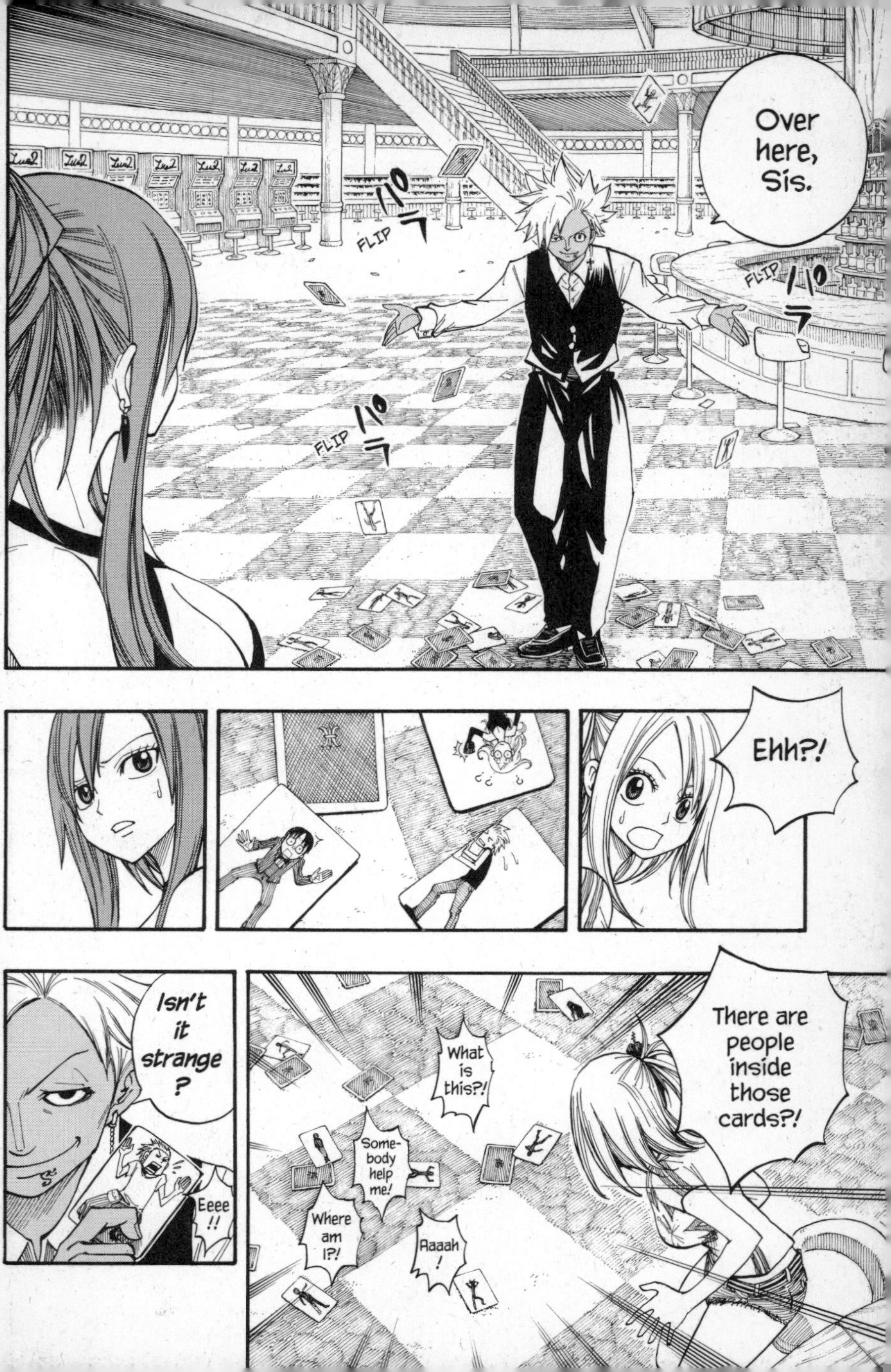

Over here, Sis.
FLIP パラ
FLIP パラ
FLIP パラ
Ehh?!
There are people inside those cards?!
What is this?!
Somebody help me!
Where am I?!
Aaaah!
Isn't it strange?
Eeee!!

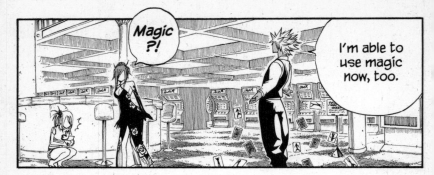

Magic ?!

I'm able to use magic now, too.

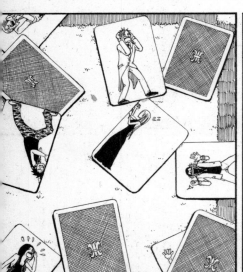

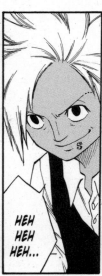

HEH HEH HEH...

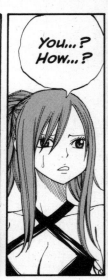

You...? How...?

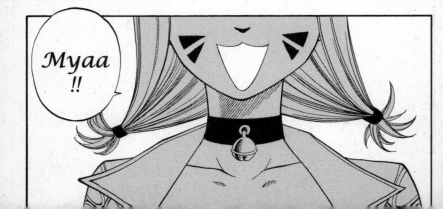

Myaa !!

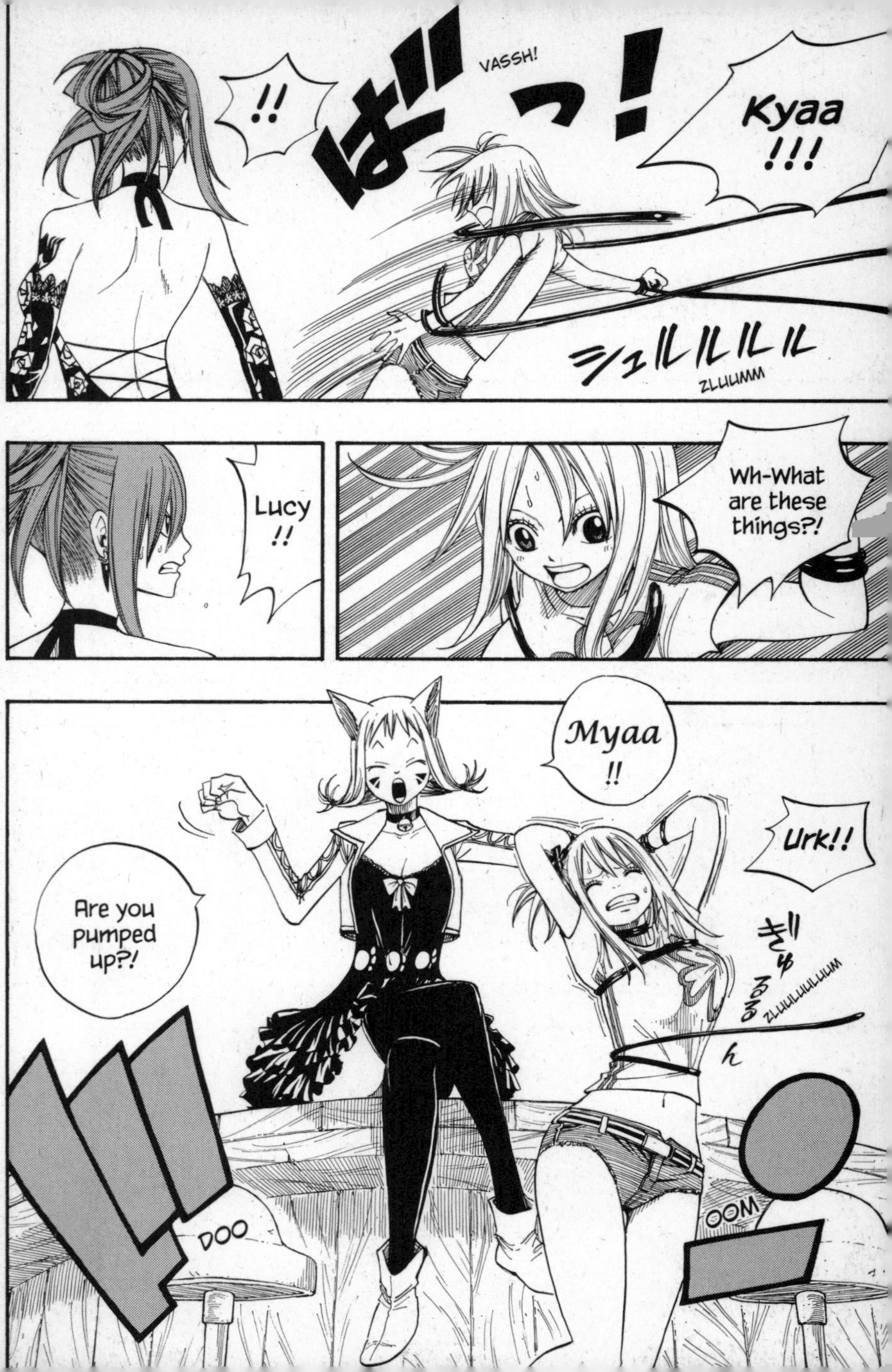
Kyaa !!!
ばっ!
VASSH!
!!
シュルルルル
ZLUUMM
Wh-What are these things?!
Lucy !!
Myaa !!
Urk!!
Are you pumped up?!
ZLULULULUM
OOM
DOO

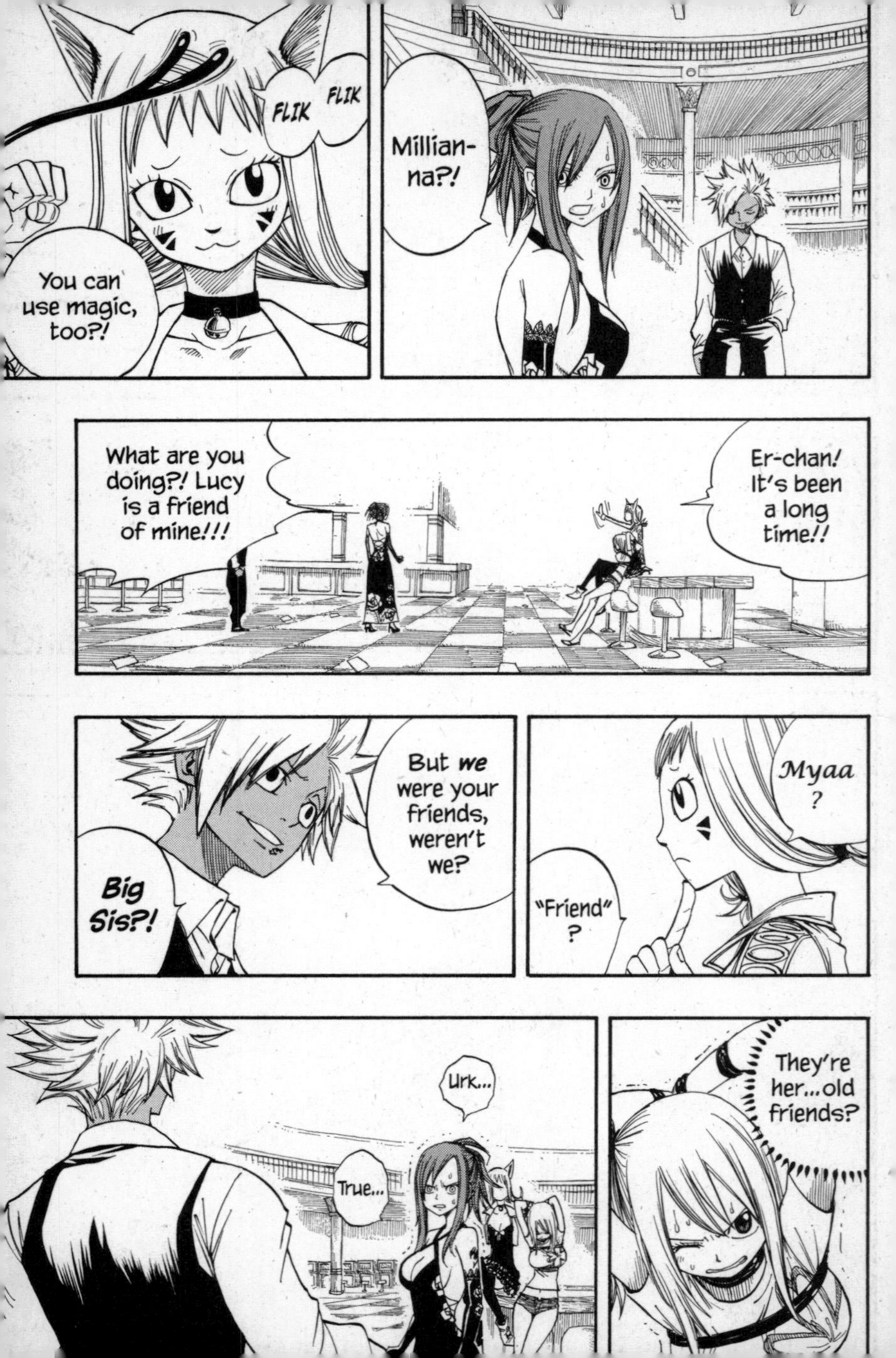
Millian-na?!
FLIK
FLIK
You can use magic, too?!
Er-chan! It's been a long time!!
What are you doing?! Lucy is a friend of mine!!!
Myaa?
"Friend"?
But we were your friends, weren't we?
Big Sis?!
They're her...old friends?
Urk...
True...

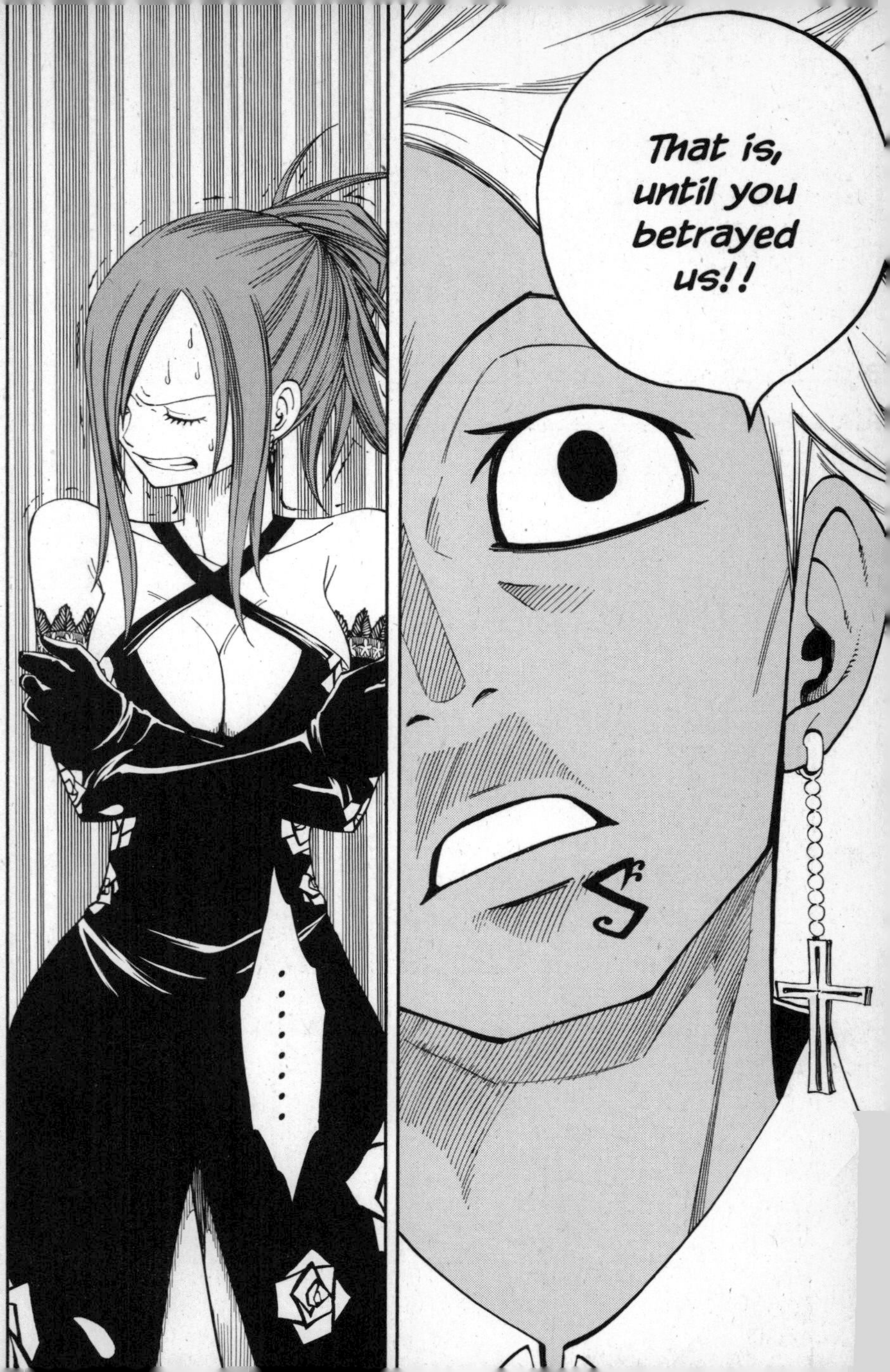
That is, until you betrayed us!!

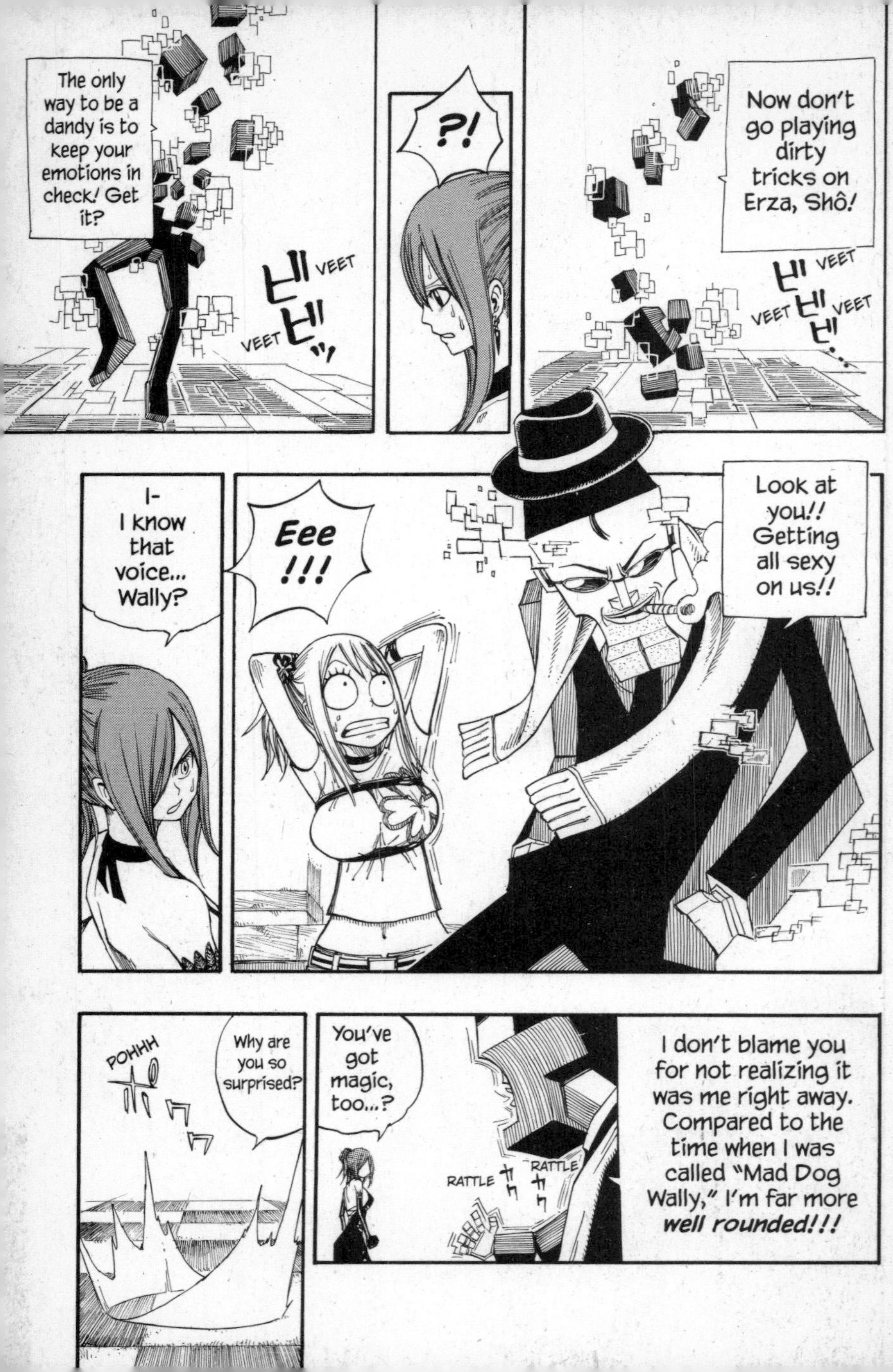

Now don't go playing dirty tricks on Erza, Shô!
VEET VEET VEET VEET
?!
The only way to be a dandy is to keep your emotions in check! Get it?
VEET VEET
Look at you!! Getting all sexy on us!!
Eee!!!
I- I know that voice... Wally?
I don't blame you for not realizing it was me right away. Compared to the time when I was called "Mad Dog Wally," I'm far more well rounded!!!
RATTLE RATTLE
You've got magic, too...?
Why are you so surprised?
POHHH

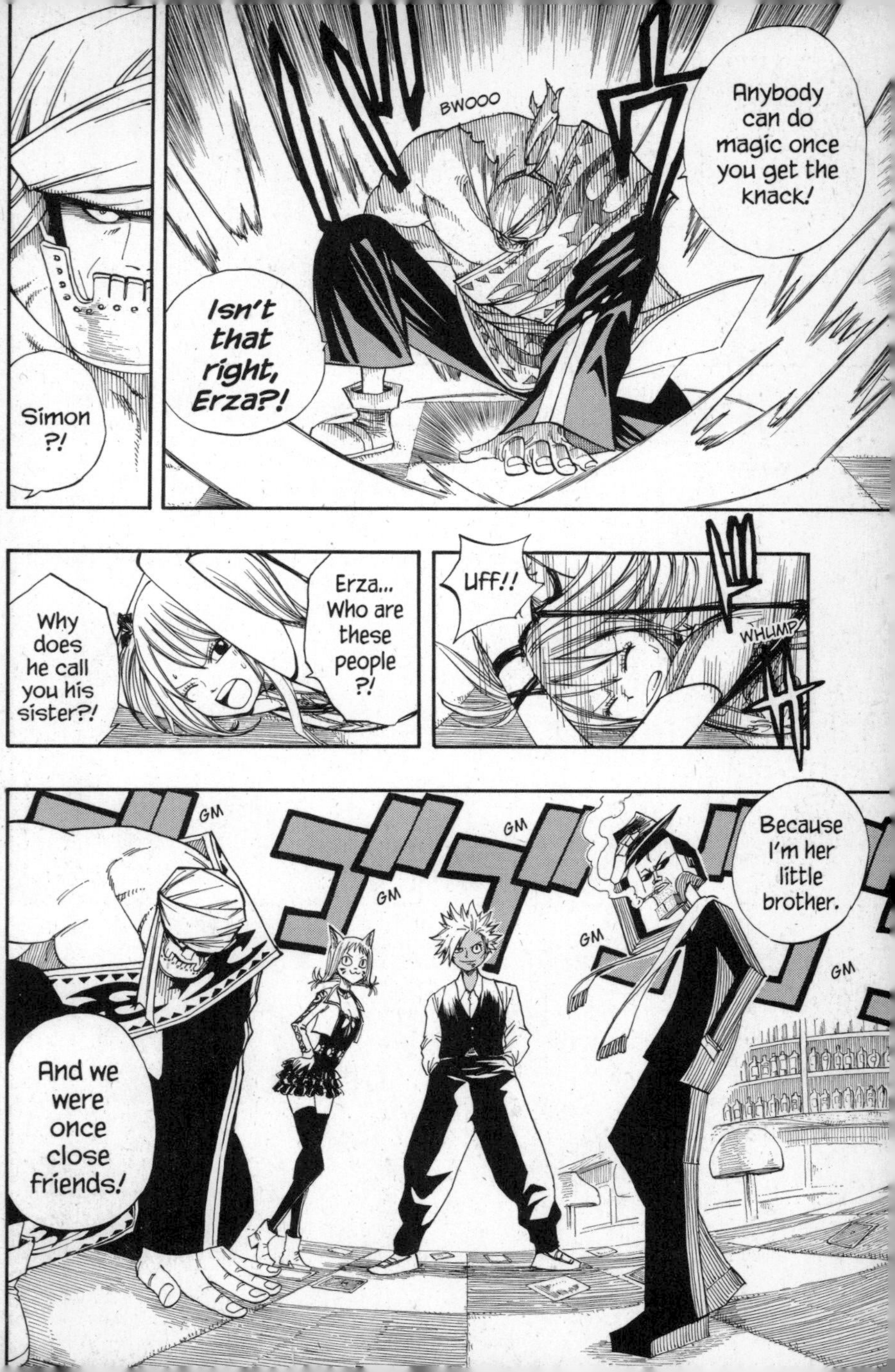
Anybody can do magic once you get the knack!
BWOOO
Isn't that right, Erza?!
Simon ?!
Uff!!
WHUMP
Erza... Who are these people ?!
Why does he call you his sister?!
Because I'm her little brother.
GM
GM
GM
GM
GM
And we were once close friends!

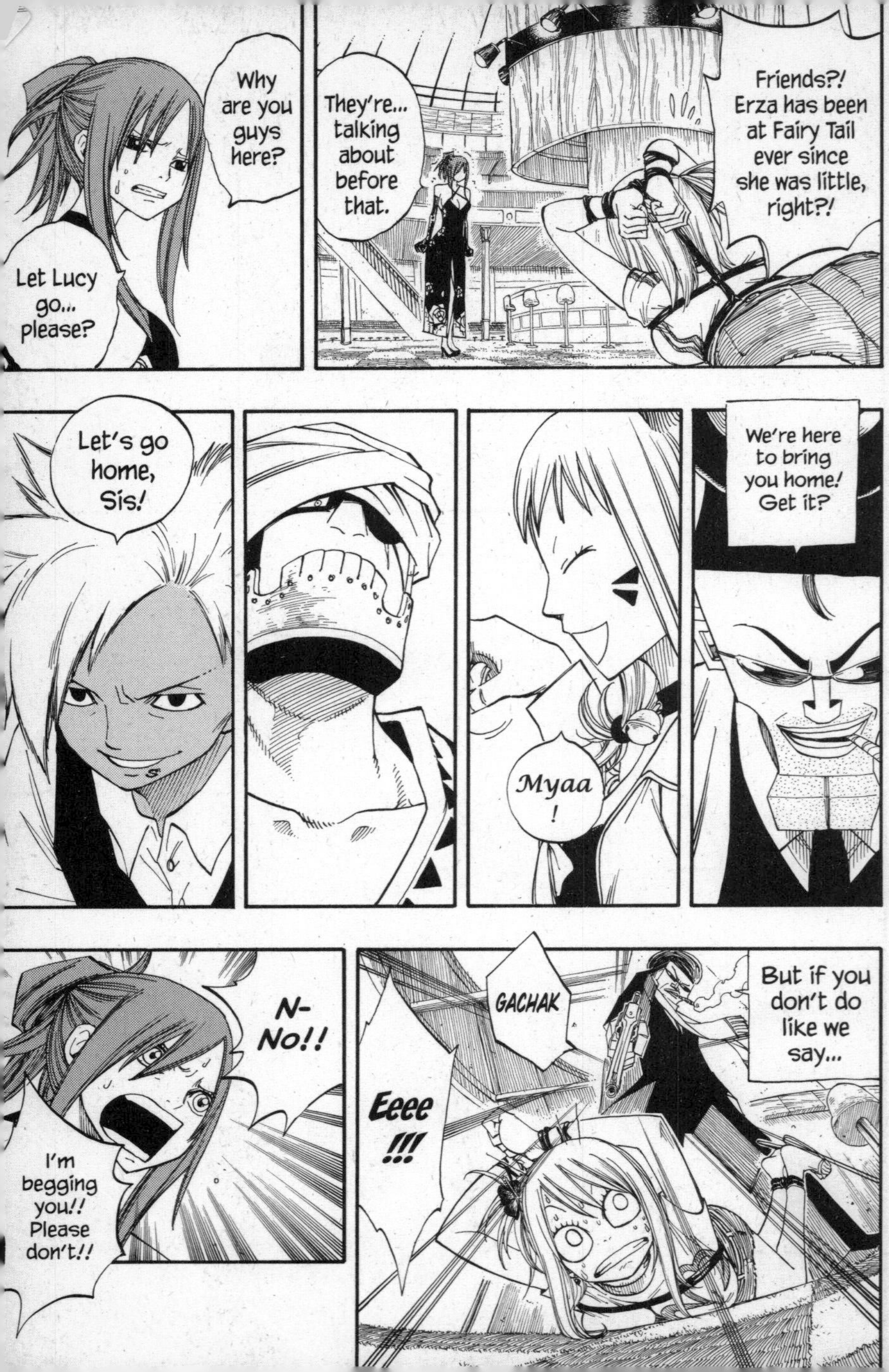
Friends?! Erza has been at Fairy Tail ever since she was little, right?!
They're... talking about before that.
Why are you guys here?
Let Lucy go... please?
We're here to bring you home! Get it?
Myaa!
Let's go home, Sis!
But if you don't do like we say...
GACHAK
Eeee!!!
N-No!!
I'm begging you!! Please don't!!

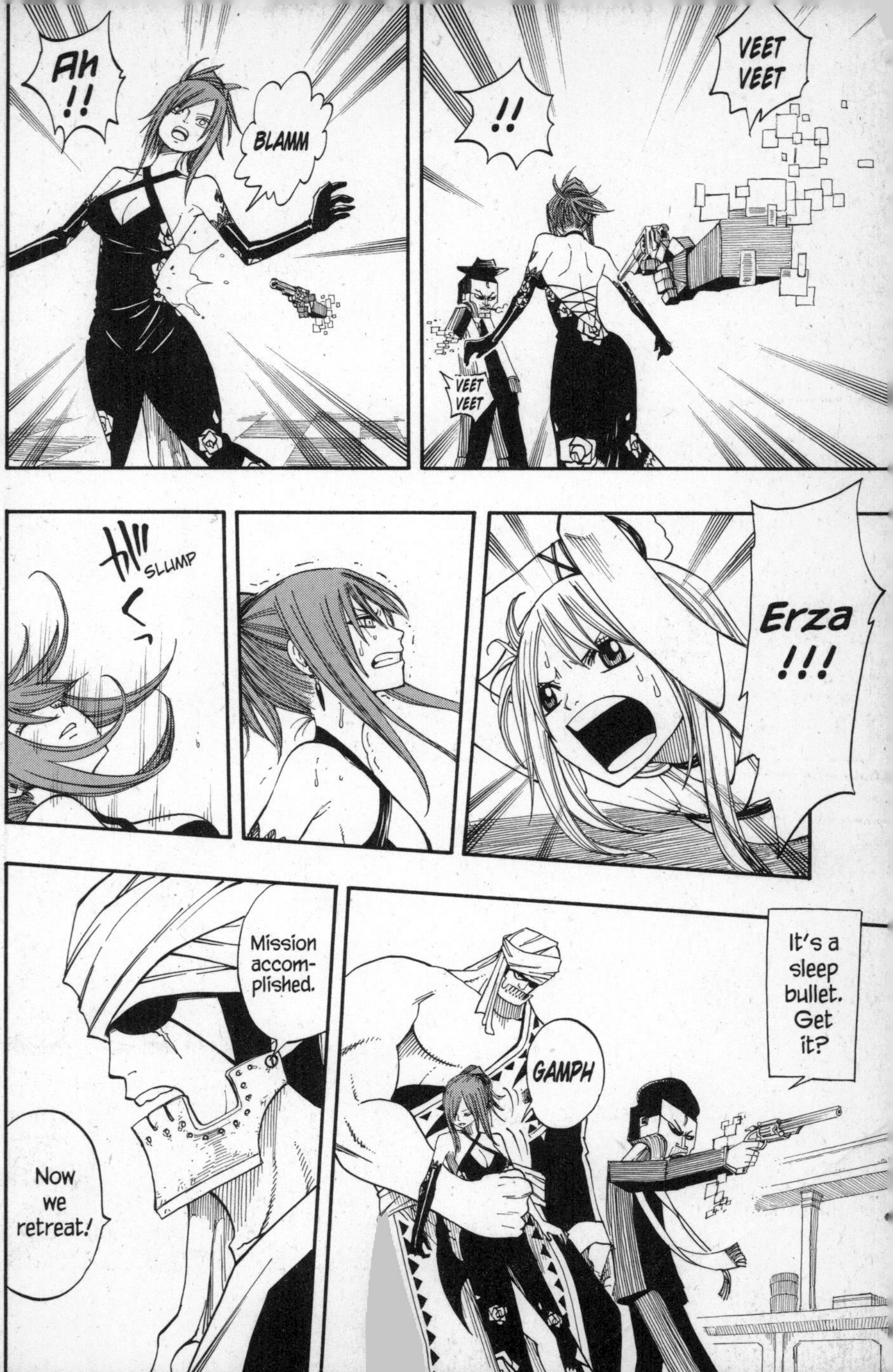
VEET VEET
!!
VEET VEET
Ah!!
BLAMM
Erza!!!
SLUMP
It's a sleep bullet. Get it?
GAMPH
Mission accomplished.
Now we retreat!

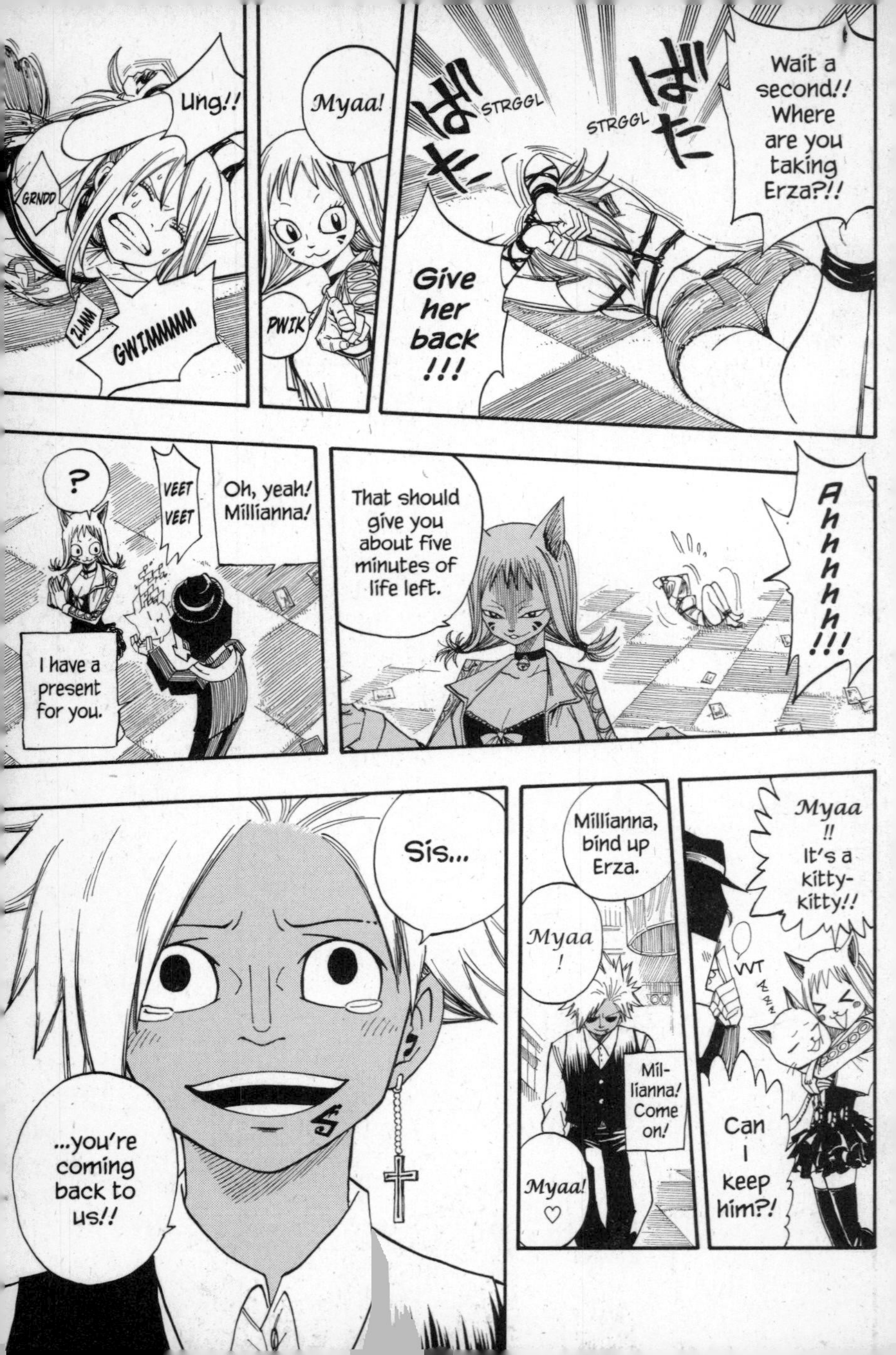
Wait a second!! Where are you taking Erza?!!
STRGGL
STRGGL
Give her back!!!
Myaa!
PWIK
Ung!!
GRNDD
ZLMM
GWIMMMM
Ahhhhhh!!!
That should give you about five minutes of life left.
Oh, yeah! Millianna!
VEET VEET
?
I have a present for you.
Myaa!! It's a kitty-kitty!!
VVT
Can I keep him?!
Millianna, bind up Erza.
Myaa!
Millianna! Come on!
Myaa! ♡
Sis...
...you're coming back to us!!

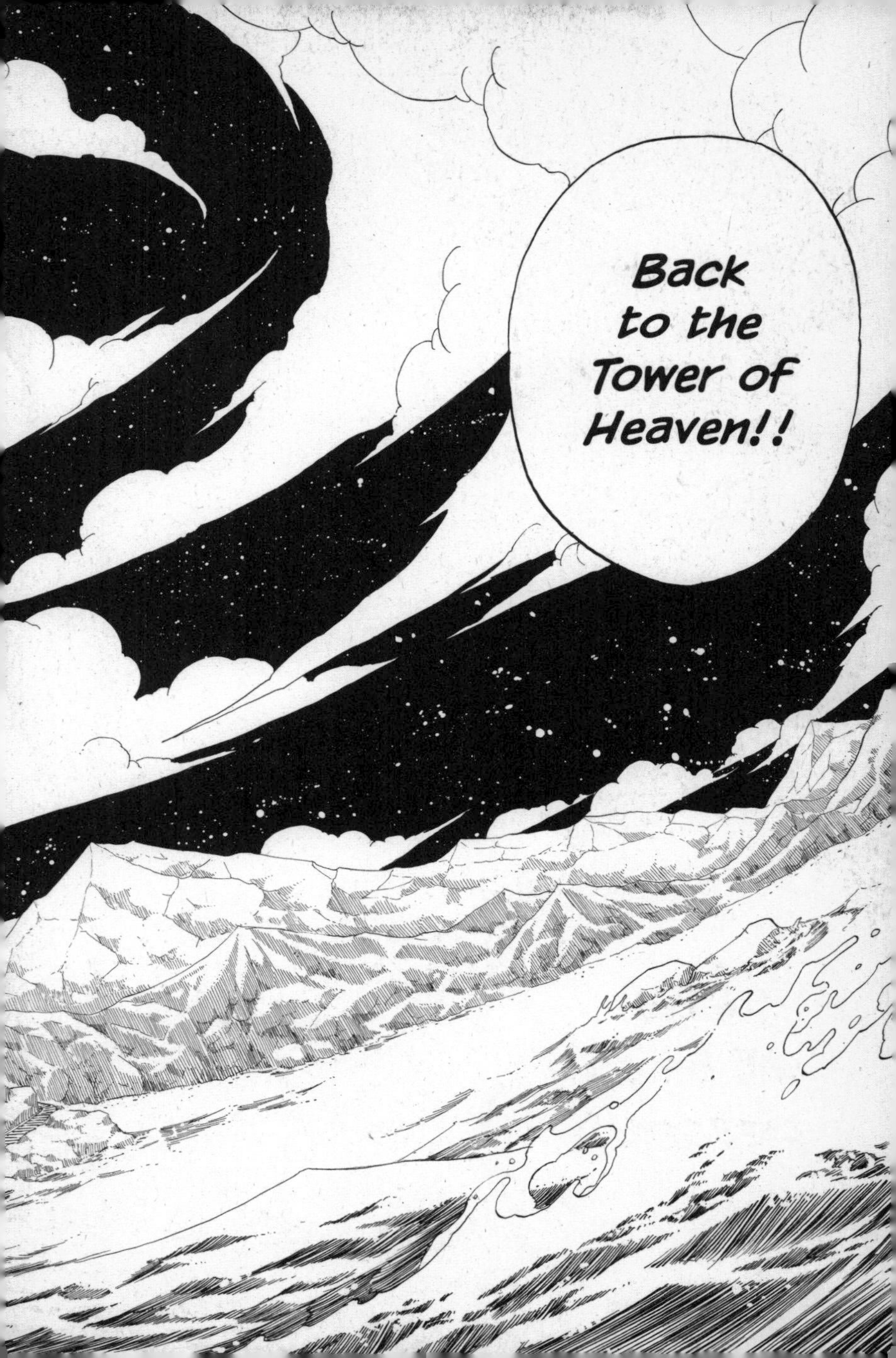
Back to the Tower of Heaven!!

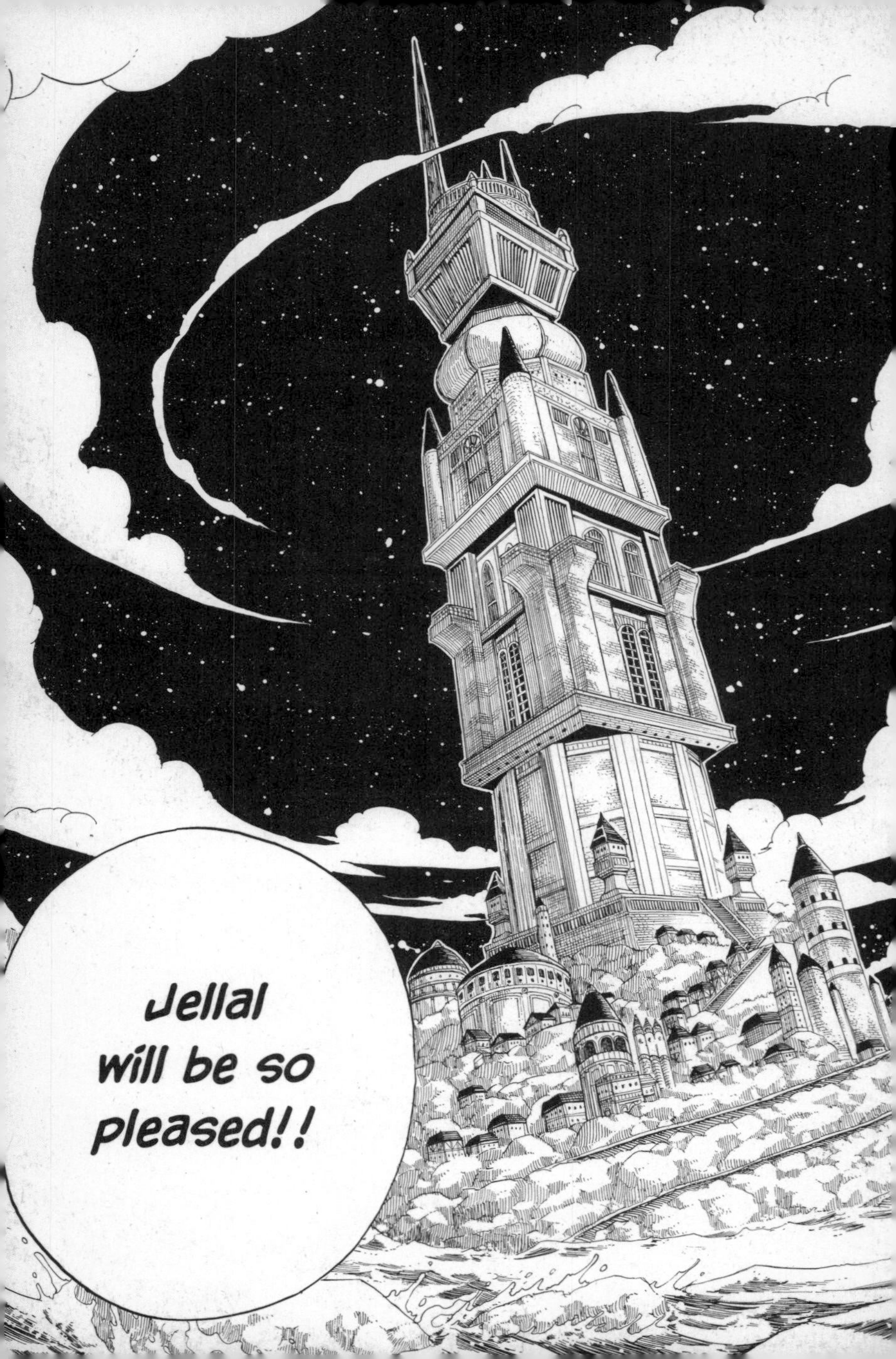
Jellal will be so pleased!!

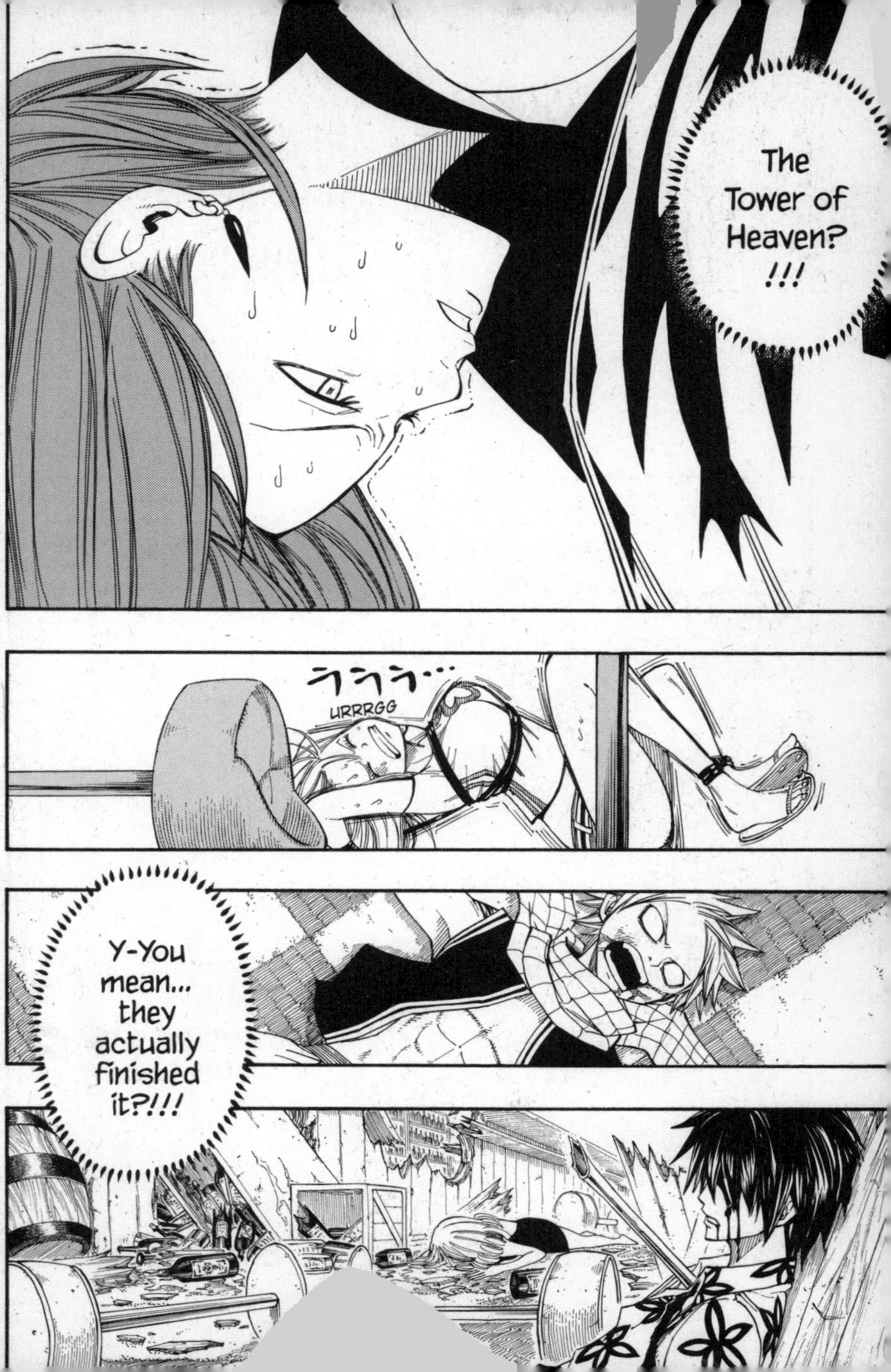
The Tower of Heaven? !!!
ラララ…
URRRGG
Y-You mean... they actually finished it?!!!

FAIRY TAIL

Chapter 77: Jellal

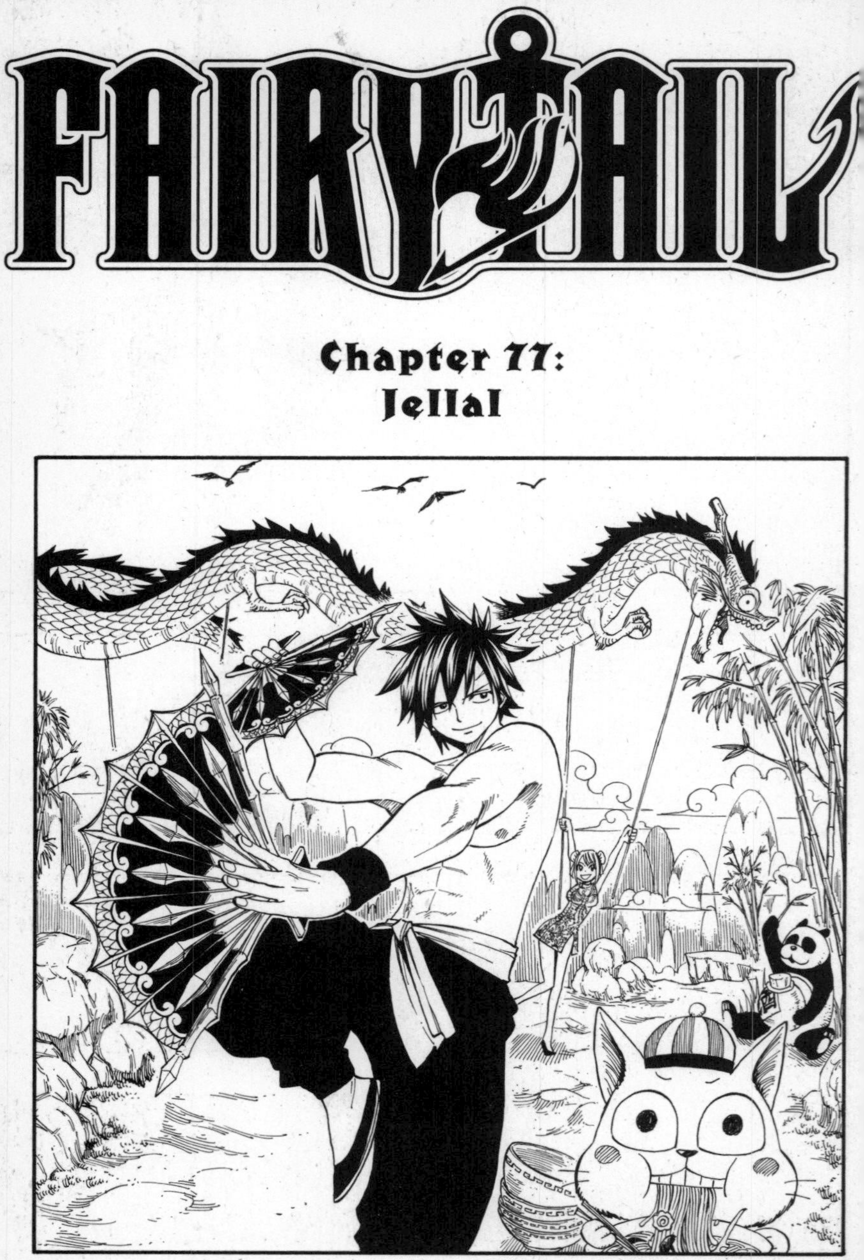

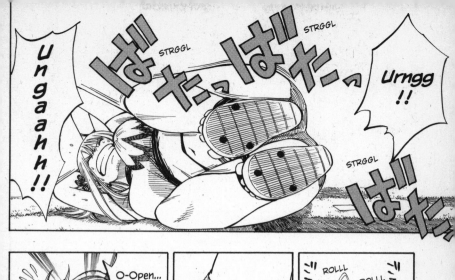

Un gaaahh!!

STRGGL

STRGGL

Urngg!!

STRGGL

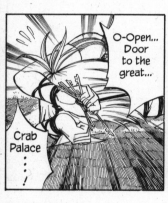

O-Open... Door to the great...

Crab Palace ...!

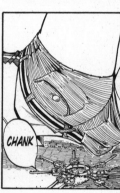

CHANK

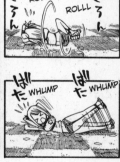

ROLLL

ROLLL

WHUMP

WHUMP

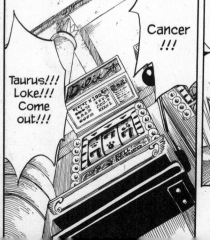

Cancer!!!

Taurus!!! Loke!!! Come out!!!

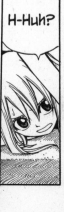

H-Huh?

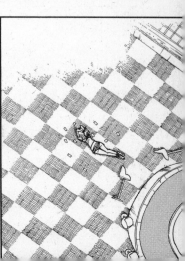

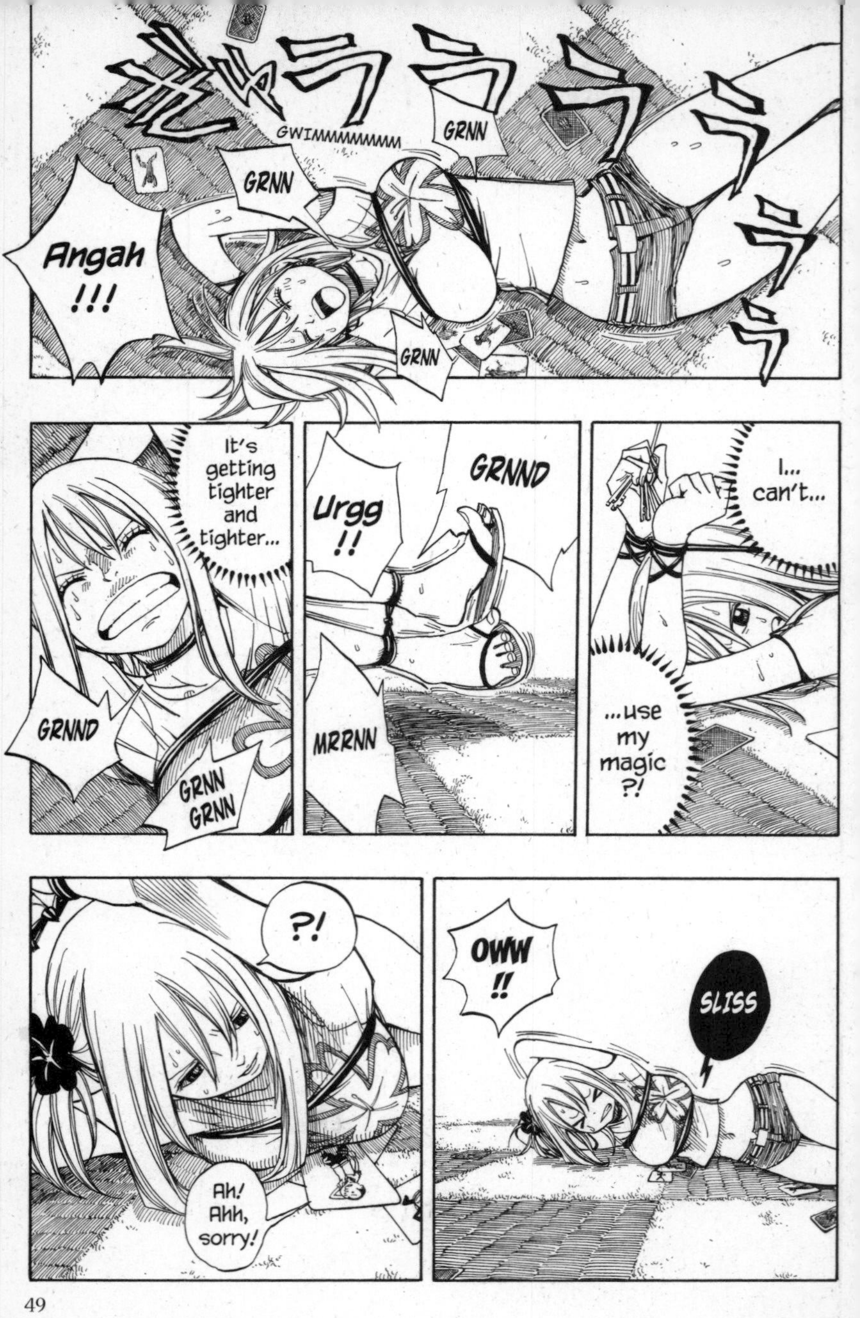
GRNN
GWIMMMMMMMM
GRNN
Angah!!!
GRNN
I... can't...
...use my magic?!
GRNND
Urgg!!
MRRNN
It's getting tighter and tighter...
GRNND
GRNN GRNN
OWW!!
SLISS
?!
Ah! Ahh, sorry!

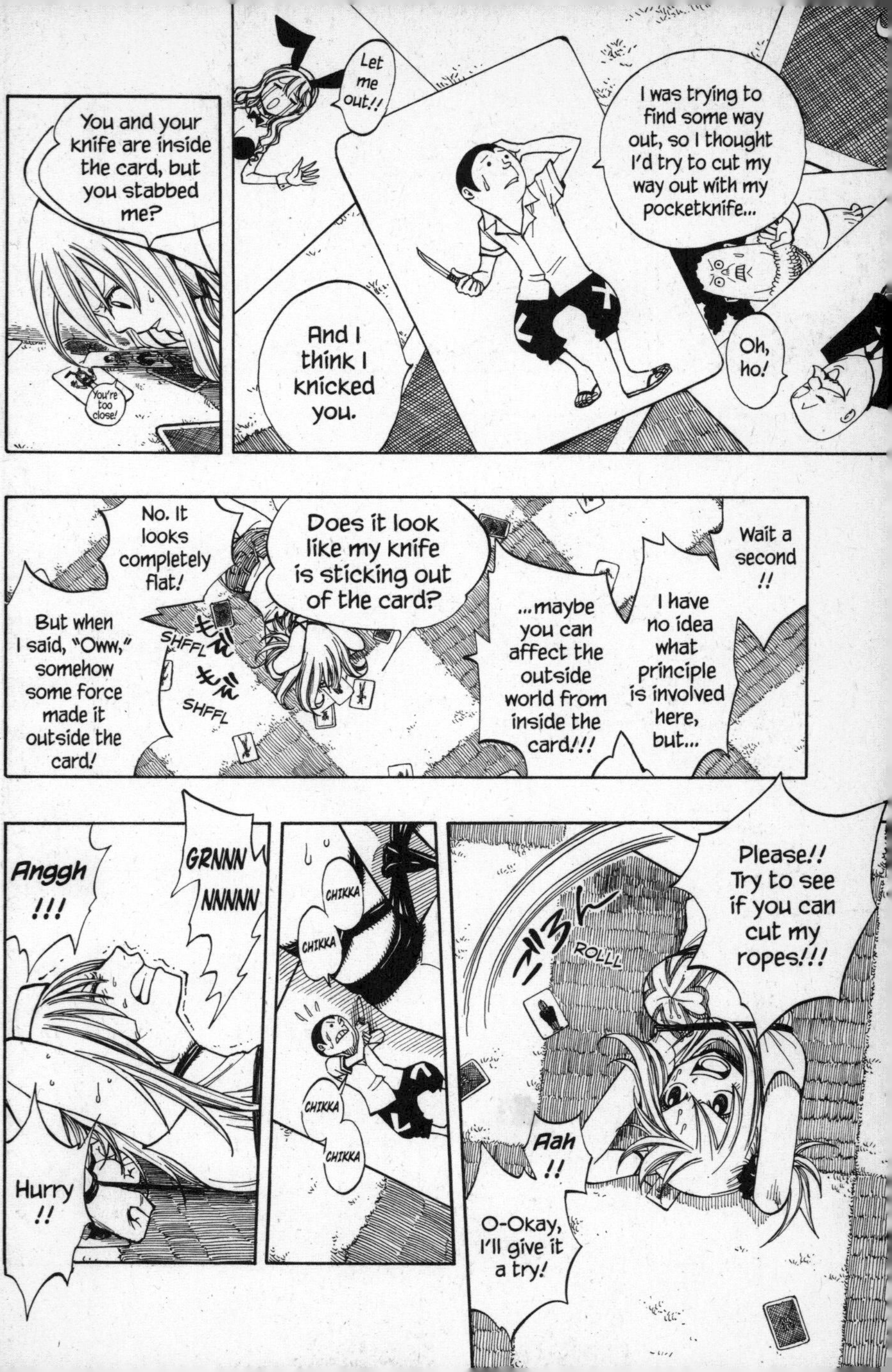
I was trying to find some way out, so I thought I'd try to cut my way out with my pocketknife...
Oh, ho!
Let me out!!
And I think I knicked you.
You and your knife are inside the card, but you stabbed me?
You're too close!
Wait a second!!
I have no idea what principle is involved here, but...
...maybe you can affect the outside world from inside the card!!!
Does it look like my knife is sticking out of the card?
No. It looks completely flat!
SHFFL
SHFFL
But when I said, "Oww," somehow some force made it outside the card!
Please!! Try to see if you can cut my ropes!!!
ROLLL
Aah!!
O-Okay, I'll give it a try!
CHIKKA
CHIKKA
CHIKKA
CHIKKA
GRNNN NNNNN
Angghh!!!
Hurry!!

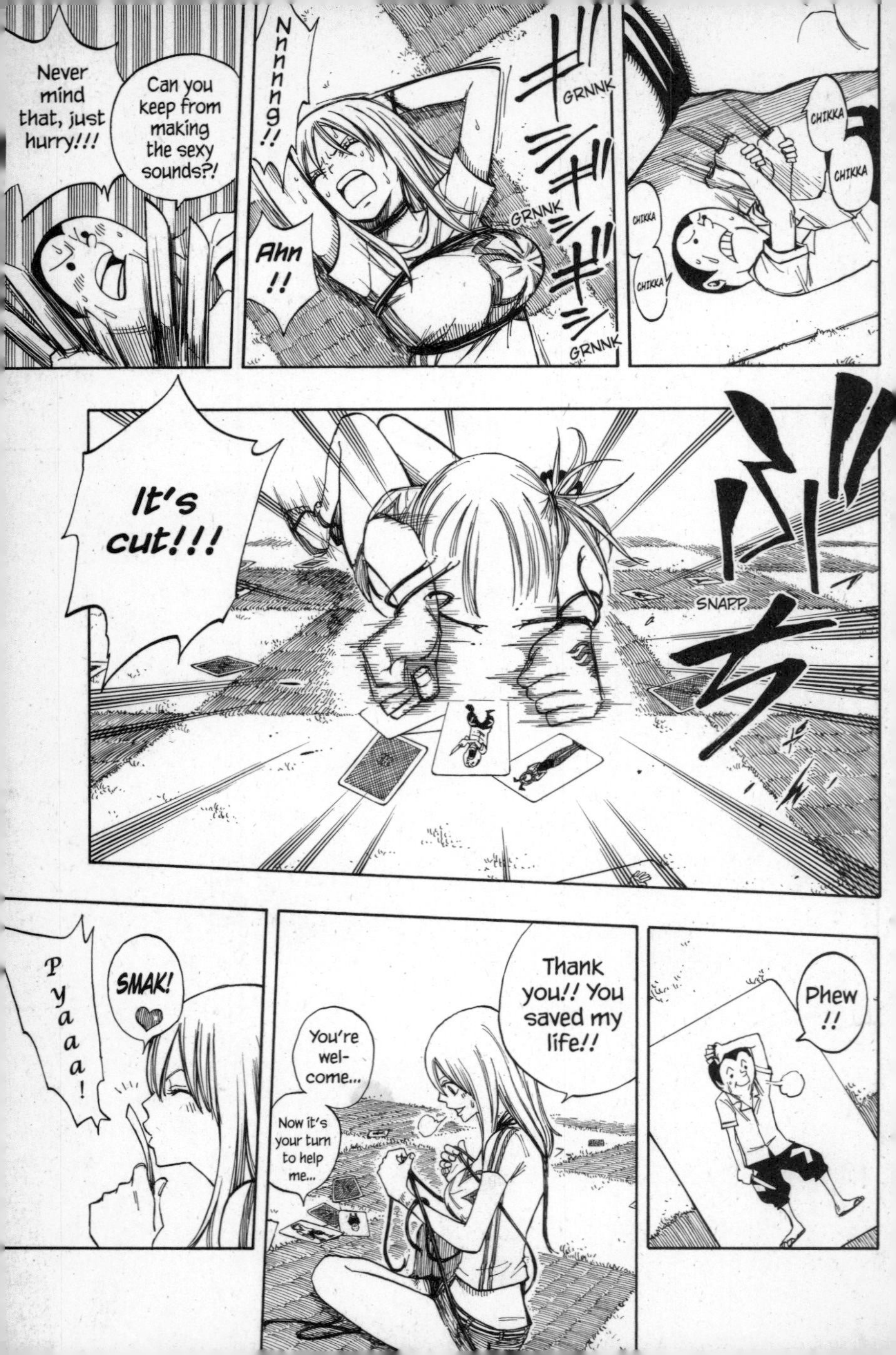
CHIKKA
CHIKKA
CHIKKA
CHIKKA
GRNNK
GRNNK
GRNNK
Nnnnng!!
Ahn!!
Can you keep from making the sexy sounds?!
Never mind that, just hurry!!!
SNAPP
It's cut!!!
Phew!!
Thank you!! You saved my life!!
You're wel-come...
Now it's your turn to help me...
SMAK! ♥
Pyaaa!

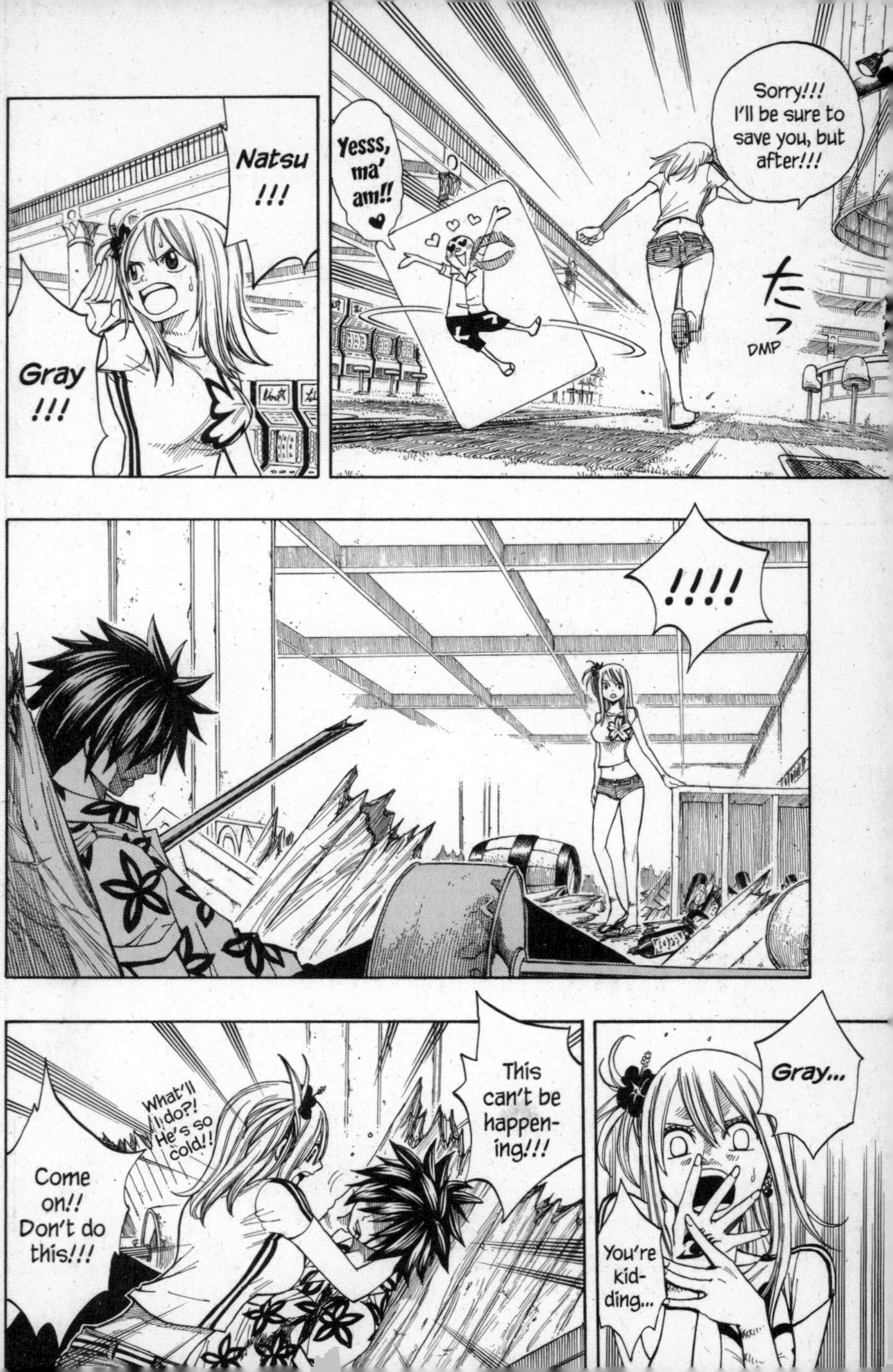
Sorry!!! I'll be sure to save you, but after!!!
Yesss, ma' am!! ♥
たっ
DMP
Natsu !!!
Gray !!!
!!!!
Gray...
You're kid-ding...
This can't be happen-ing!!!
What'll I do?! He's so cold!!
Come on!! Don't do this!!!

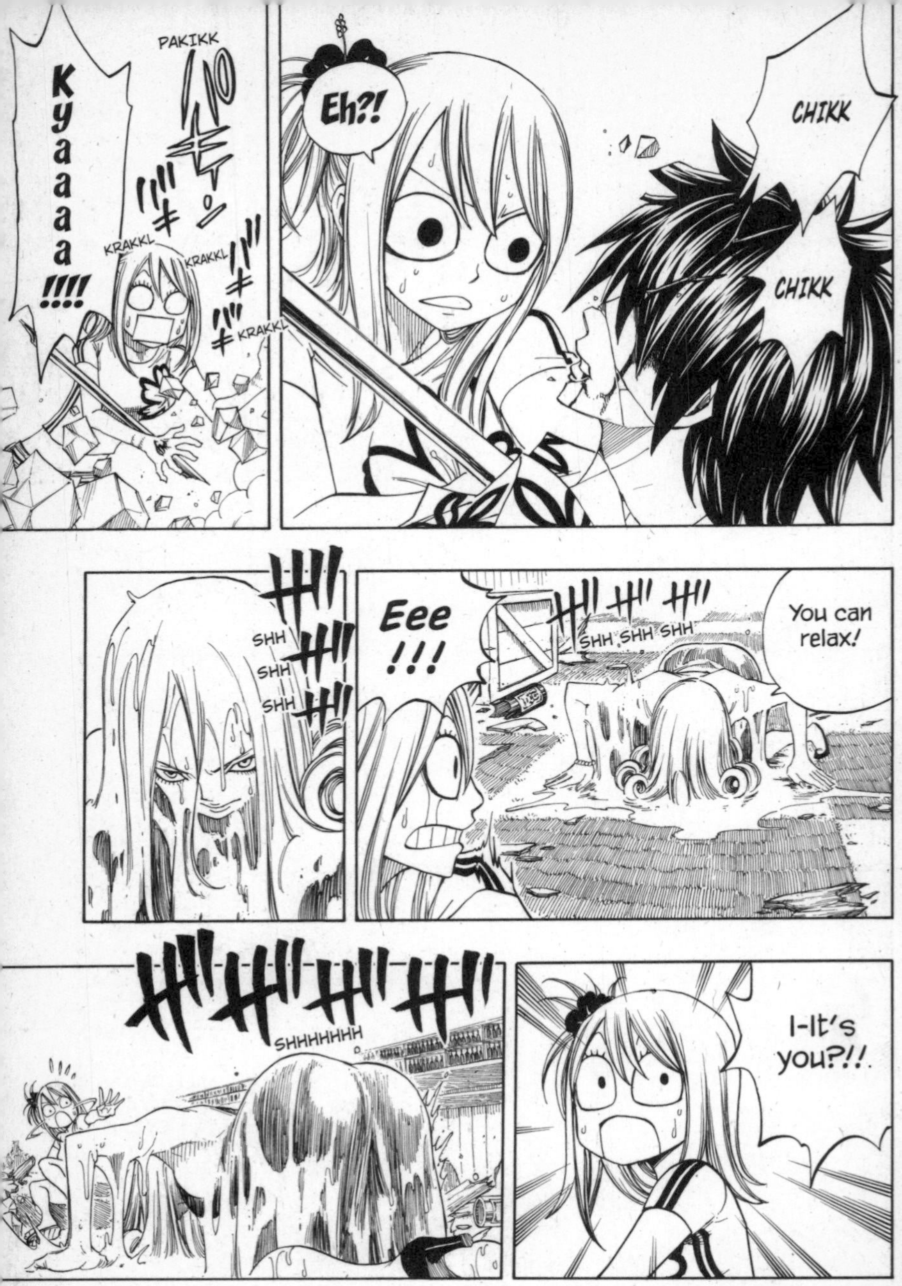
CHIKK
CHIKK
Eh?!
PAKIKK
Kyaaaaa!!!!
KRAKKL
KRAKKL
KRAKKL
You can relax!
SHH SHH SHH
Eee!!!
SHH
SHH
SHH
I-It's you?!!
SHHHHHHH

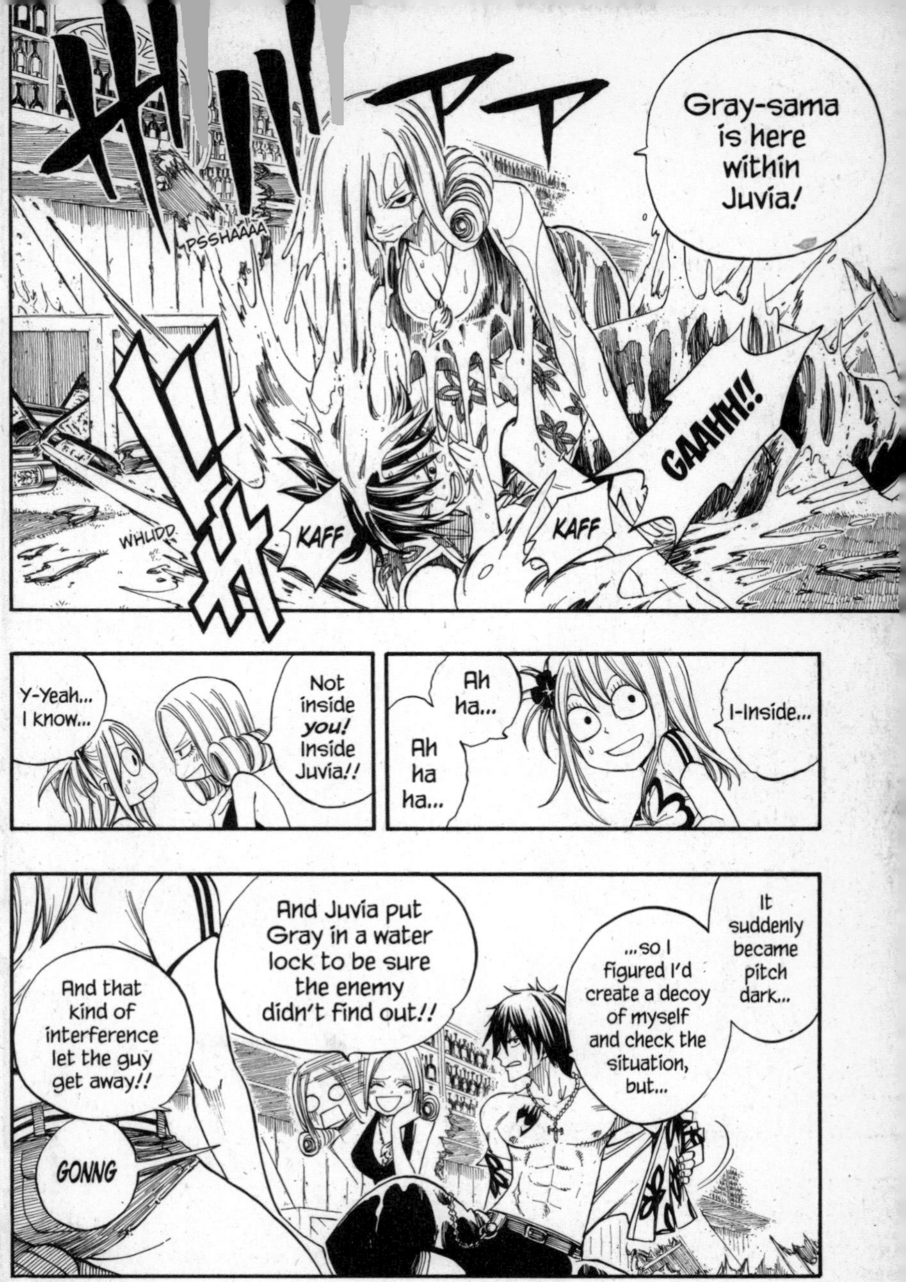
Gray-sama is here within Juvia!
PSSHAAAA
GAAHH!!
KAFF
KAFF
WHUDD
I-Inside...
Ah ha...
Ah ha ha...
Not inside *you!* Inside Juvia!!
Y-Yeah... I know...
It suddenly became pitch dark...
...so I figured I'd create a decoy of myself and check the situation, but...
And Juvia put Gray in a water lock to be sure the enemy didn't find out!!
And that kind of interference let the guy get away!!
GONNG

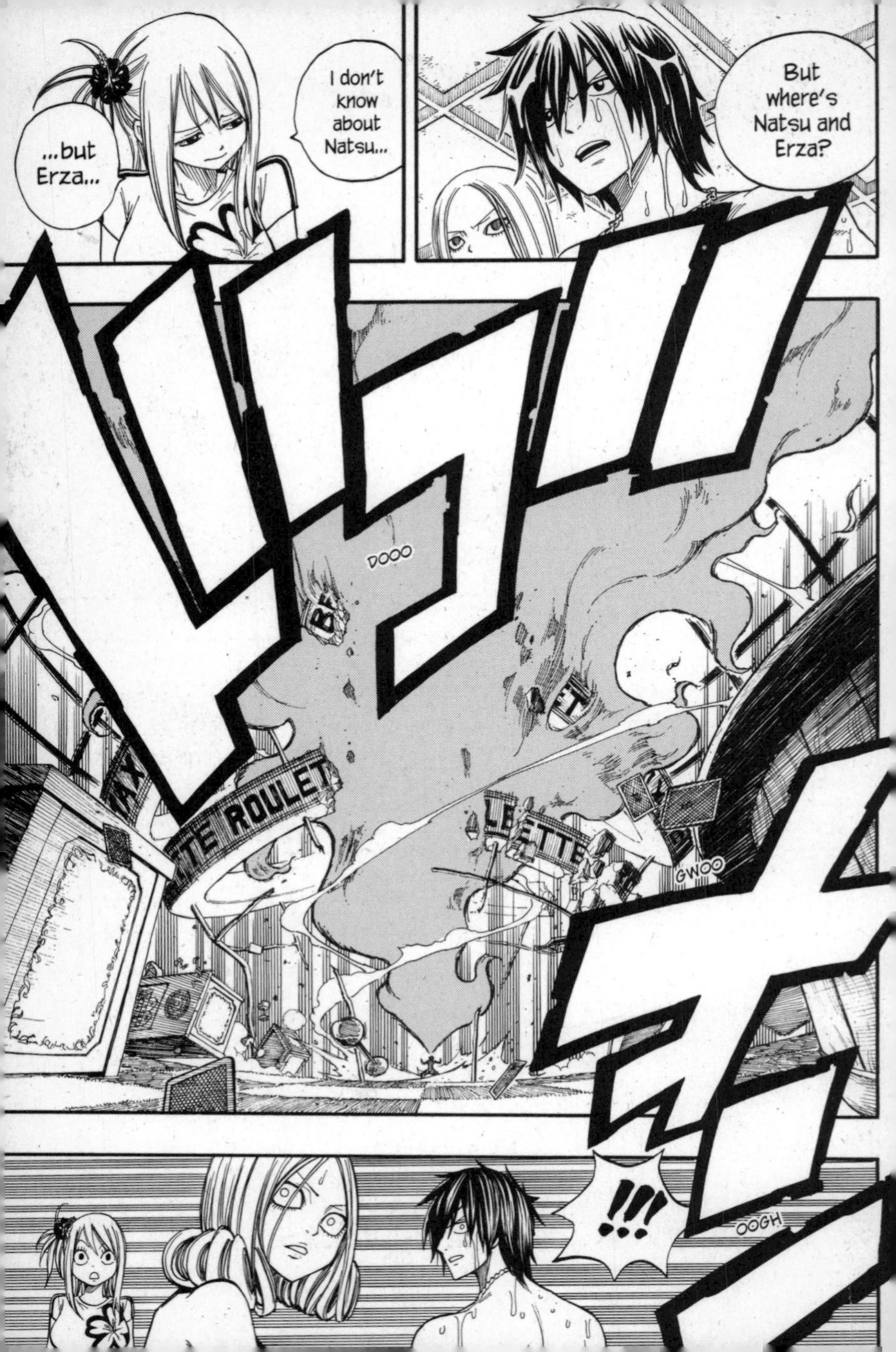
But where's Natsu and Erza?
I don't know about Natsu...
...but Erza...
DOOO
TE ROULET
LETTE
GWOO
OOGH
!!!

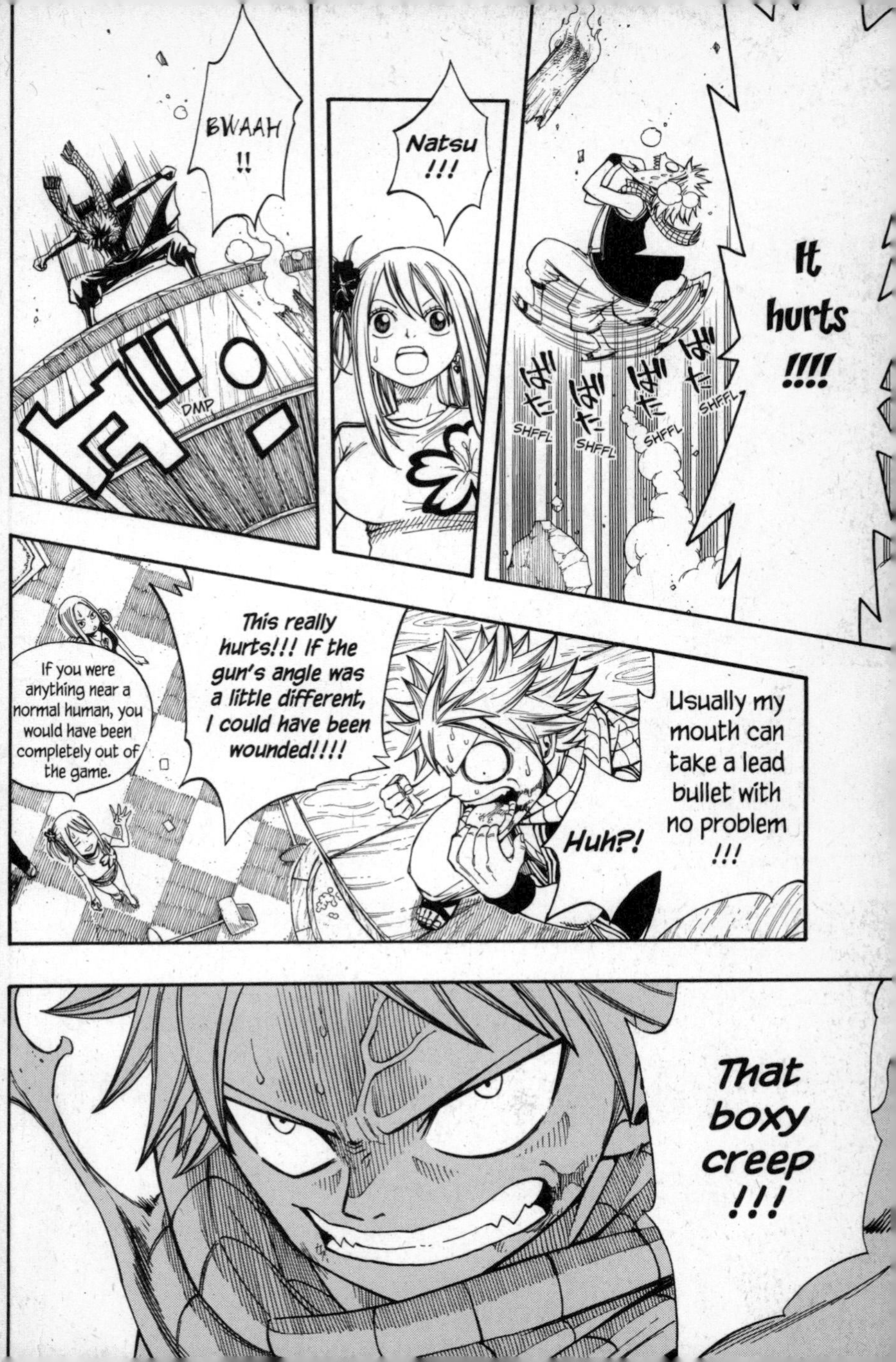

It hurts!!!!
SHFFL
SHFFL
SHFFL
SHFFL
Natsu!!!
BWAAH!!
DMP
Usually my mouth can take a lead bullet with no problem!!!
Huh?!
This really hurts!!! If the gun's angle was a little different, I could have been wounded!!!!
If you were anything near a normal human, you would have been completely out of the game.
That boxy creep!!!

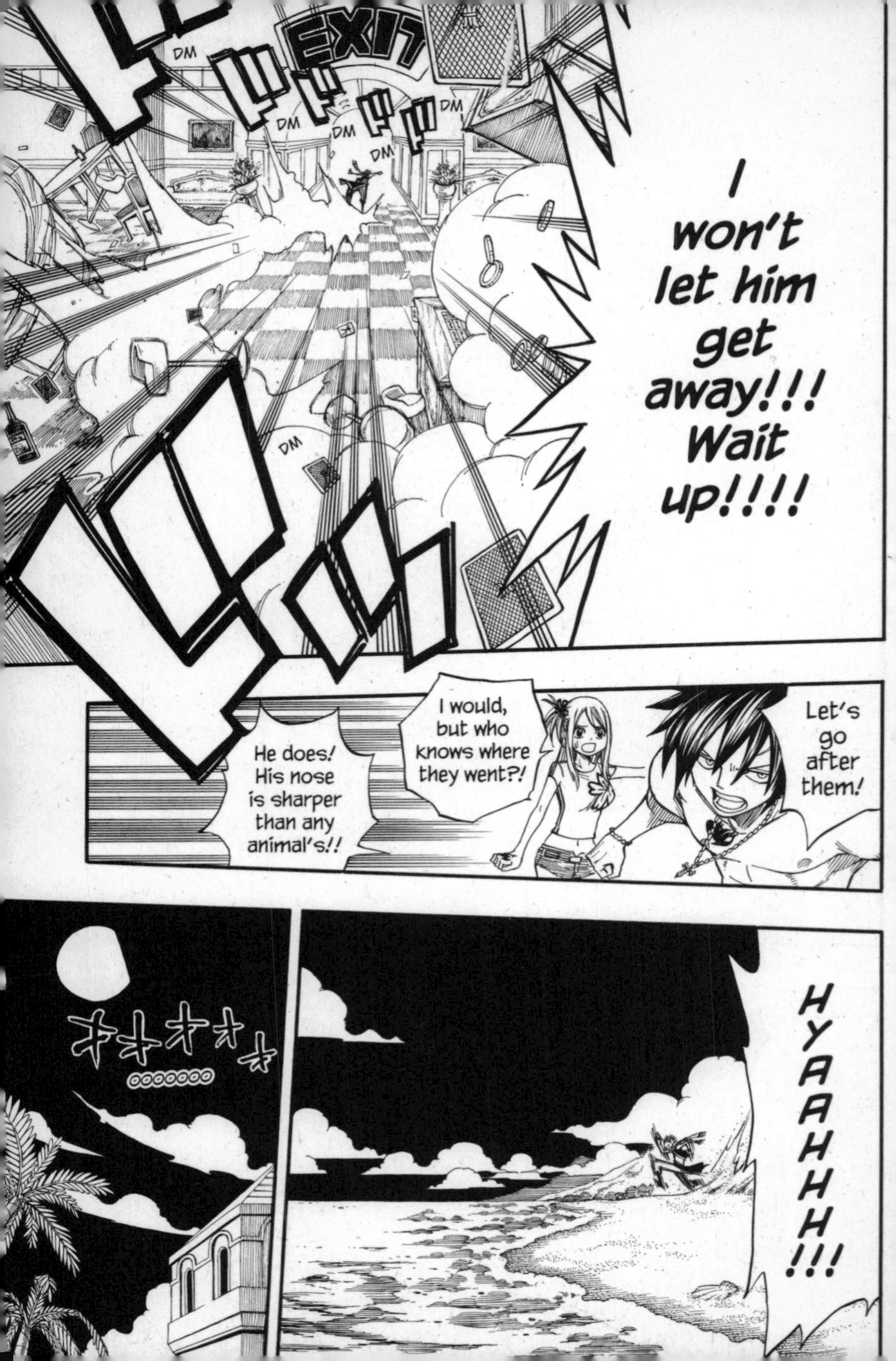
EXIT
DM
DM
DM
DM
DM
DM
I won't let him get away!!! Wait up!!!!
Let's go after them!
I would, but who knows where they went?!
He does! His nose is sharper than any animal's!!
HYAAAHHHH!!!
オオオオオ
oooooooo

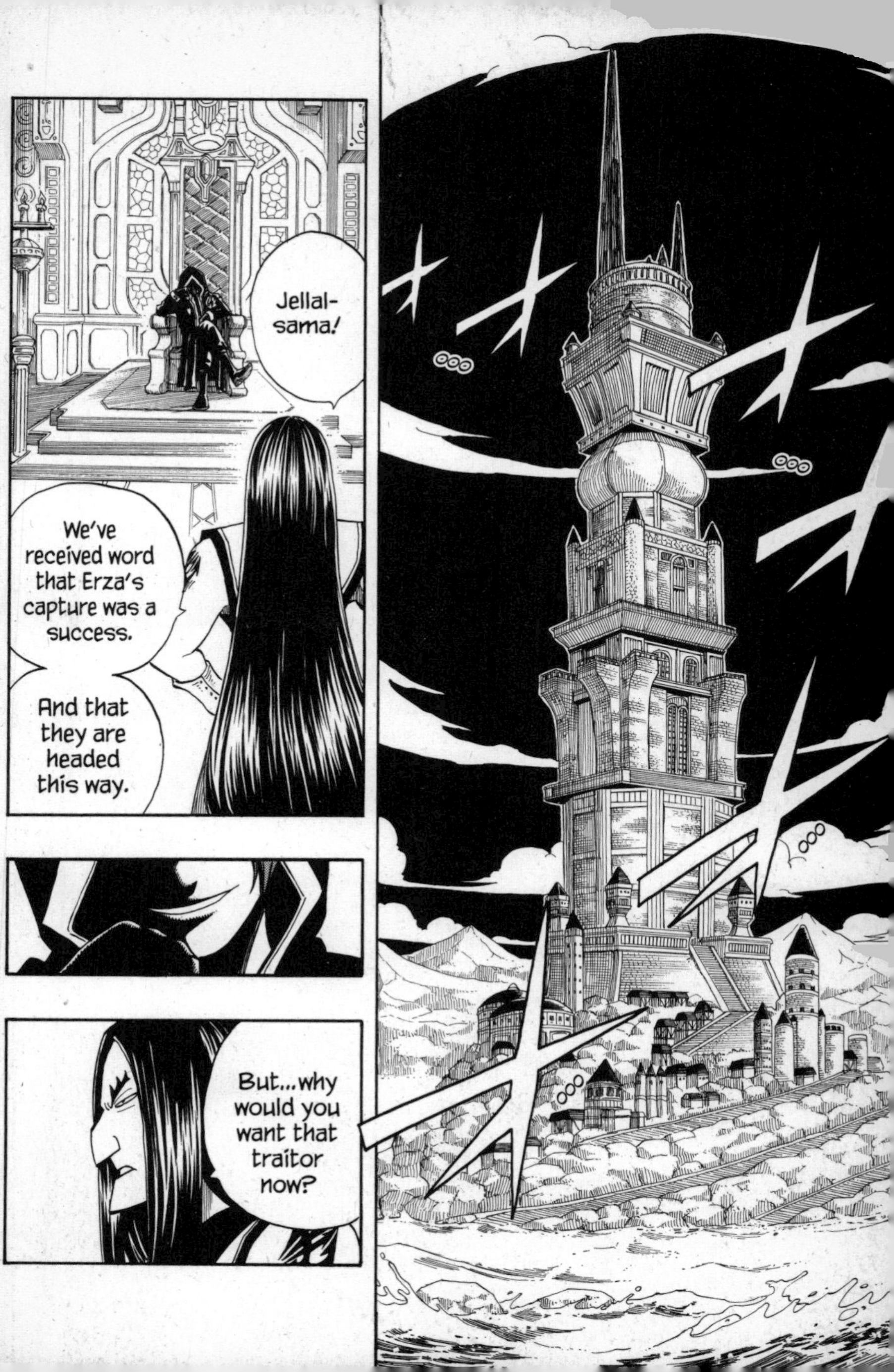
Jellal-sama!
We've received word that Erza's capture was a success.
And that they are headed this way.
But...why would you want that traitor now?

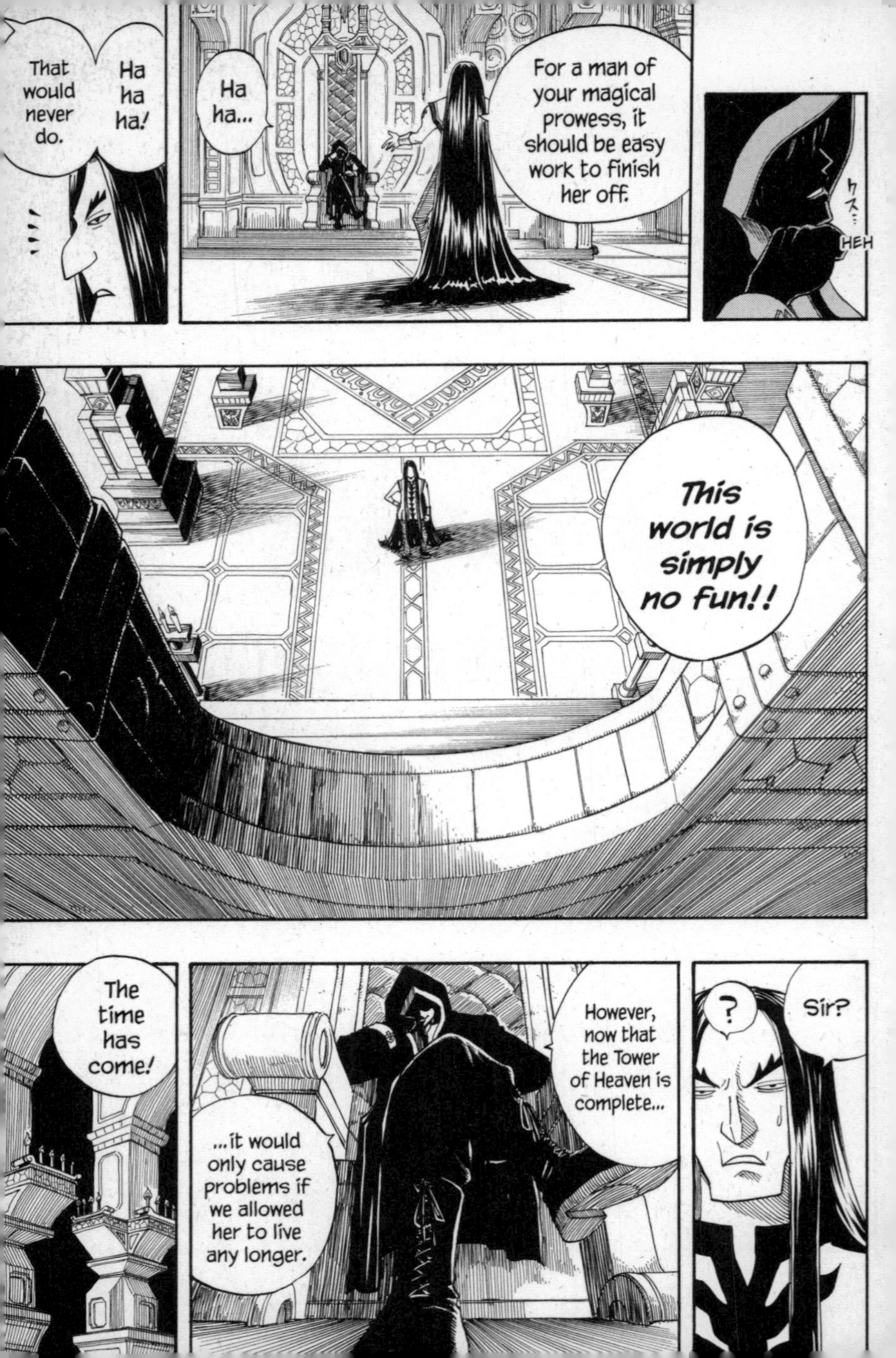
クス…
HEH
For a man of your magical prowess, it should be easy work to finish her off.
Ha ha...
Ha ha ha!
That would never do.
This world is simply no fun!!
Sir?
?
However, now that the Tower of Heaven is complete...
...it would only cause problems if we allowed her to live any longer.
The time has come!

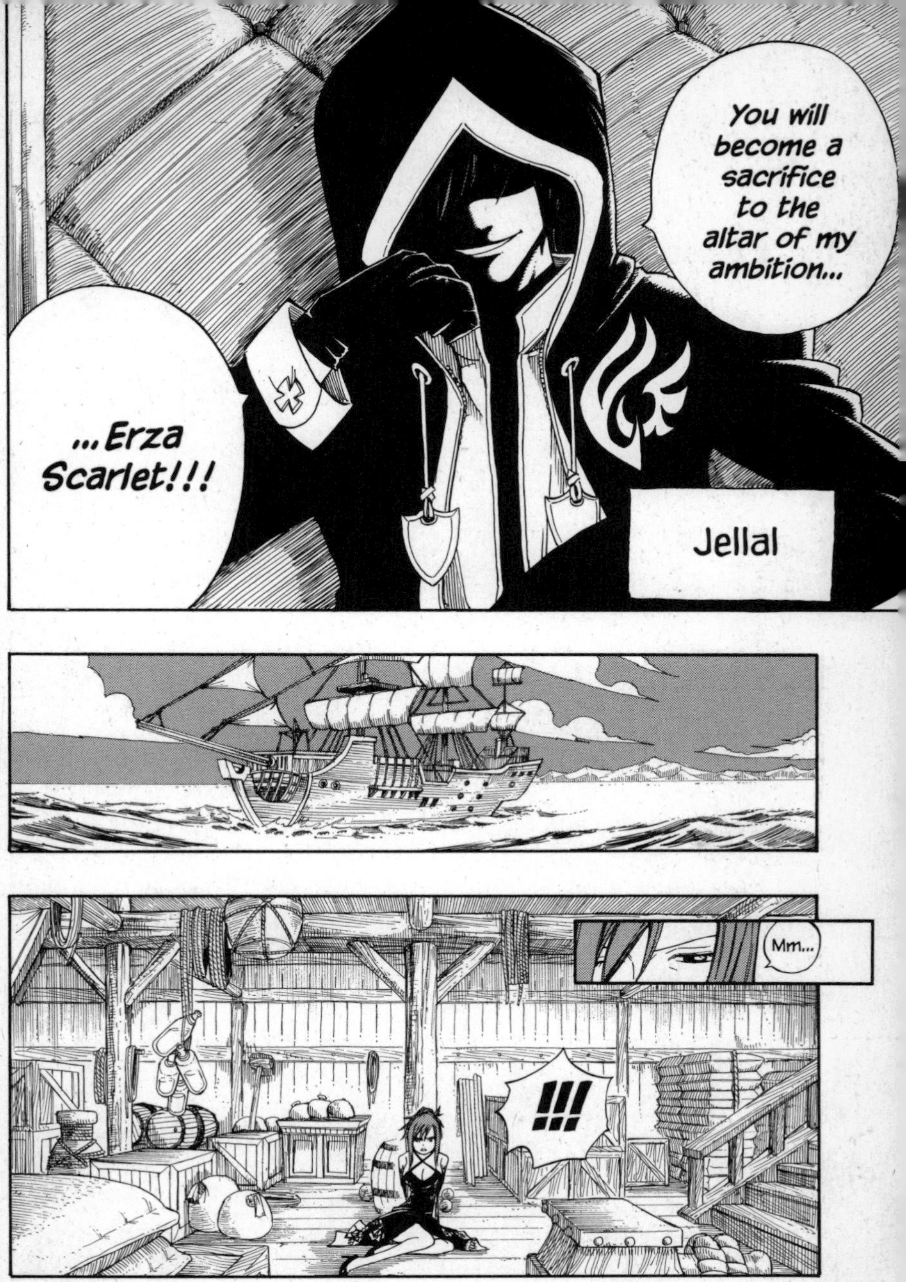
You will become a sacrifice to the altar of my ambition...
...Erza Scarlet!!!
Jellal
Mm...
!!!

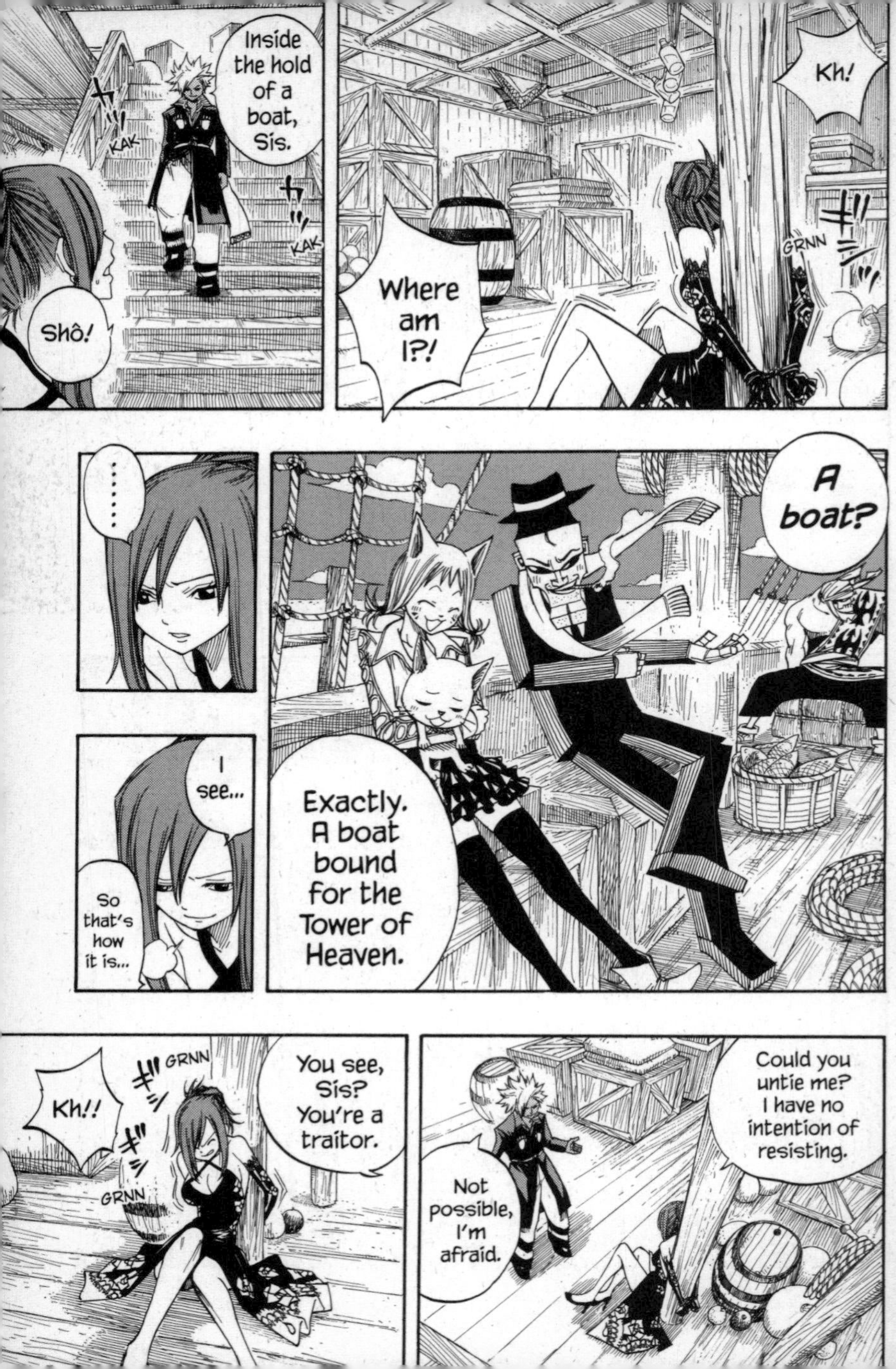
Kh!
GRNN
Where am I?!
Inside the hold of a boat, Sis.
KAK
KAK
Shô!
A boat?
Exactly. A boat bound for the Tower of Heaven.
......
I see...
So that's how it is...
Could you untie me? I have no intention of resisting.
Not possible, I'm afraid.
You see, Sis? You're a traitor.
GRNN
Kh!!
GRNN

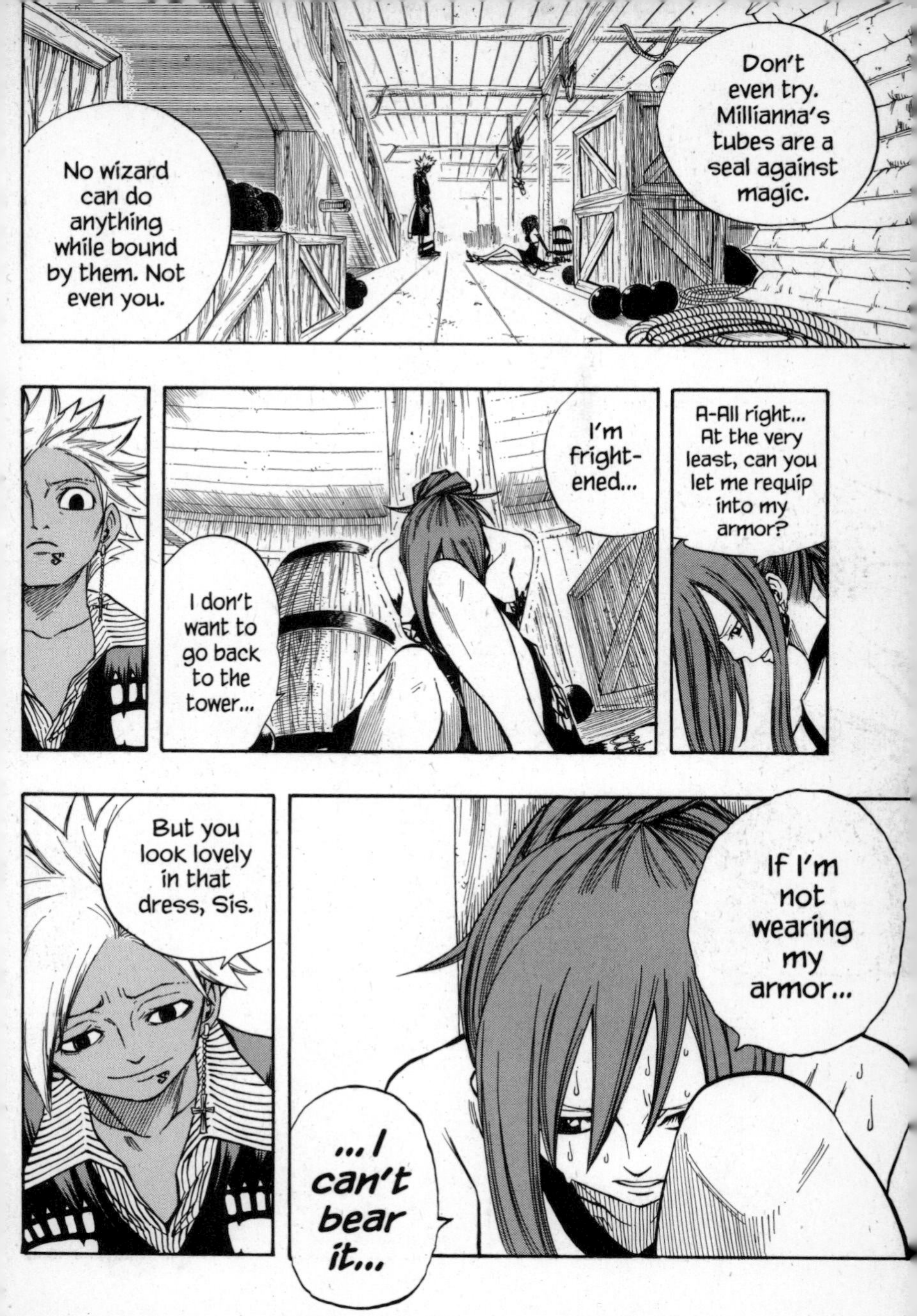
Don't even try. Millianna's tubes are a seal against magic.
No wizard can do anything while bound by them. Not even you.
A-All right... At the very least, can you let me requip into my armor?
I'm fright-ened...
I don't want to go back to the tower...
If I'm not wearing my armor...
...I can't bear it...
But you look lovely in that dress, Sis.

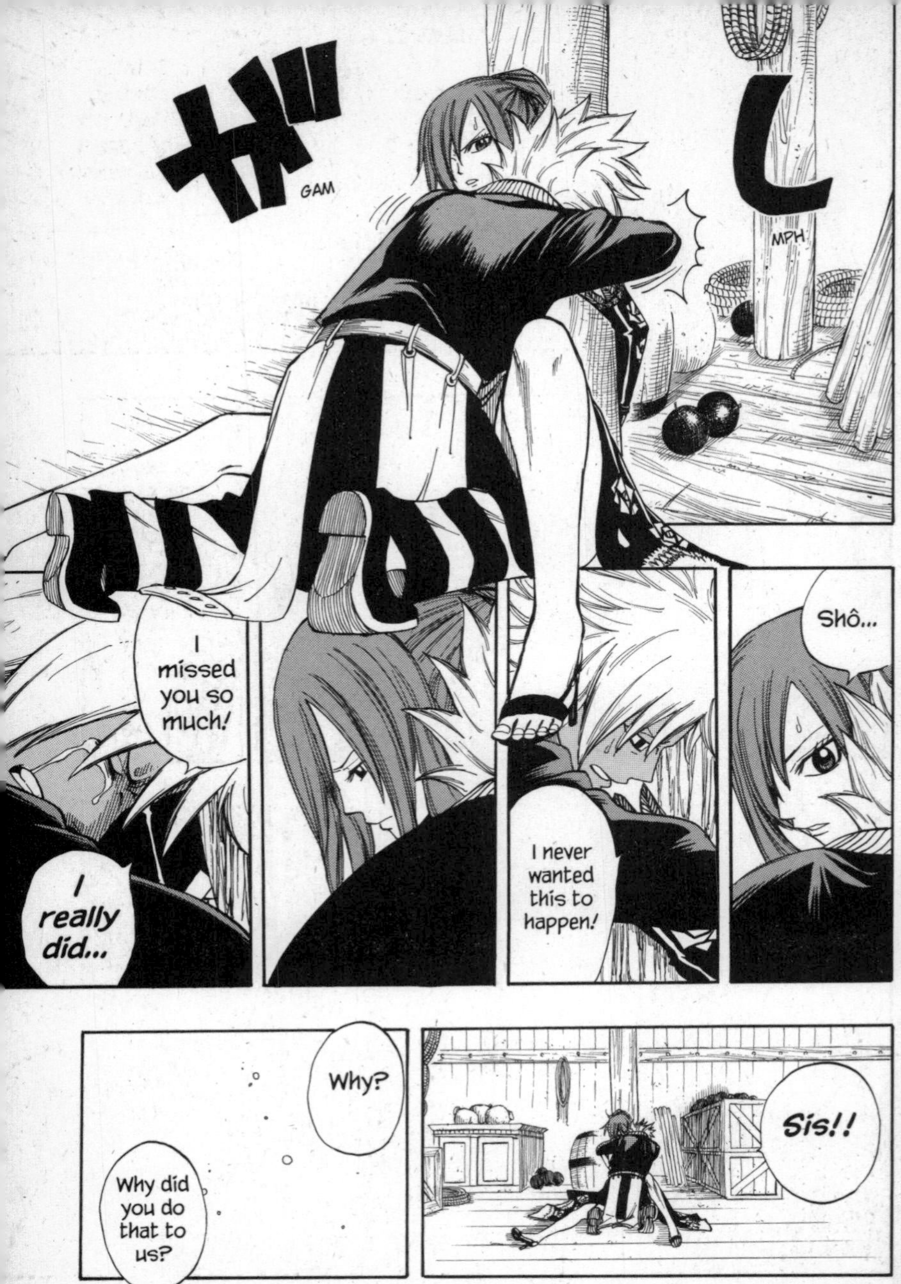

MPH
GAM
Shô...
I never wanted this to happen!
I missed you so much!
I really did...
Sis!!
Why?
Why did you do that to us?

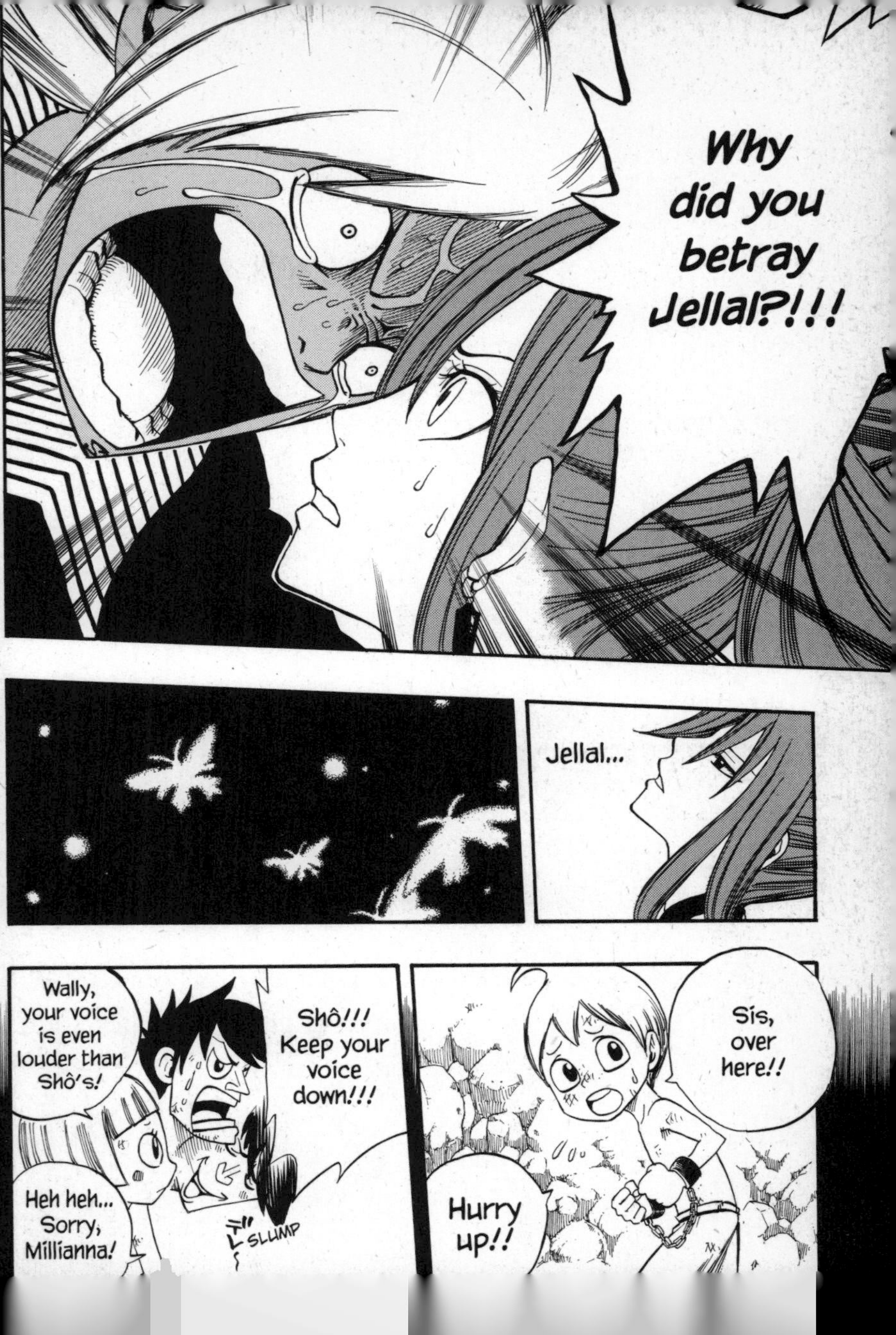
Why did you betray Jellal?!!!
Jellal...
Sis, over here!!
Hurry up!!
Shô!!! Keep your voice down!!!
Wally, your voice is even louder than Shô's!
Heh heh... Sorry, Millianna!
SLUMP

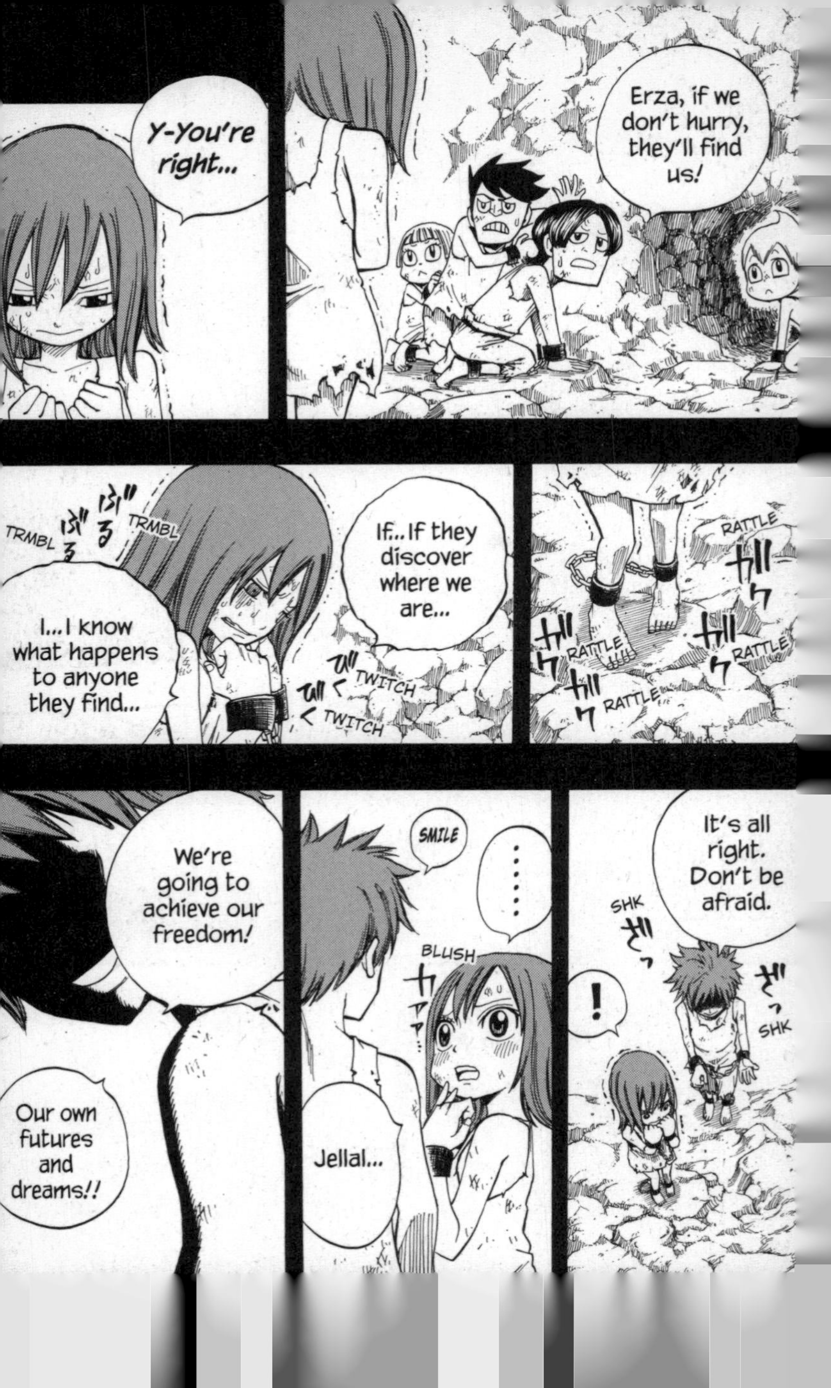
Erza, if we don't hurry, they'll find us!
Y-You're right...
RATTLE
RATTLE
RATTLE
RATTLE
If... If they discover where we are...
TRMBL
TRMBL
I...I know what happens to anyone they find...
TWITCH
TWITCH
It's all right. Don't be afraid.
SHK
SHK
!
......
SMILE
BLUSH
Jellal...
We're going to achieve our freedom!
Our own futures and dreams!!

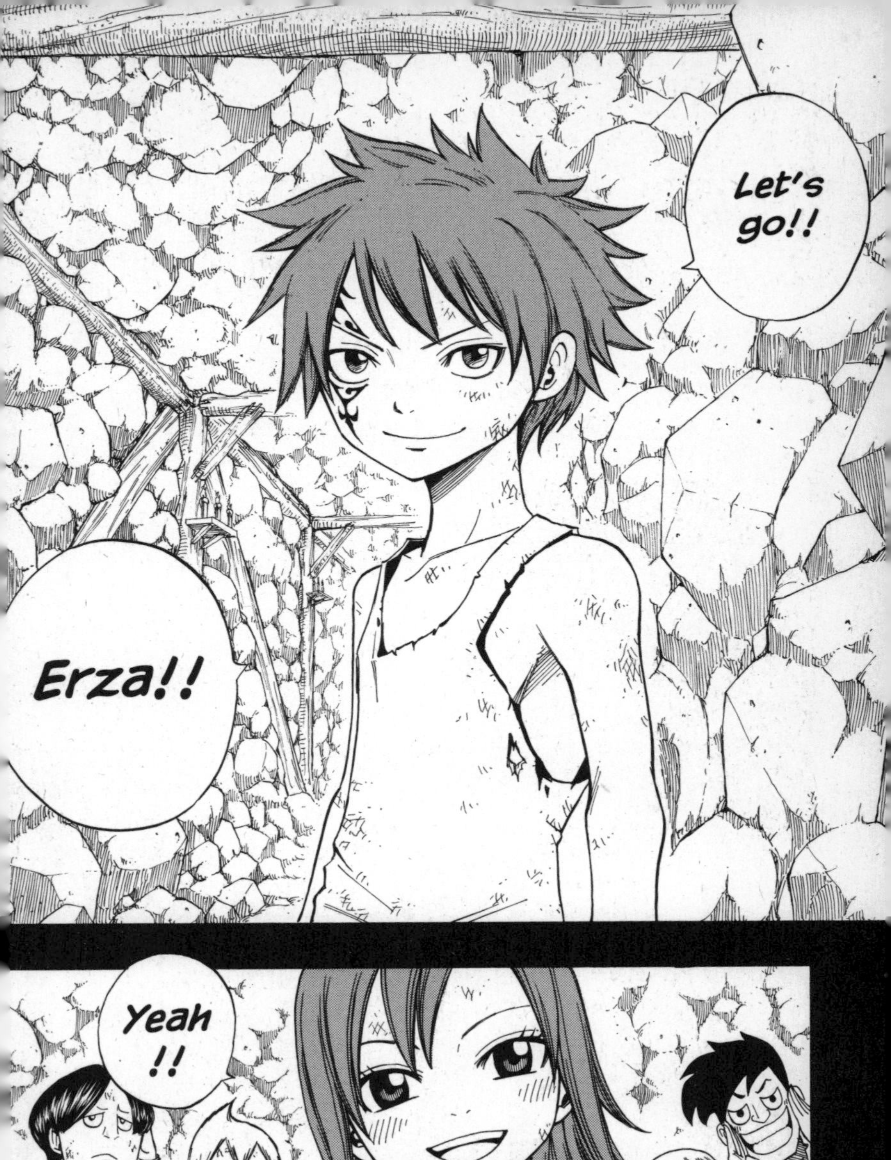
Let's go!!
Erza!!
Yeah !!

FAIRY TAIL

Chapter 78: Heaven Over There

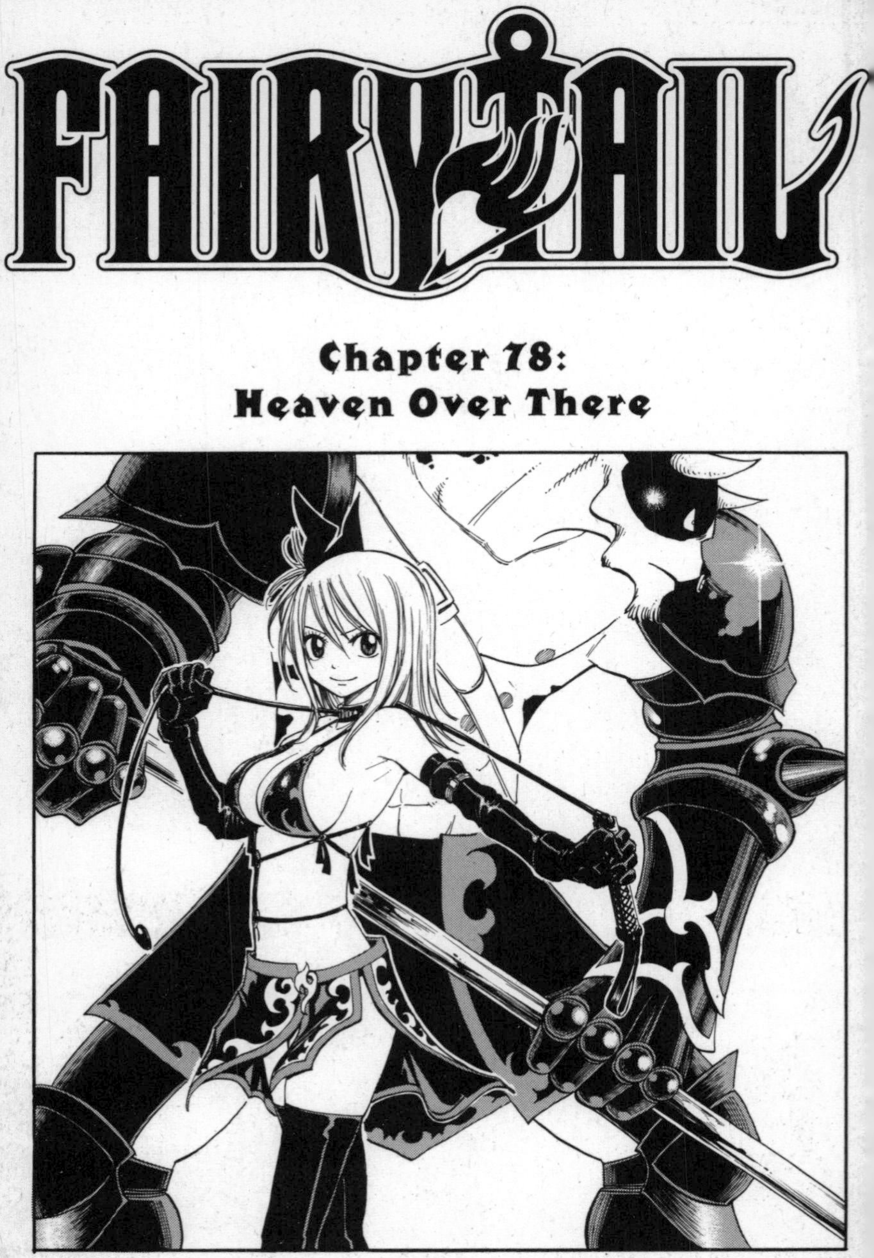

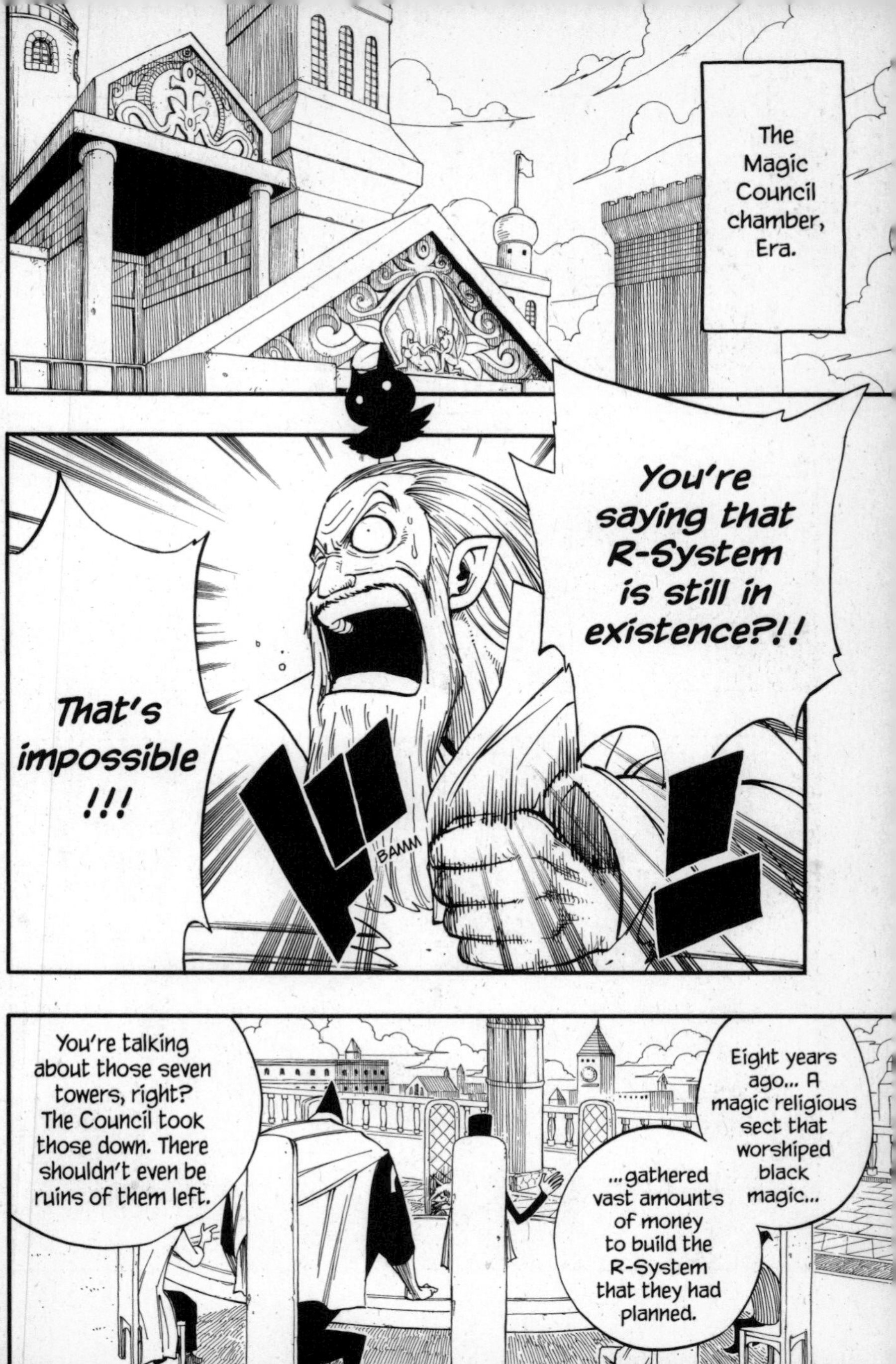
The Magic Council chamber, Era.
You're saying that R-System is still in existence?!!
That's impossible!!!
BAMM
Eight years ago... A magic religious sect that worshiped black magic...
...gathered vast amounts of money to build the R-System that they had planned.
You're talking about those seven towers, right? The Council took those down. There shouldn't even be ruins of them left.

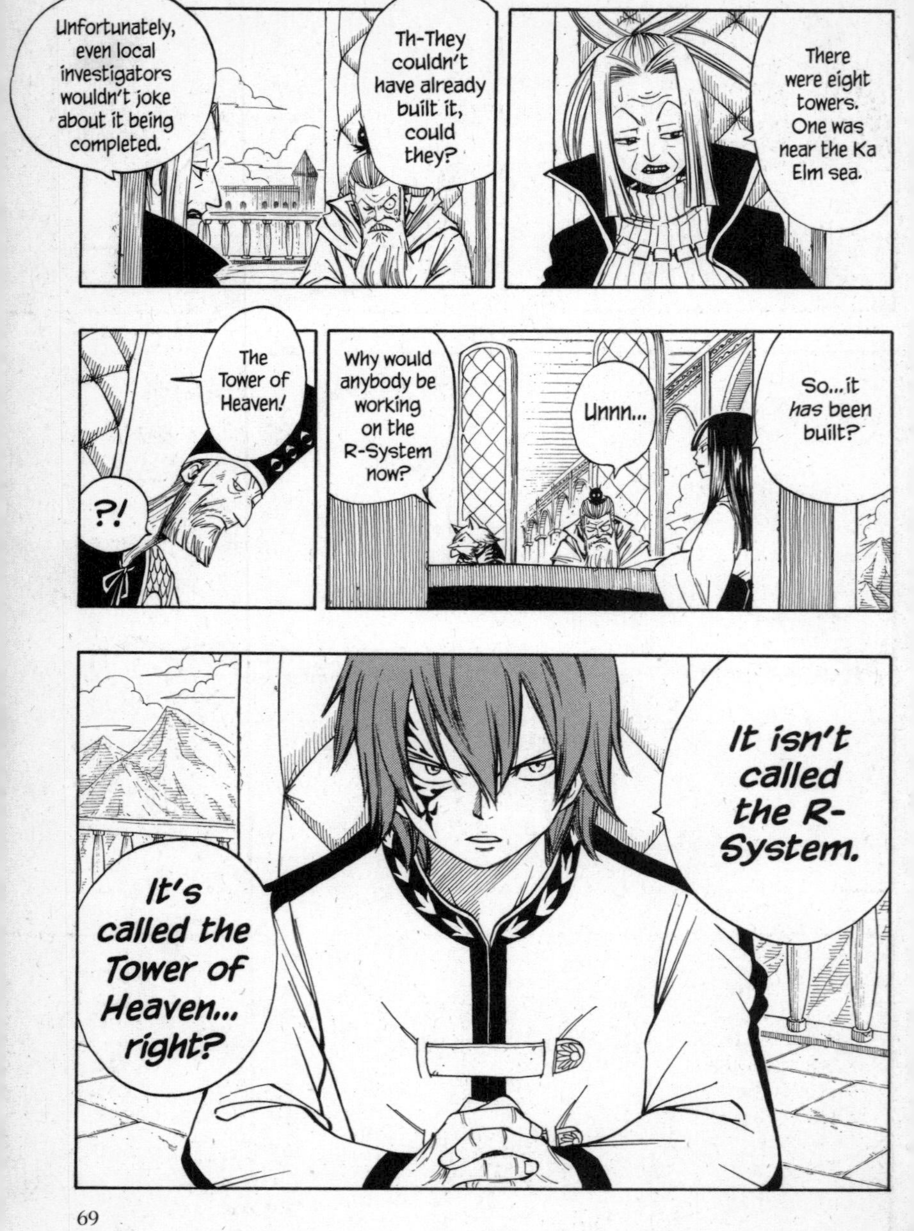
There were eight towers. One was near the Ka Elm sea.
Th-They couldn't have already built it, could they?
Unfortunately, even local investigators wouldn't joke about it being completed.
So...it *has* been built?
Unnn...
Why would anybody be working on the R-System now?
The Tower of Heaven!
?!
It isn't called the R-System.
It's called the Tower of Heaven... right?

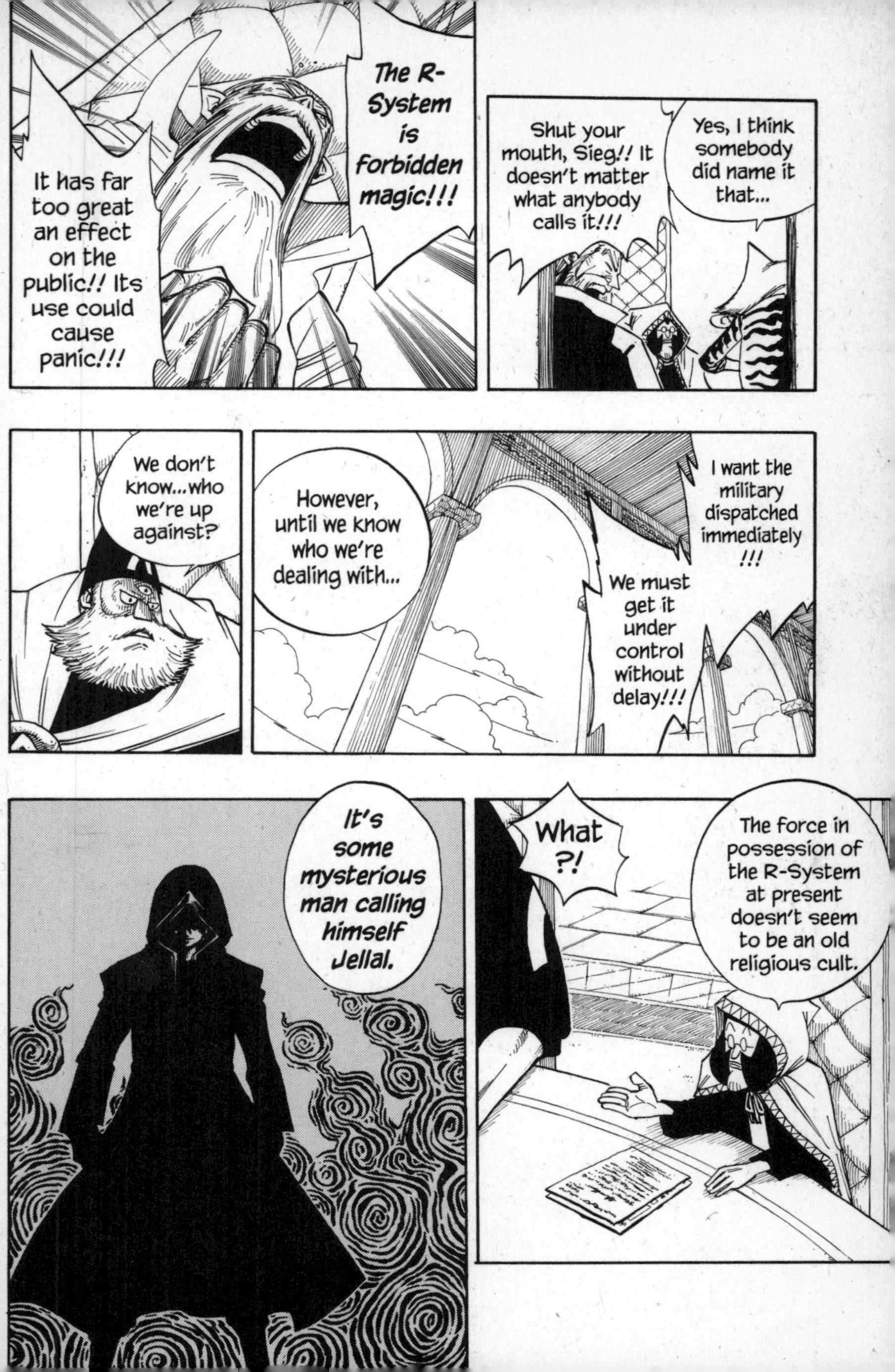
Yes, I think somebody did name it that...
Shut your mouth, Sieg!! It doesn't matter what anybody calls it!!!
The R-System is forbidden magic!!!
It has far too great an effect on the public!! Its use could cause panic!!!
I want the military dispatched immediately!!!
We must get it under control without delay!!!
However, until we know who we're dealing with...
We don't know...who we're up against?
The force in possession of the R-System at present doesn't seem to be an old religious cult.
What?!
It's some mysterious man calling himself Jellal.

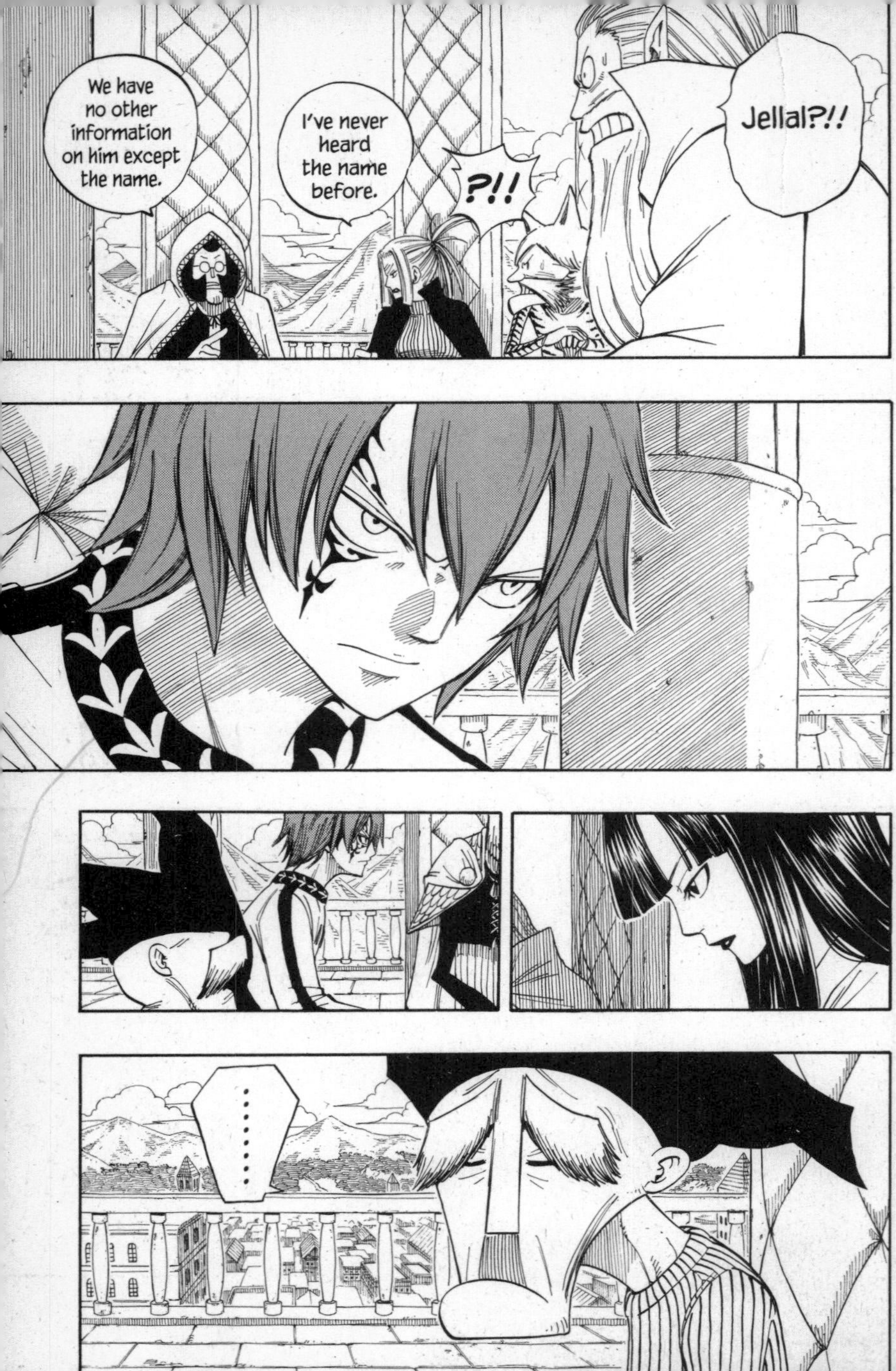
Jellal?!!
?!!
I've never heard the name before.
We have no other information on him except the name.
......

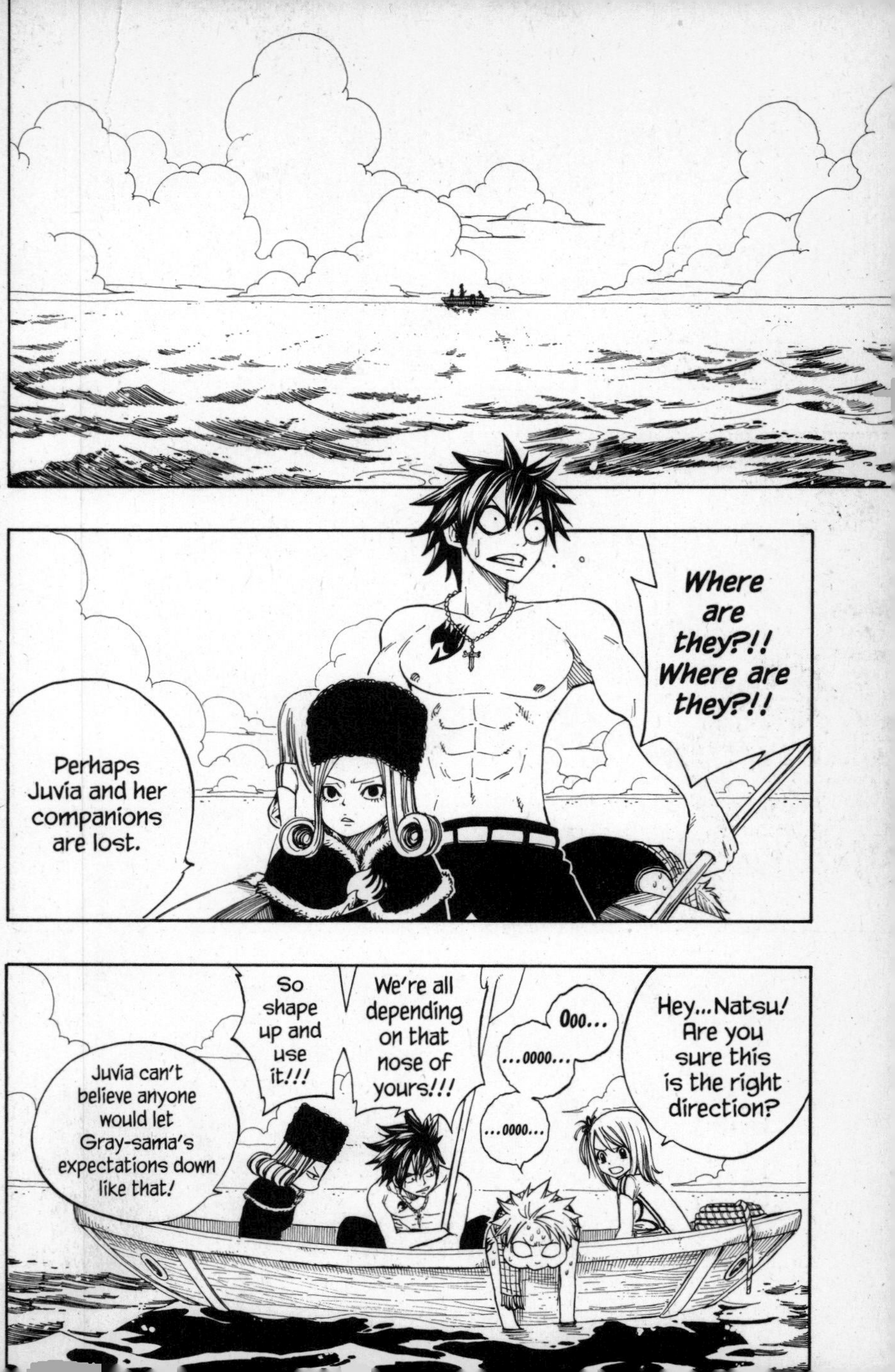
Where are they?!! Where are they?!!
Perhaps Juvia and her companions are lost.
Hey...Natsu! Are you sure this is the right direction?
Ooo...
...oooo...
...oooo...
We're all depending on that nose of yours!!!
So shape up and use it!!!
Juvia can't believe anyone would let Gray-sama's expectations down like that!

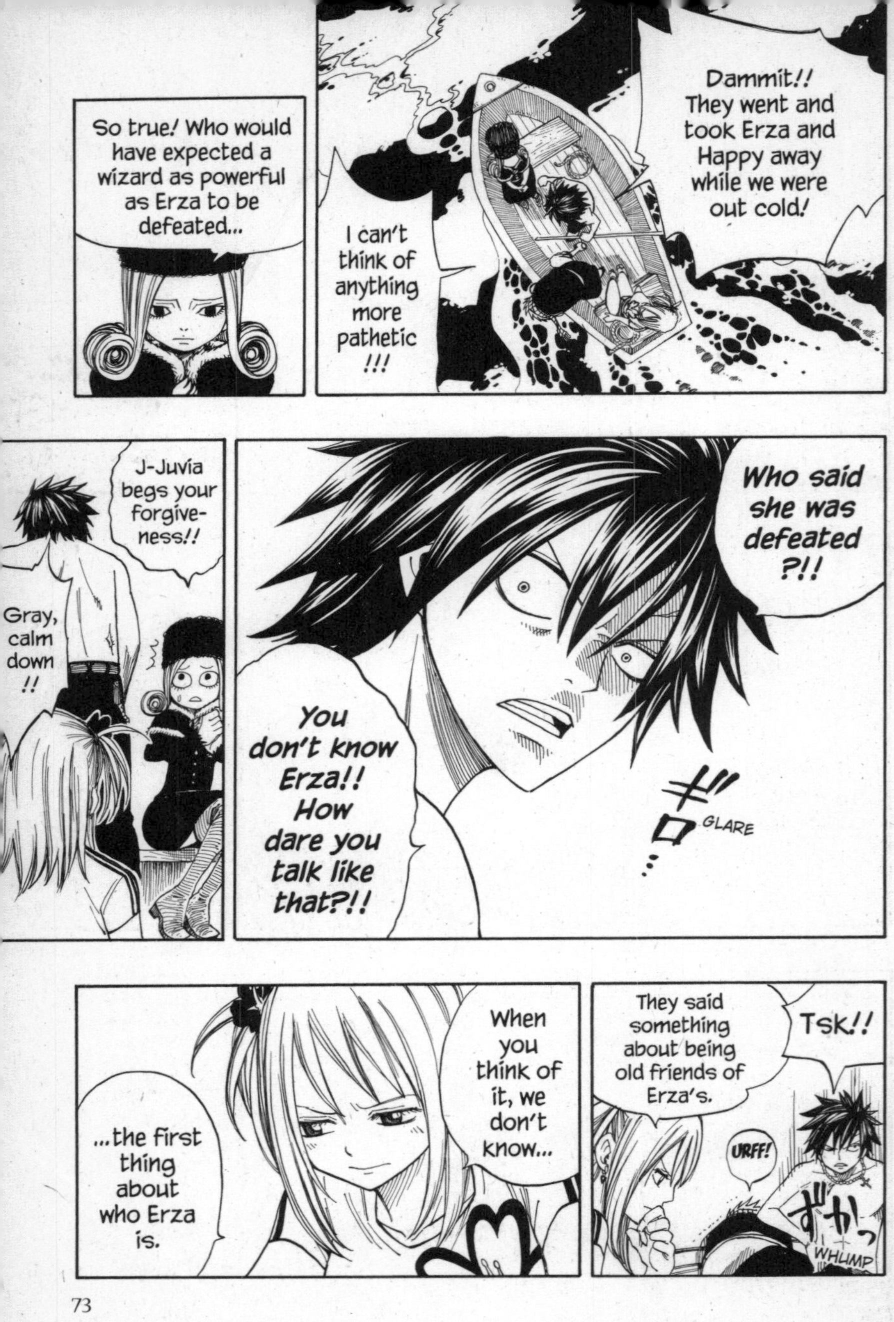
Dammit!! They went and took Erza and Happy away while we were out cold!
I can't think of anything more pathetic!!!
So true! Who would have expected a wizard as powerful as Erza to be defeated...
Who said she was defeated?!!
You don't know Erza!! How dare you talk like that?!!
GLARE
J-Juvia begs your forgive-ness!!
Gray, calm down!!
Tsk!!
They said something about being old friends of Erza's.
URFF!
WHUMP
When you think of it, we don't know...
...the first thing about who Erza is.

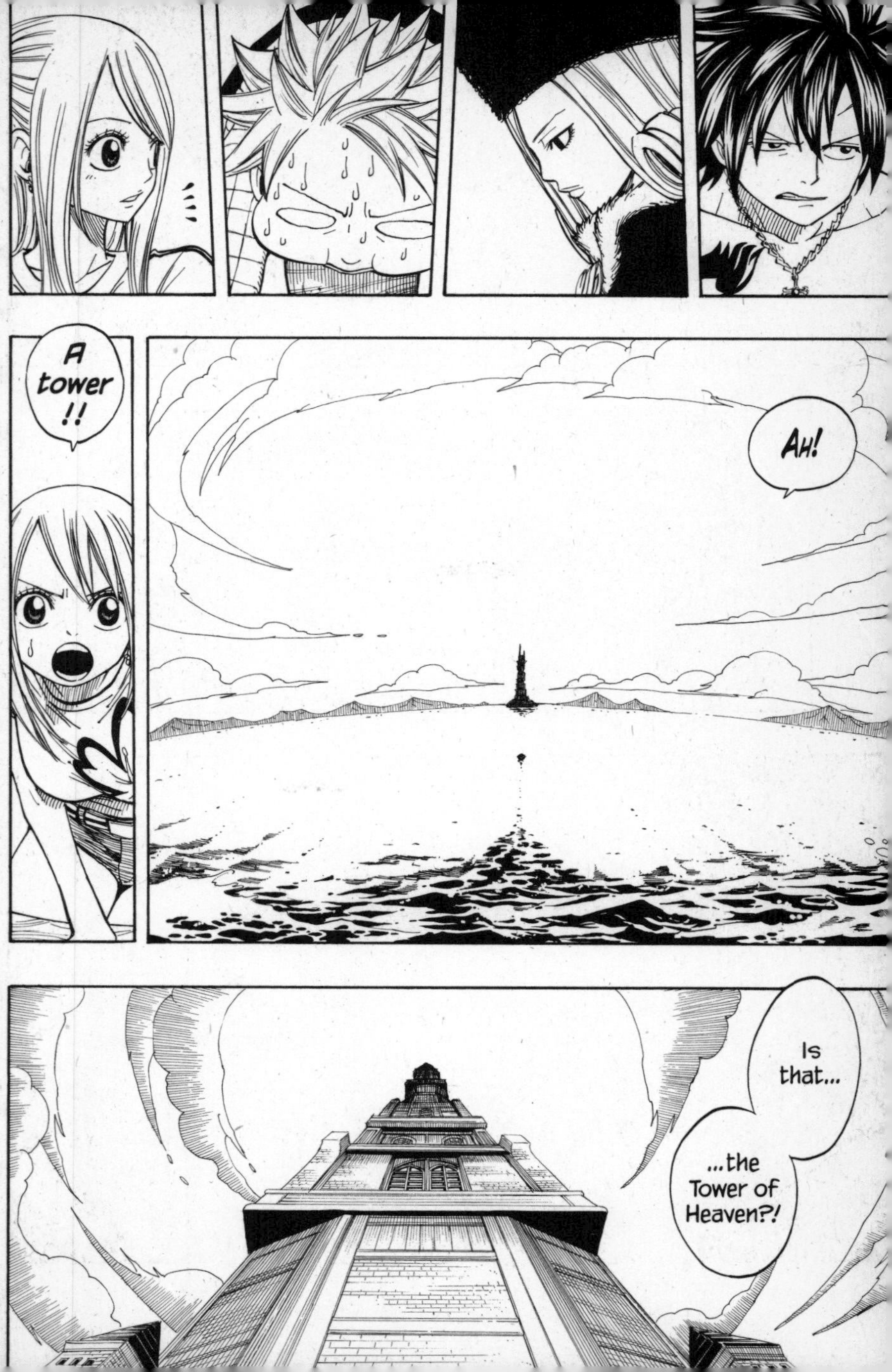
Ah!
A tower !!
Is that...
...the Tower of Heaven?!

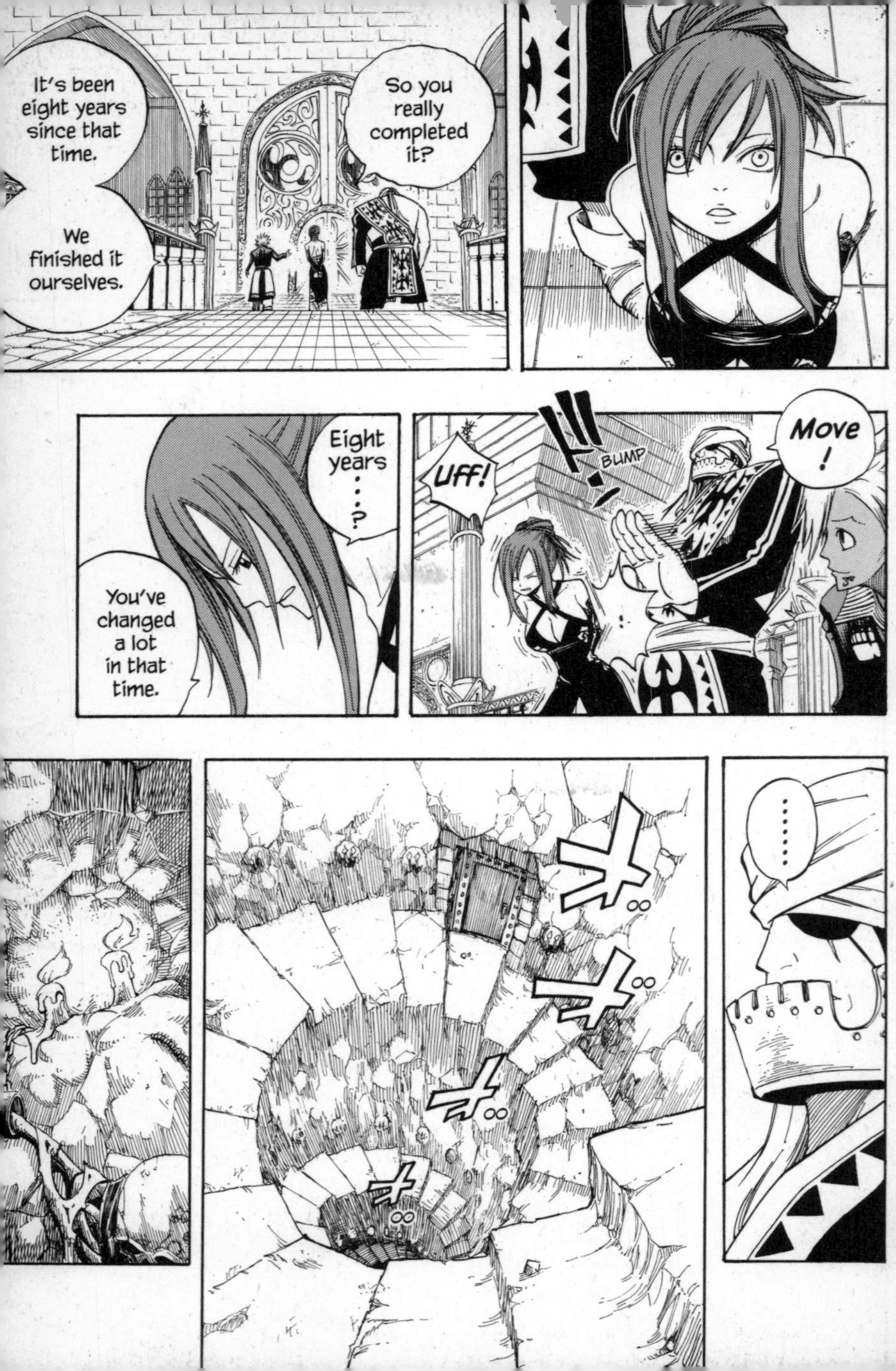
So you really completed it?
It's been eight years since that time.
We finished it ourselves.
Move!
BUMP
UFF!
Eight years...?
You've changed a lot in that time.
......

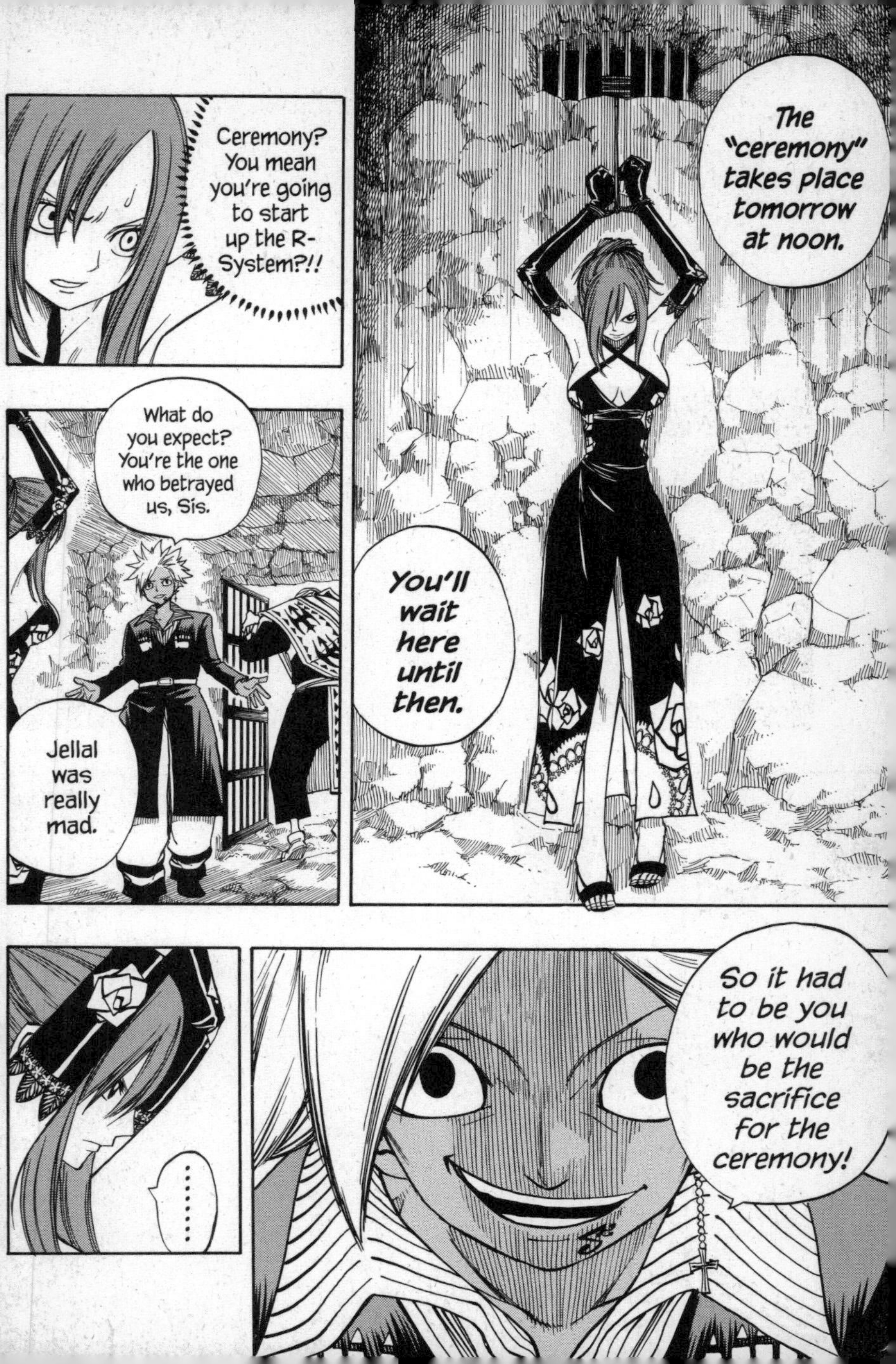
The "ceremony" takes place tomorrow at noon.
You'll wait here until then.
Ceremony? You mean you're going to start up the R-System?!!
What do you expect? You're the one who betrayed us, Sis.
Jellal was really mad.
So it had to be you who would be the sacrifice for the ceremony!
......

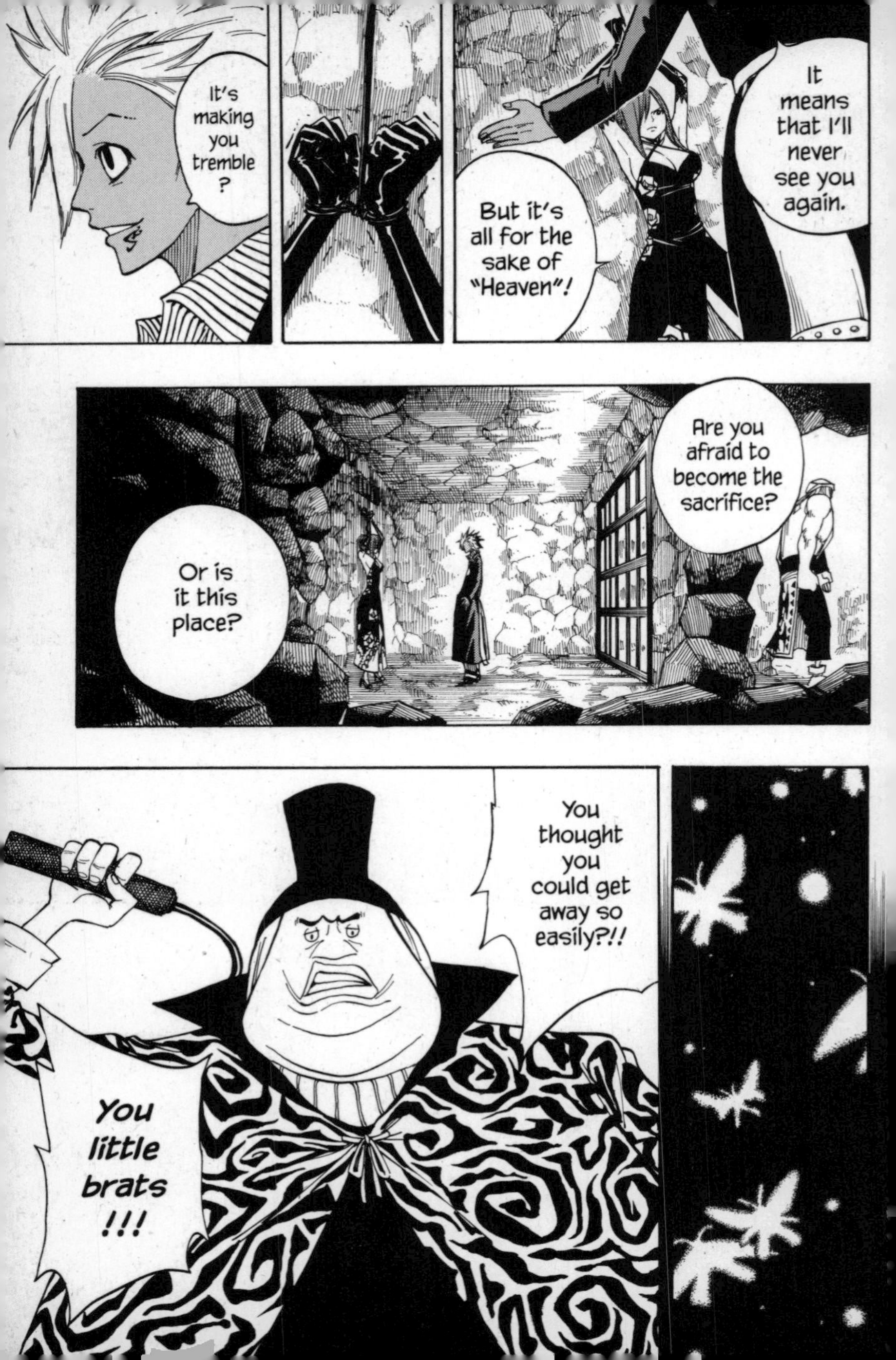
It means that I'll never see you again.
But it's all for the sake of "Heaven"!
It's making you tremble?
Are you afraid to become the sacrifice?
Or is it this place?
You thought you could get away so easily?!!
You little brats!!!

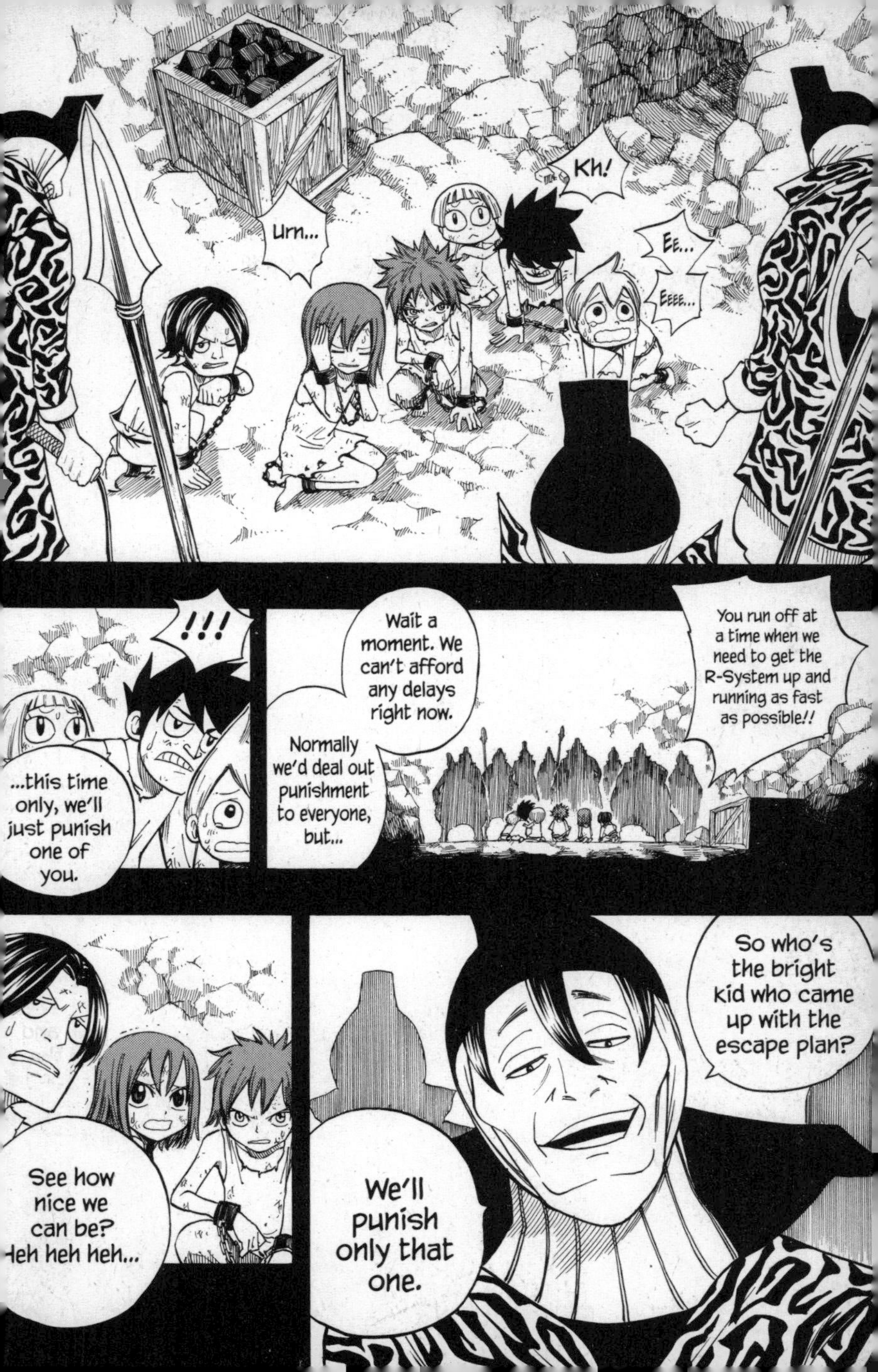
Ee...
Eeee...
Kh!
Urn...
You run off at a time when we need to get the R-System up and running as fast as possible!!
Wait a moment. We can't afford any delays right now.
Normally we'd deal out punishment to everyone, but...
!!!
...this time only, we'll just punish one of you.
So who's the bright kid who came up with the escape plan?
We'll punish only that one.
See how nice we can be? Heh heh heh...

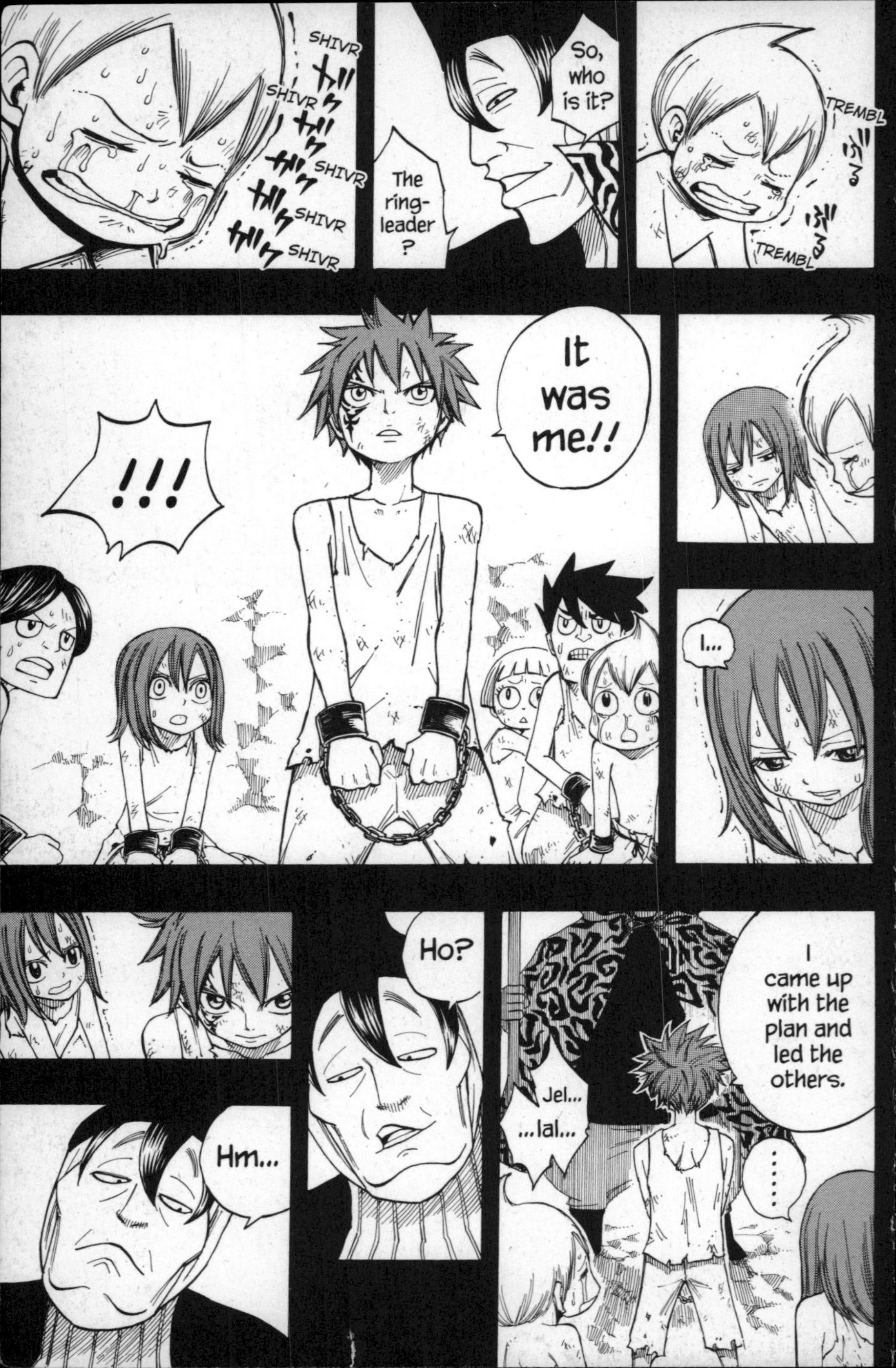
TREMBL
TREMBL
So, who is it?
The ring-leader?
SHIVR
SHIVR
SHIVR
SHIVR
SHIVR
I...
It was me!!
!!!
I came up with the plan and led the others.
......
Jel...
...lal...
Ho?
Hm...

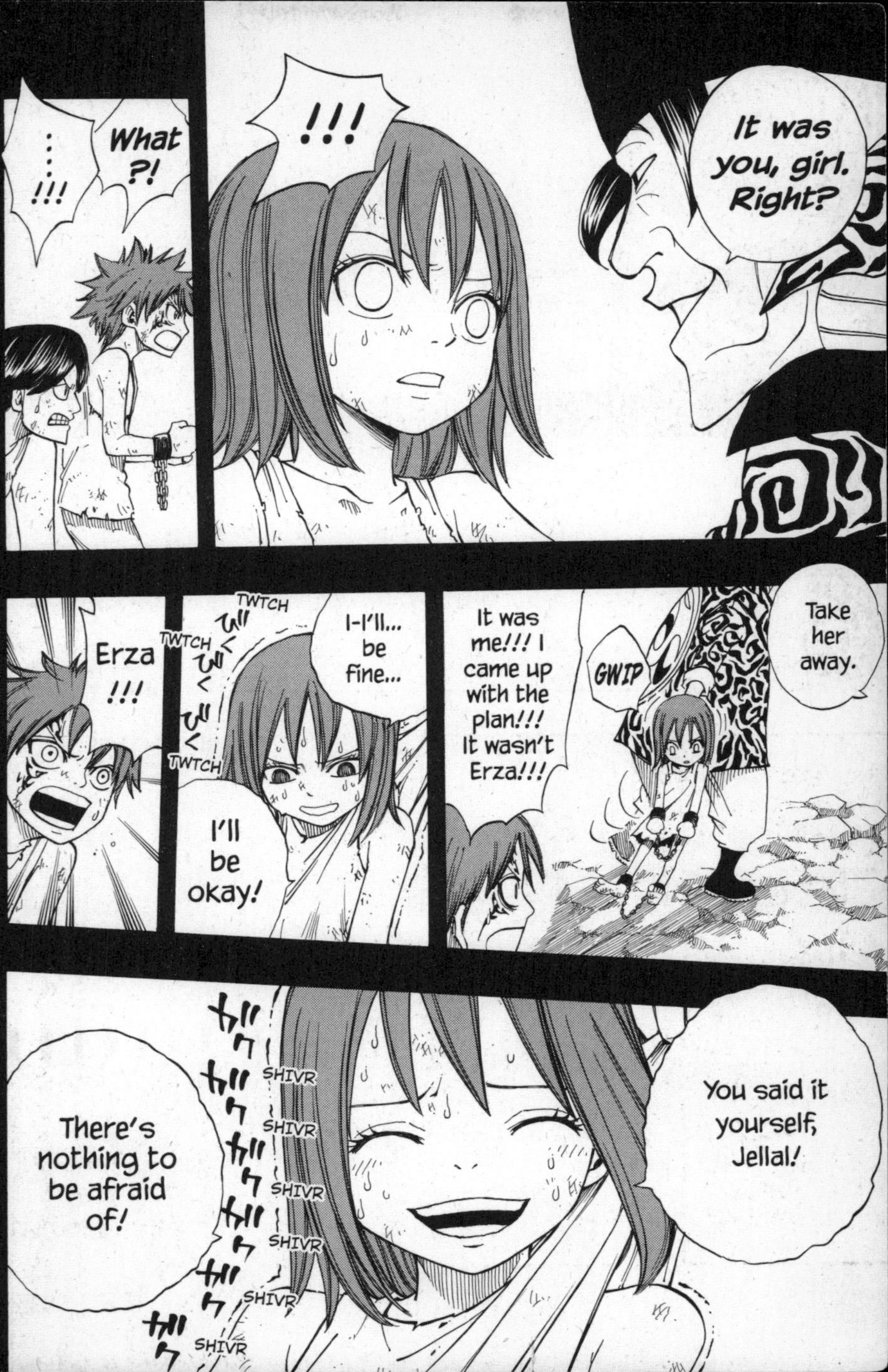
It was you, girl. Right?
!!!
What ?!
......!!!
Take her away.
GWIP
It was me!!! I came up with the plan!!! It wasn't Erza!!!
TWTCH
TWTCH
TWTCH
I-I'll... be fine...
I'll be okay!
Erza !!!
You said it yourself, Jellal!
There's nothing to be afraid of!
SHIVR
SHIVR
SHIVR
SHIVR
SHIVR
SHIVR

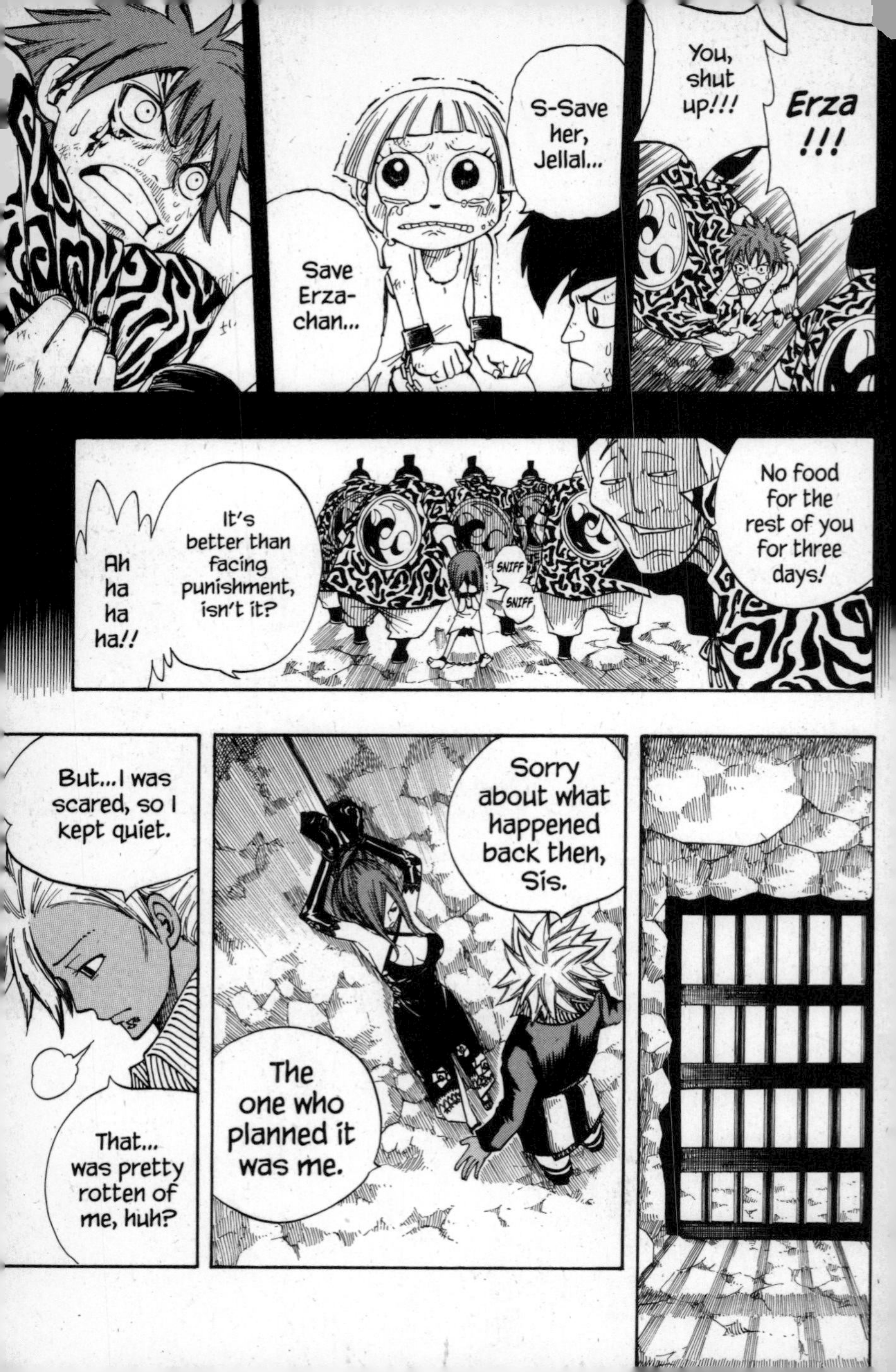
Erza!!!
You, shut up!!!
S-Save her, Jellal...
Save Erza-chan...
No food for the rest of you for three days!
SNIFF
SNIFF
It's better than facing punishment, isn't it?
Ah ha ha ha!!
Sorry about what happened back then, Sis.
The one who planned it was me.
But...I was scared, so I kept quiet.
That... was pretty rotten of me, huh?

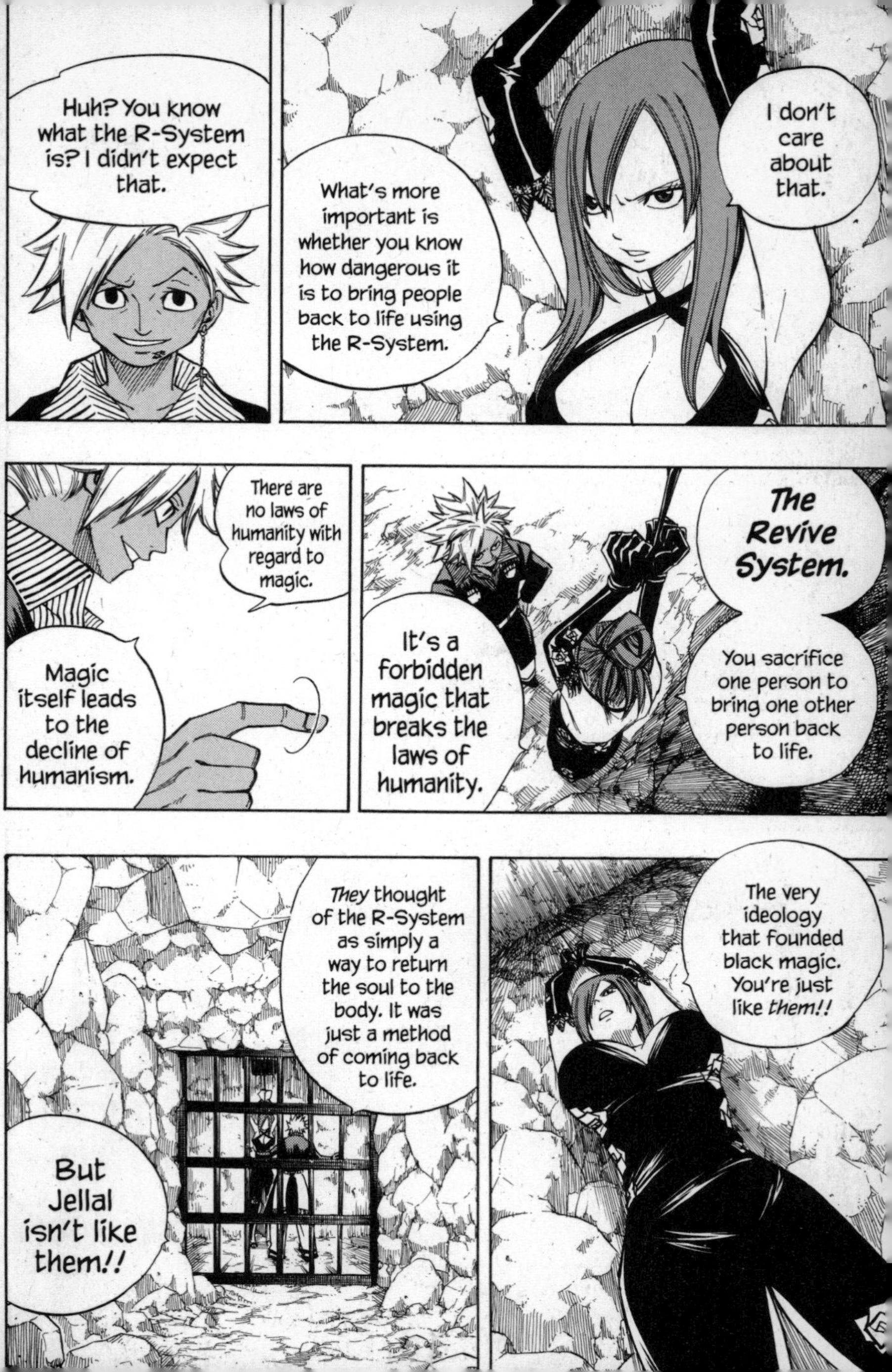
I don't care about that.
What's more important is whether you know how dangerous it is to bring people back to life using the R-System.
Huh? You know what the R-System is? I didn't expect that.
The Revive System.
You sacrifice one person to bring one other person back to life.
It's a forbidden magic that breaks the laws of humanity.
There are no laws of humanity with regard to magic.
Magic itself leads to the decline of humanism.
The very ideology that founded black magic. You're just like *them!!*
They thought of the R-System as simply a way to return the soul to the body. It was just a method of coming back to life.
But Jellal isn't like them!!

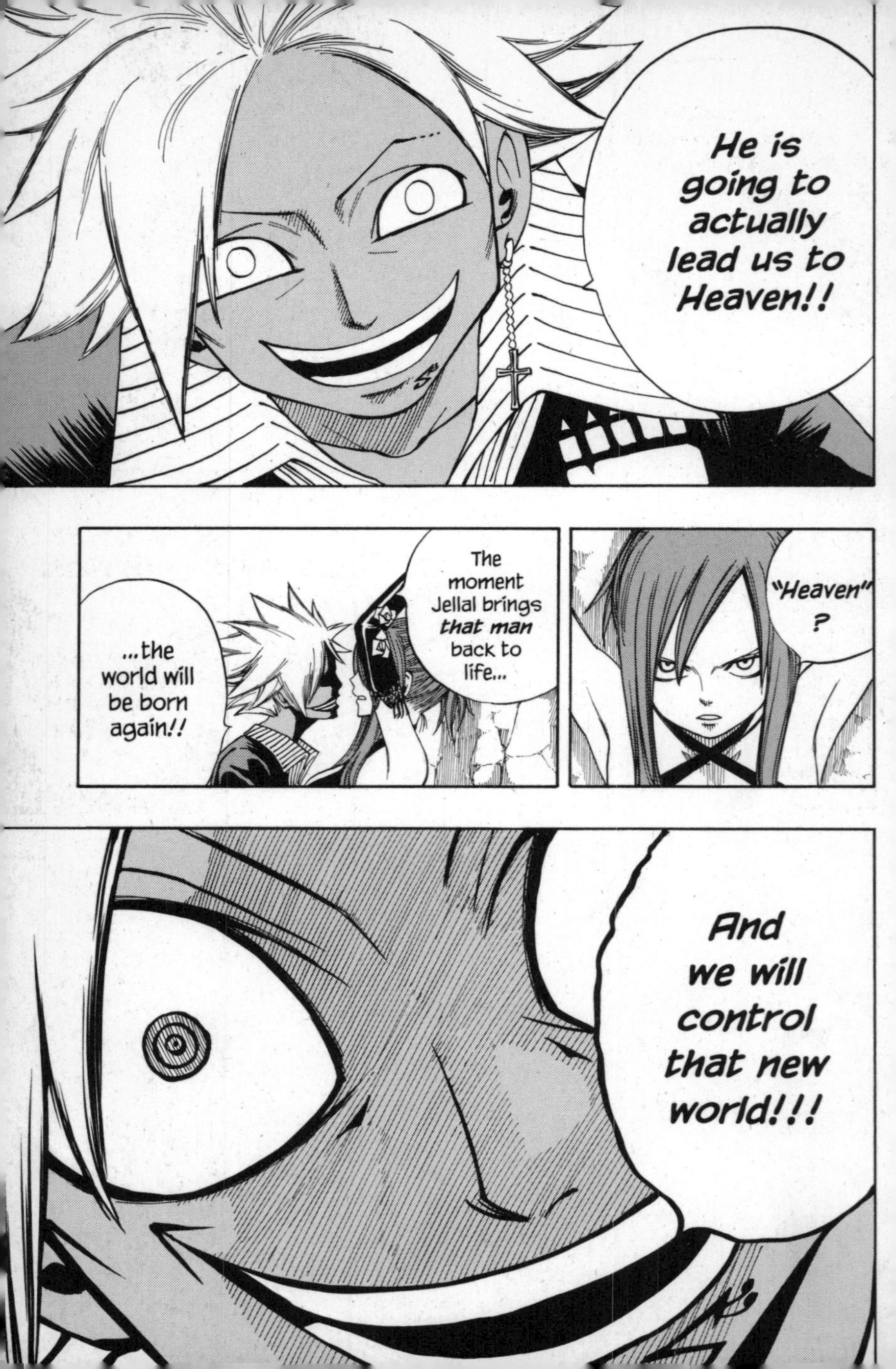
He is going to actually lead us to Heaven!!
"Heaven"?
The moment Jellal brings *that man* back to life...
...the world will be born again!!
And we will control that new world!!!

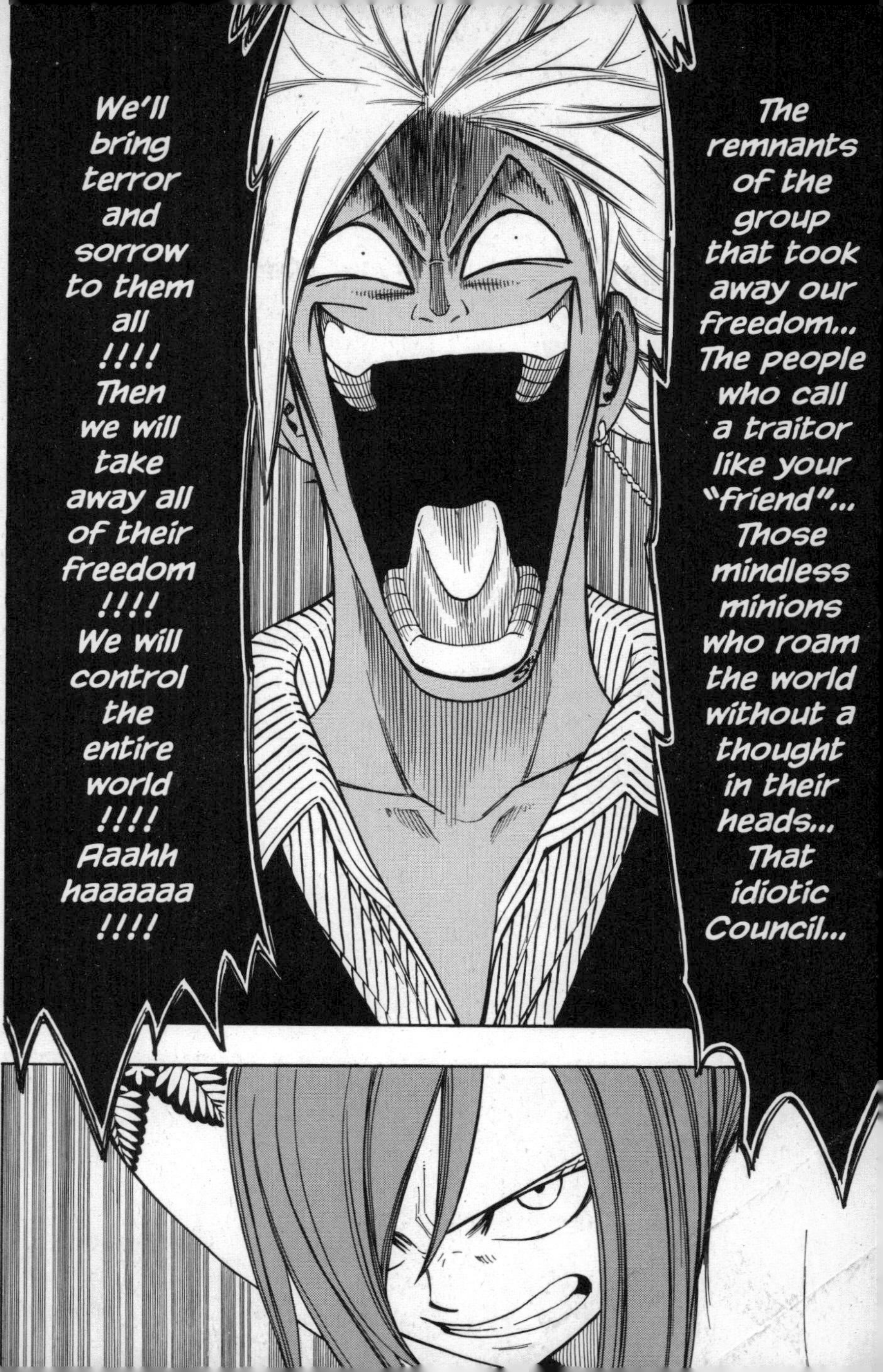

The remnants of the group that took away our freedom... The people who call a traitor like your "friend"... Those mindless minions who roam the world without a thought in their heads... That idiotic Council...
We'll bring terror and sorrow to them all !!!! Then we will take away all of their freedom !!!! We will control the entire world !!!! Aaahh haaaaaa !!!!

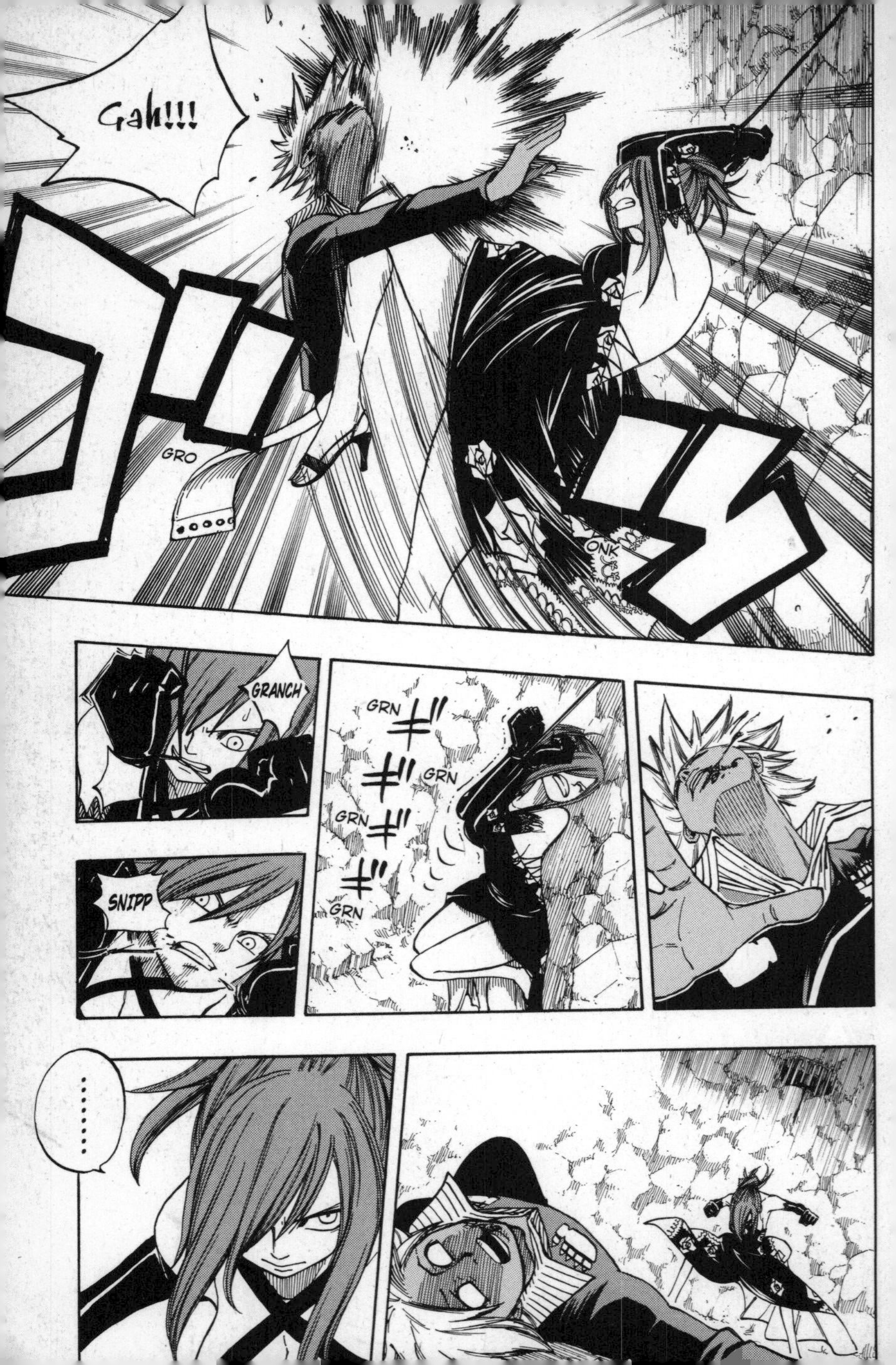
Gah!!!
GRO
ONK
GRN
GRN
GRN
GRN
GRANCH
SNIPP
......

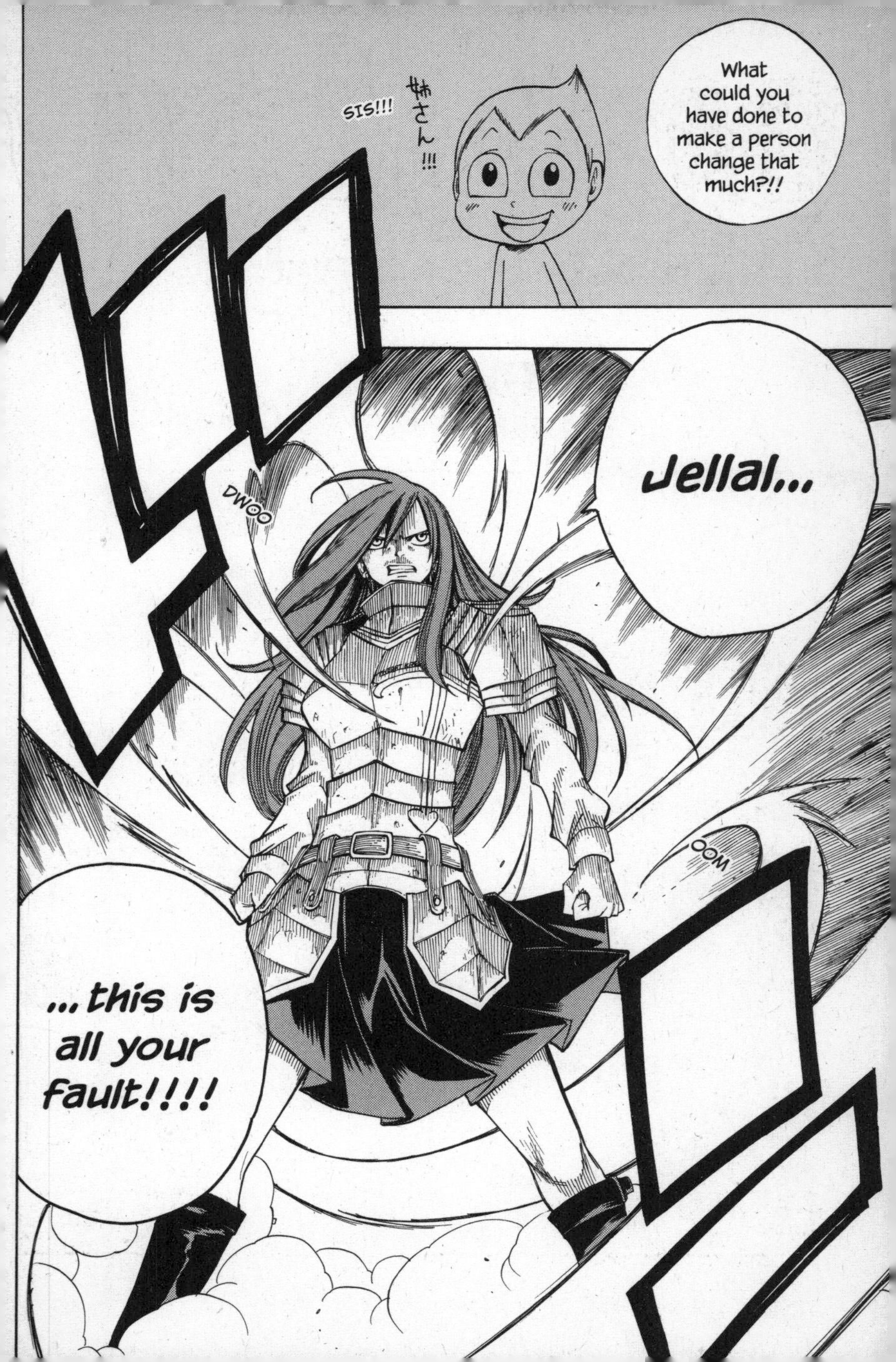
What could you have done to make a person change that much?!!
姉さん!!!
SIS!!!
Jellal...
DWOO
OOM
...this is all your fault!!!!

FAIRY TAIL

Chapter 79: Siegrain's Decision

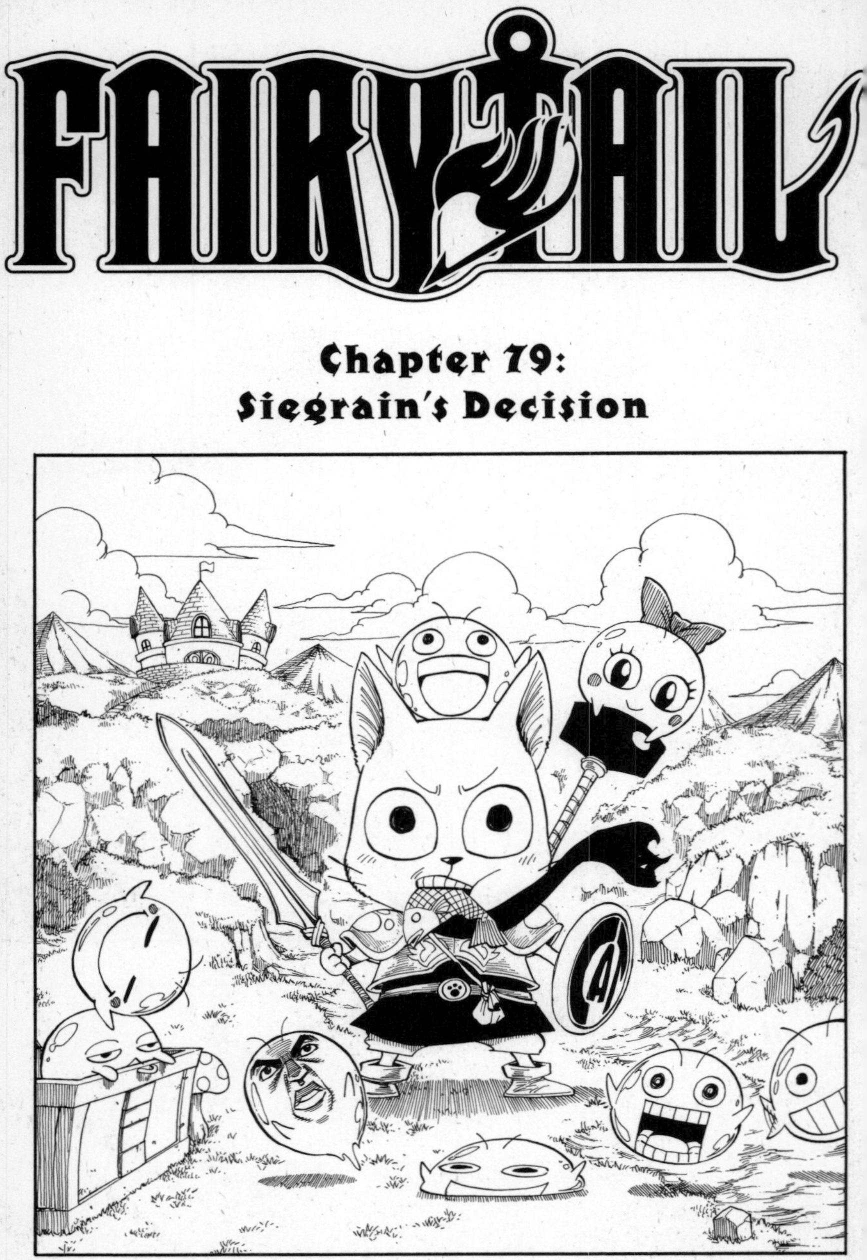

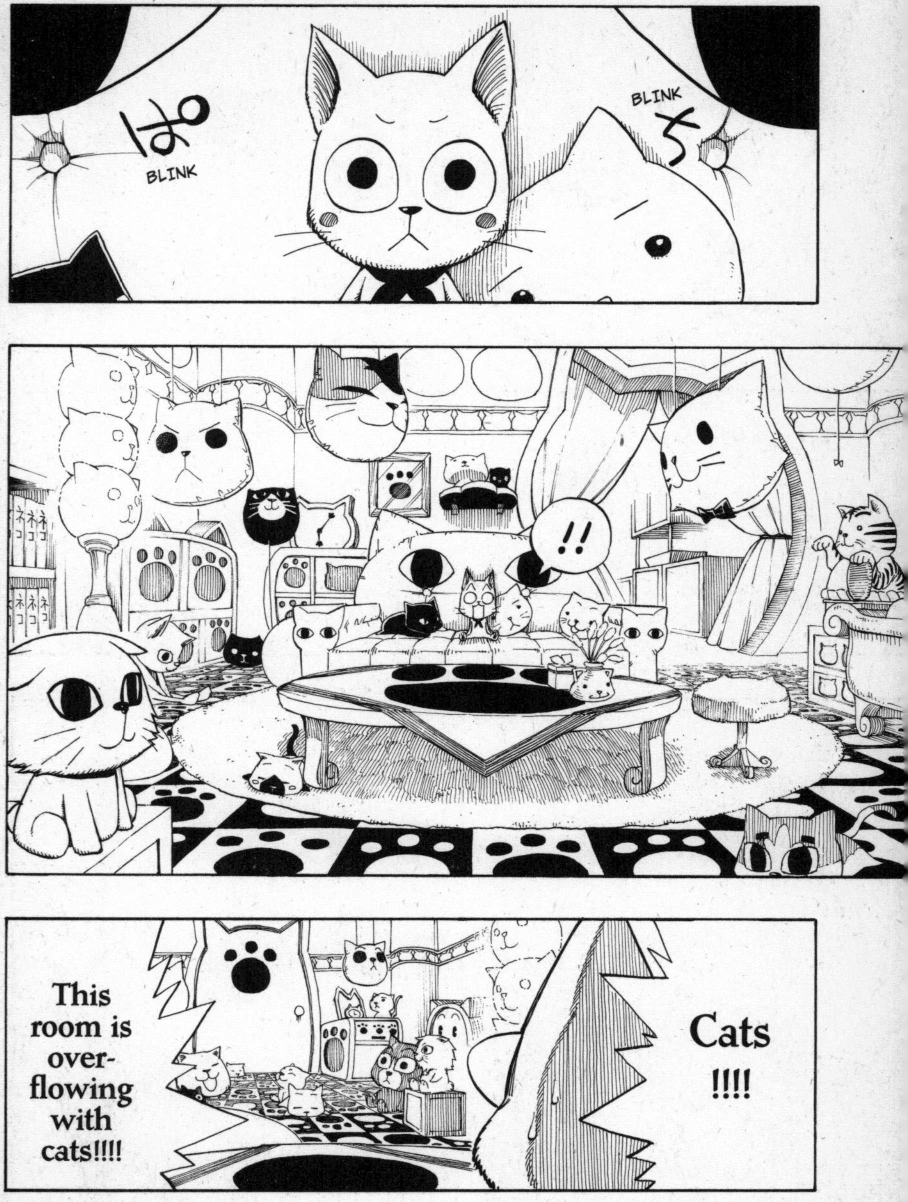
BLINK
ち
ぱ
BLINK
!!
Cats
!!!!
This room is over-flowing with cats!!!!

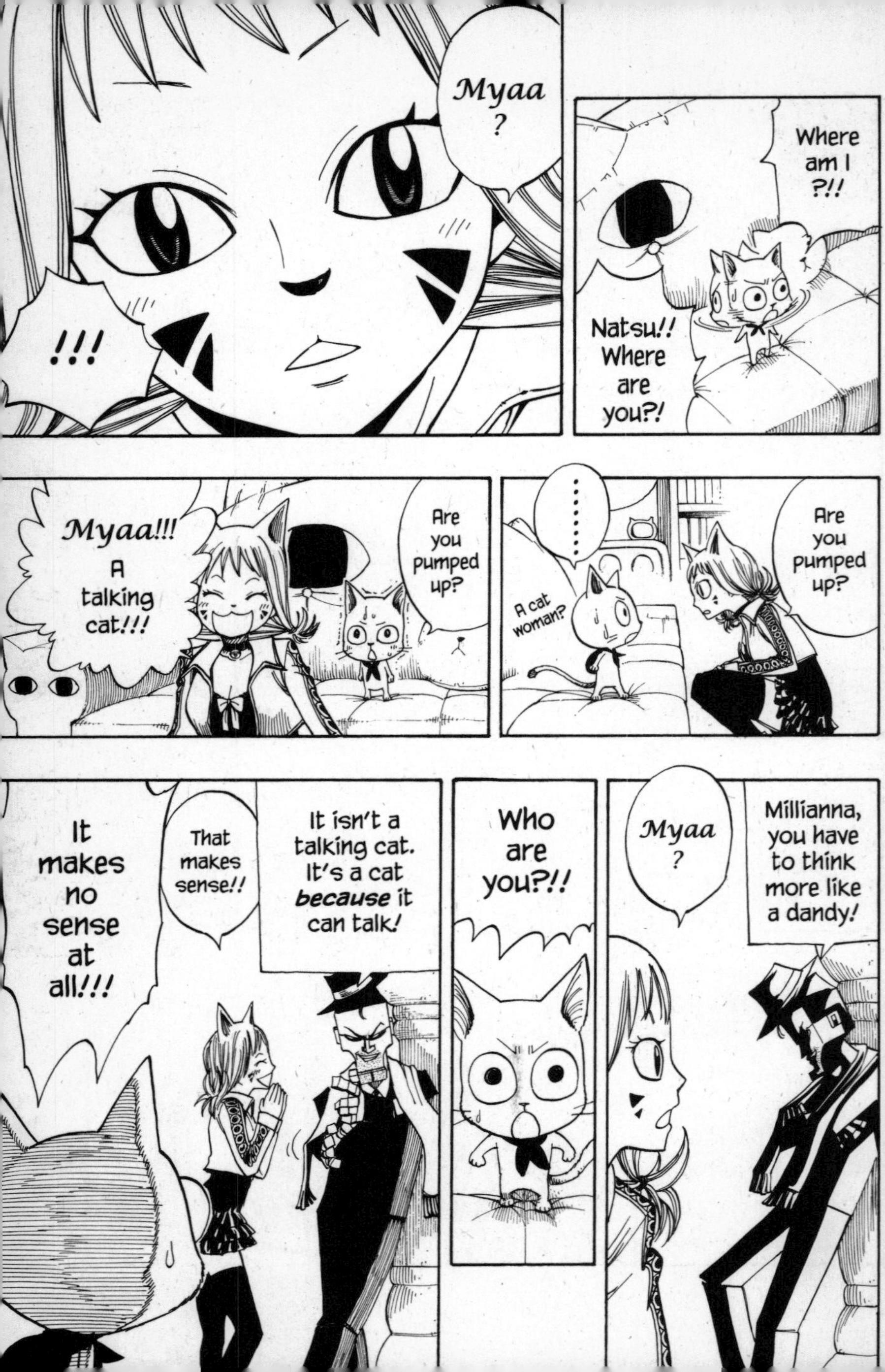
Where am I ?!!
Natsu!! Where are you?!
Myaa ?
!!!
Are you pumped up?
......
A cat woman?
Are you pumped up?
Myaa!!! A talking cat!!!
Millianna, you have to think more like a dandy!
Myaa ?
Who are you?!!
It isn't a talking cat. It's a cat *because* it can talk!
That makes sense!!
It makes no sense at all!!!

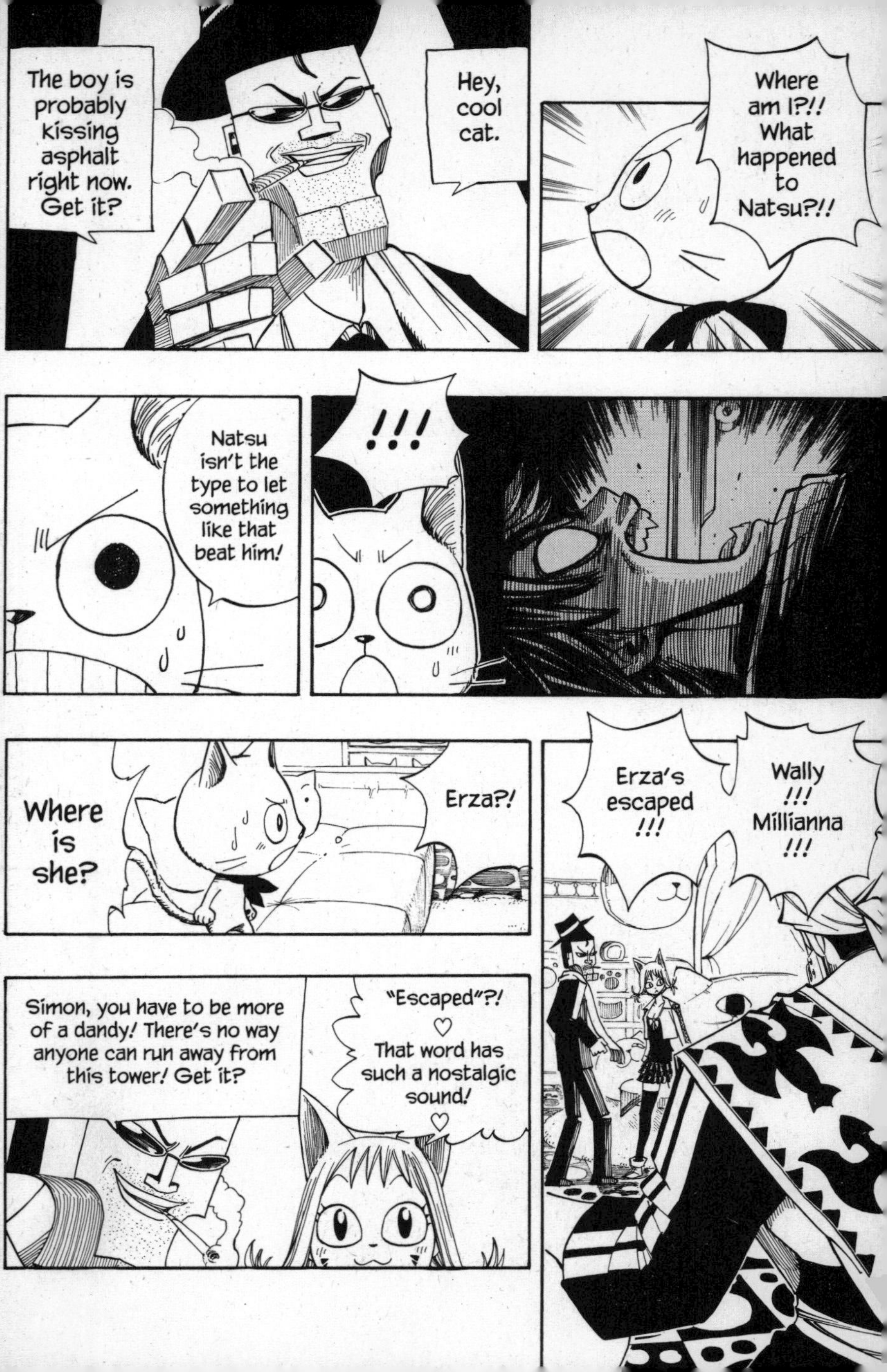

Where am I?!! What happened to Natsu?!!
Hey, cool cat.
The boy is probably kissing asphalt right now. Get it?
!!!
Natsu isn't the type to let something like that beat him!
Wally!!! Millianna!!!
Erza's escaped!!!
Erza?!
Where is she?
"Escaped"?! ♡ That word has such a nostalgic sound! ♡
Simon, you have to be more of a dandy! There's no way anyone can run away from this tower! Get it?

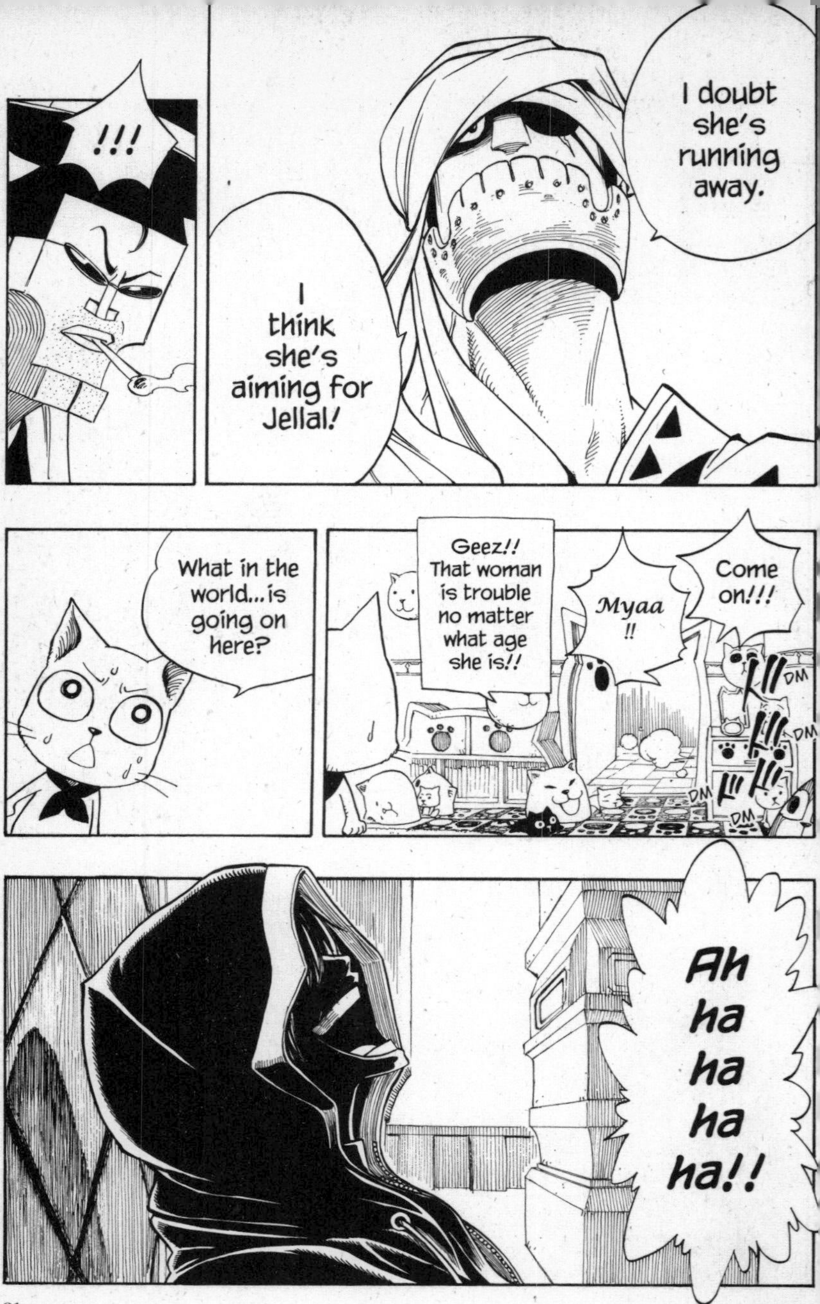
I doubt she's running away.
I think she's aiming for Jellal!
!!!
Come on!!!
Myaa !!
Geez!! That woman is trouble no matter what age she is!!
DM
DM
DM
DM
What in the world...is going on here?
Ah ha ha ha ha!!

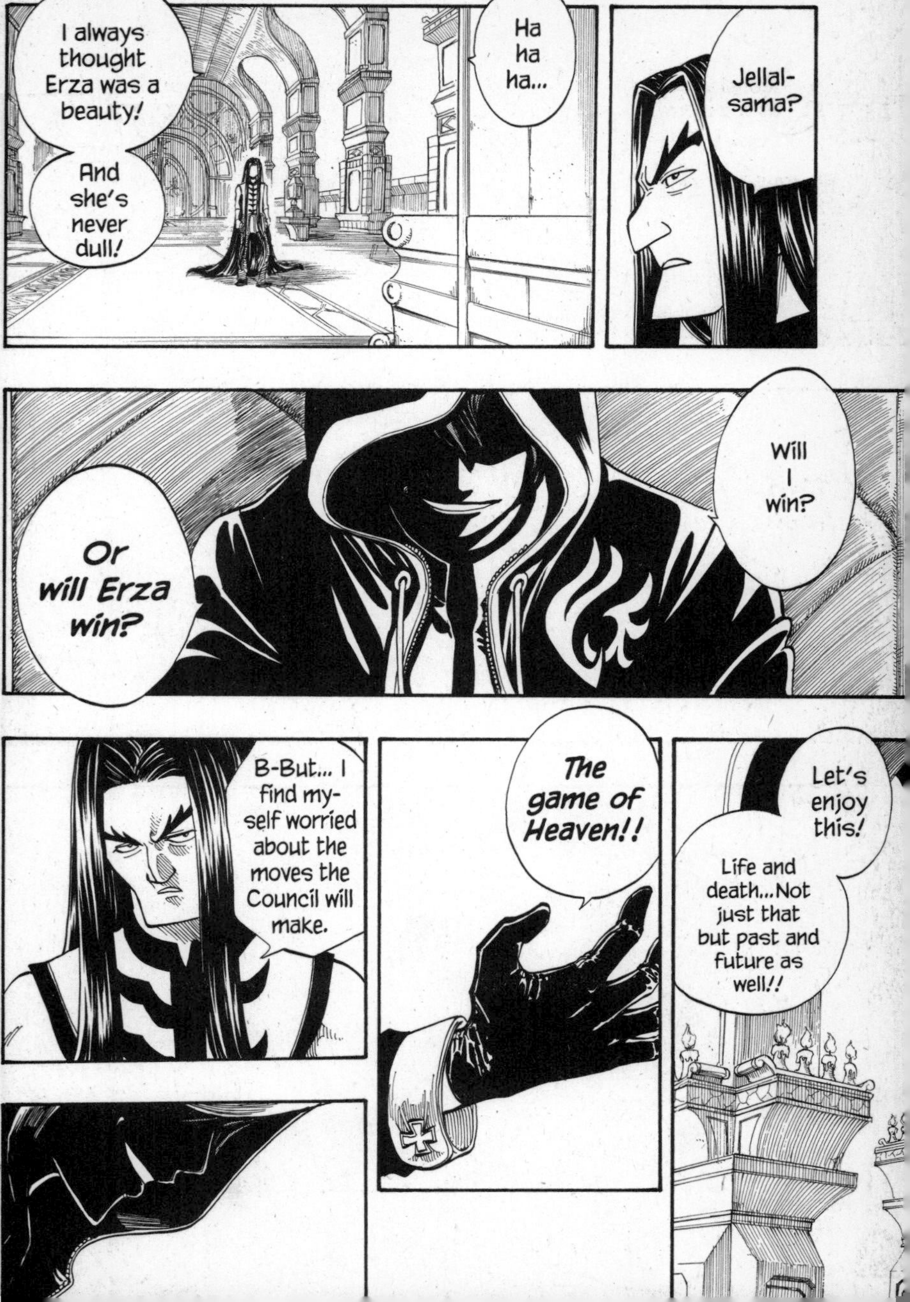
Jellal-sama?
Ha ha ha...
I always thought Erza was a beauty!
And she's never dull!
Will I win?
Or will Erza win?
Let's enjoy this!
Life and death...Not just that but past and future as well!!
The game of Heaven!!
B-But... I find my-self worried about the moves the Council will make.

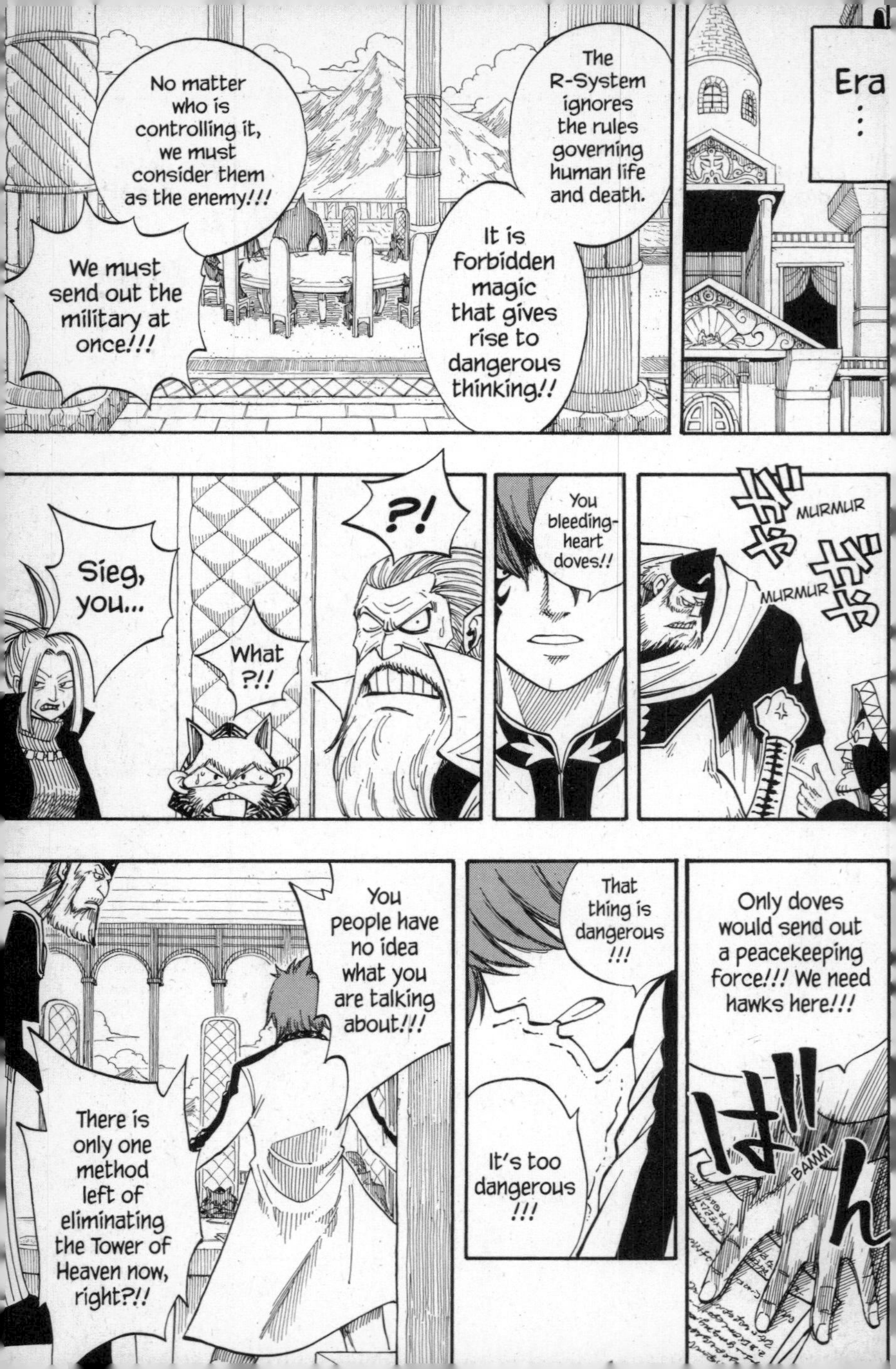
Era...
The R-System ignores the rules governing human life and death.
No matter who is controlling it, we must consider them as the enemy!!!
It is forbidden magic that gives rise to dangerous thinking!!
We must send out the military at once!!!
MURMUR
MURMUR
You bleeding-heart doves!!
?!
Sieg, you...
What ?!!
Only doves would send out a peacekeeping force!!! We need hawks here!!!
BAMM
That thing is dangerous !!!
It's too dangerous !!!
You people have no idea what you are talking about!!!
There is only one method left of eliminating the Tower of Heaven now, right?!!

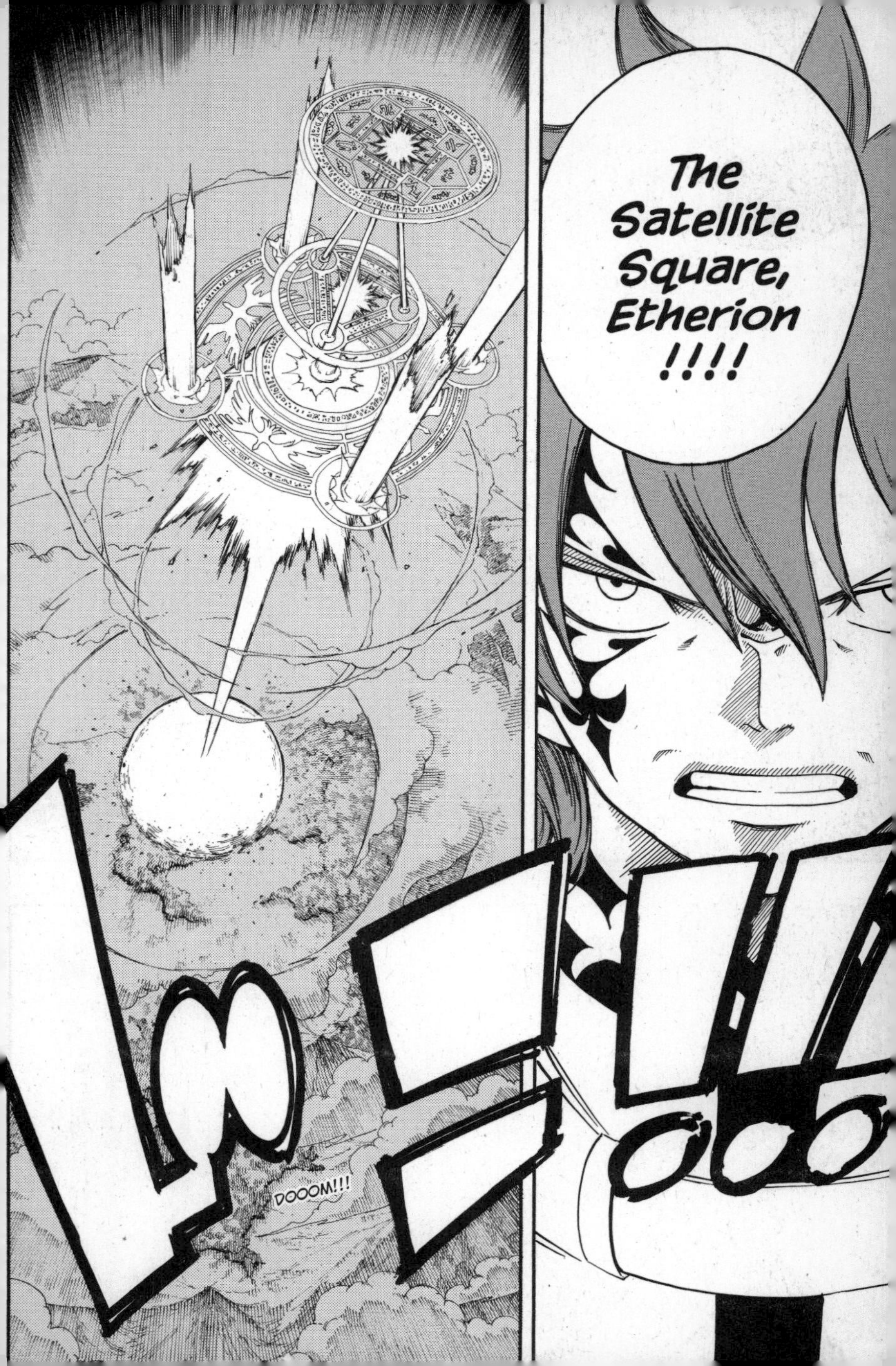
The Satellite Square, Etherion !!!!
DOOOM!!!

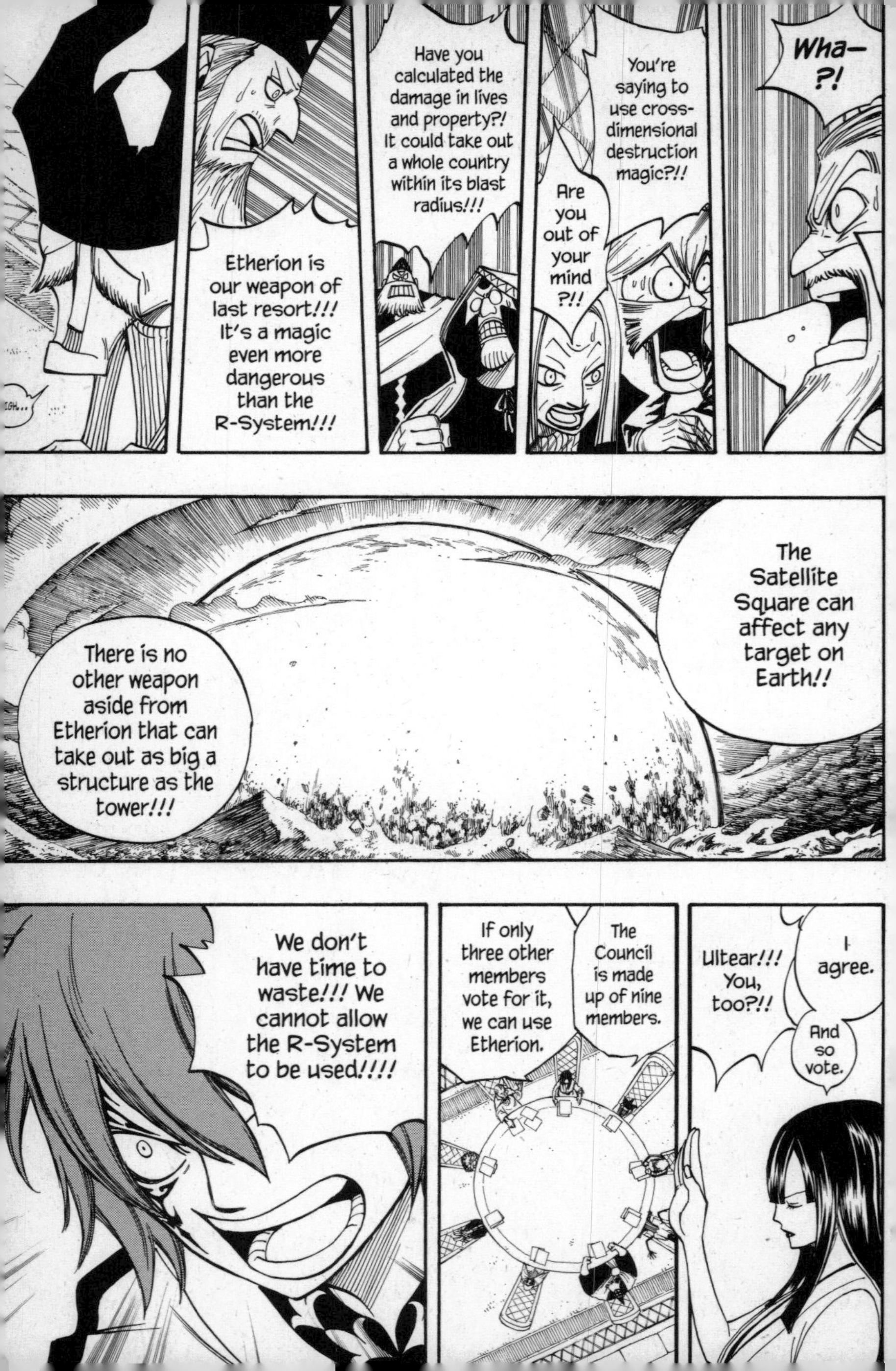

Wha— ?!
You're saying to use cross-dimensional destruction magic?!!
Are you out of your mind ?!!
Have you calculated the damage in lives and property?! It could take out a whole country within its blast radius!!!
Etherion is our weapon of last resort!!! It's a magic even more dangerous than the R-System!!!
The Satellite Square can affect any target on Earth!!
There is no other weapon aside from Etherion that can take out as big a structure as the tower!!!
I agree.
And so vote.
Ultear!!! You, too?!!
The Council is made up of nine members.
If only three other members vote for it, we can use Etherion.
We don't have time to waste!!! We cannot allow the R-System to be used!!!!

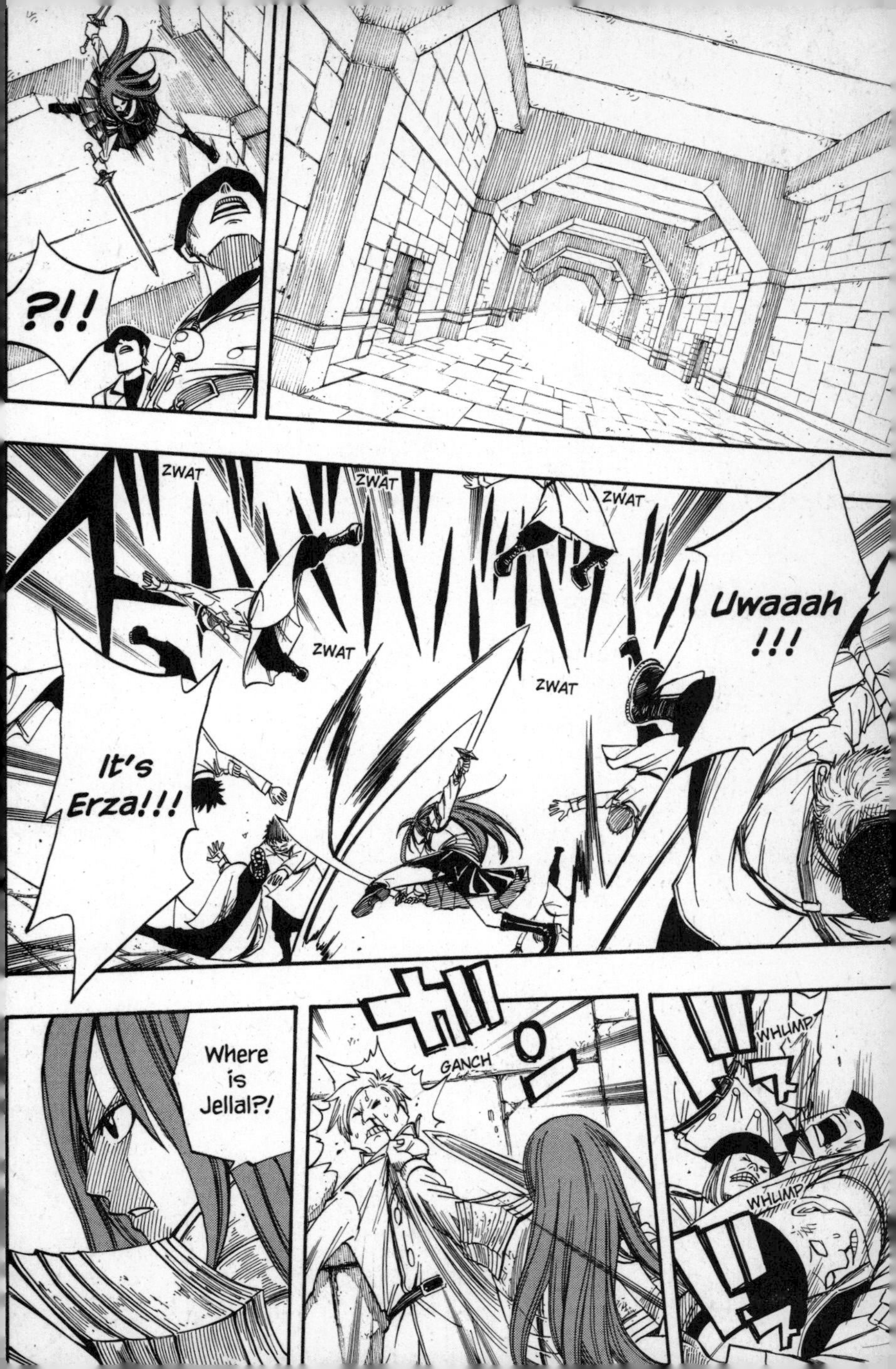
?!!
ZWAT
Uwaaah !!!
ZWAT
ZWAT
ZWAT
ZWAT
It's Erza!!!
WHLUMP
WHLUMP
GANCH
Where is Jellal?!

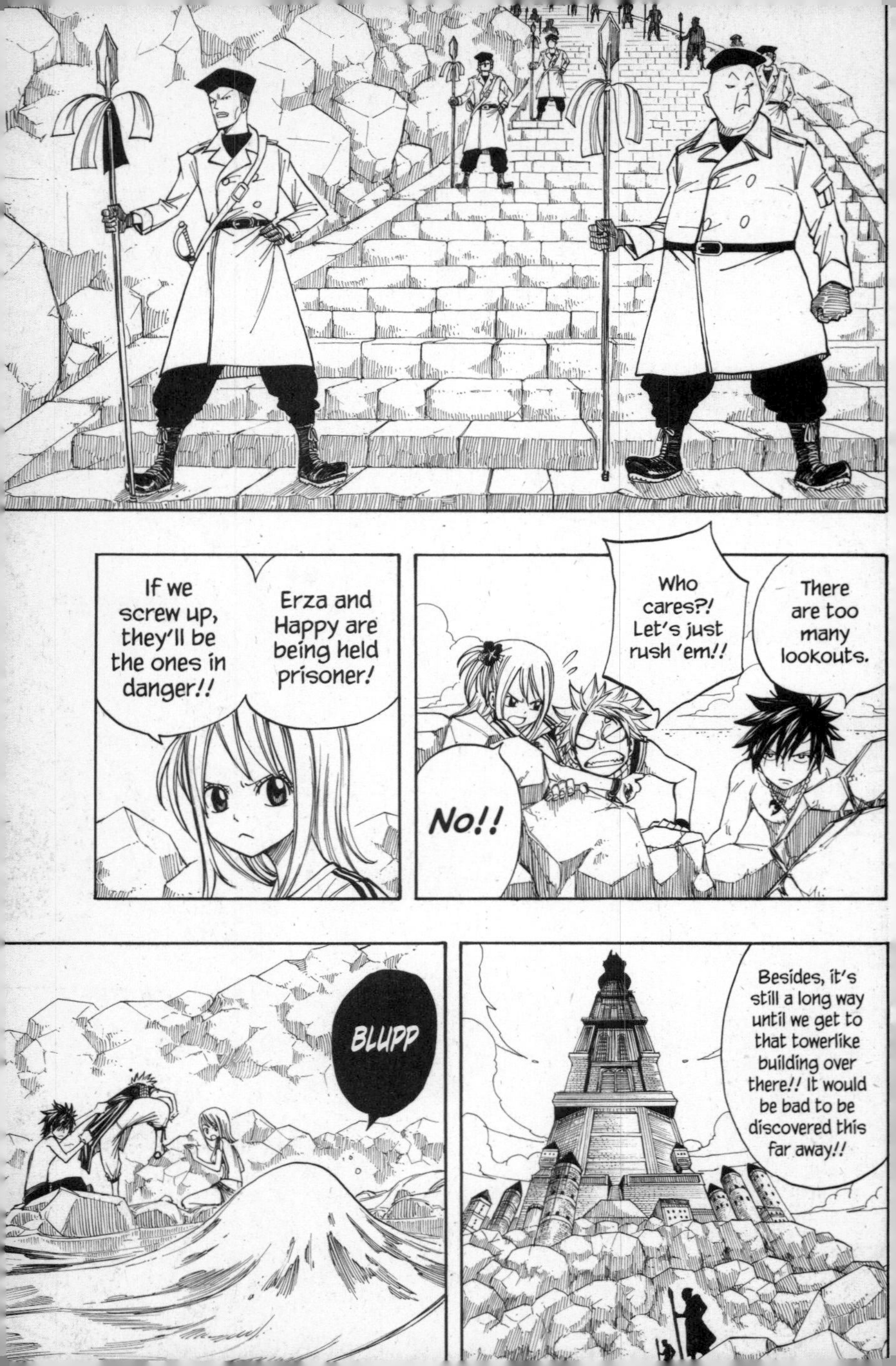
There are too many lookouts.
Who cares?! Let's just rush 'em!!
No!!
Erza and Happy are being held prisoner!
If we screw up, they'll be the ones in danger!!
Besides, it's still a long way until we get to that towerlike building over there!! It would be bad to be discovered this far away!!
BLUPP

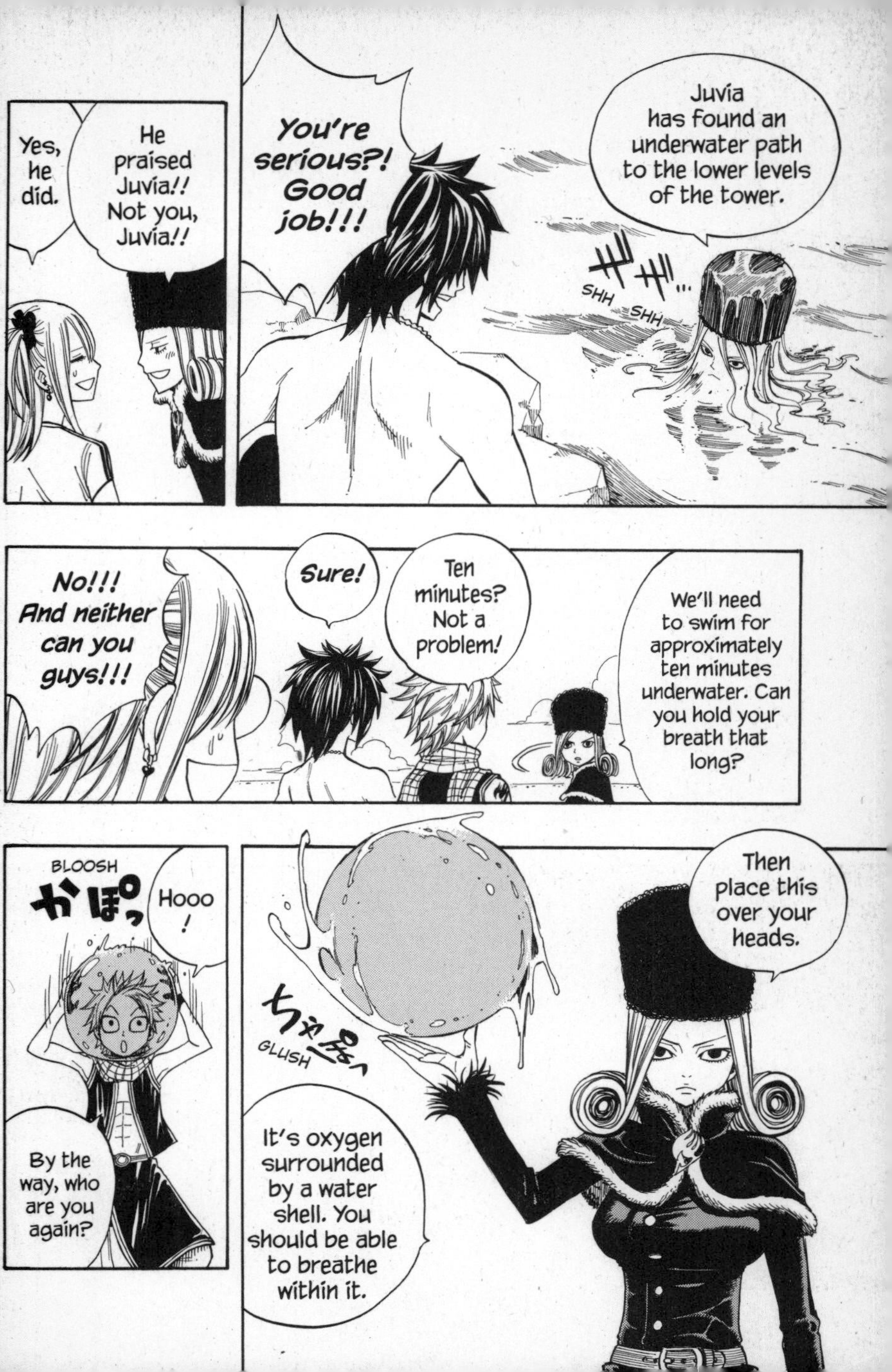
Juvia has found an underwater path to the lower levels of the tower.
ギギ…
SHH SHH
You're serious?! Good job!!!
He praised Juvia!! Not you, Juvia!!
Yes, he did.
We'll need to swim for approximately ten minutes underwater. Can you hold your breath that long?
Ten minutes? Not a problem!
Sure!
No!!! And neither can you guys!!!
Then place this over your heads.
ちゃぷ
GLUSH
It's oxygen surrounded by a water shell. You should be able to breathe within it.
Hooo!
かぽっ
BLOOSH
By the way, who are you again?

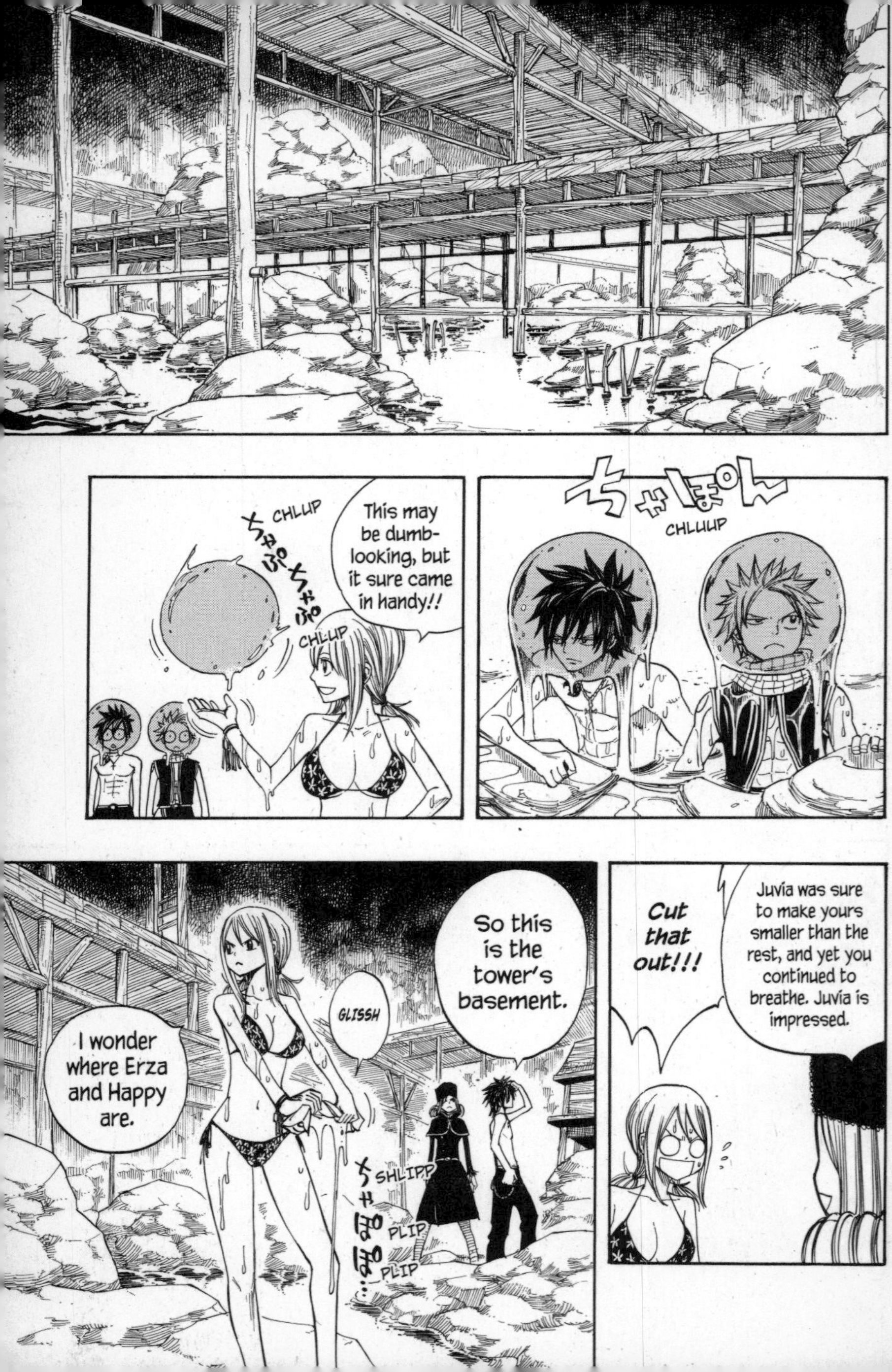
ちゃぽん
CHLUUP
CHLUP
ちゃぷちゃぷ
This may be dumb-looking, but it sure came in handy!!
CHLUP
Juvia was sure to make yours smaller than the rest, and yet you continued to breathe. Juvia is impressed.
Cut that out!!!
So this is the tower's basement.
GLISSH
I wonder where Erza and Happy are.
ちゃぽぽ…
SHLIPP
PLIP
PLIP

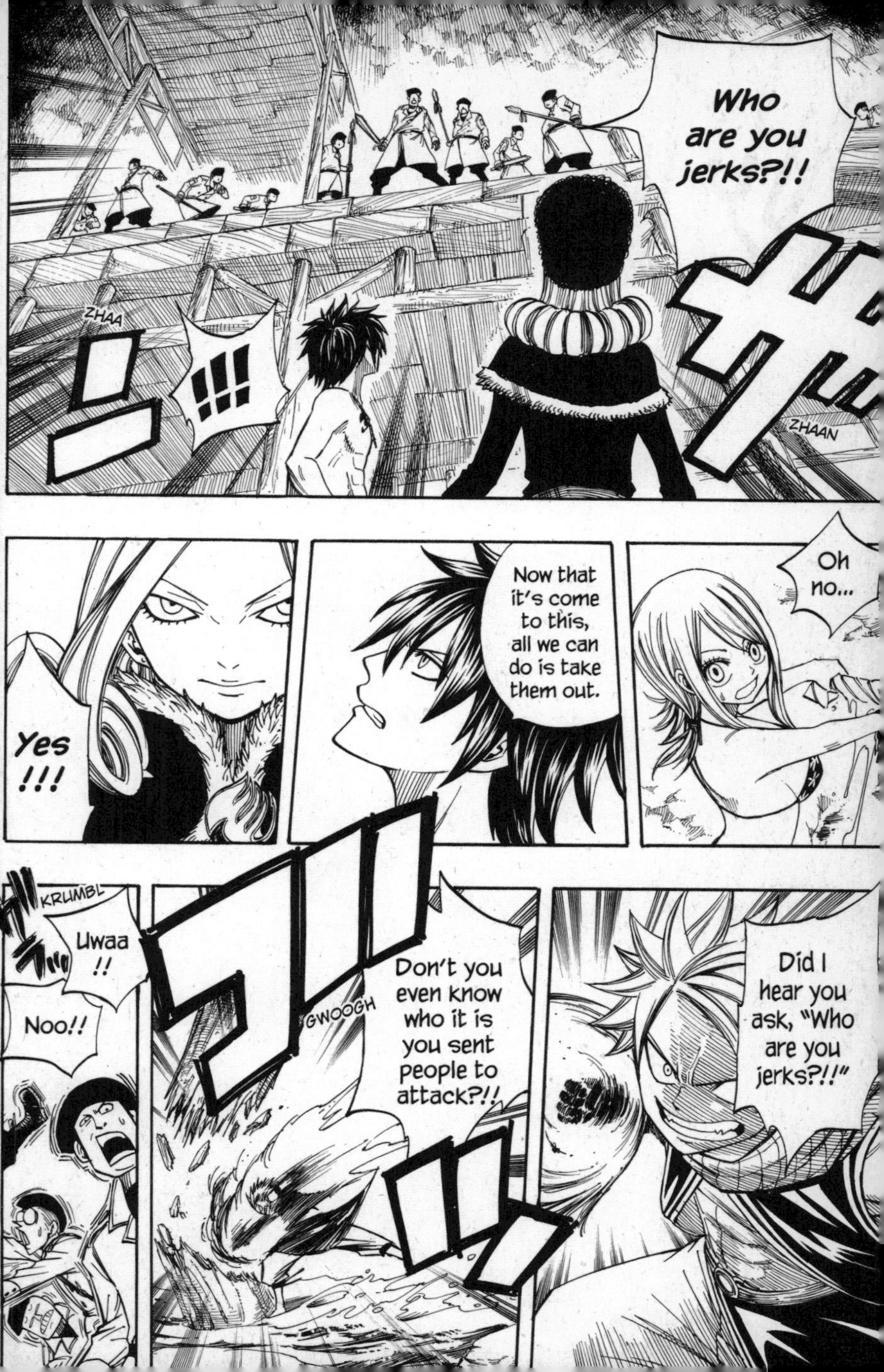
Who are you jerks?!!
ZHAAN
!!!
ZHAA
Oh no...
Now that it's come to this, all we can do is take them out.
Yes !!!
Did I hear you ask, "Who are you jerks?!!"
Don't you even know who it is you sent people to attack?!!
GWOOGH
KRUMBL
Uwaa !!
Noo!!

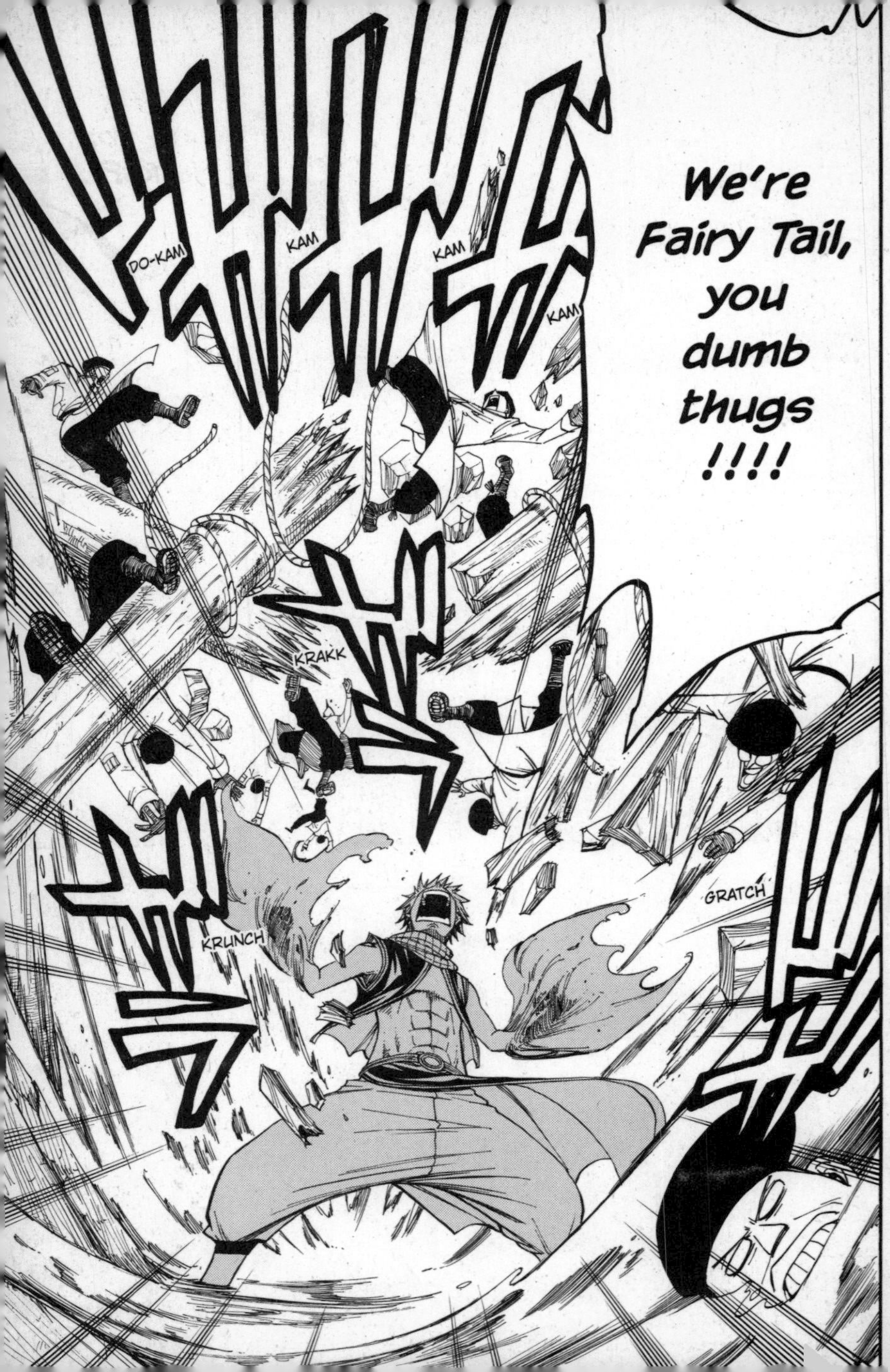
We're Fairy Tail, you dumb thugs!!!!
DO-KAM
KAM
KAM
KAM
KRAKK
KRUNCH
GRATCH

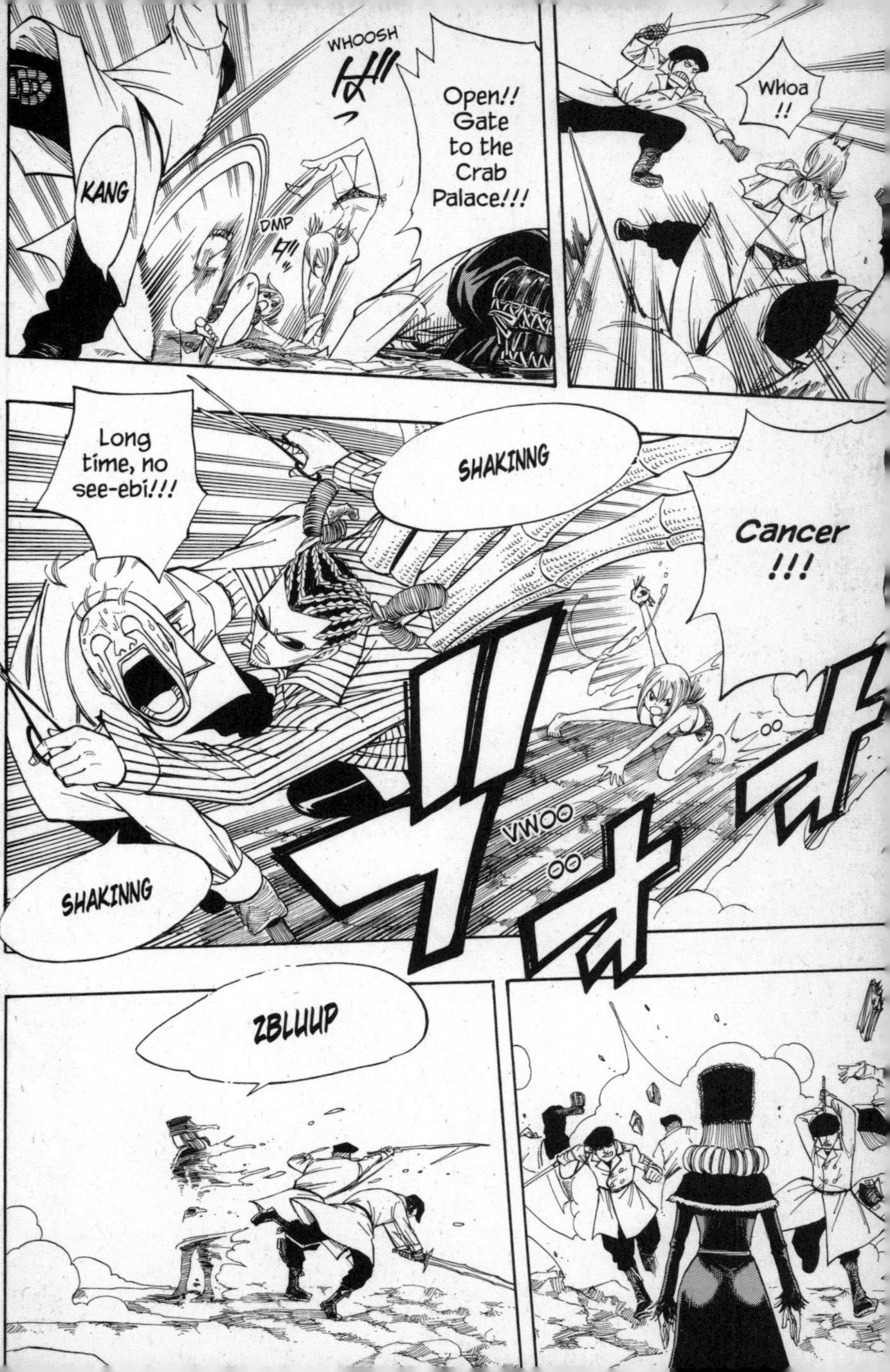
Whoa !!
Open!! Gate to the Crab Palace!!!
WHOOSH
DMP
KANG
Cancer !!!
SHAKINNG
Long time, no see-ebi!!!
VWOO OO
SHAKINNG
ZBLUUP

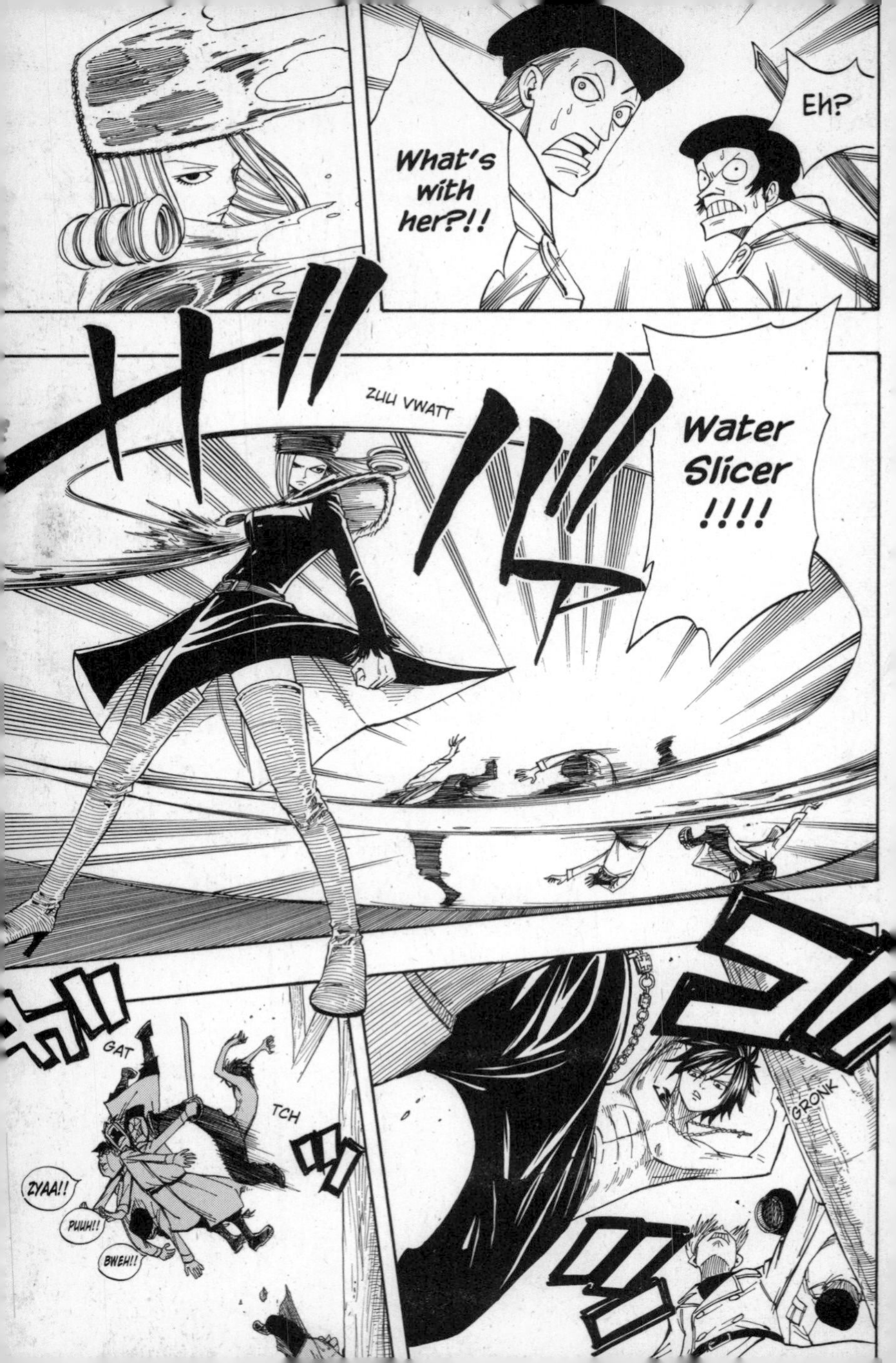

Eh?
What's with her?!!
Water Slicer !!!!
ZULI VWATT
GRONK
GAT
TCH
ZYAA!!
PUUH!!
BWEH!!

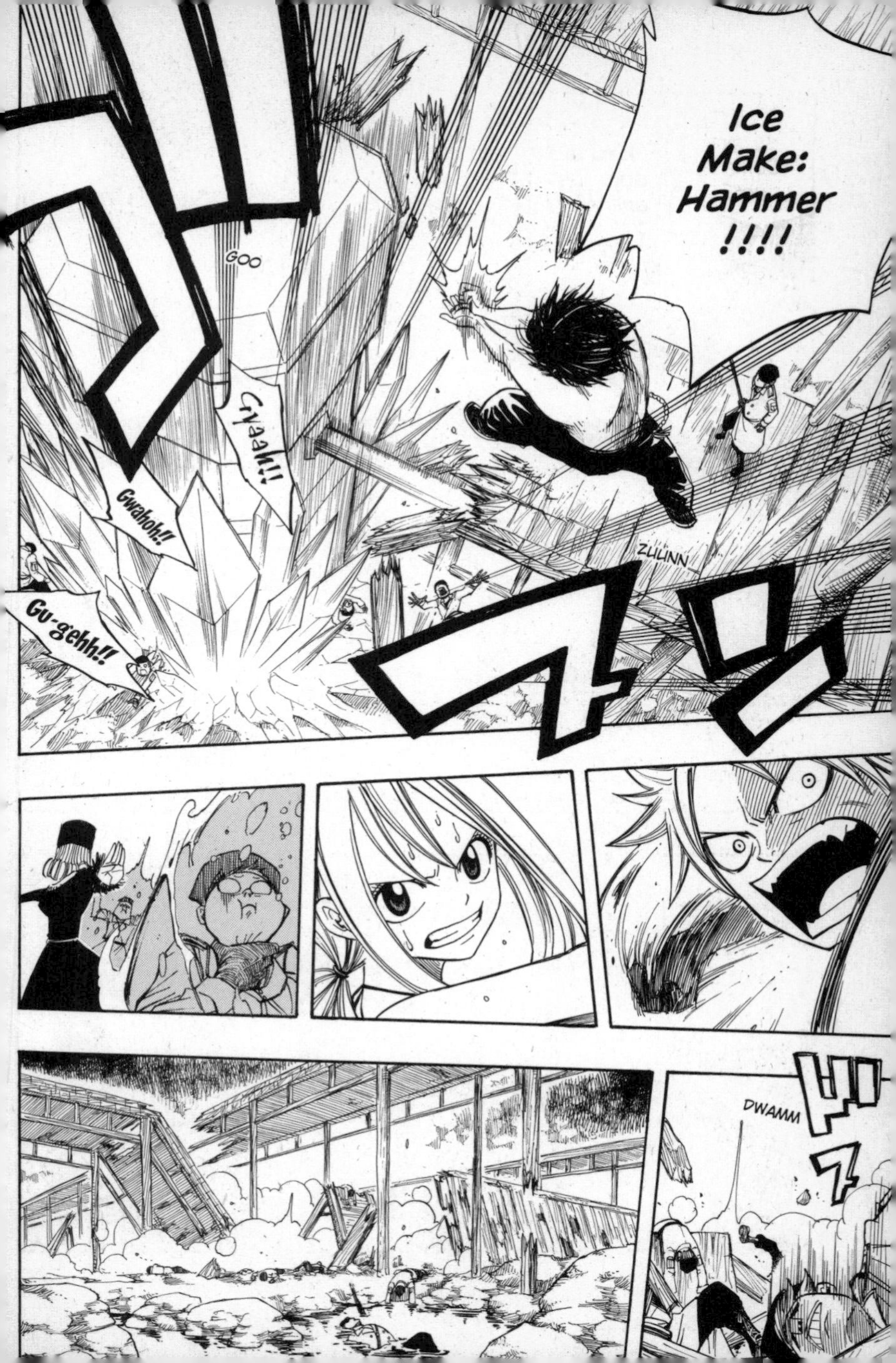
Ice Make: Hammer !!!!
ZULINN
GOO
Gyaah!!
Gwahoh!!
Gu-gehh!!
DWAMM

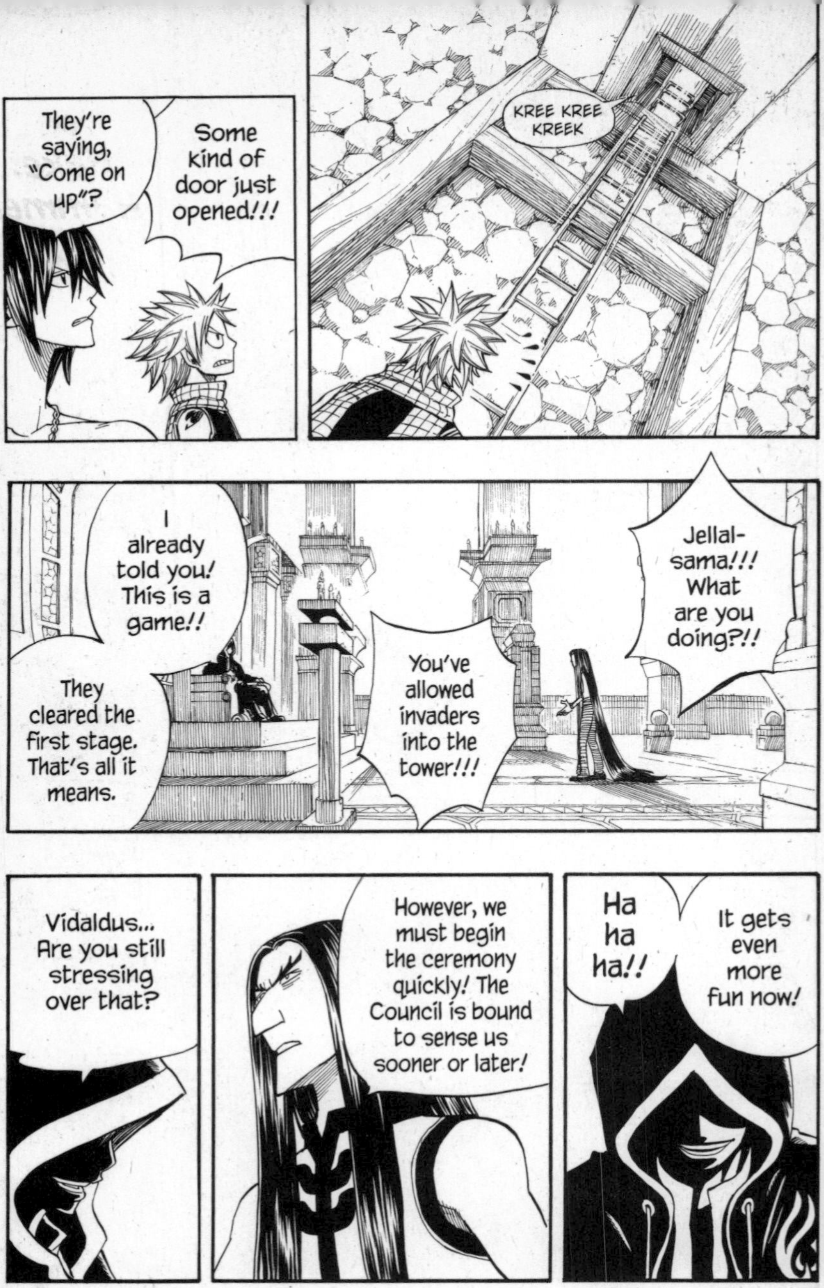
KREE KREE KREEK
Some kind of door just opened!!!
They're saying, "Come on up"?
Jellal-sama!!! What are you doing?!!
You've allowed invaders into the tower!!!
I already told you! This is a game!!
They cleared the first stage. That's all it means.
It gets even more fun now!
Ha ha ha!!
However, we must begin the ceremony quickly! The Council is bound to sense us sooner or later!
Vidaldus... Are you still stressing over that?

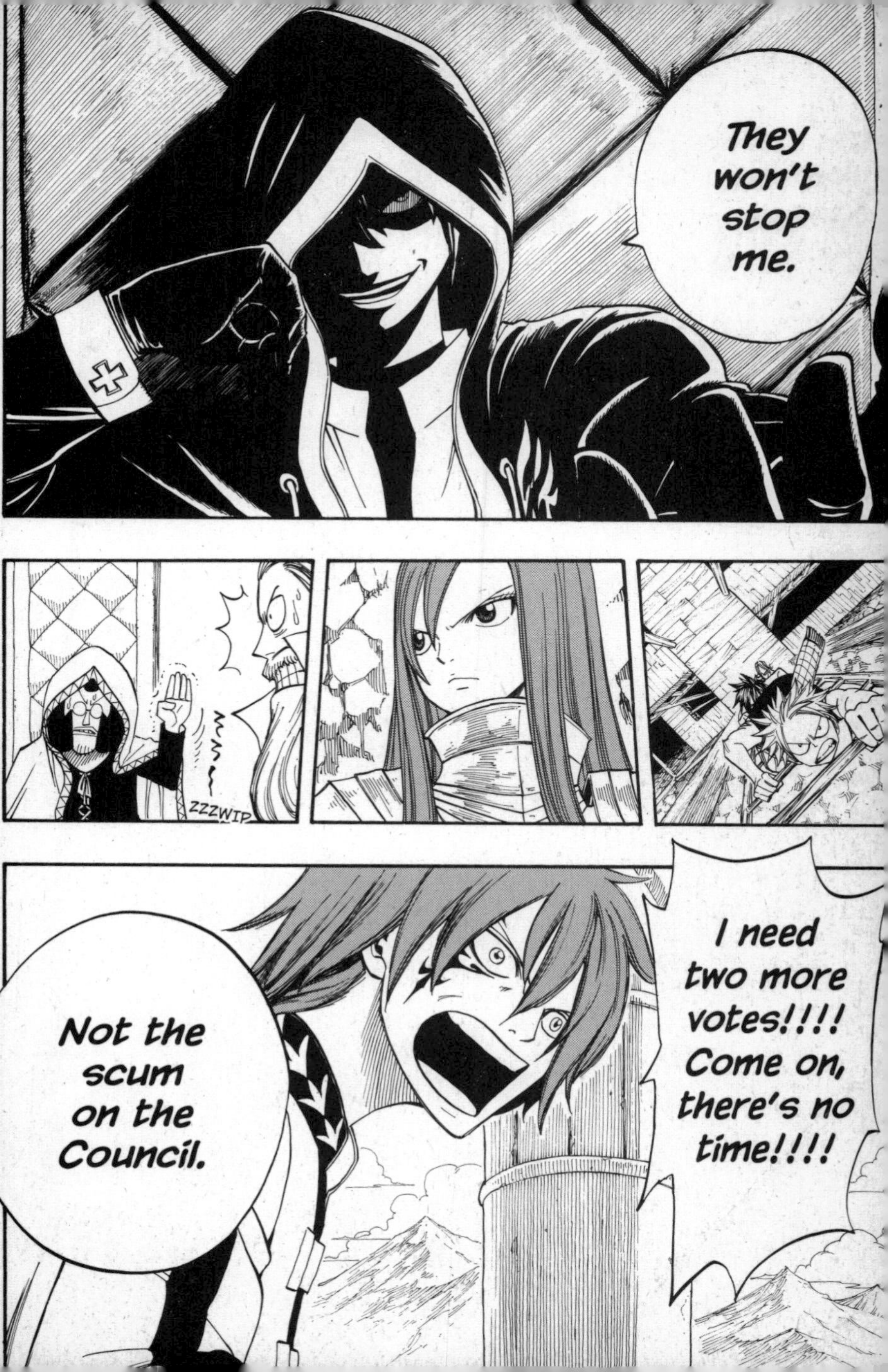
They won't stop me.
ZZZWIP
I need two more votes!!!! Come on, there's no time!!!!
Not the scum on the Council.

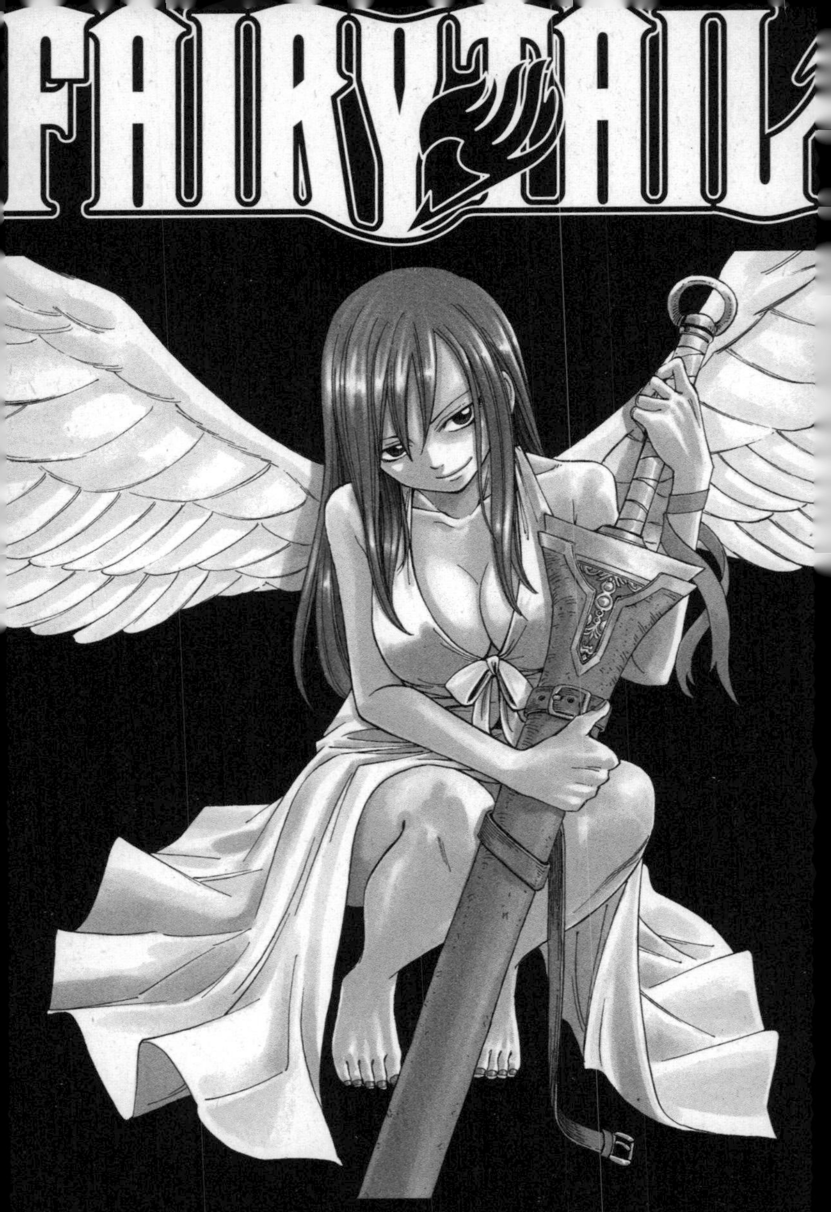
FAIRY TAIL

Chapter 80: Joan of Arc

FAIRY TAIL

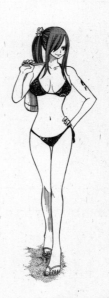

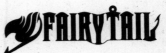

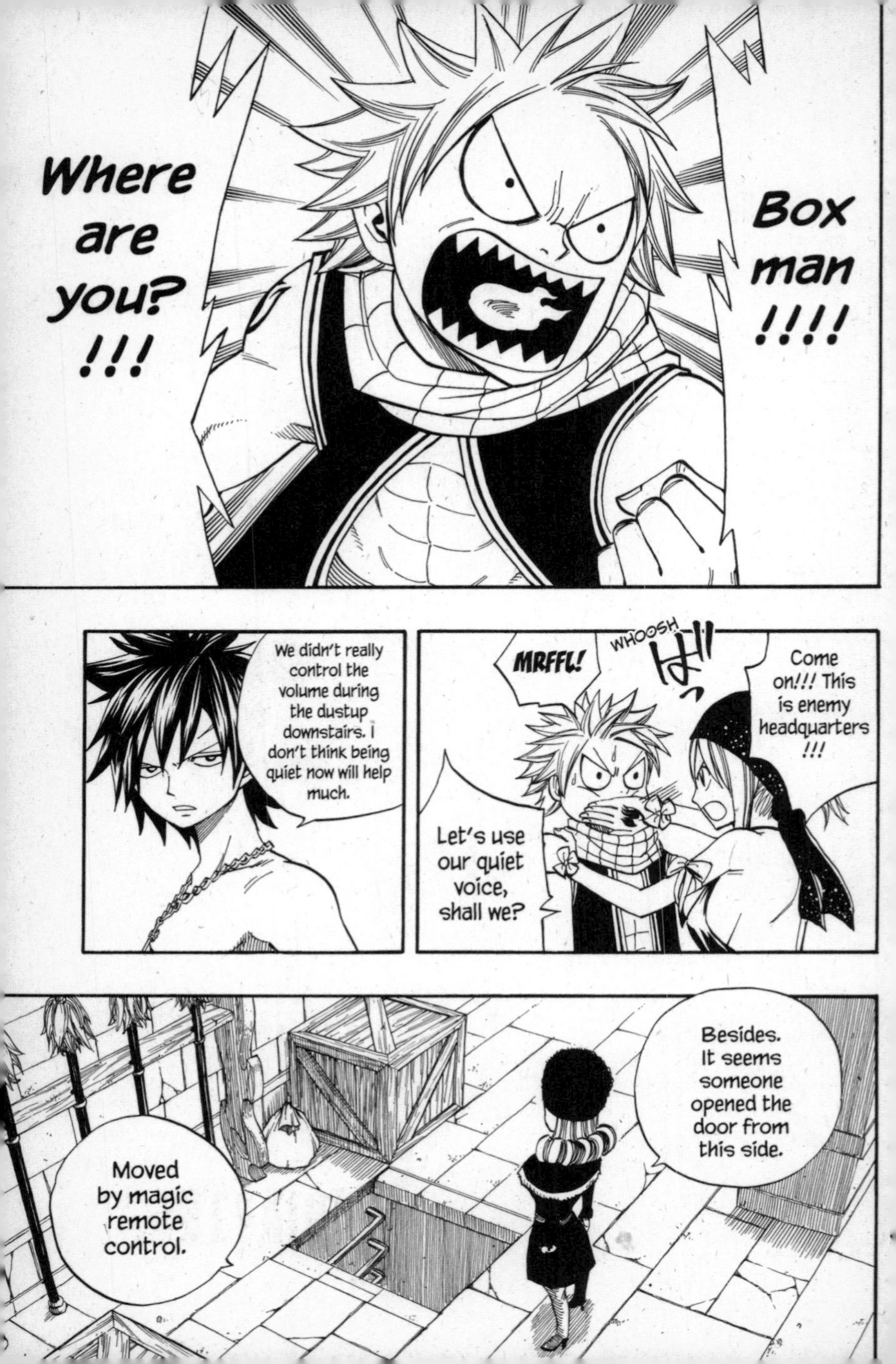

Box man!!!!
Where are you?!!!
Come on!!! This is enemy headquarters!!!
WHOOSH
MRFFL!
Let's use our quiet voice, shall we?
We didn't really control the volume during the dustup downstairs. I don't think being quiet now will help much.
Besides. It seems someone opened the door from this side.
Moved by magic remote control.

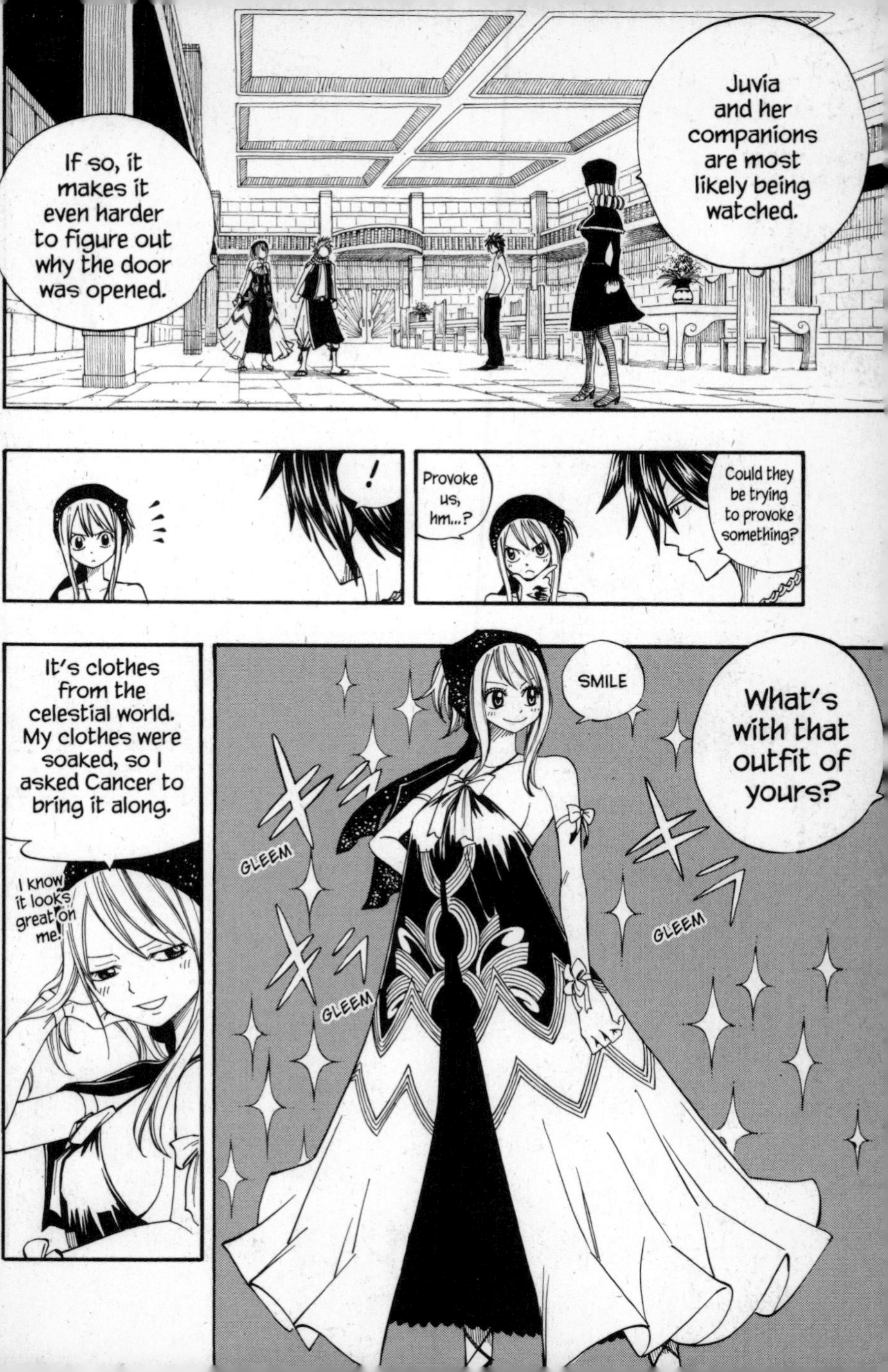
Juvia and her companions are most likely being watched.
If so, it makes it even harder to figure out why the door was opened.
Could they be trying to provoke something?
Provoke us, hm...?
!
What's with that outfit of yours?
SMILE
GLEEM
GLEEM
GLEEM
It's clothes from the celestial world. My clothes were soaked, so I asked Cancer to bring it along.
I know it looks great on me!

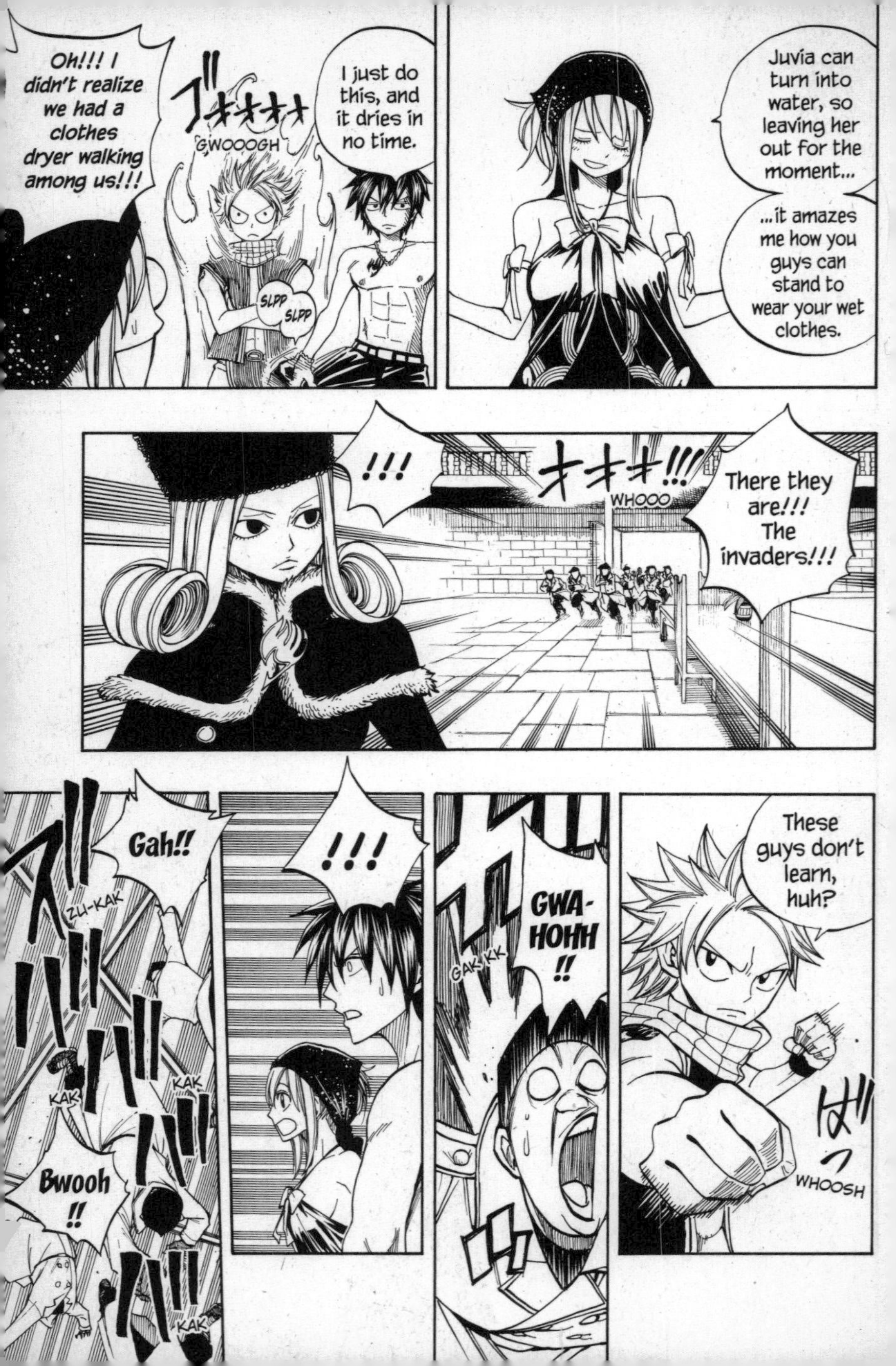

Juvia can turn into water, so leaving her out for the moment...
...it amazes me how you guys can stand to wear your wet clothes.
I just do this, and it dries in no time.
GWOOOGH
SLPP
SLPP
Oh!!! I didn't realize we had a clothes dryer walking among us!!!
There they are!!! The invaders!!!
WHOOO
!!!
These guys don't learn, huh?
WHOOSH
GWA-HOHH!!
GAK KK
!!!
Gah!!
ZU-KAK
KAK
KAK
Bwooh!!
KAK

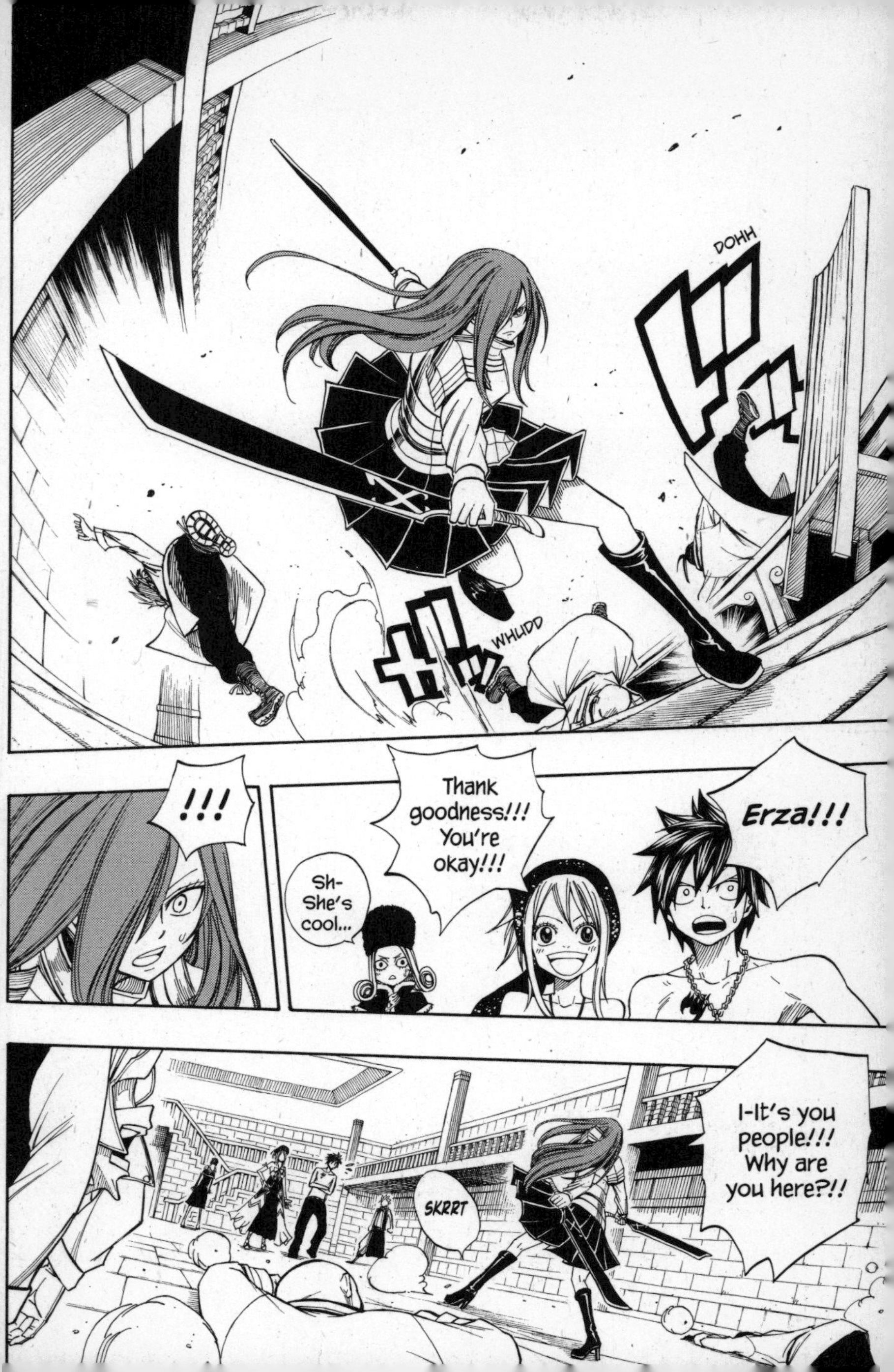
DOHH
WHUDD
Erza!!!
Thank goodness!!! You're okay!!!
Sh-She's cool...
!!!
I-It's you people!!! Why are you here?!!
SKRRT

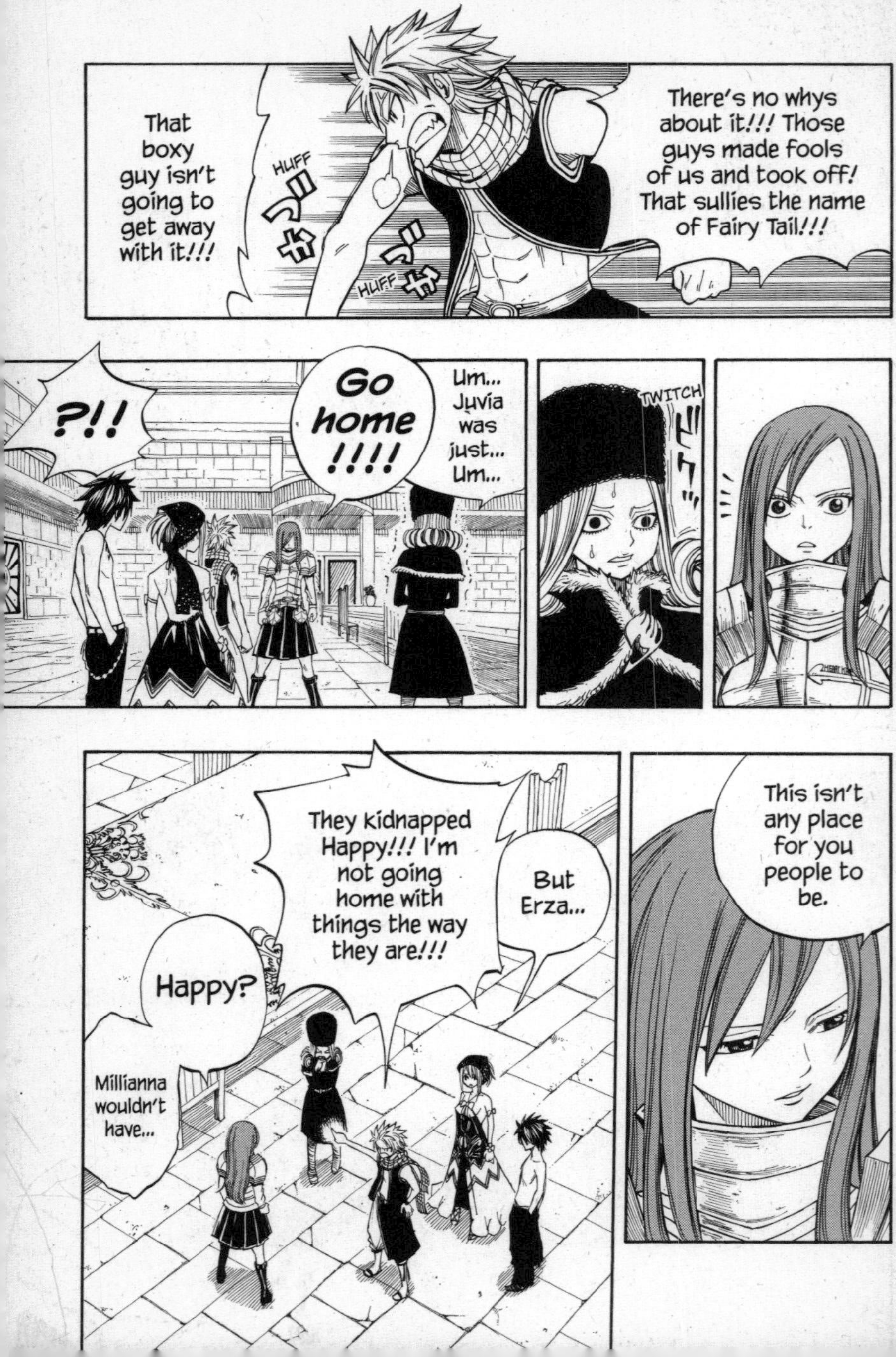
There's no whys about it!!! Those guys made fools of us and took off! That sullies the name of Fairy Tail!!!
That boxy guy isn't going to get away with it!!!
HUFF
HUFF
TWITCH
Um... Juvia was just... Um...
Go home!!!!
?!!
This isn't any place for you people to be.
But Erza...
They kidnapped Happy!!! I'm not going home with things the way they are!!!
Happy?
Millianna wouldn't have...

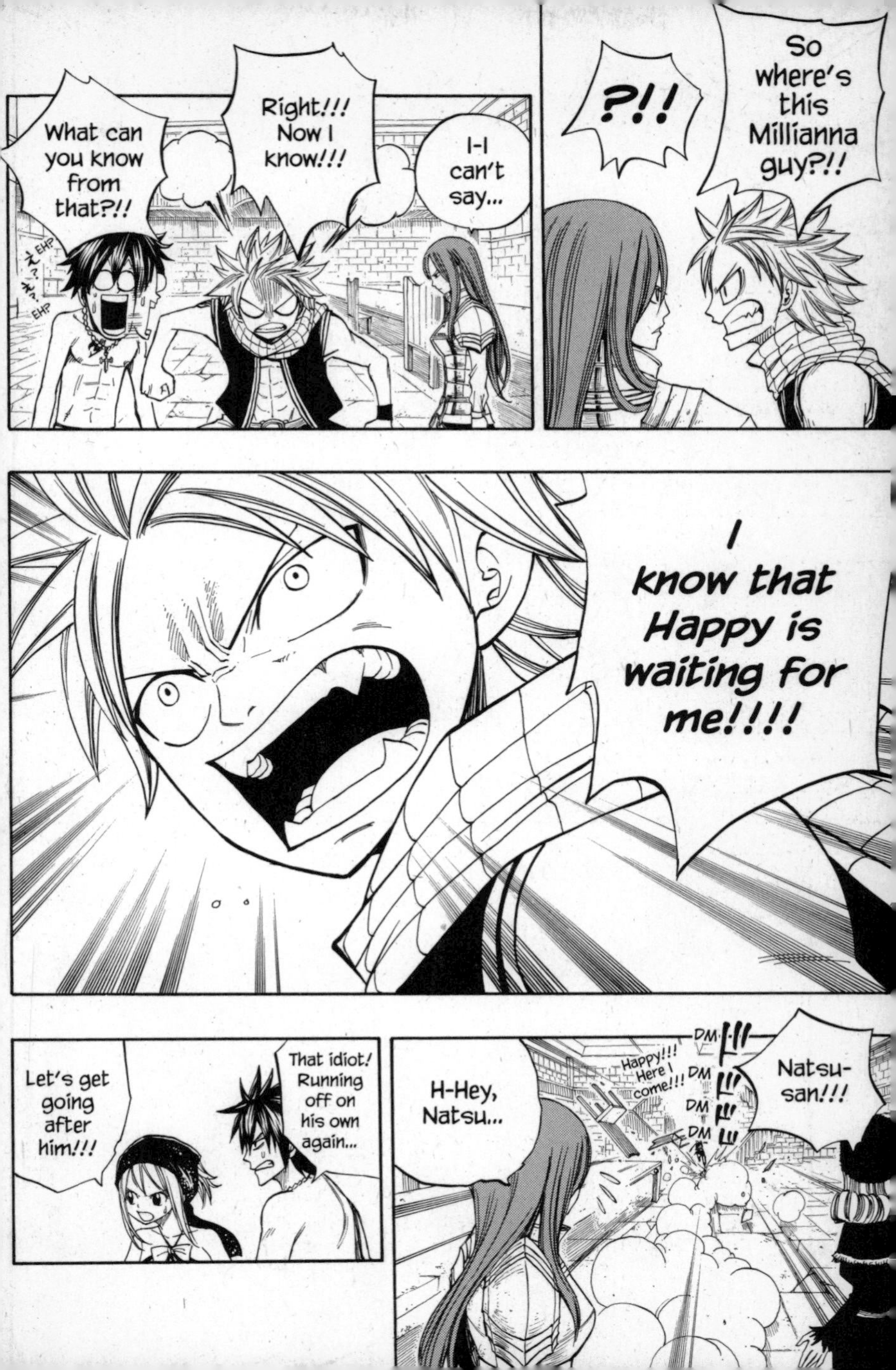
So where's this Millianna guy?!!
?!!
I-I can't say...
Right!!! Now I know!!!
What can you know from that?!!
EHP? EHP?
I know that Happy is waiting for me!!!!
Natsu-san!!!
DM DM DM DM
Happy!!! Here I come!!!
H-Hey, Natsu...
That idiot! Running off on his own again...
Let's get going after him!!!

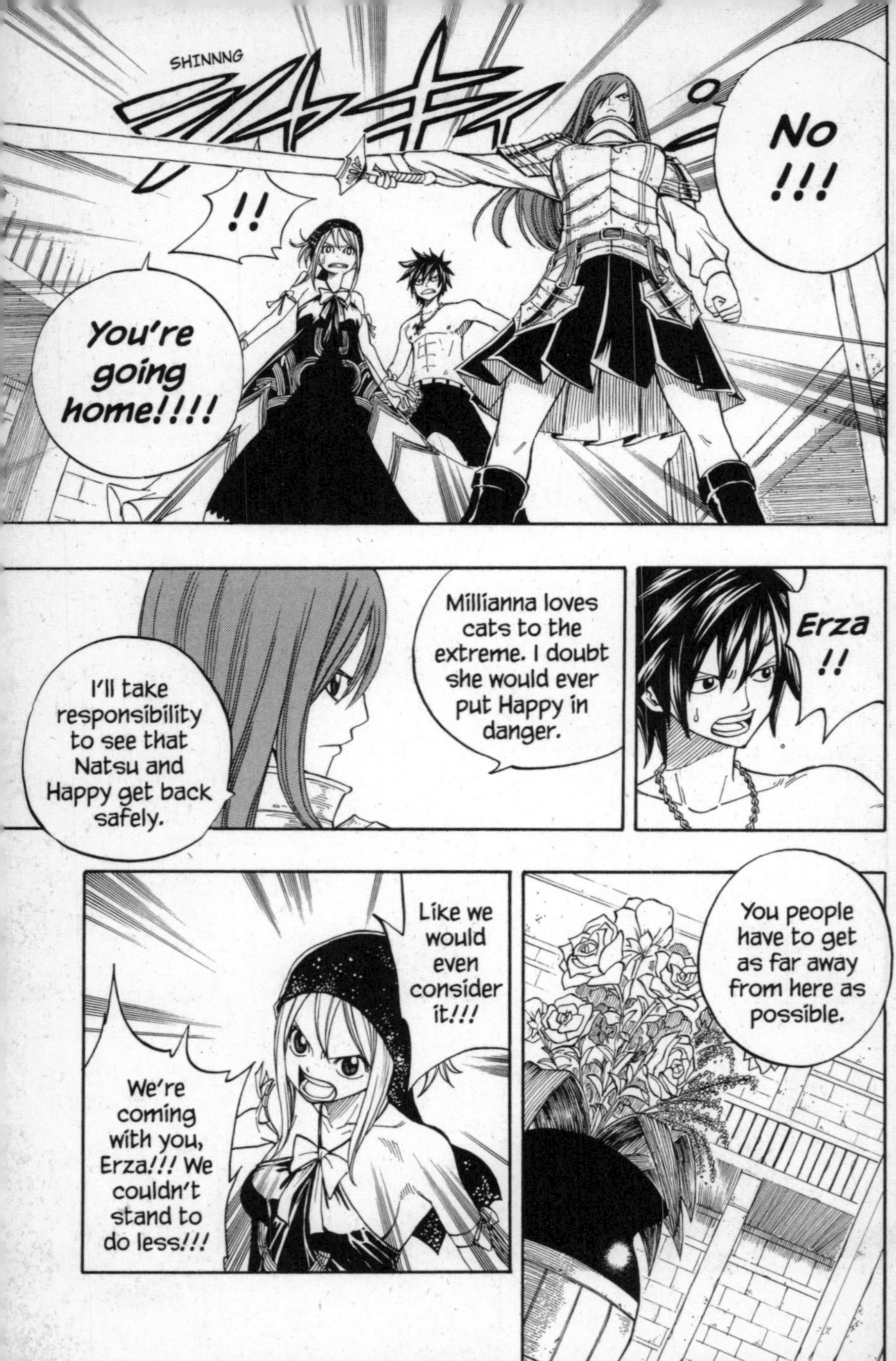
No !!!
SHINNNG
!!
You're going home!!!!
Erza !!
Millianna loves cats to the extreme. I doubt she would ever put Happy in danger.
I'll take responsibility to see that Natsu and Happy get back safely.
You people have to get as far away from here as possible.
Like we would even consider it!!!
We're coming with you, Erza!!! We couldn't stand to do less!!!

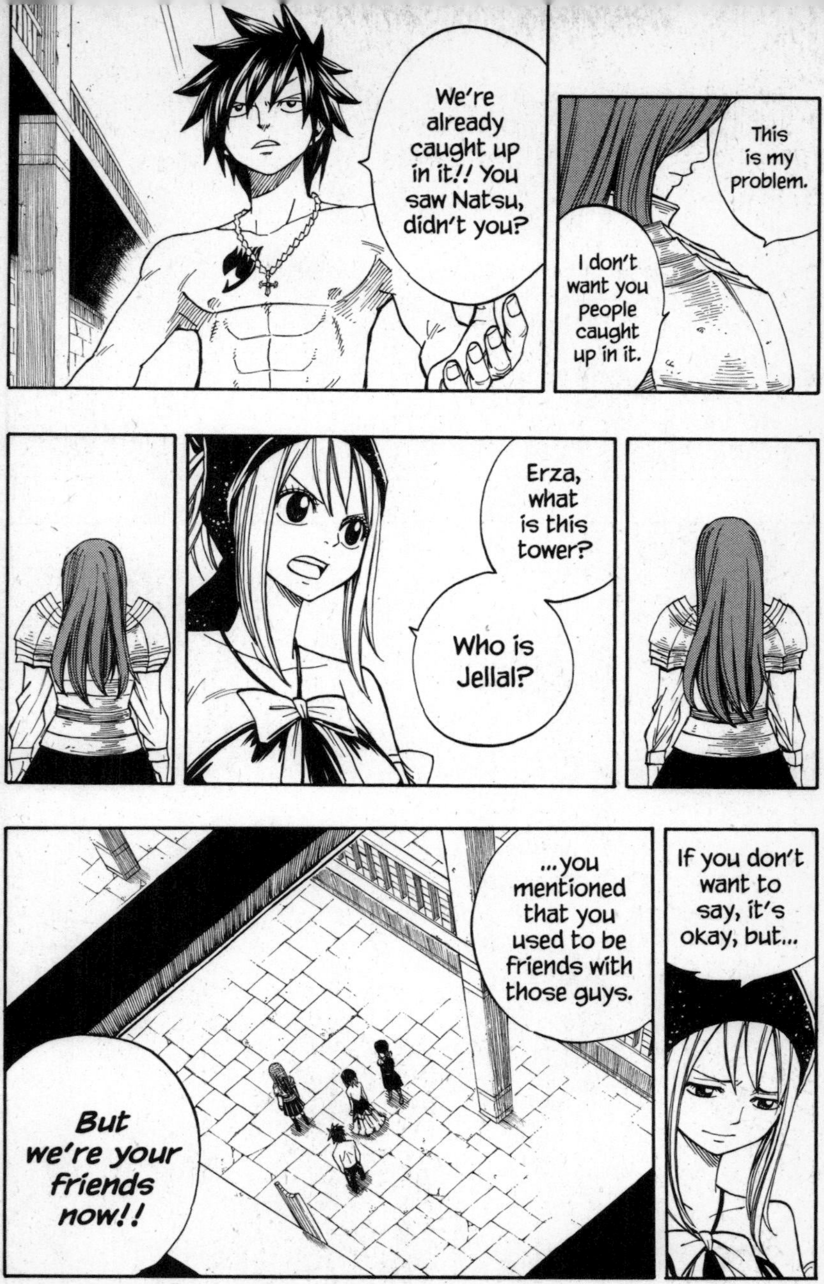
This is my problem.
I don't want you people caught up in it.
We're already caught up in it!! You saw Natsu, didn't you?
Erza, what is this tower?
Who is Jellal?
If you don't want to say, it's okay, but...
...you mentioned that you used to be friends with those guys.
But we're your friends now!!

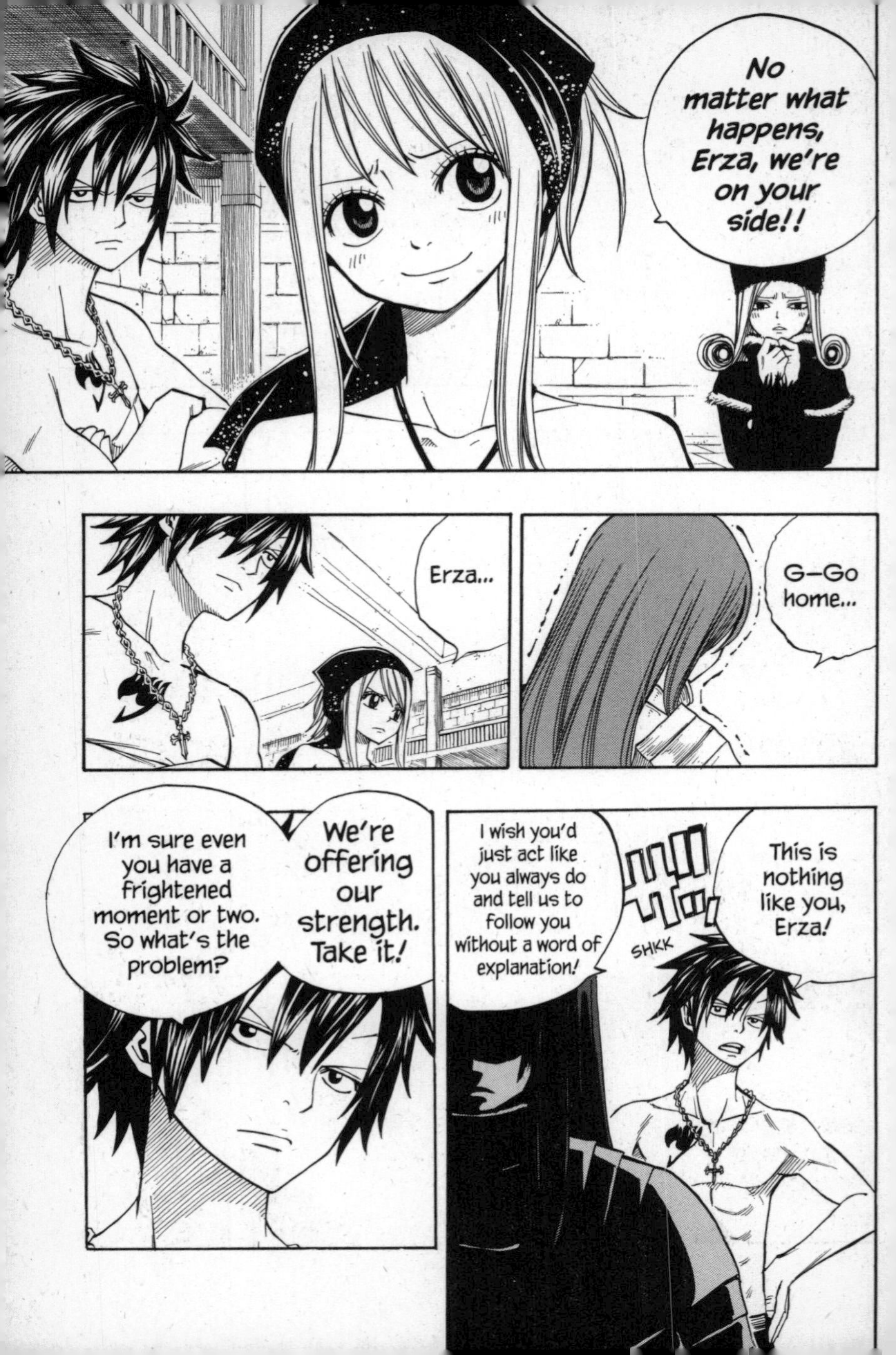
No matter what happens, Erza, we're on your side!!
G–Go home...
Erza...
This is nothing like you, Erza!
SHKK
I wish you'd just act like you always do and tell us to follow you without a word of explanation!
We're offering our strength. Take it!
I'm sure even you have a frightened moment or two. So what's the problem?

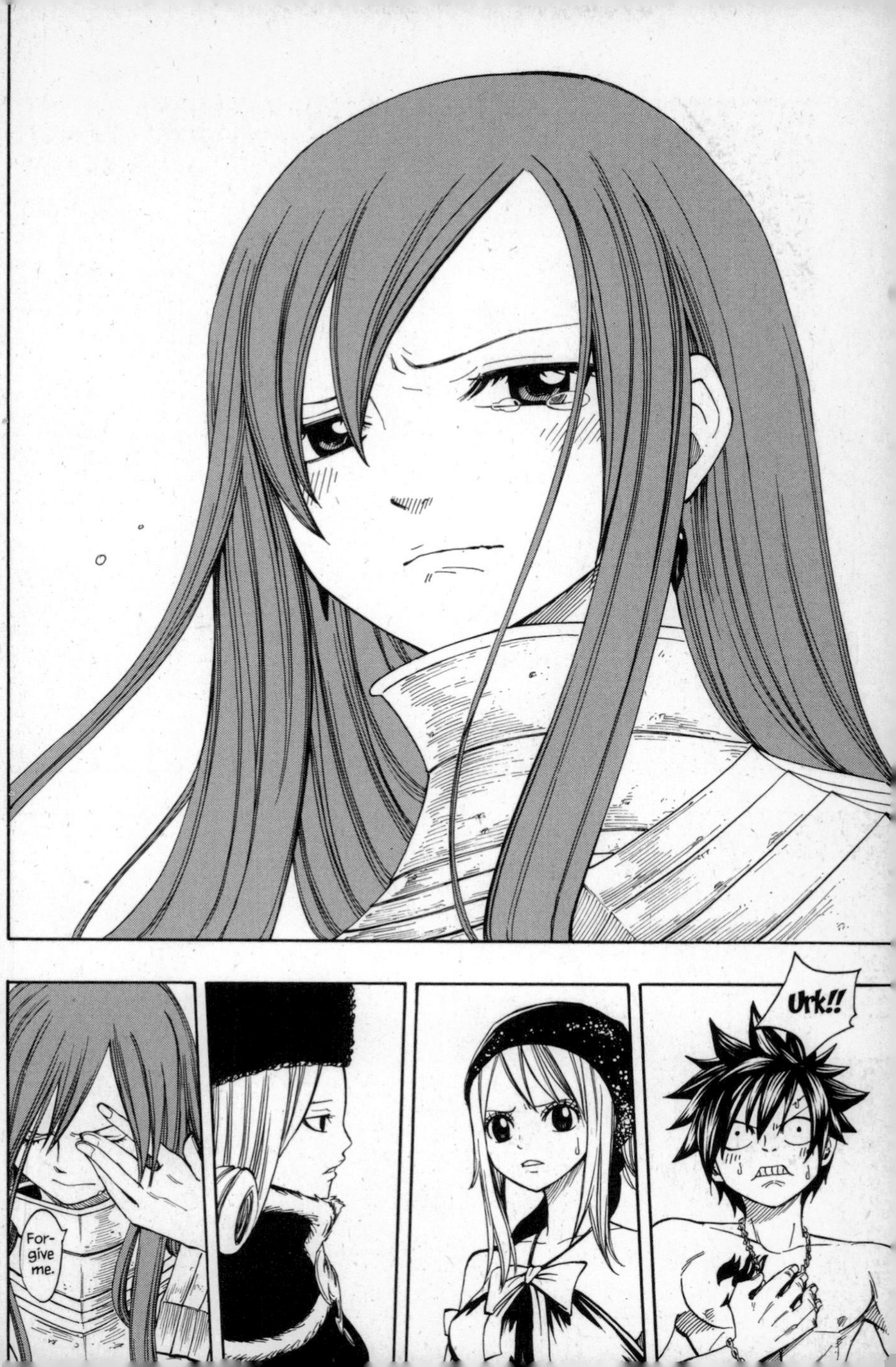
Urk!!
Forgive me.

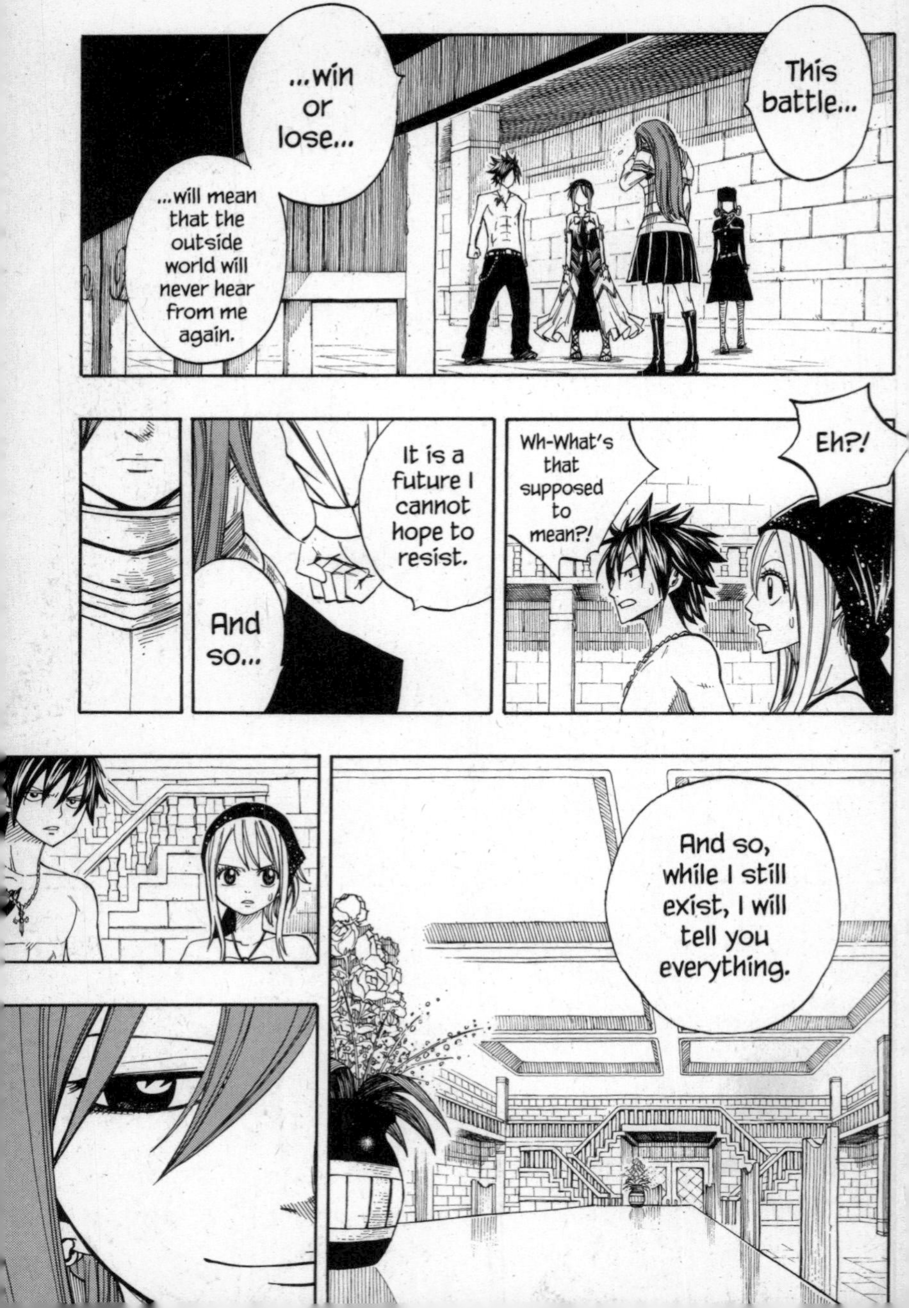

This battle...
...win or lose...
...will mean that the outside world will never hear from me again.
Eh?!
Wh-What's that supposed to mean?!
It is a future I cannot hope to resist.
And so...
And so, while I still exist, I will tell you everything.

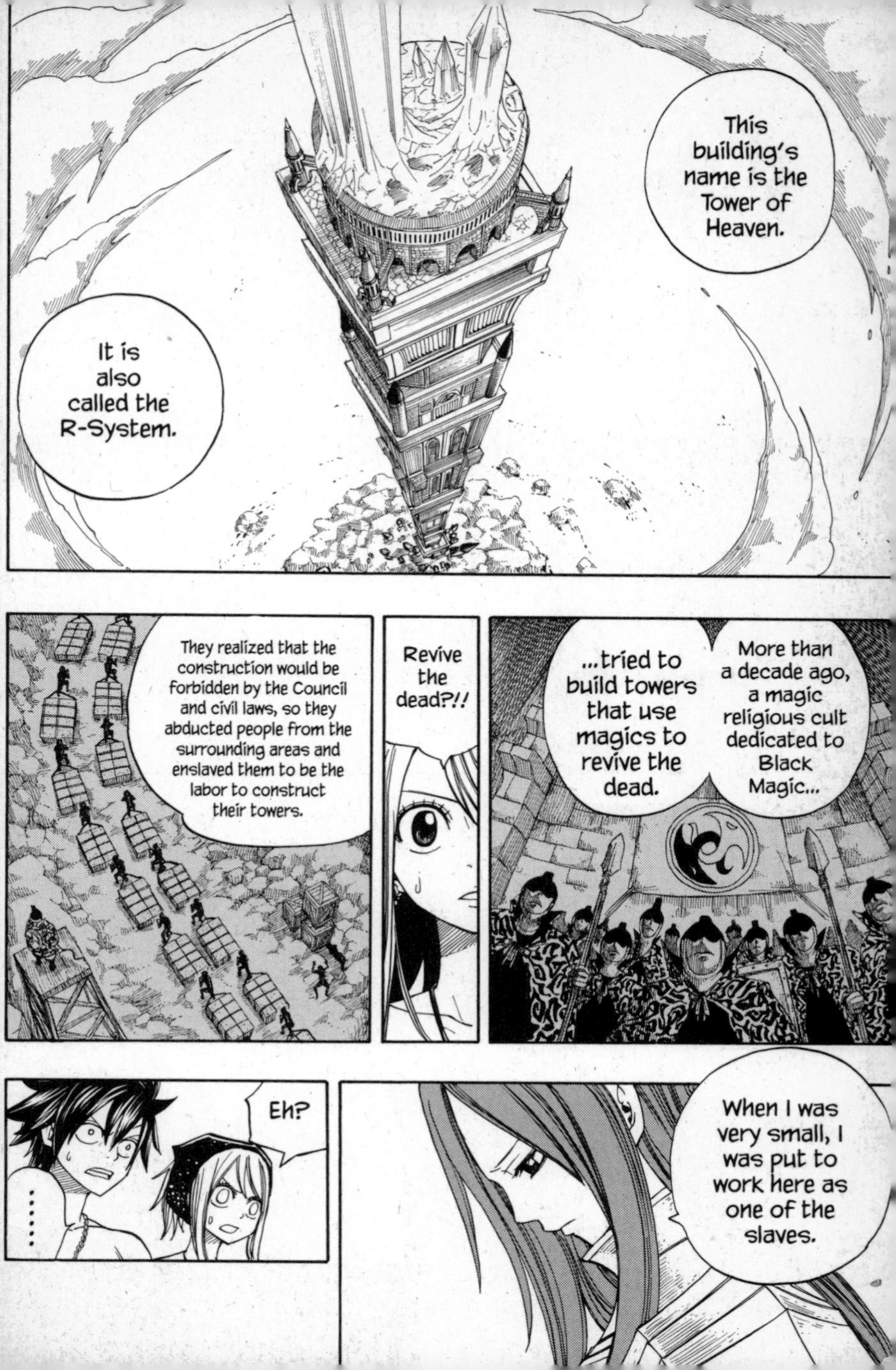
This building's name is the Tower of Heaven.
It is also called the R-System.
More than a decade ago, a magic religious cult dedicated to Black Magic...
...tried to build towers that use magics to revive the dead.
Revive the dead?!!
They realized that the construction would be forbidden by the Council and civil laws, so they abducted people from the surrounding areas and enslaved them to be the labor to construct their towers.
When I was very small, I was put to work here as one of the slaves.
Eh?
......

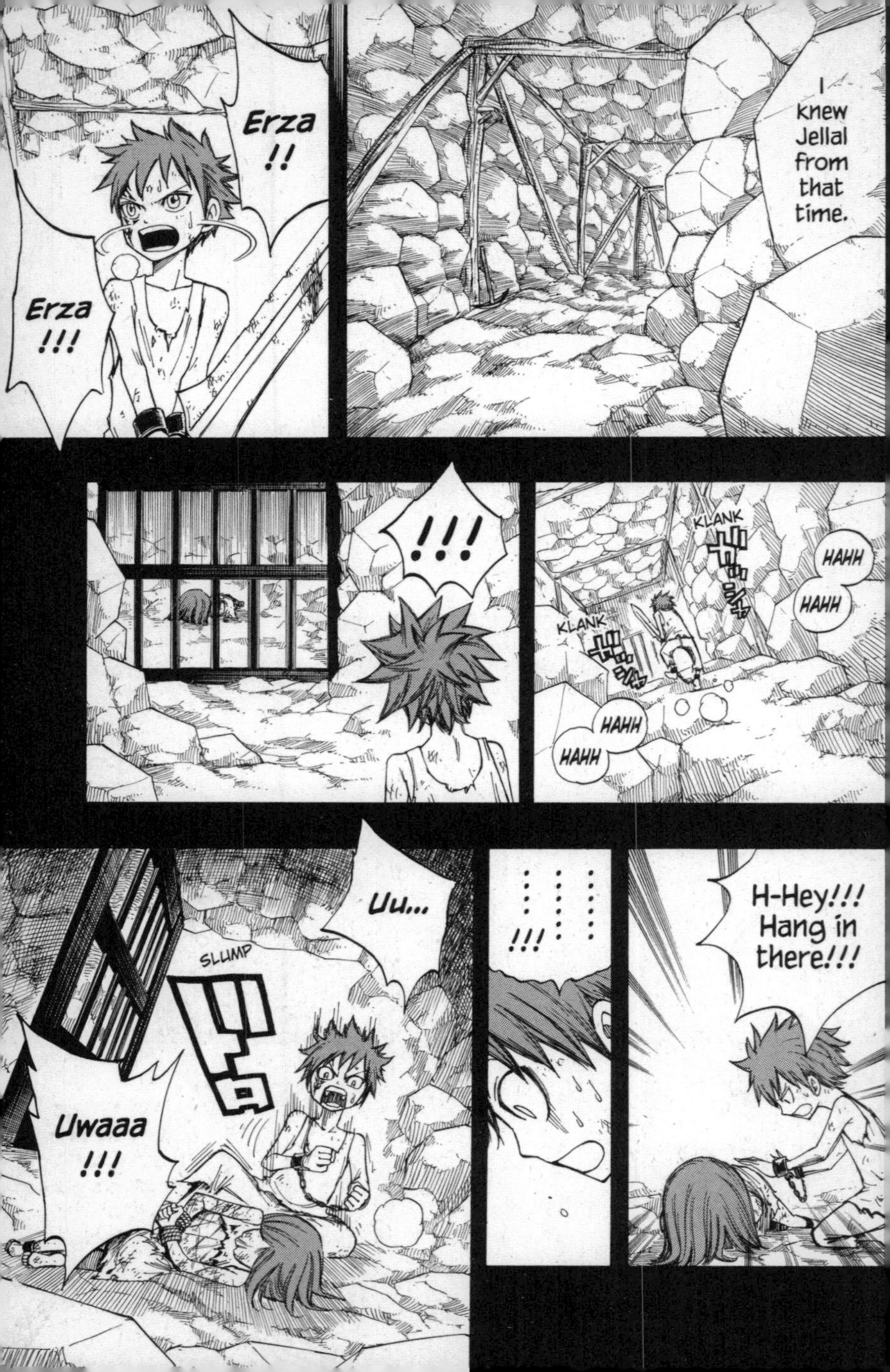
I knew Jellal from that time.
Erza!!
Erza!!!
KLANK
KLANK
HAHH
HAHH
HAHH
HAHH
!!!
H-Hey!!! Hang in there!!!
......!!!
Uu...
SLUMP
Uwaaa!!!

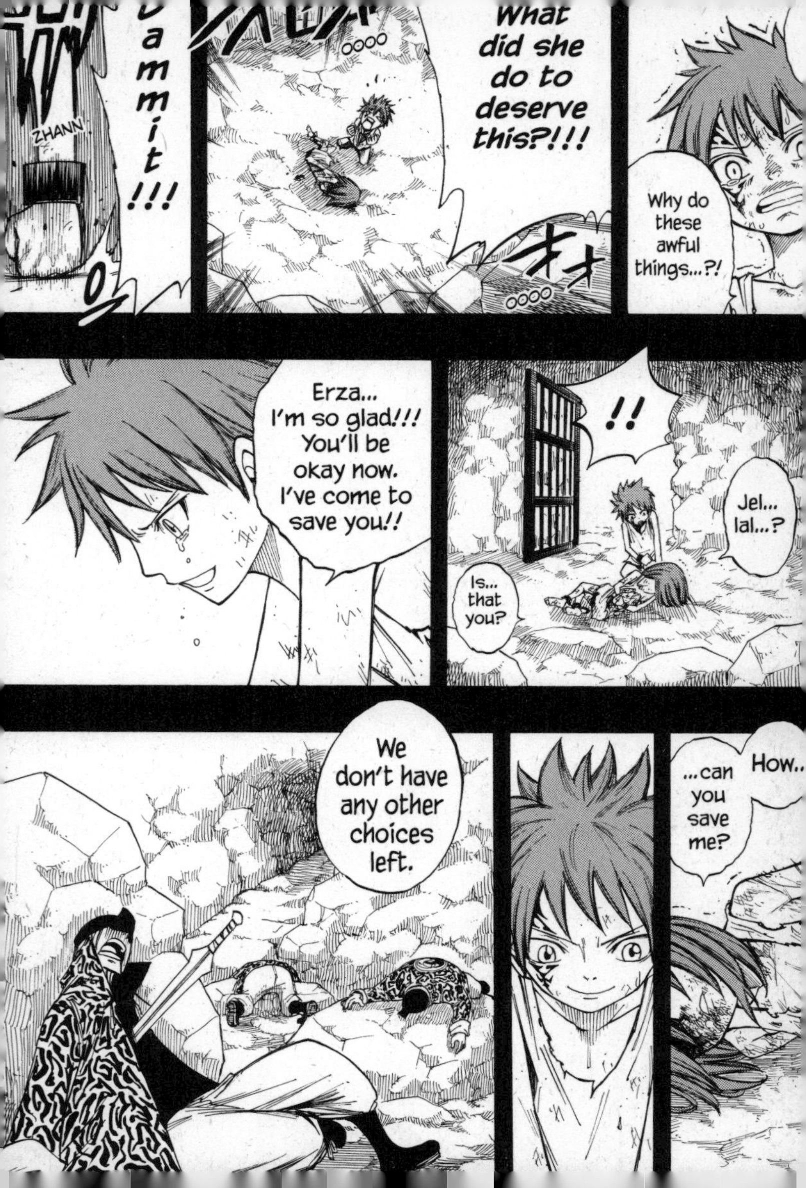
Why do these awful things...?!
What did she do to deserve this?!!!
Dammit!!!
ZHANN
!!
Jel... lal...?
Is... that you?
Erza... I'm so glad!!! You'll be okay now. I've come to save you!!
How..
...can you save me?
We don't have any other choices left.

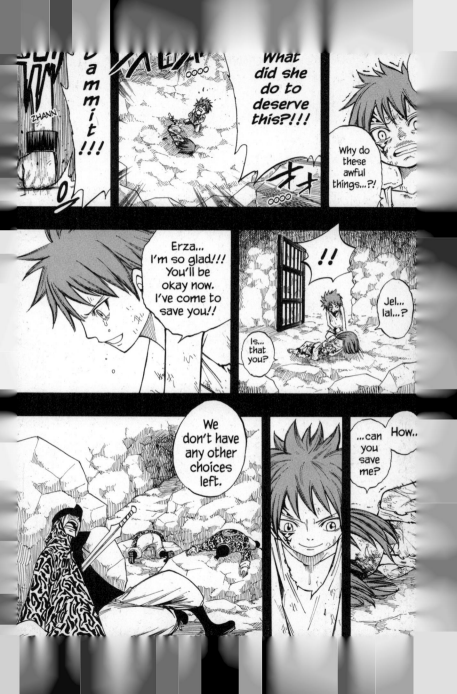

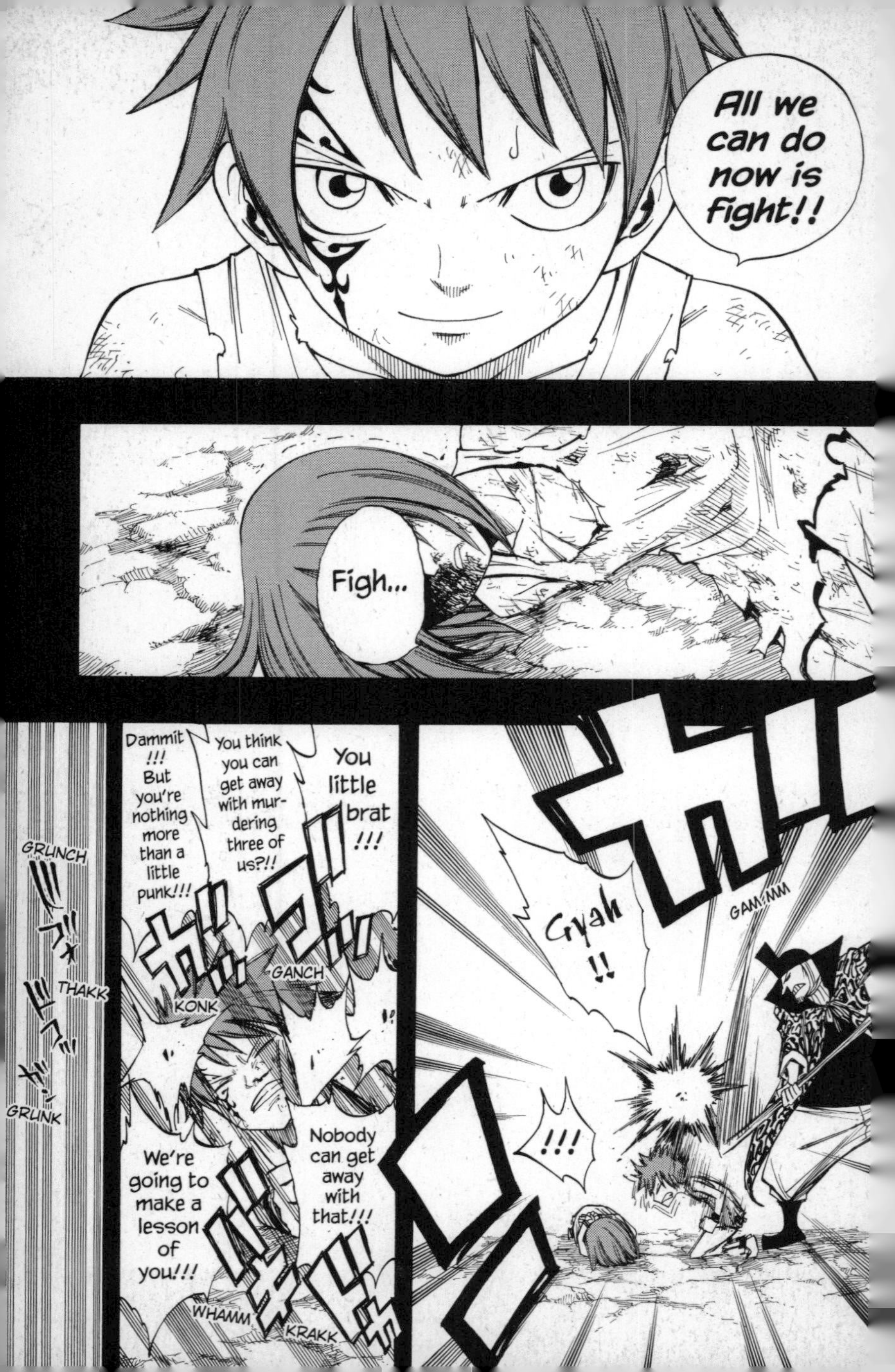
All we can do now is fight!!
Figh...
GAM MM
Gyah!!
!!!
You little brat!!!
You think you can get away with murdering three of us?!!
Dammit!!! But you're nothing more than a little punk!!!
GANCH
KONK
Nobody can get away with that!!!
We're going to make a lesson of you!!!
WHAMM
KRAKK
GRUNCH
THAKK
GRUNK

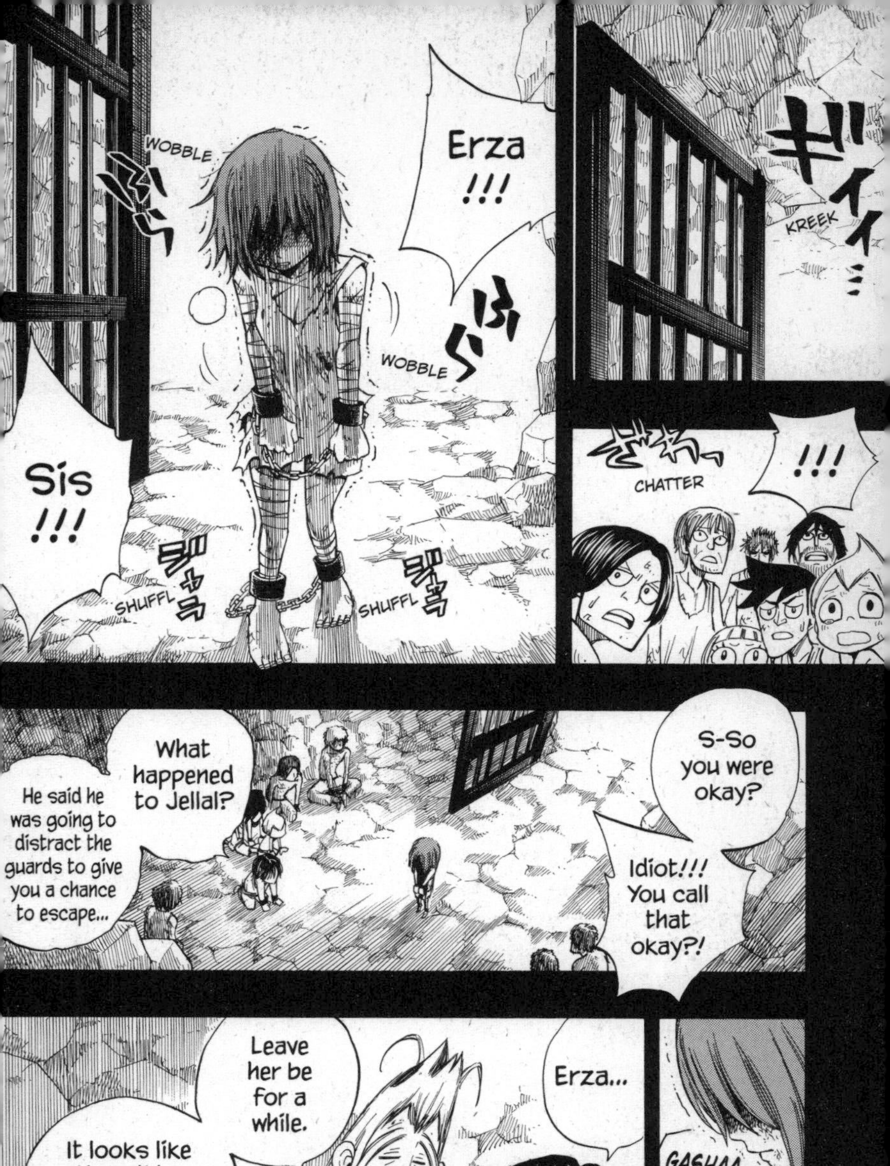
KREEK
CHATTER
!!!
Erza !!!
WOBBLE
WOBBLE
Sis !!!
SHUFFL
SHUFFL
S-So you were okay?
Idiot!!! You call that okay?!
What happened to Jellal?
He said he was going to distract the guards to give you a chance to escape...
GASHAA
......
Erza...
Leave her be for a while.
It looks like they did a thorough job in her punishment. Poor girl.

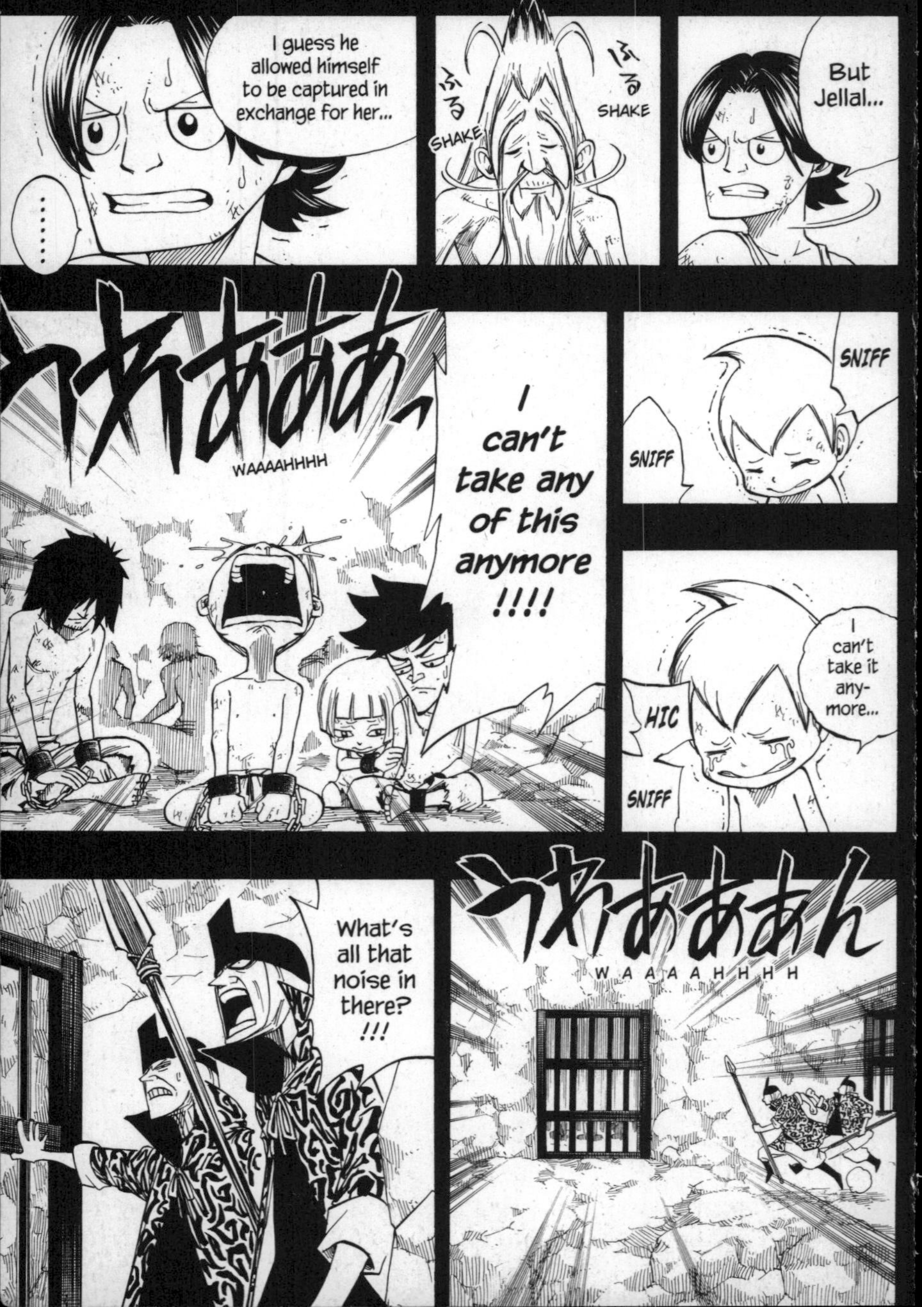
But Jellal...
ふる
SHAKE
ふる
SHAKE
I guess he allowed himself to be captured in exchange for her...
......
SNIFF
SNIFF
I can't take it anymore...
HIC
SNIFF
うわあああ
WAAAAHHHH
I can't take any of this anymore !!!!
うわあああん
WAAAAHHHH
What's all that noise in there? !!!

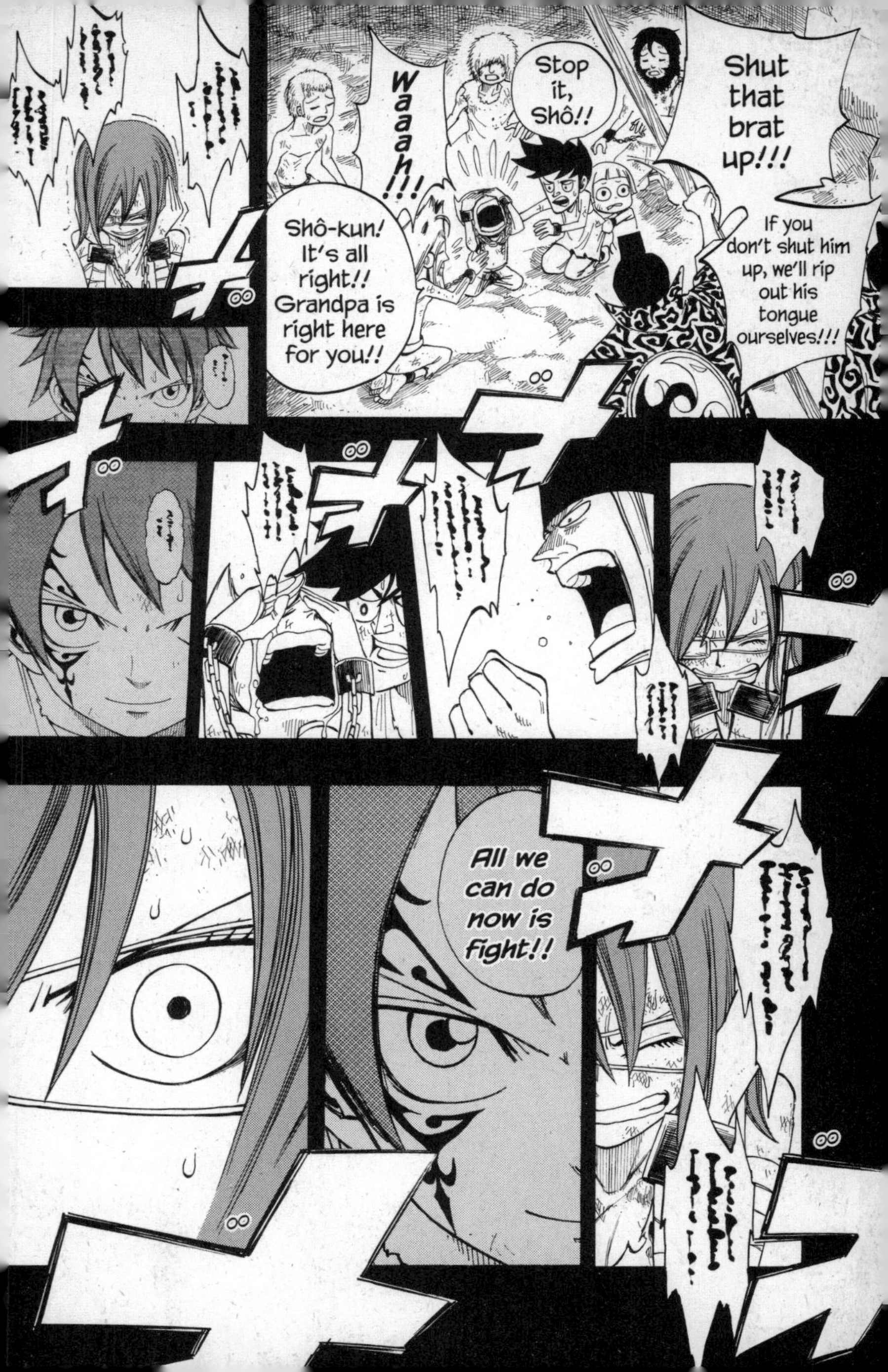
Shut that brat up!!!
If you don't shut him up, we'll rip out his tongue ourselves!!!
Stop it, Shô!!
Waaaah!!!
Shô-kun! It's all right!! Grandpa is right here for you!!
All we can do now is fight!!

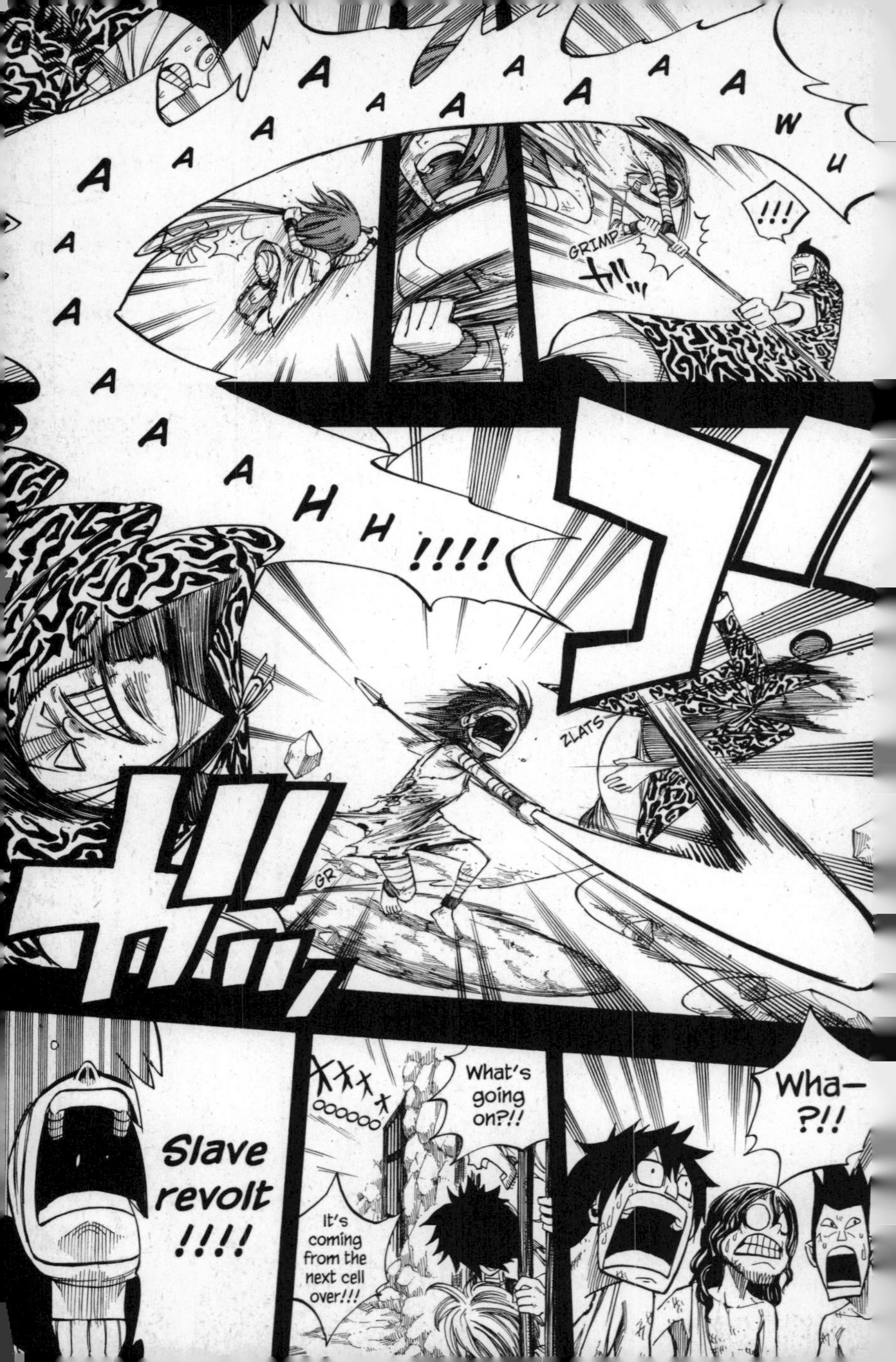

UWAAAAAAAAAAAAAAAHH!!!!
!!!
GRIMP
ZLATS
GR
Wha—?!!
What's going on?!!
It's coming from the next cell over!!!
Slave revolt!!!!

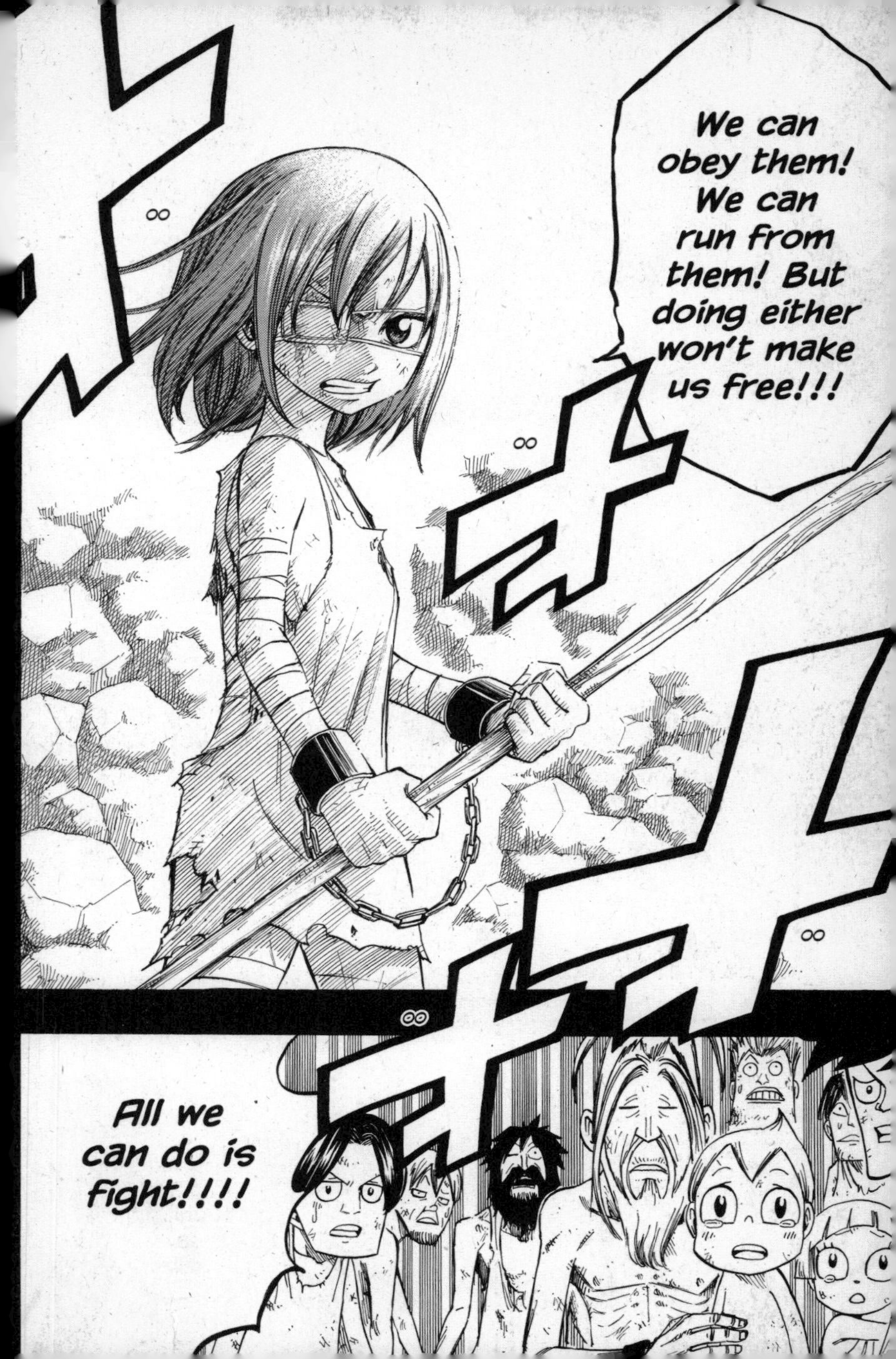
We can obey them! We can run from them! But doing either won't make us free!!!
All we can do is fight!!!!

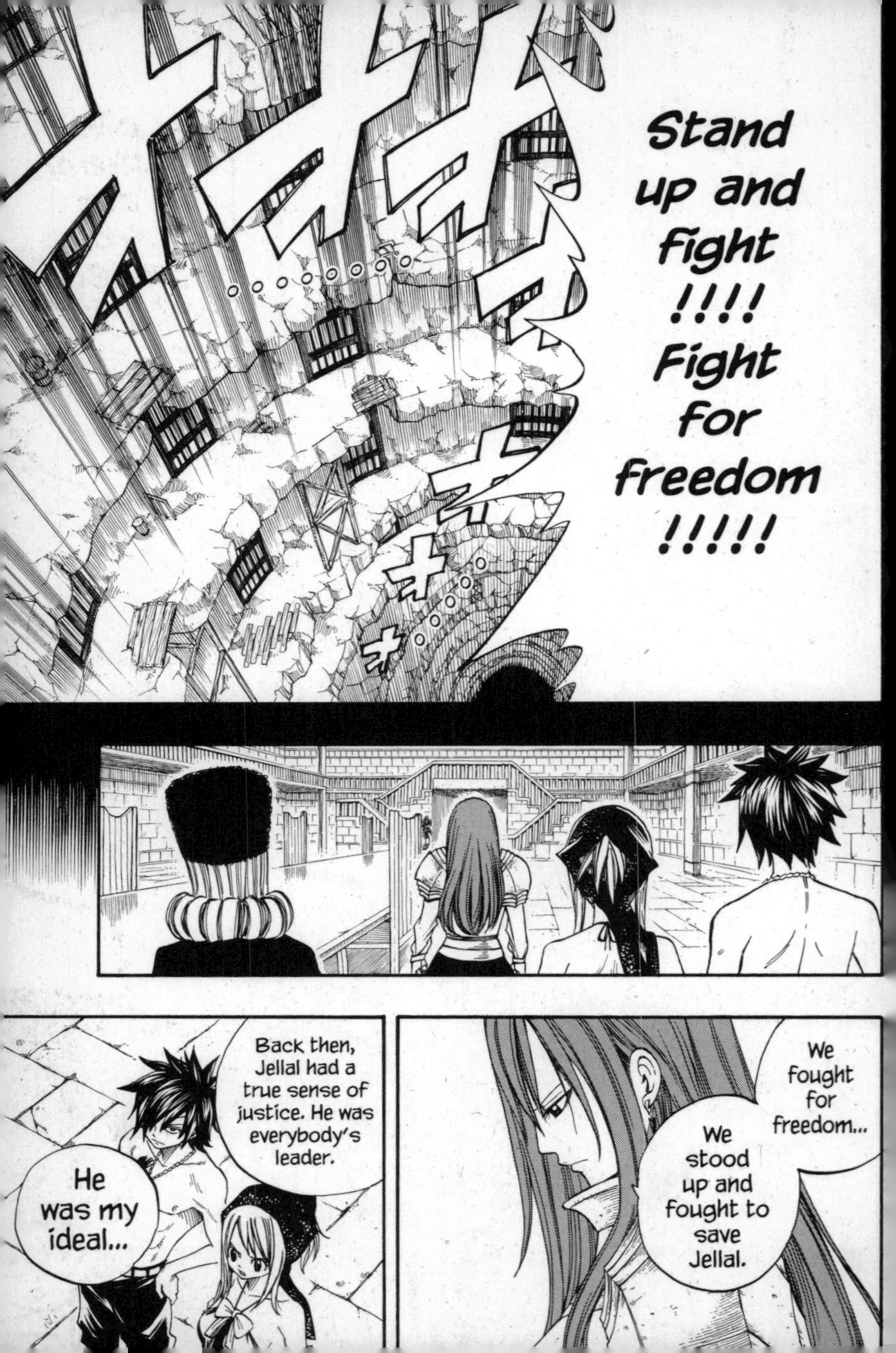
Stand up and fight!!!! Fight for freedom!!!!!
We fought for freedom...
We stood up and fought to save Jellal.
Back then, Jellal had a true sense of justice. He was everybody's leader.
He was my ideal...

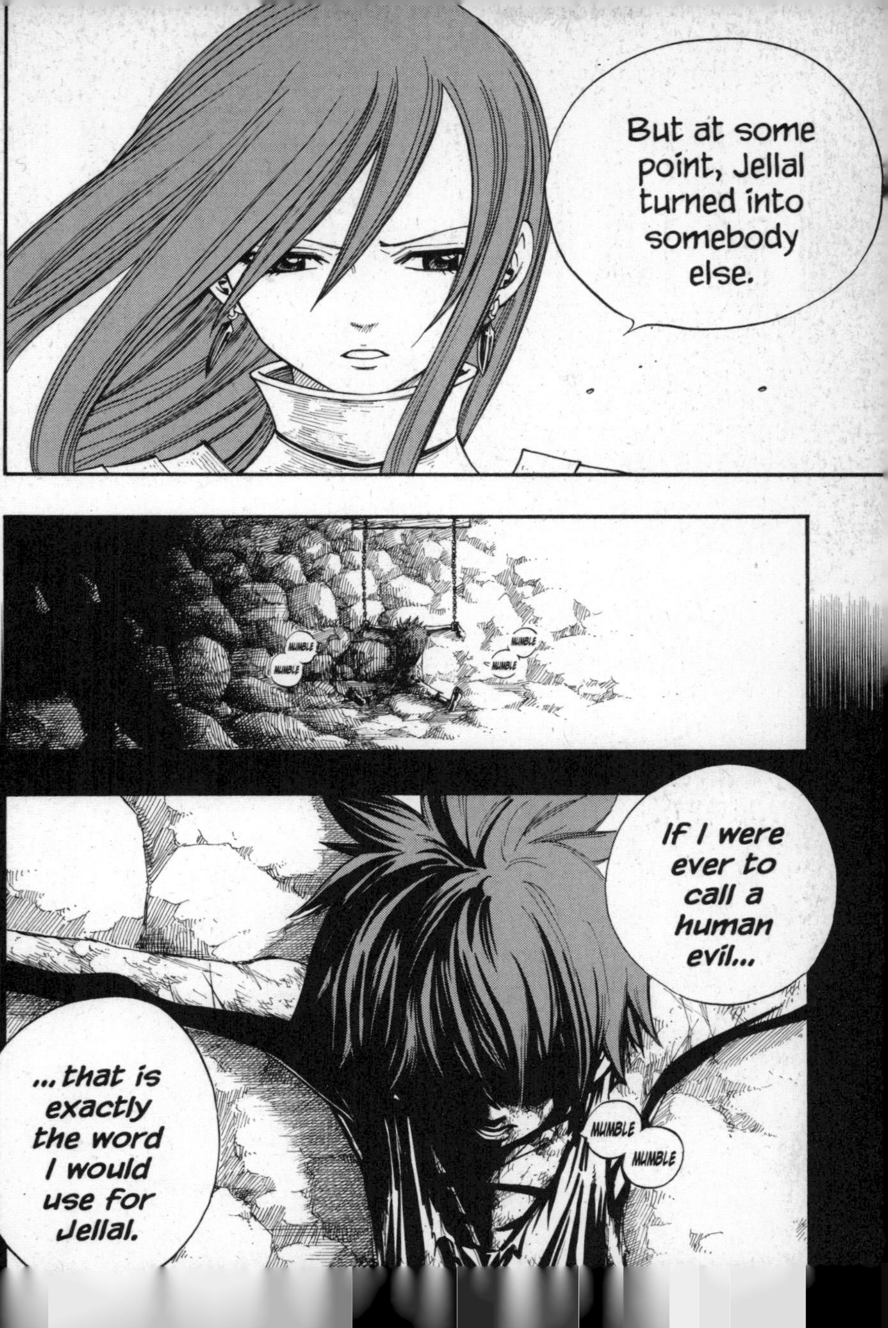
But at some point, Jellal turned into somebody else.
MUMBLE
MUMBLE
MUMBLE
MUMBLE
If I were ever to call a human evil...
...that is exactly the word I would use for Jellal.
MUMBLE
MUMBLE

FAIRY TAIL

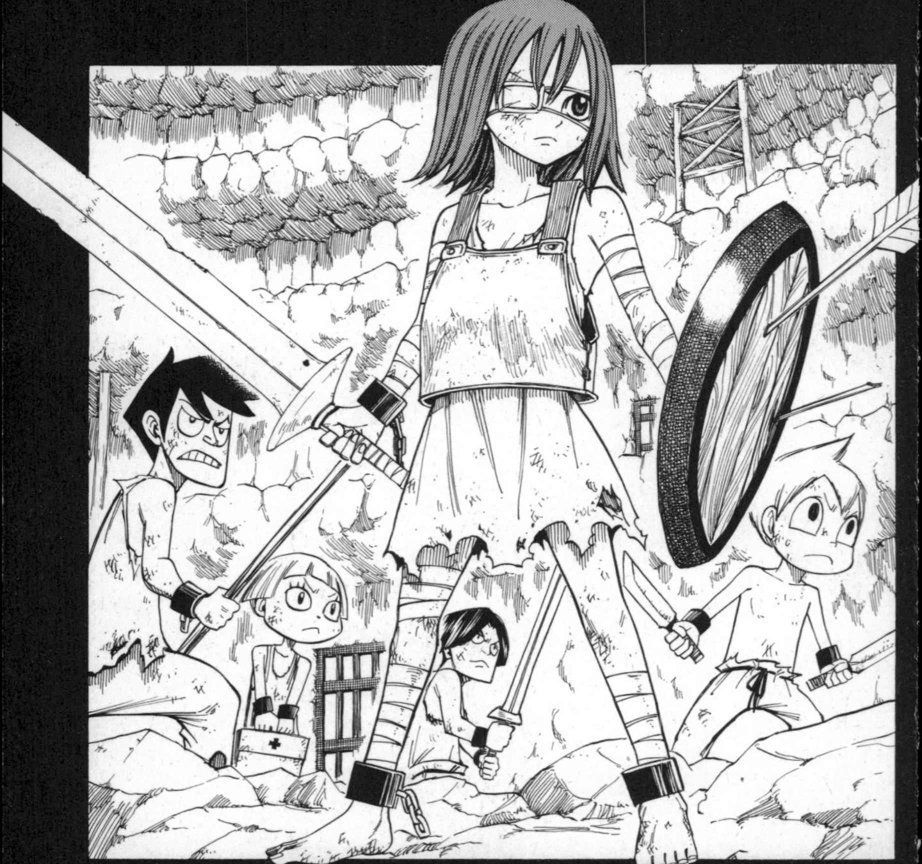

Chapter 81: The Voice in the Darkness

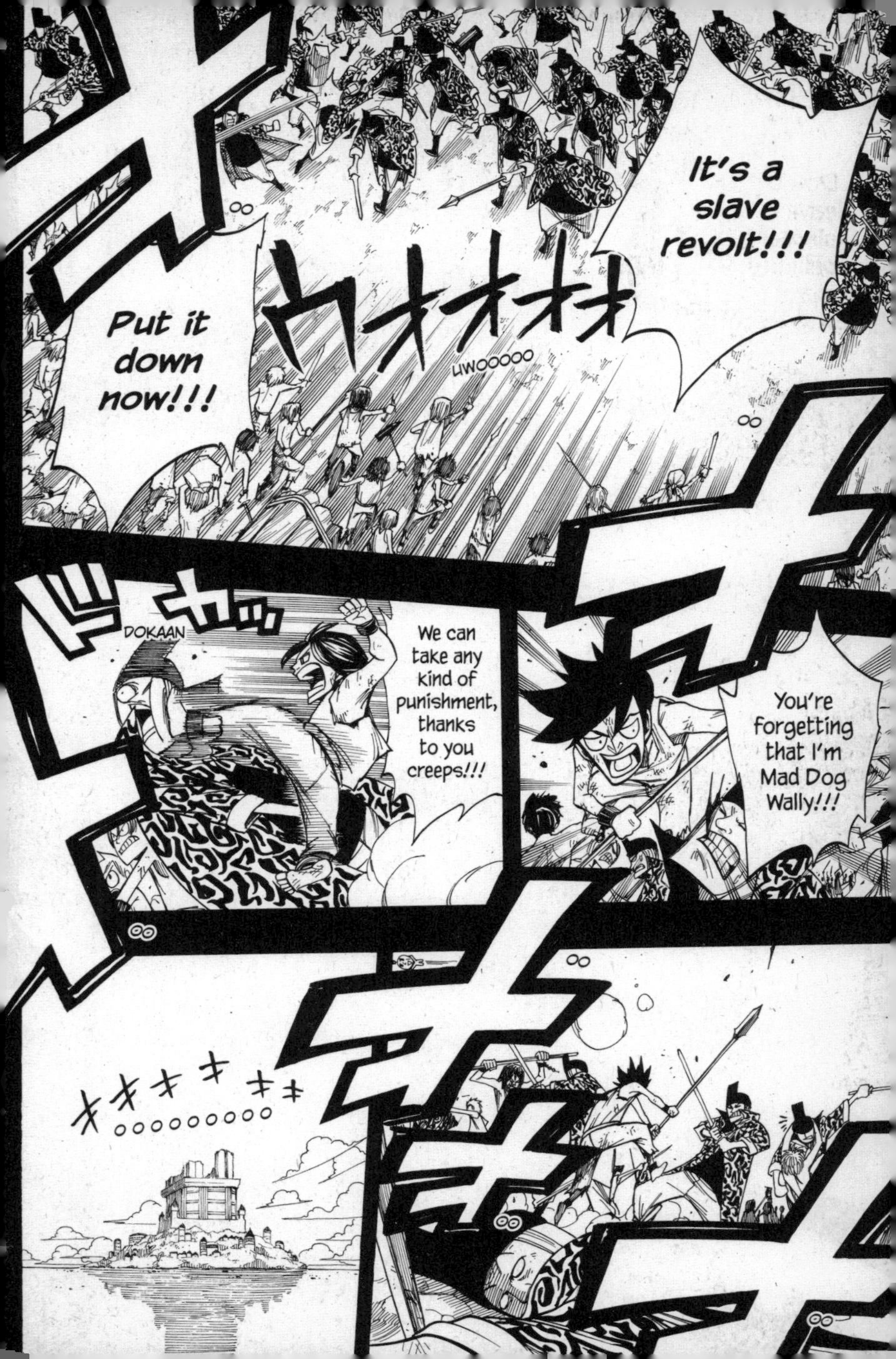
It's a slave revolt!!!
ウオオオオオ
UWOOOOO
Put it down now!!!
You're forgetting that I'm Mad Dog Wally!!!
DOKAAN
We can take any kind of punishment, thanks to you creeps!!!
ooooooooo

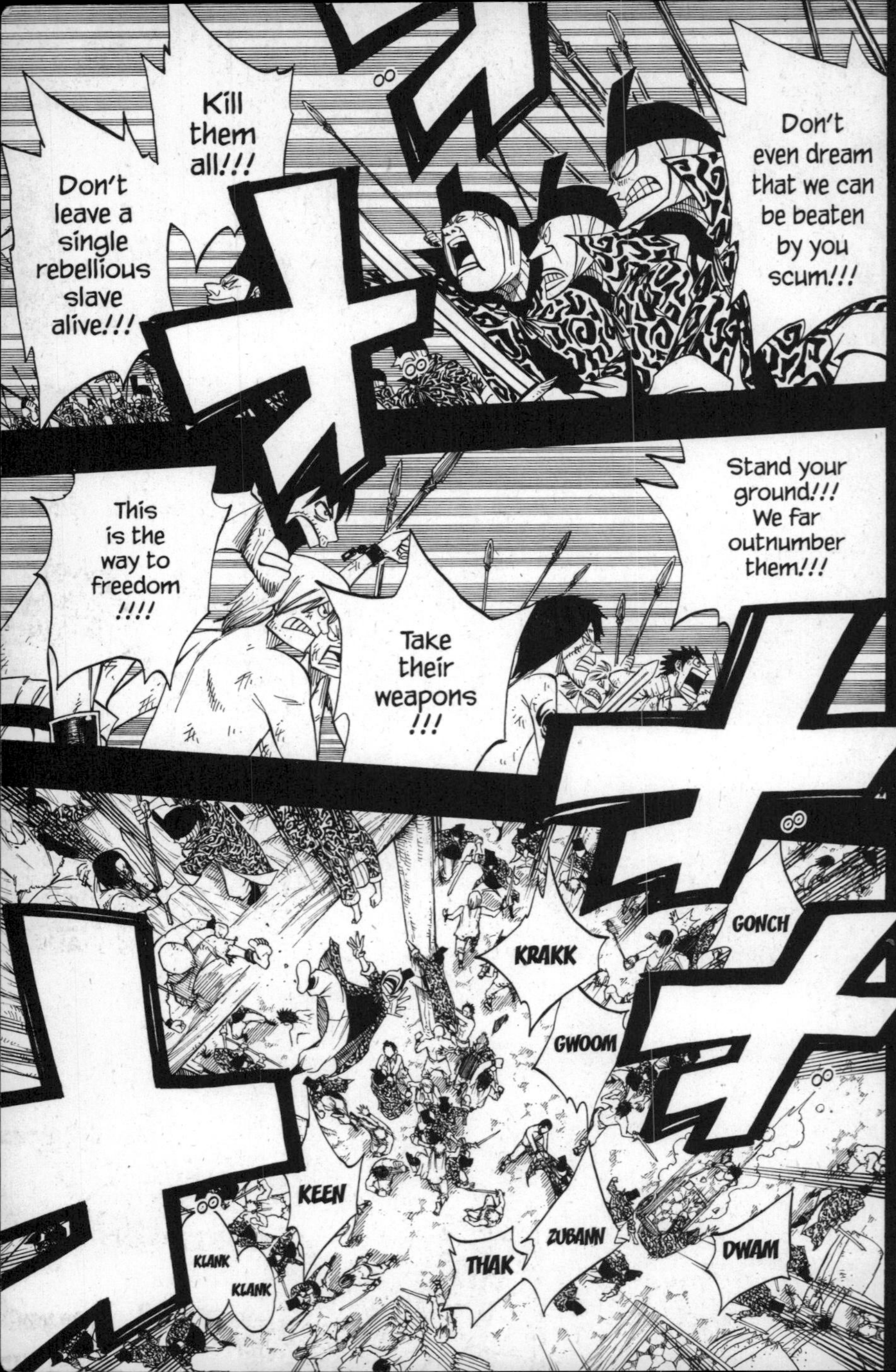
Don't even dream that we can be beaten by you scum!!!
Kill them all!!!
Don't leave a single rebellious slave alive!!!
Stand your ground!!! We far outnumber them!!!
Take their weapons!!!
This is the way to freedom!!!!
GONCH
KRAKK
GWOOM
DWAM
ZUBANN
THAK
KEEN
KLANK
KLANK

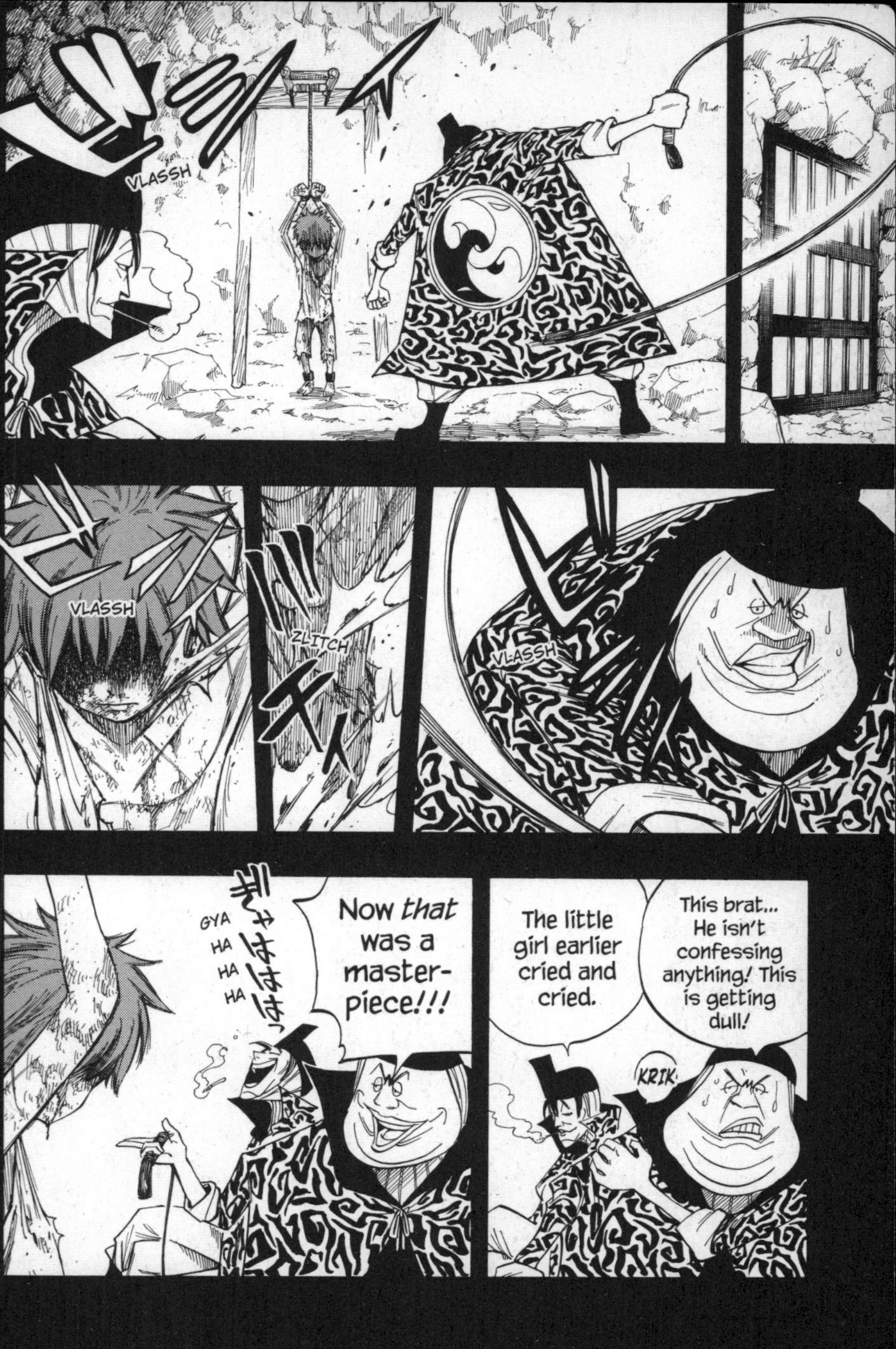
VLASSH
VLASSH
ZLITCH
VLASSH
This brat... He isn't confessing anything! This is getting dull!
KRIK
The little girl earlier cried and cried.
Now *that* was a master-piece!!!
GYA HA HA HA
ぎゃはははっ

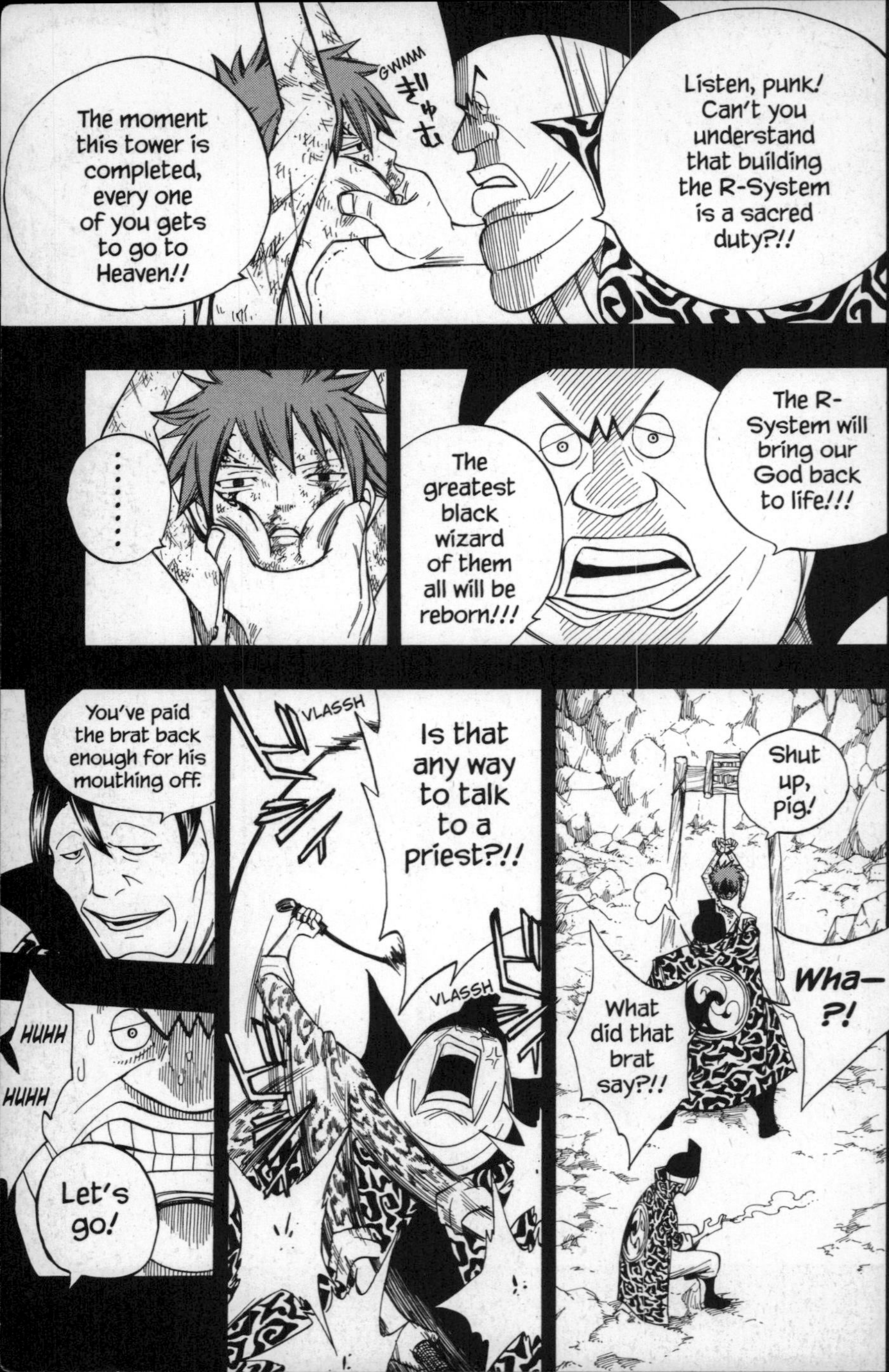
Listen, punk! Can't you understand that building the R-System is a sacred duty?!!
GWMM
The moment this tower is completed, every one of you gets to go to Heaven!!
The R-System will bring our God back to life!!!
The greatest black wizard of them all will be reborn!!!
......
Shut up, pig!
Wha—?!
What did that brat say?!!
VLASSH
Is that any way to talk to a priest?!!
VLASSH
You've paid the brat back enough for his mouthing off.
HUHH
HUHH
Let's go!

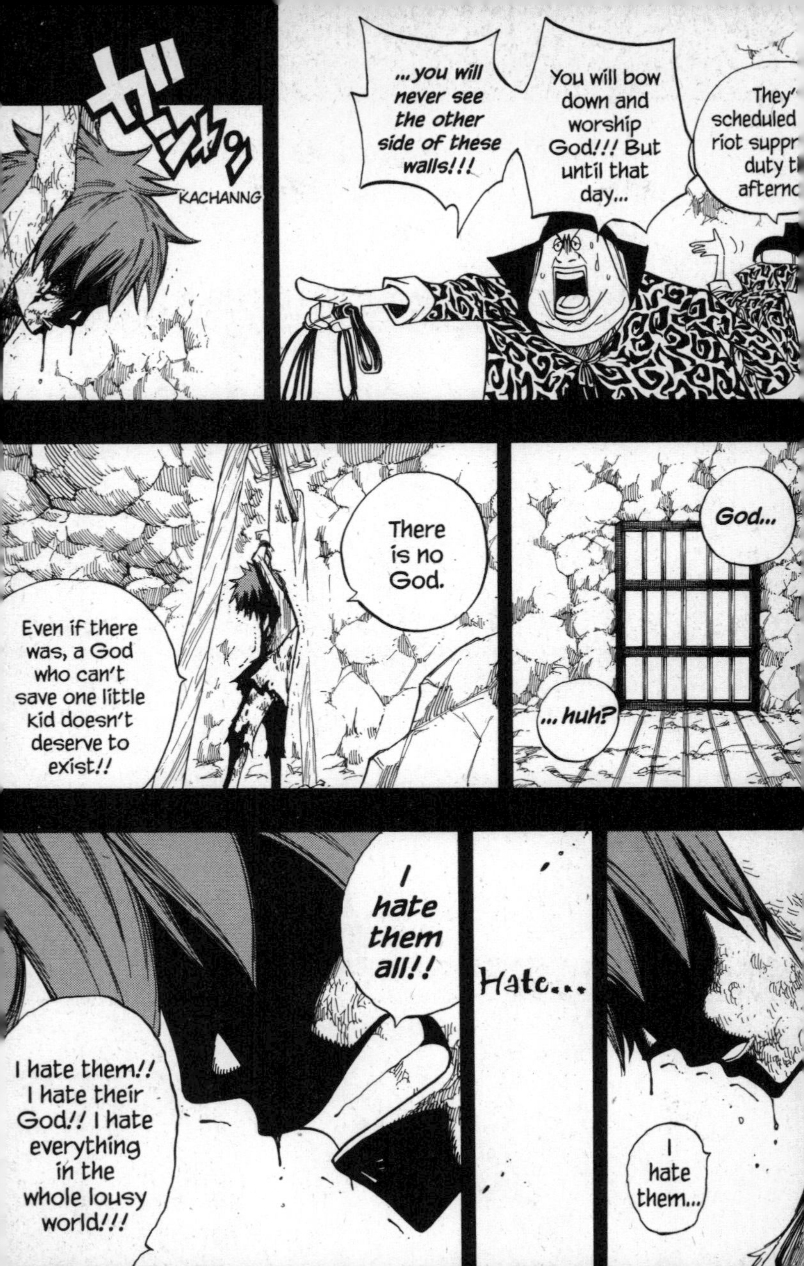
They'
scheduled
riot suppr
duty t
afterno
You will bow down and worship God!!! But until that day...
...you will never see the other side of these walls!!!
KACHANNG
God...
...huh?
There is no God.
Even if there was, a God who can't save one little kid doesn't deserve to exist!!
I hate them...
Hate...
I hate them all!!
I hate them!! I hate their God!! I hate everything in the whole lousy world!!!

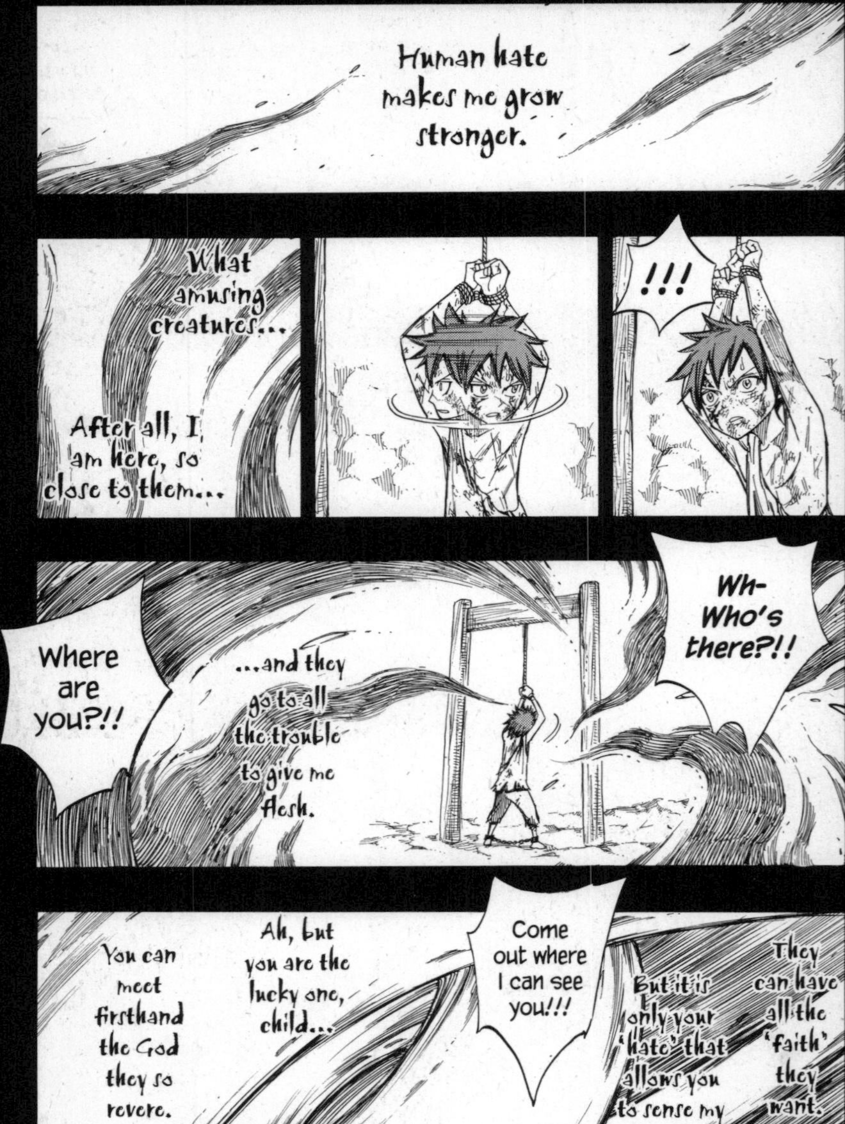
Human hate makes me grow stronger.
!!!
What amusing creatures...
After all, I am here, so close to them...
Wh- Who's there?!!
...and they go to all the trouble to give me flesh.
Where are you?!!
They can have all the 'faith' they want.
But it is only your 'hate' that allows you to sense my presence.
Come out where I can see you!!!
Ah, but you are the lucky one, child...
You can meet firsthand the God they so revere.

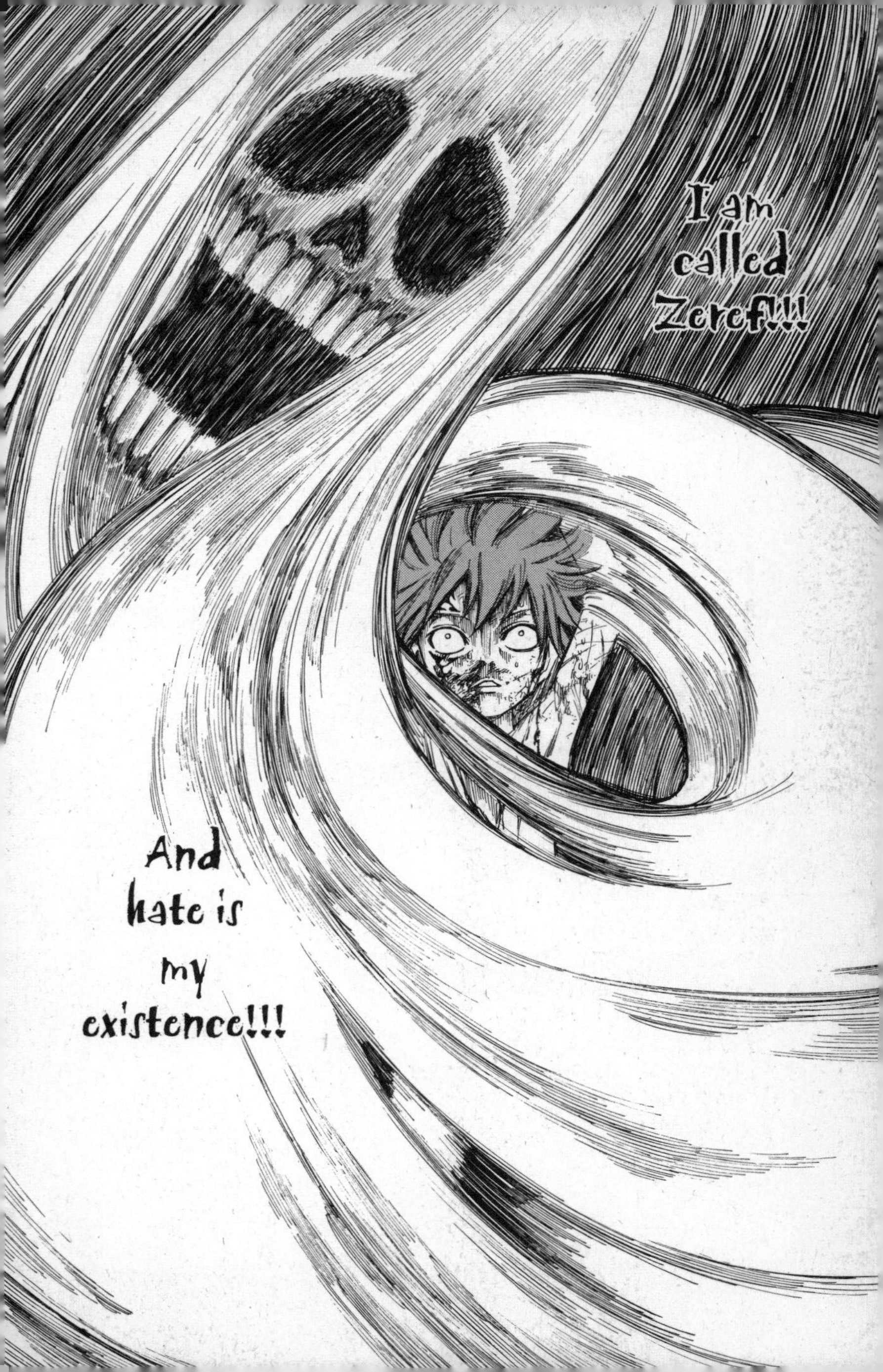
I am called Zeref!!!
And hate is my existence!!!

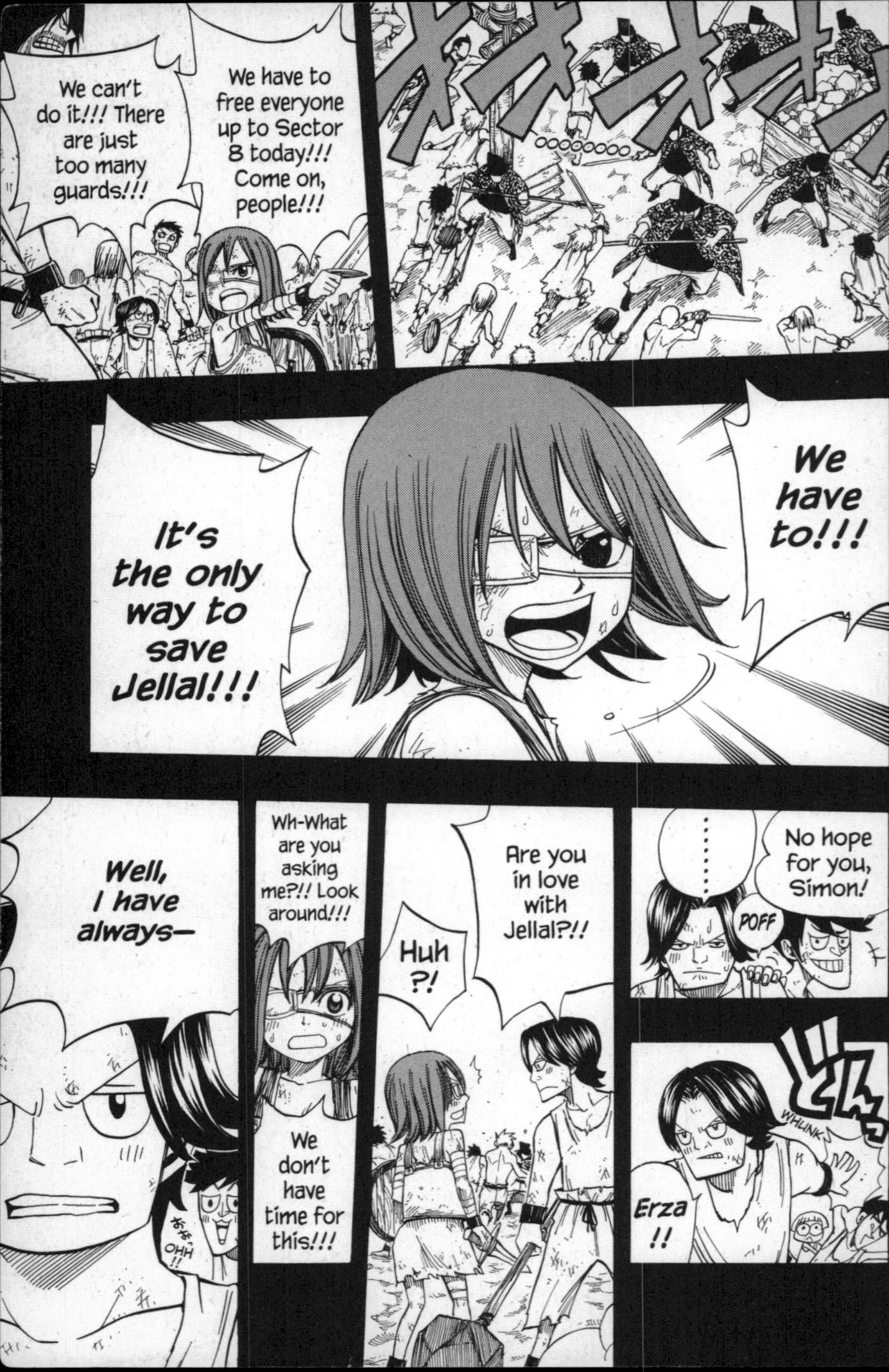
OOOOOOOOO
We have to free everyone up to Sector 8 today!!! Come on, people!!!
We can't do it!!! There are just too many guards!!!
We have to!!!
It's the only way to save Jellal!!!
No hope for you, Simon!
POFF
WHUNK
Erza !!
Are you in love with Jellal?!!
Huh ?!
Wh-What are you asking me?!! Look around!!!
We don't have time for this!!!
Well, I have always—
OHH !!

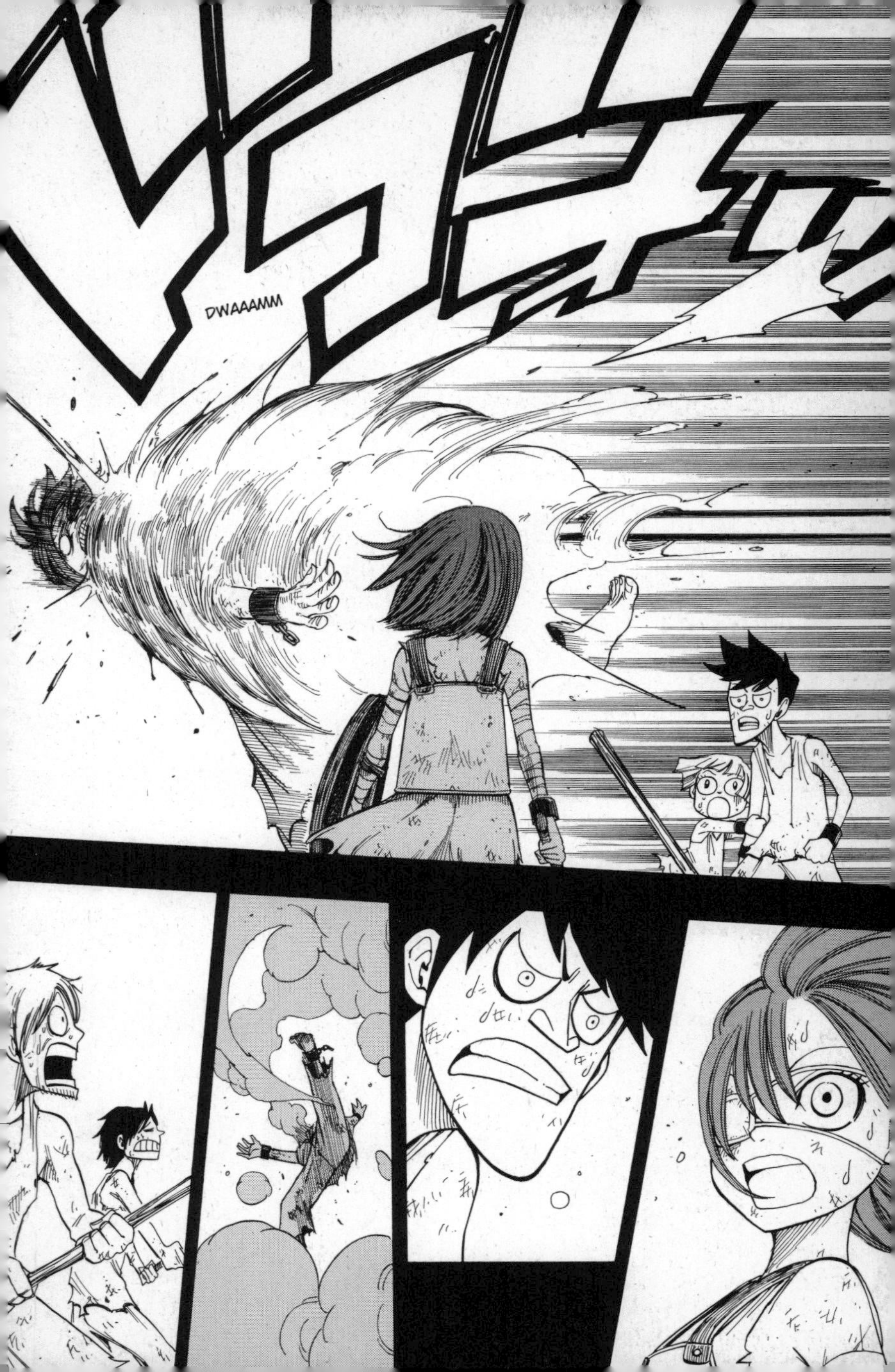
DWAAAMM

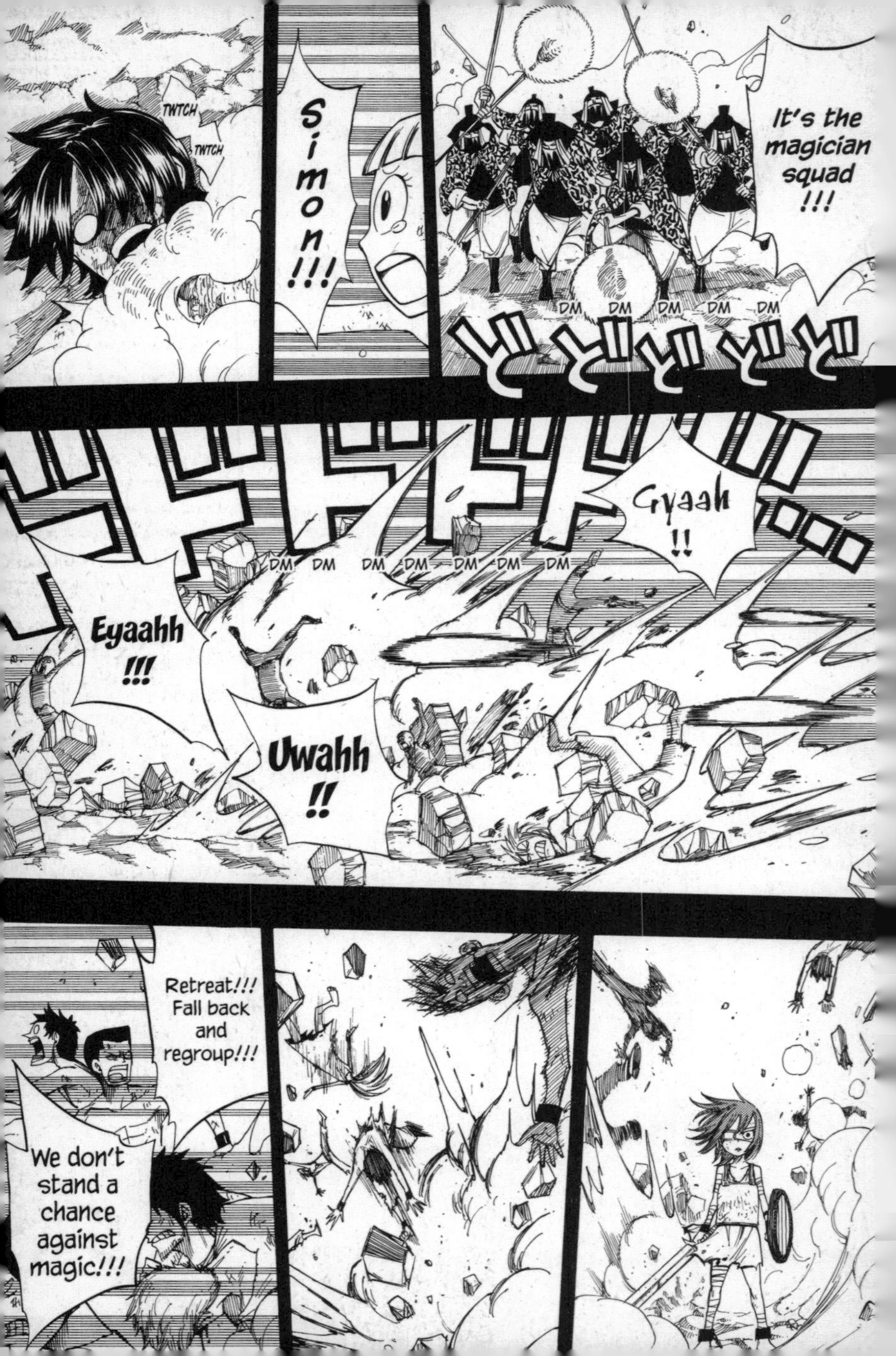

It's the magician squad!!!
DM DM DM DM DM
Simon!!!
TWTCH
TWTCH
Gyaah!!
DM DM DM DM DM DM DM
Uwahh!!
Eyaahh!!!
Retreat!!! Fall back and regroup!!!
We don't stand a chance against magic!!!

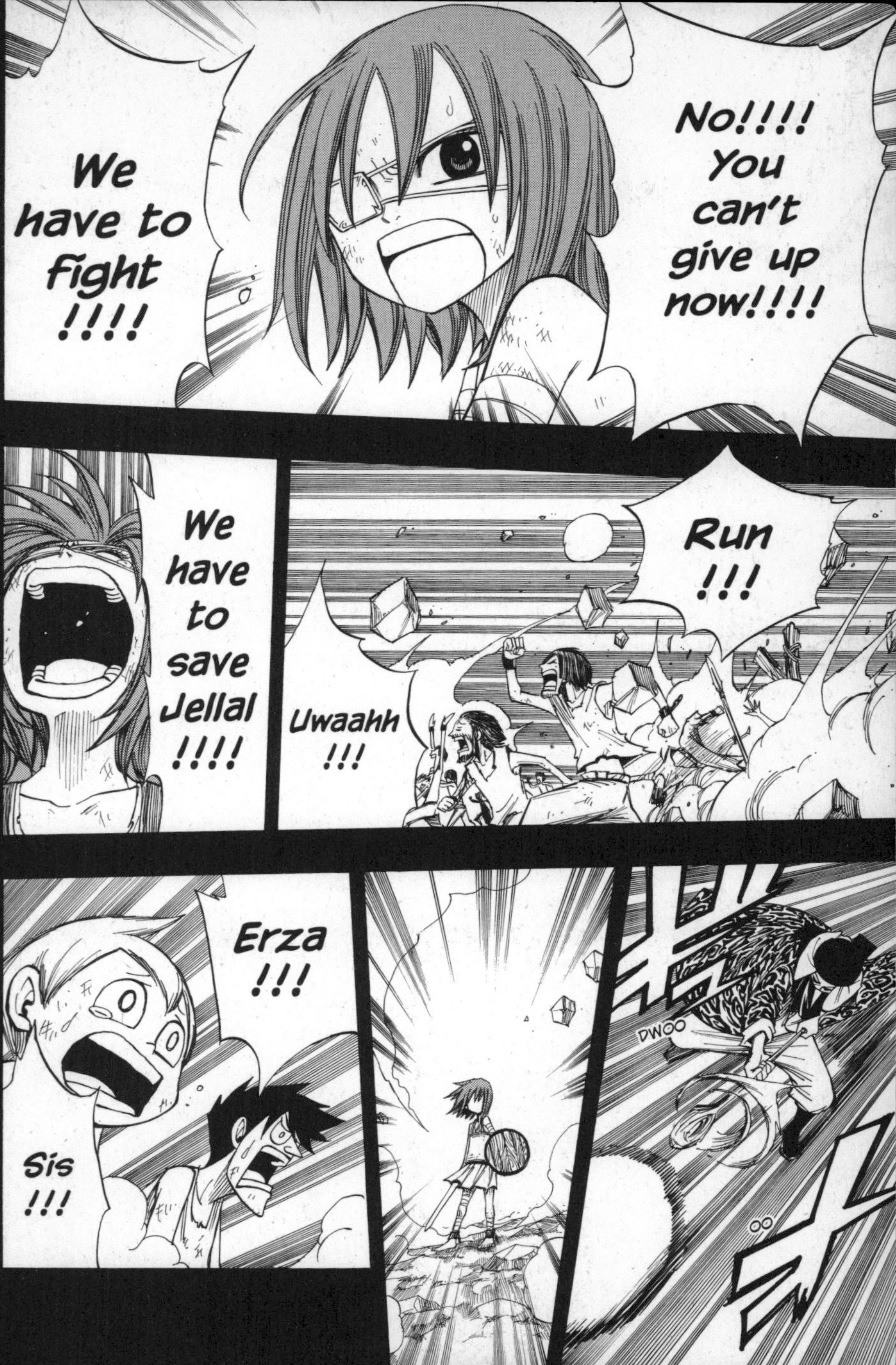
No!!!! You can't give up now!!!!
We have to fight !!!!
Run !!!
Uwaahh !!!
We have to save Jellal !!!!
DWOO
Erza !!!
Sis !!!

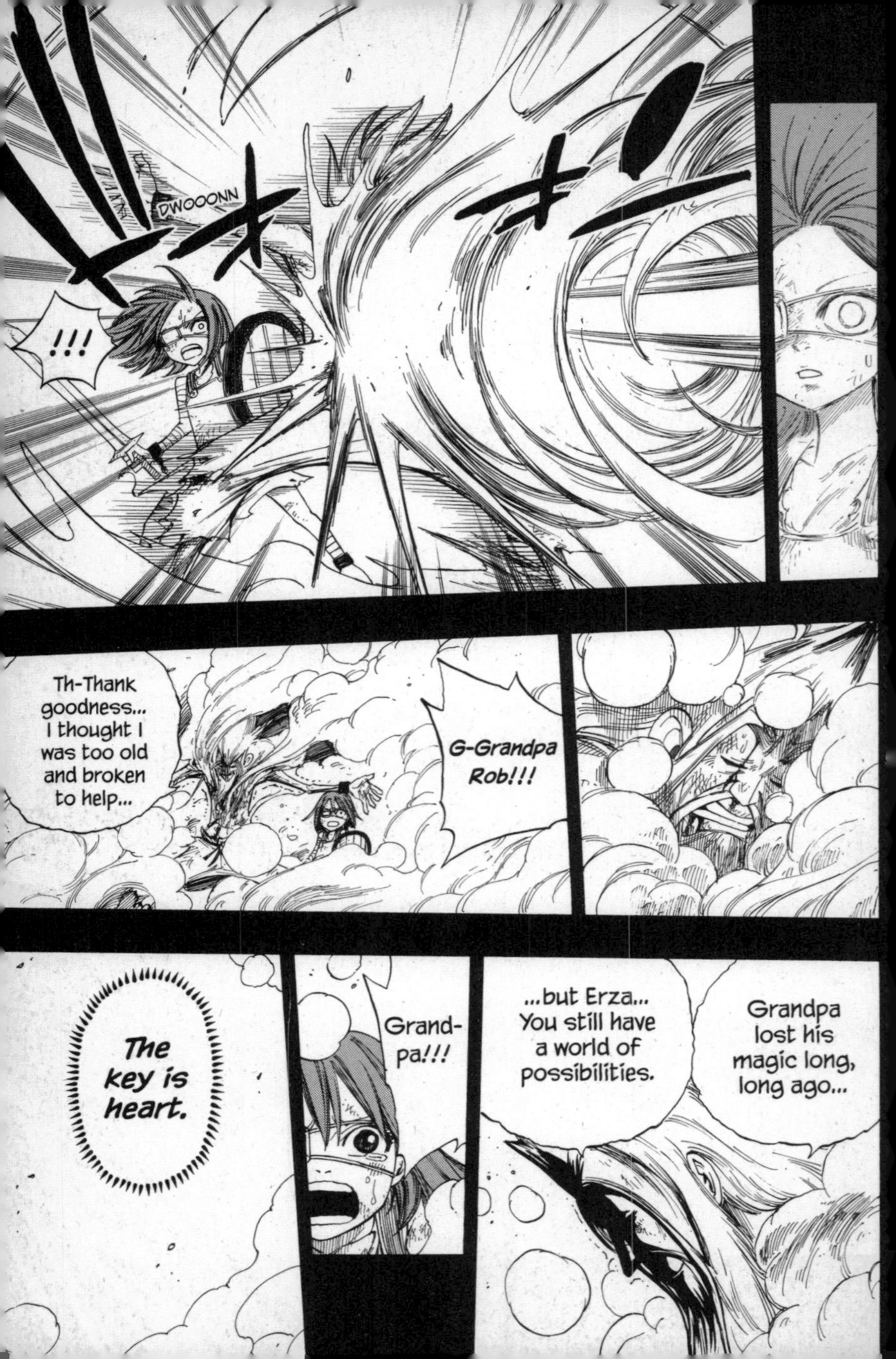
DWOOONN
!!!
G-Grandpa Rob!!!
Th-Thank goodness... I thought I was too old and broken to help...
Grandpa lost his magic long, long ago...
...but Erza... You still have a world of possibilities.
Grand-pa!!!
The key is heart.

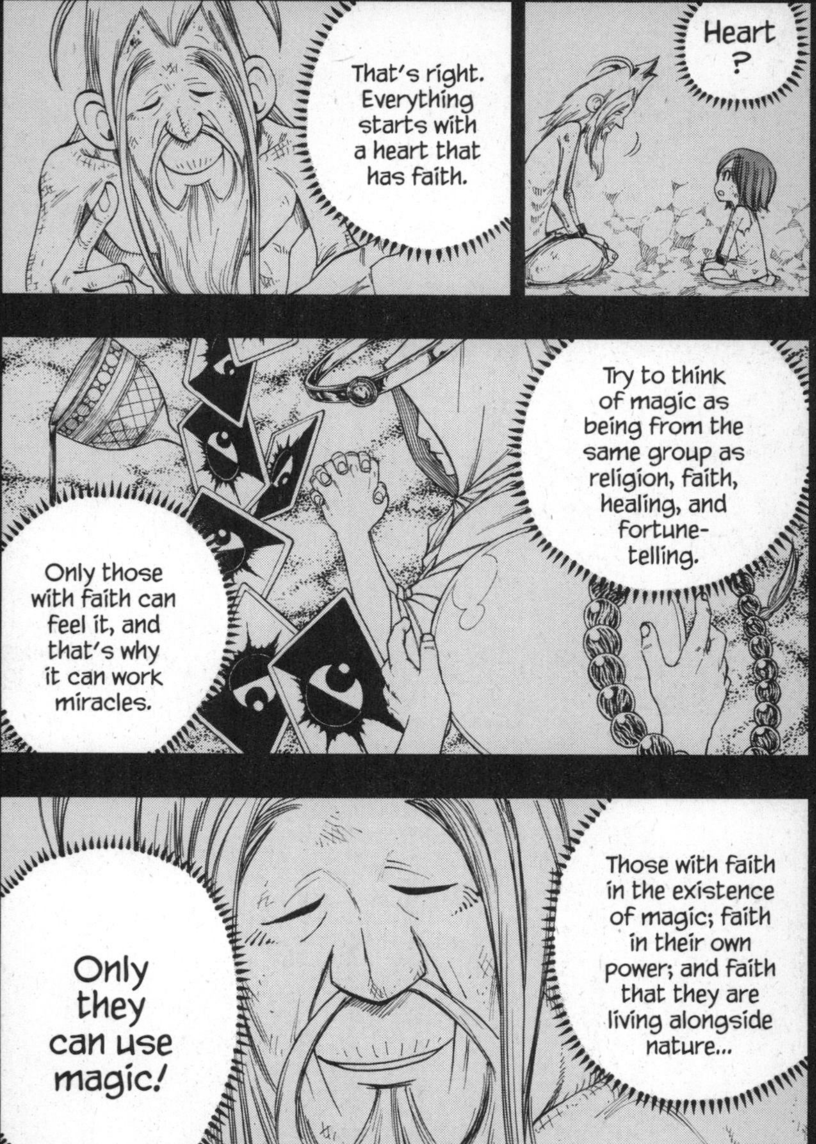
Heart ?
That's right. Everything starts with a heart that has faith.
Try to think of magic as being from the same group as religion, faith, healing, and fortune-telling.
Only those with faith can feel it, and that's why it can work miracles.
Those with faith in the existence of magic; faith in their own power; and faith that they are living alongside nature...
Only they can use magic!

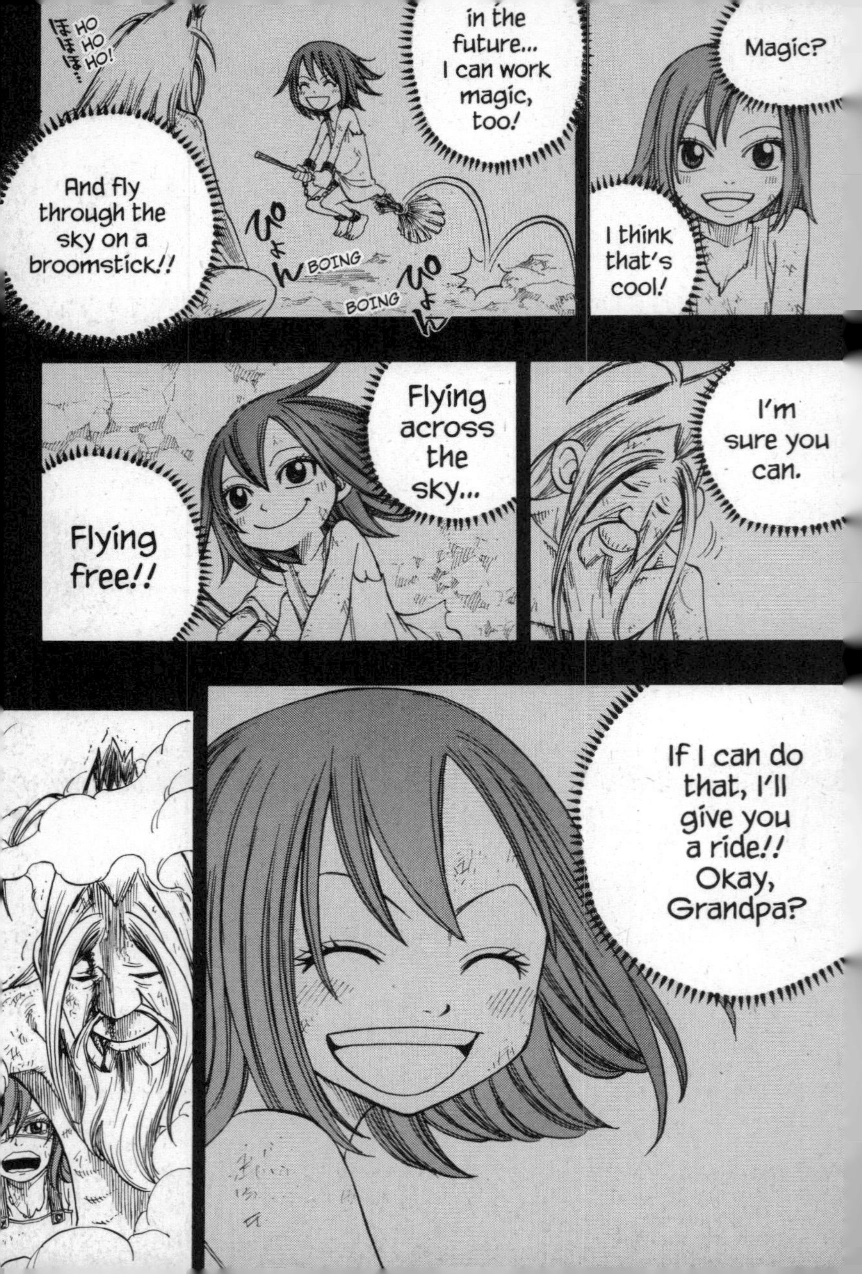

Magic?
I think that's cool!
in the future... I can work magic, too!
HO HO HO!
And fly through the sky on a broomstick!!
BOING
BOING
I'm sure you can.
Flying across the sky...
Flying free!!
If I can do that, I'll give you a ride!! Okay, Grandpa?

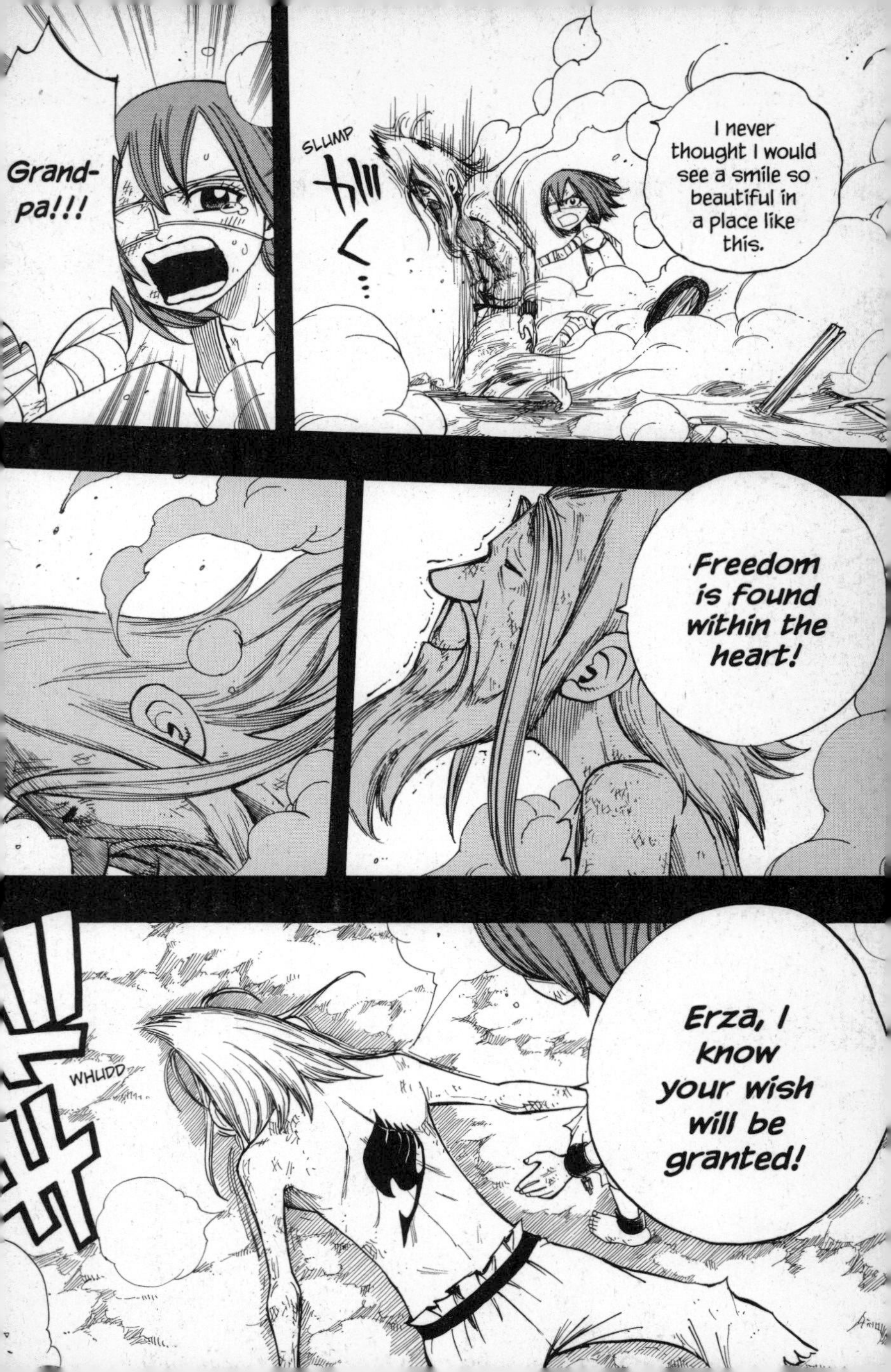
I never thought I would see a smile so beautiful in a place like this.
SLUMP
Grand-pa!!!
Freedom is found within the heart!
Erza, I know your wish will be granted!
WHUDD

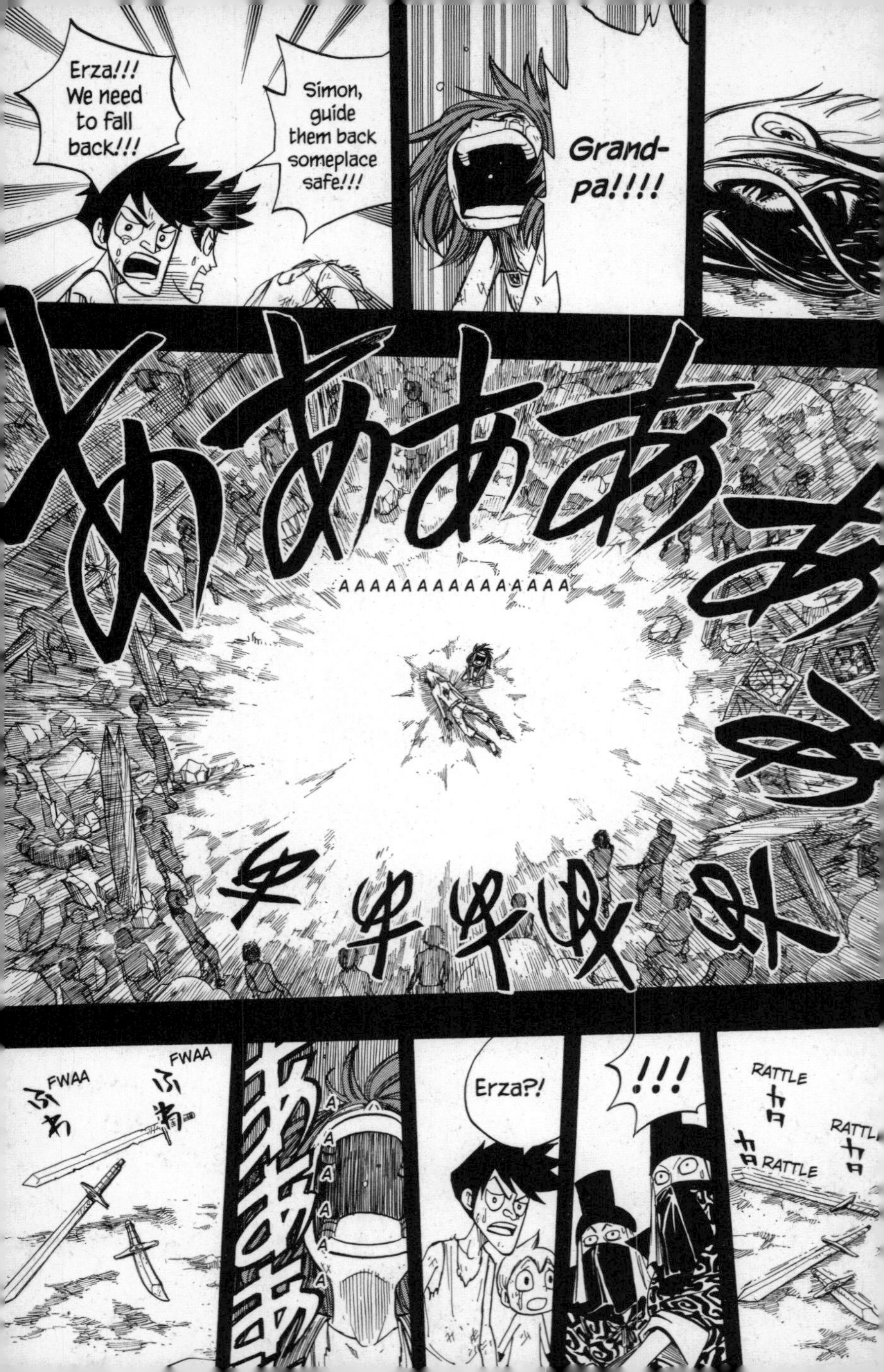
Grand-pa!!!!
Simon, guide them back someplace safe!!!
Erza!!! We need to fall back!!!
AAAAAAAAAAAAAAAA
RATTLE
RATTL
RATTLE
!!!
Erza?!
AAAAAAA
FWAA
FWAA

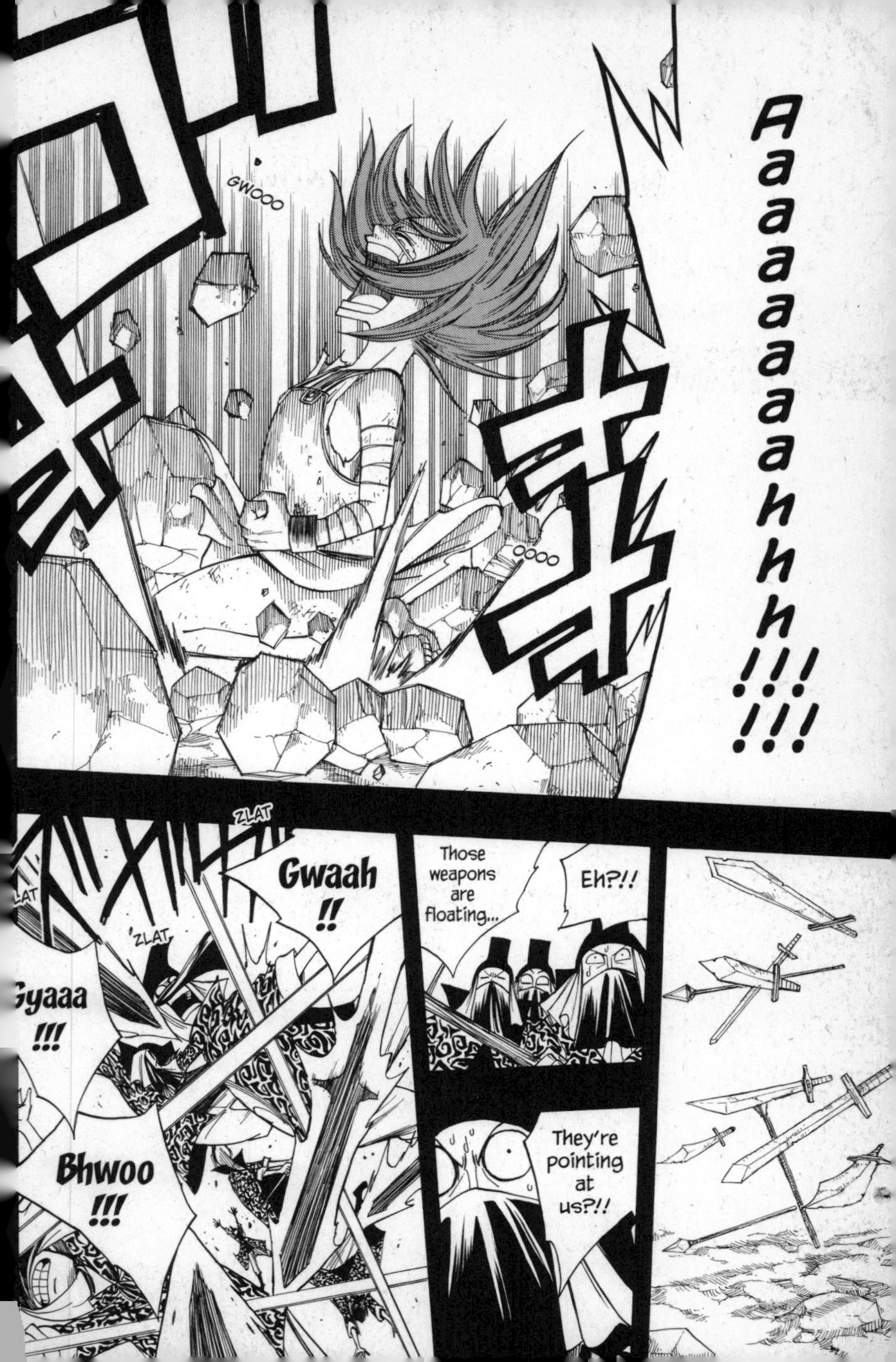
Aaaaaaaahhh!!!!!!
GWOOO
OOOO
Eh?!!
Those weapons are floating...
They're pointing at us?!!
ZLAT
Gwaah!!
ZLAT
ZLAT
Gyaaa!!!
Bhwoo!!!

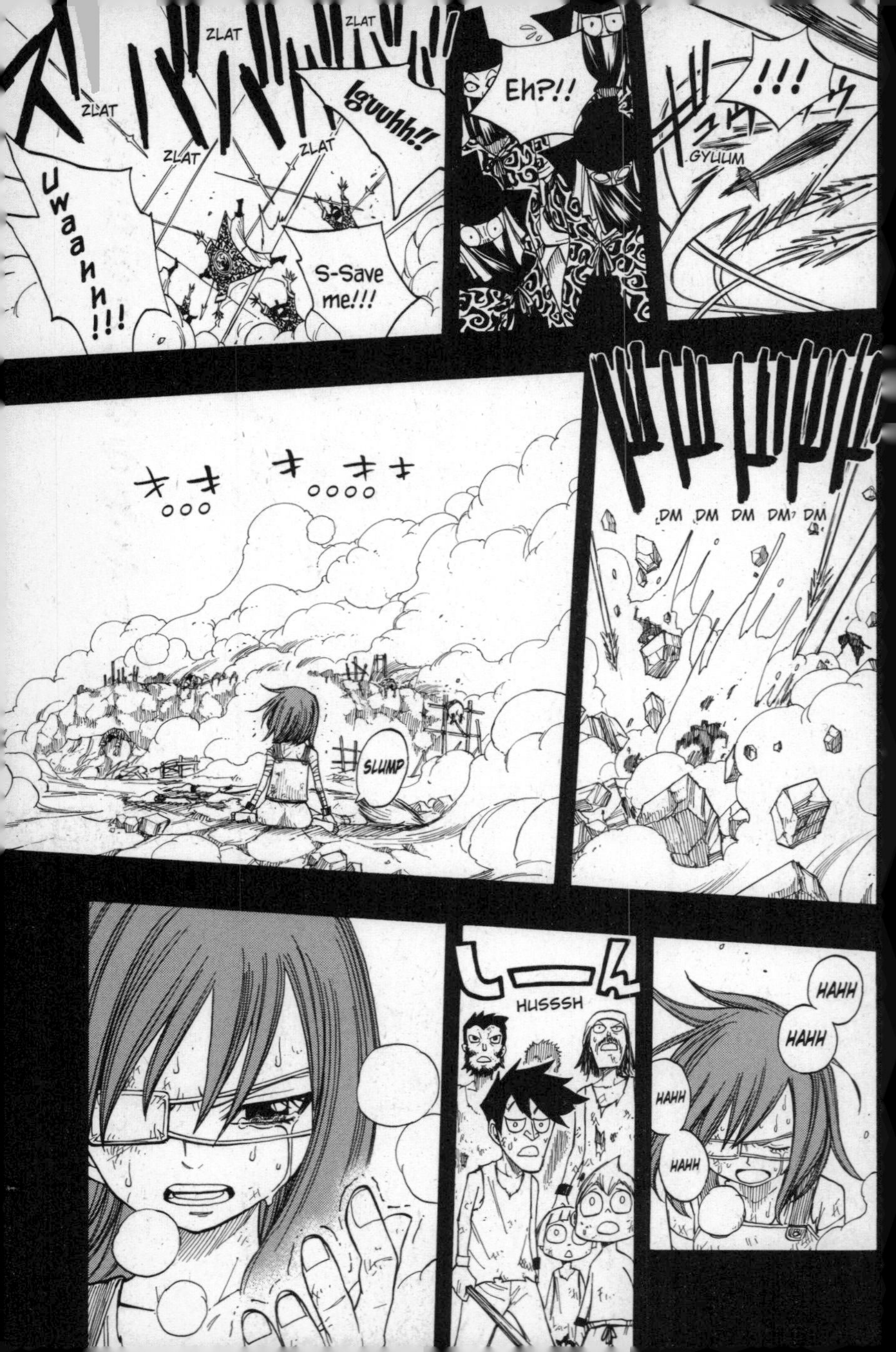
!!!
GYUUM
Eh?!!
ZLAT
ZLAT
Iguuhh!!
ZLAT
ZLAT
ZLAT
Uwaahh!!!
S-Save me!!!
DM DM DM DM DM
SLUMP
HAHH
HAHH
HAHH
HAHH
しーん
HUSSSH

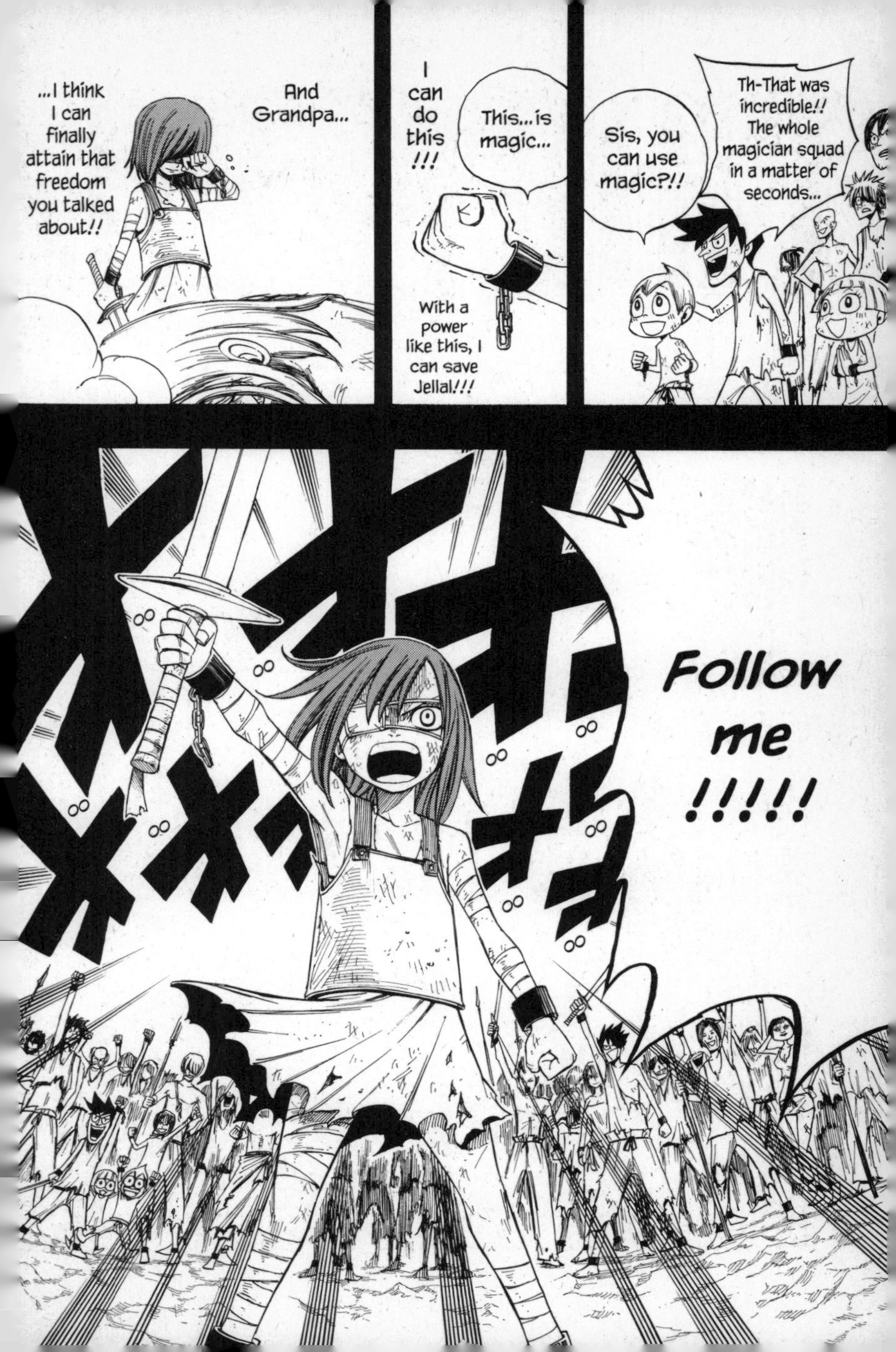
Th-That was incredible!! The whole magician squad in a matter of seconds...
Sis, you can use magic?!!
This...is magic...
I can do this!!!
With a power like this, I can save Jellal!!!
And Grandpa...
...I think I can finally attain that freedom you talked about!!
Follow me!!!!!

FAIRY TAIL

Chapter 82: Howling at the Moon

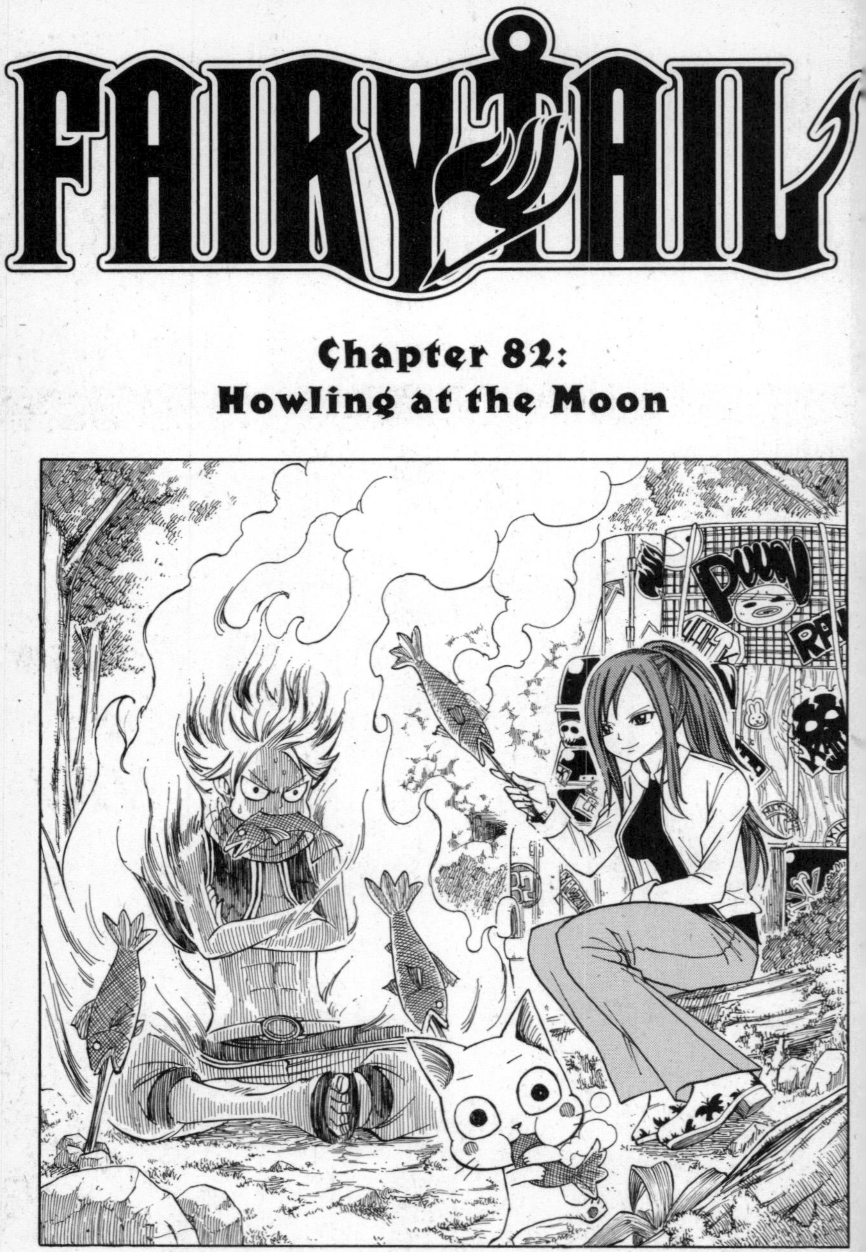
PUUN

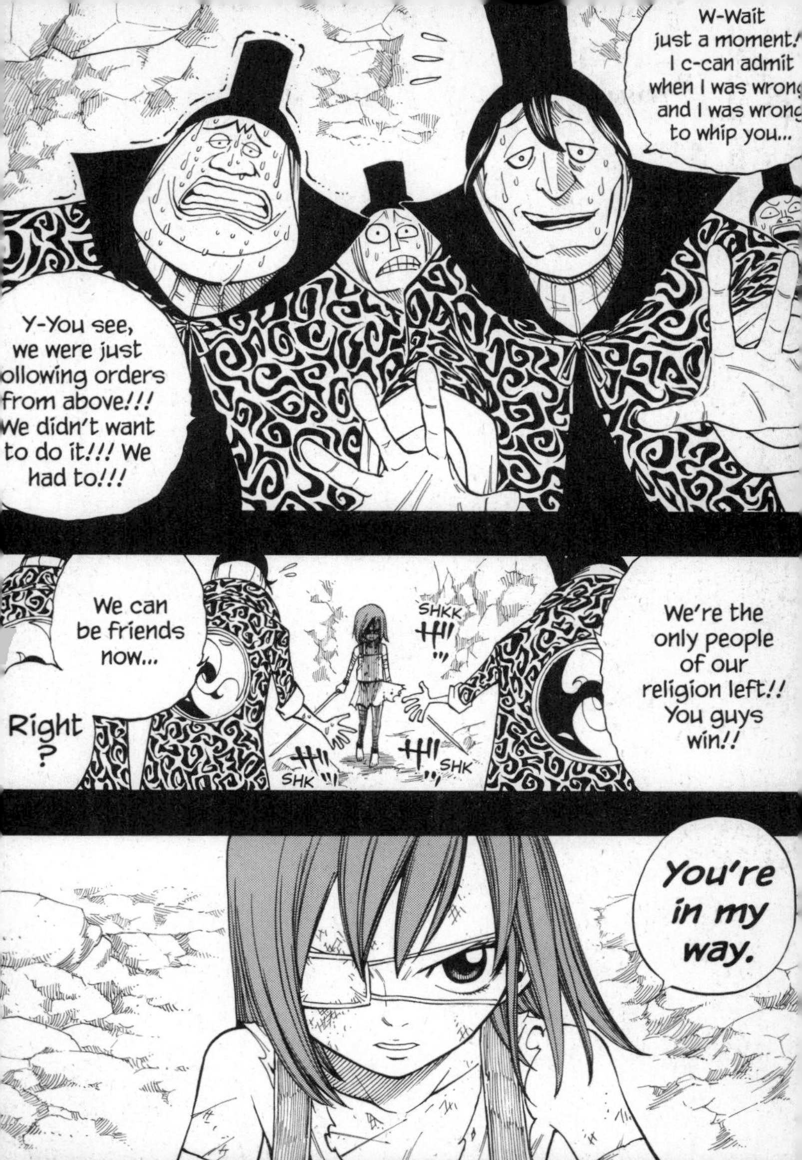
W-Wait just a moment! I c-can admit when I was wrong and I was wrong to whip you...
Y-You see, we were just ollowing orders from above!!! We didn't want to do it!!! We had to!!!
We're the only people of our religion left!! You guys win!!
SHKK
SHK
SHK
We can be friends now...
Right?
You're in my way.

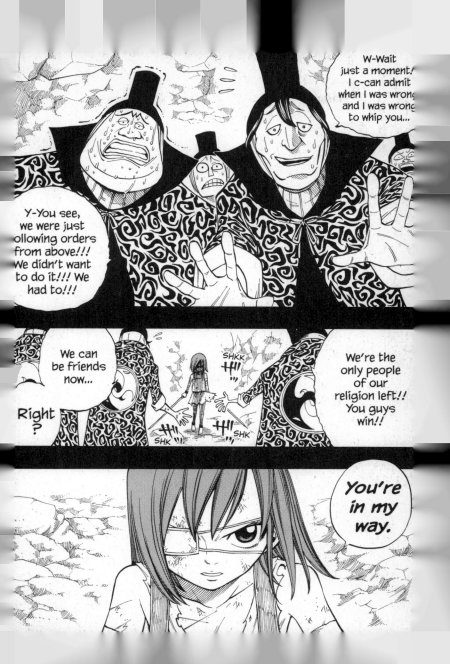

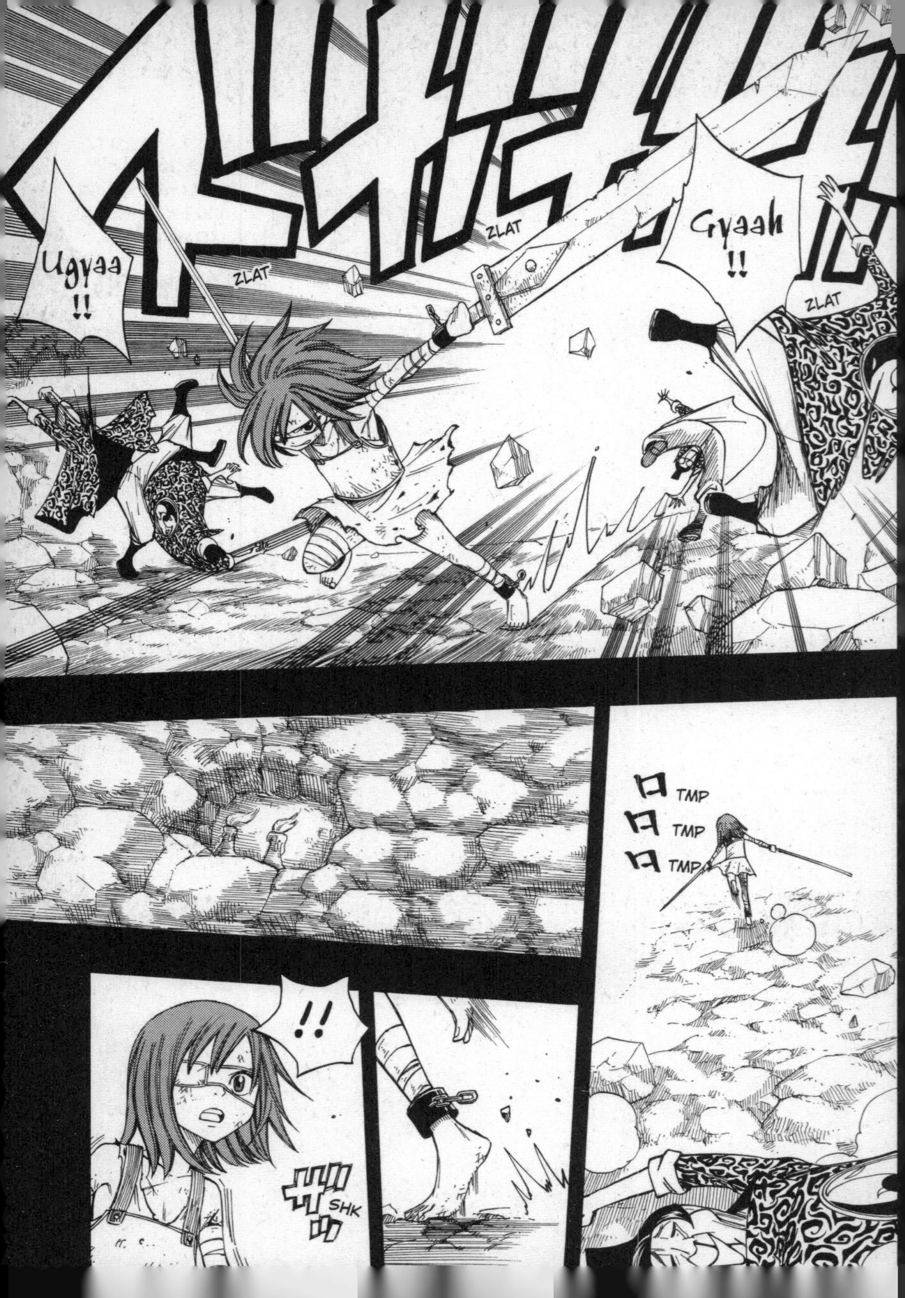
Gyaah !!
ZLAT
ZLAT
ZLAT
Ugyaa !!
TMP
TMP
TMP
!!
SHK

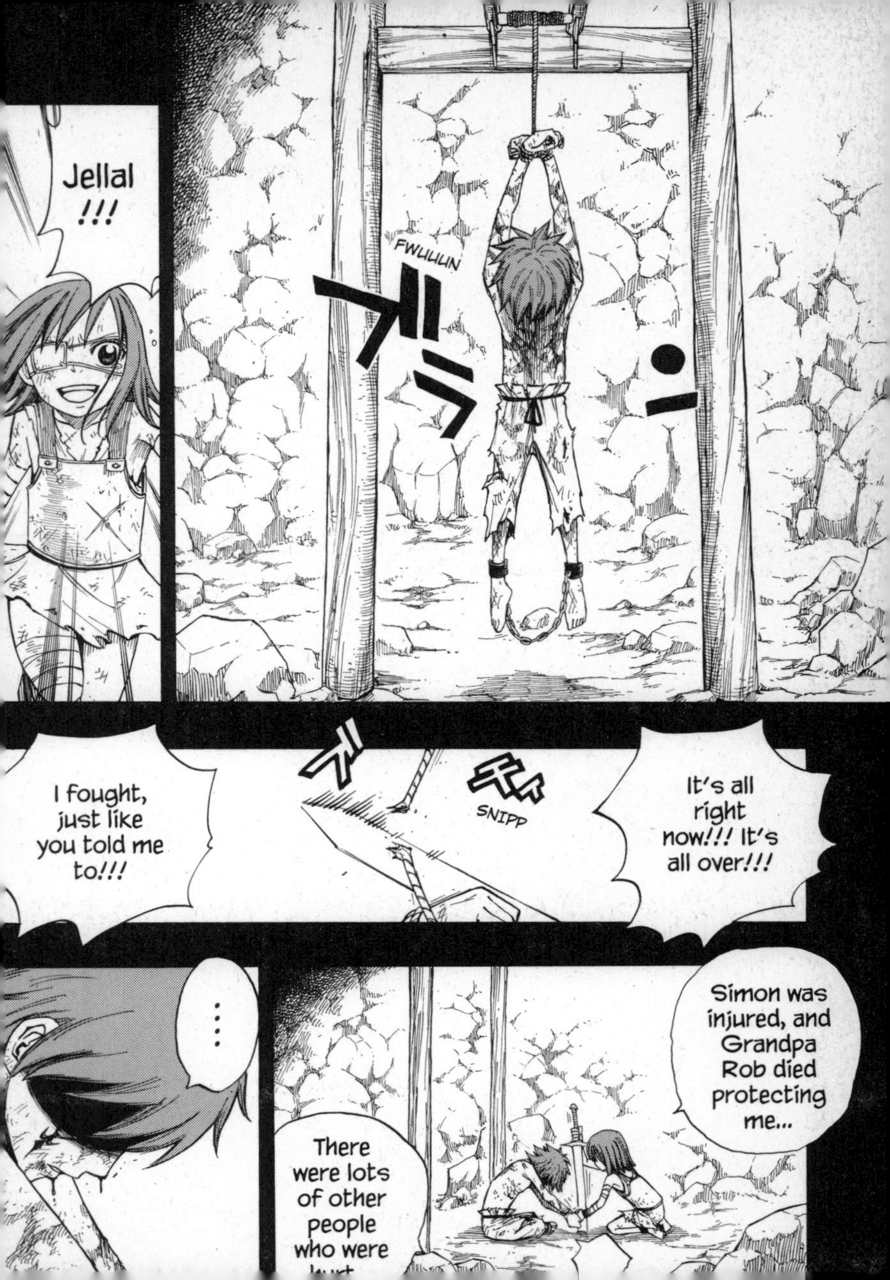

FWUUUN
Jellal !!!
It's all right now!!! It's all over!!!
SNIPP
I fought, just like you told me to!!!
Simon was injured, and Grandpa Rob died protecting me...
There were lots of other people who were
....

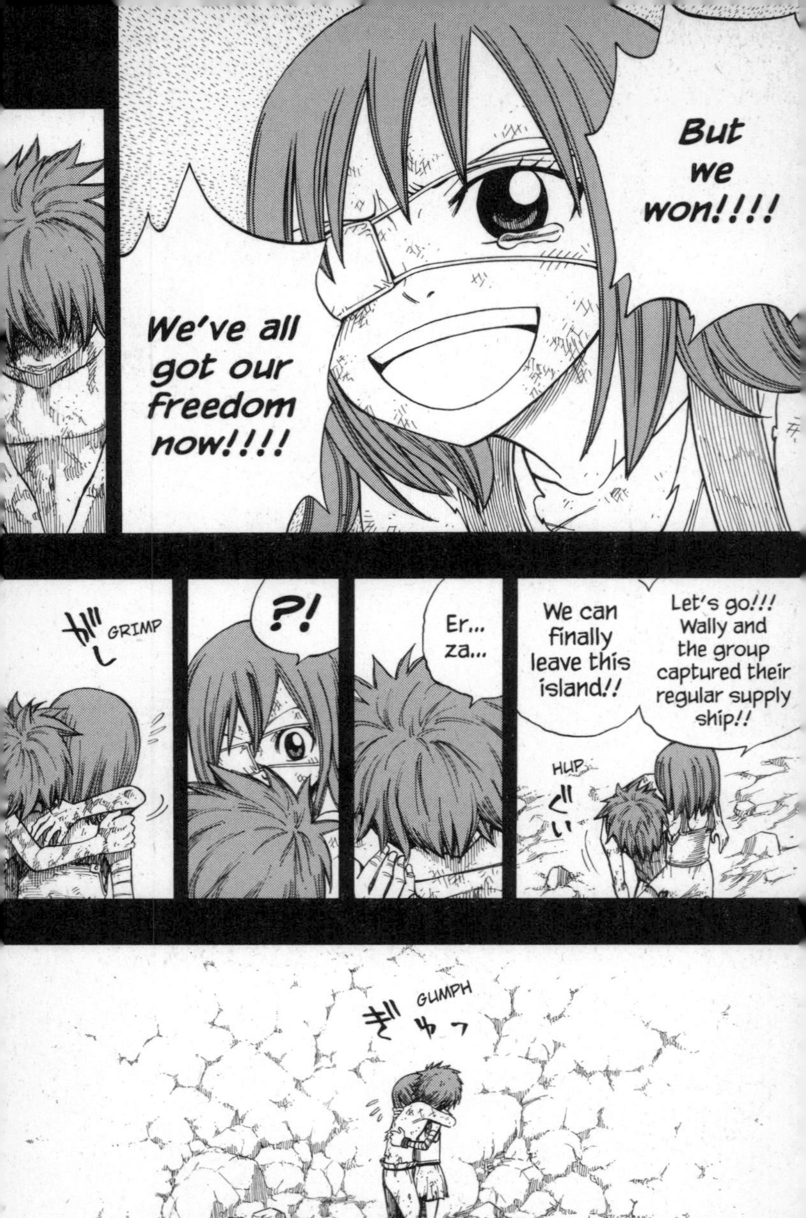
But we won!!!!
We've all got our freedom now!!!!
Let's go!!! Wally and the group captured their regular supply ship!!
We can finally leave this island!!
ぐい HUP
Er... za...
?!
がし GRIMP
ぎゅっ GUMPH

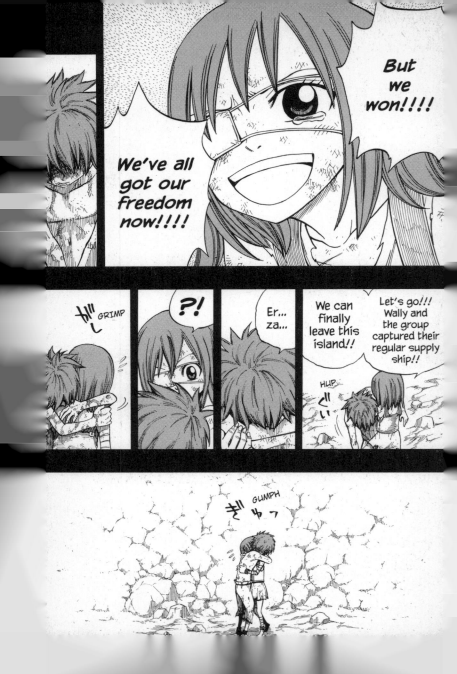

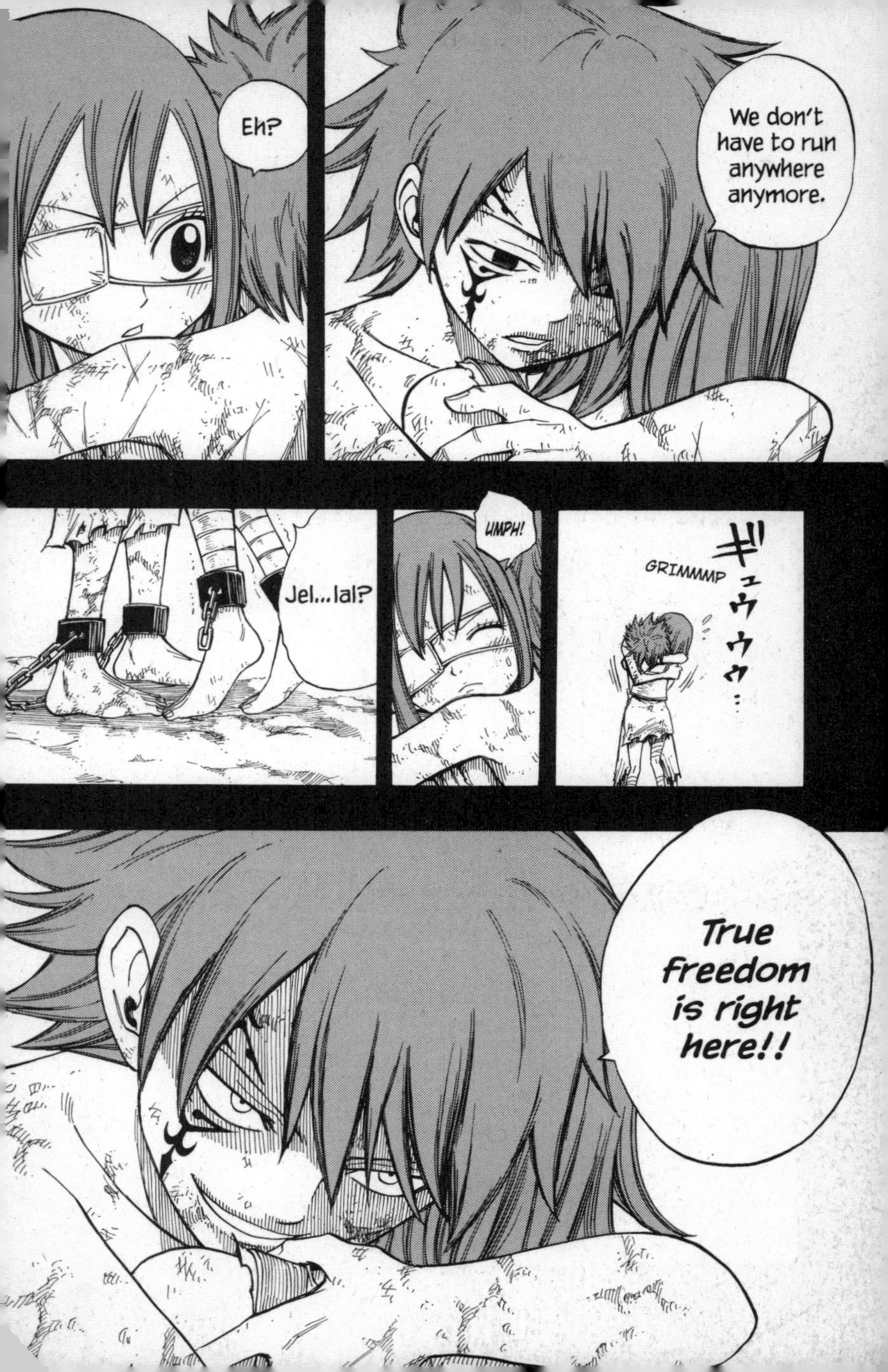
We don't have to run anywhere anymore.
Eh?
ギュウウウ…
GRIMMMMP
UMPH!
Jel...lal?
True freedom is right here!!

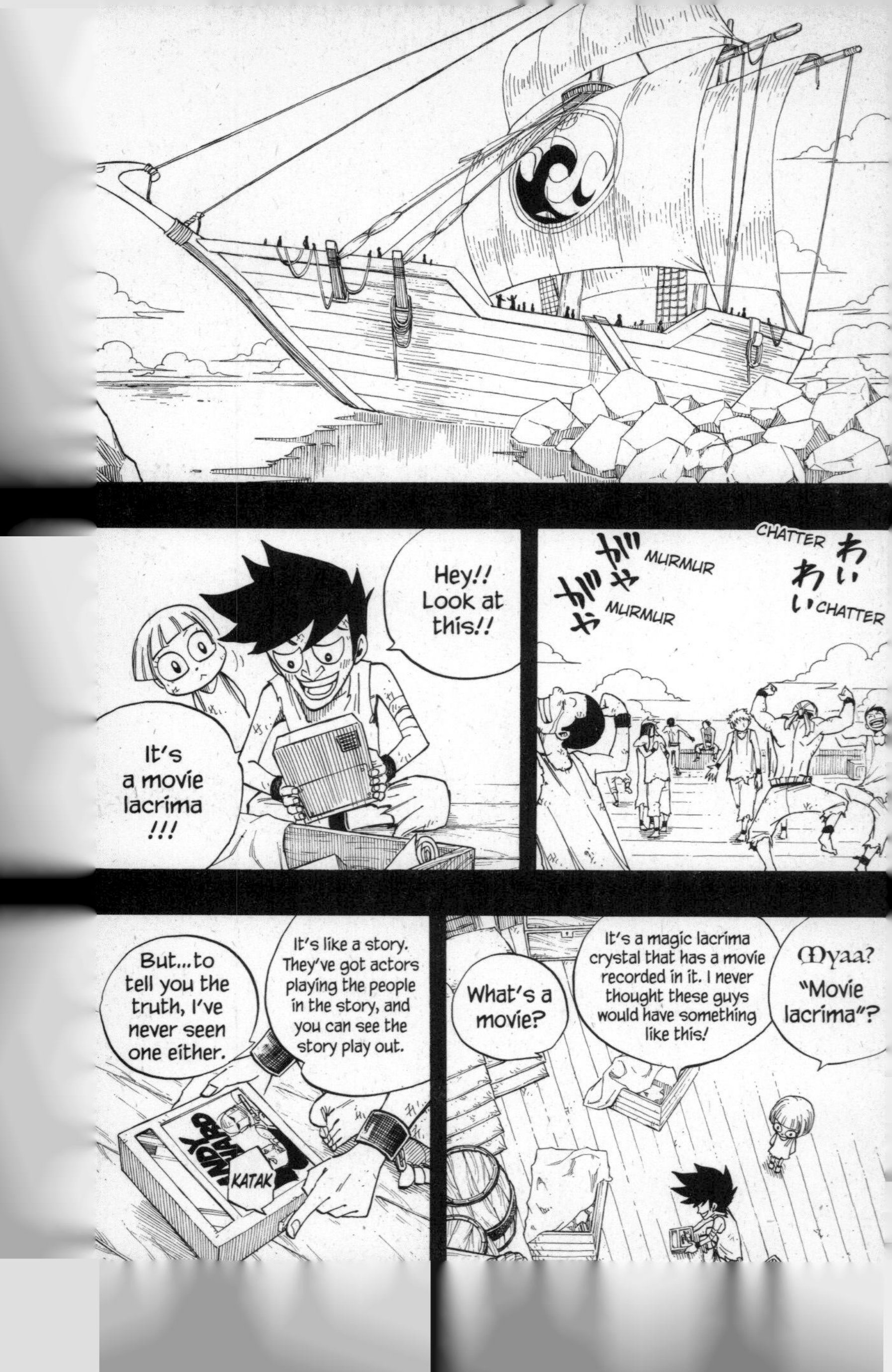

わいわい
CHATTER
CHATTER
ガヤガヤ
MURMUR
MURMUR
Hey!! Look at this!!
It's a movie lacrima!!!
Myaa? "Movie lacrima"?
It's a magic lacrima crystal that has a movie recorded in it. I never thought these guys would have something like this!
What's a movie?
It's like a story. They've got actors playing the people in the story, and you can see the story play out.
But...to tell you the truth, I've never seen one either.
KATAK

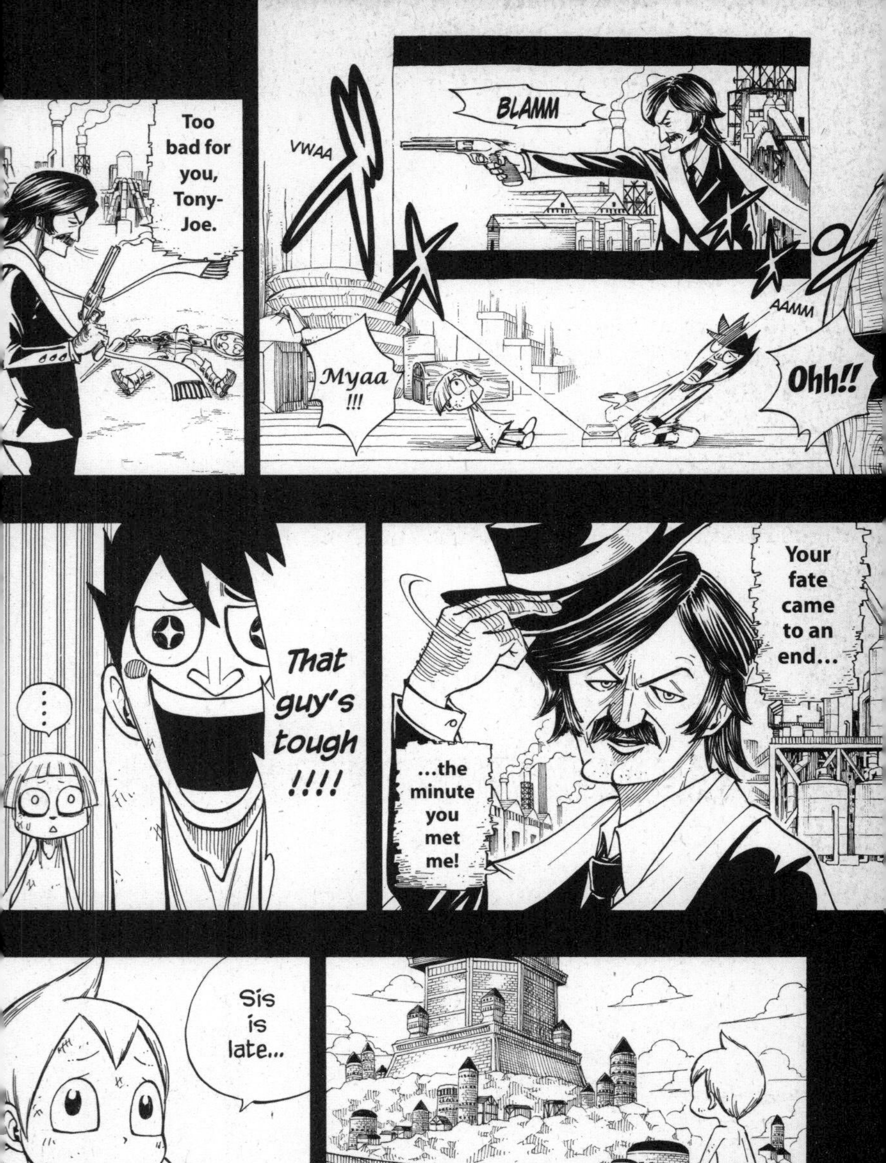
BLAMM
VWAA
AAMM
Ohh!!
Myaa !!!
Too bad for you, Tony-Joe.
Your fate came to an end...
...the minute you met me!
That guy's tough!!!!
....
Sis is late...

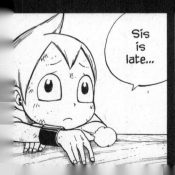

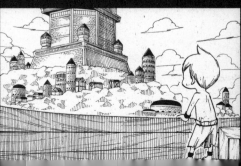

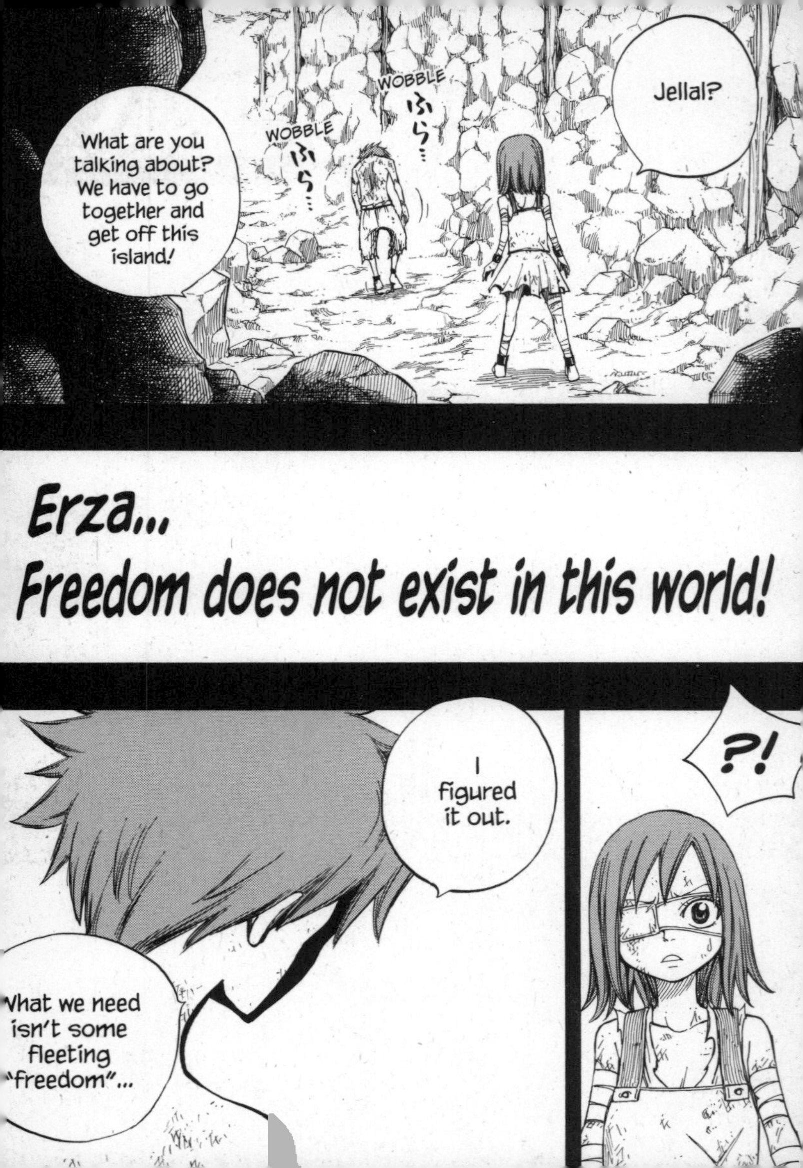
Jellal?
WOBBLE
ふら…
WOBBLE
ふら…
What are you talking about? We have to go together and get off this island!
Erza... Freedom does not exist in this world!
?!
I figured it out.
What we need isn't some fleeting "freedom"...

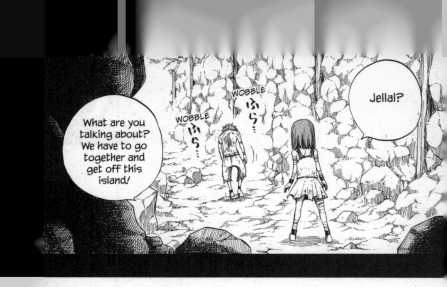

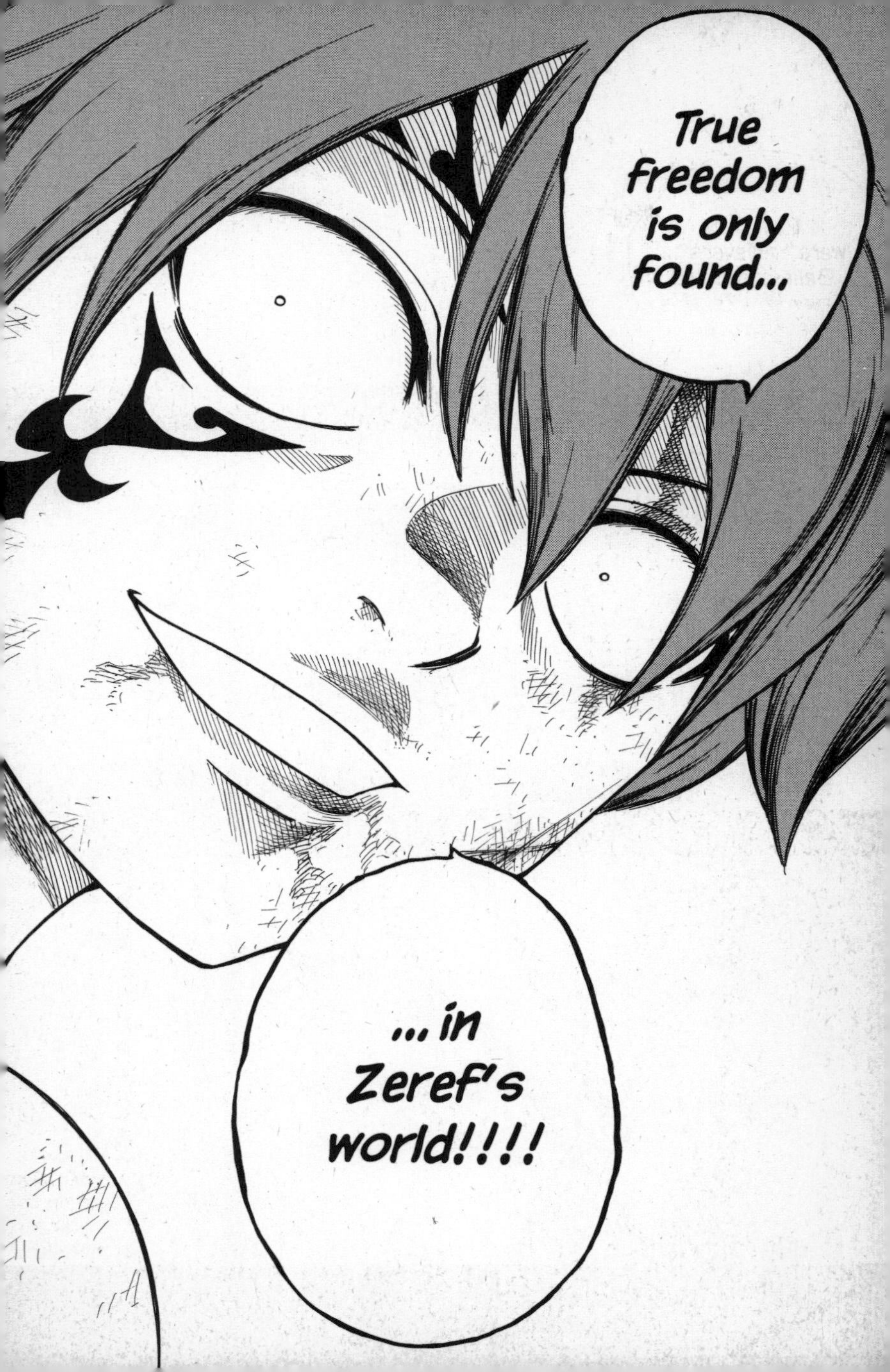
True freedom is only found...
...in Zeref's world!!!!

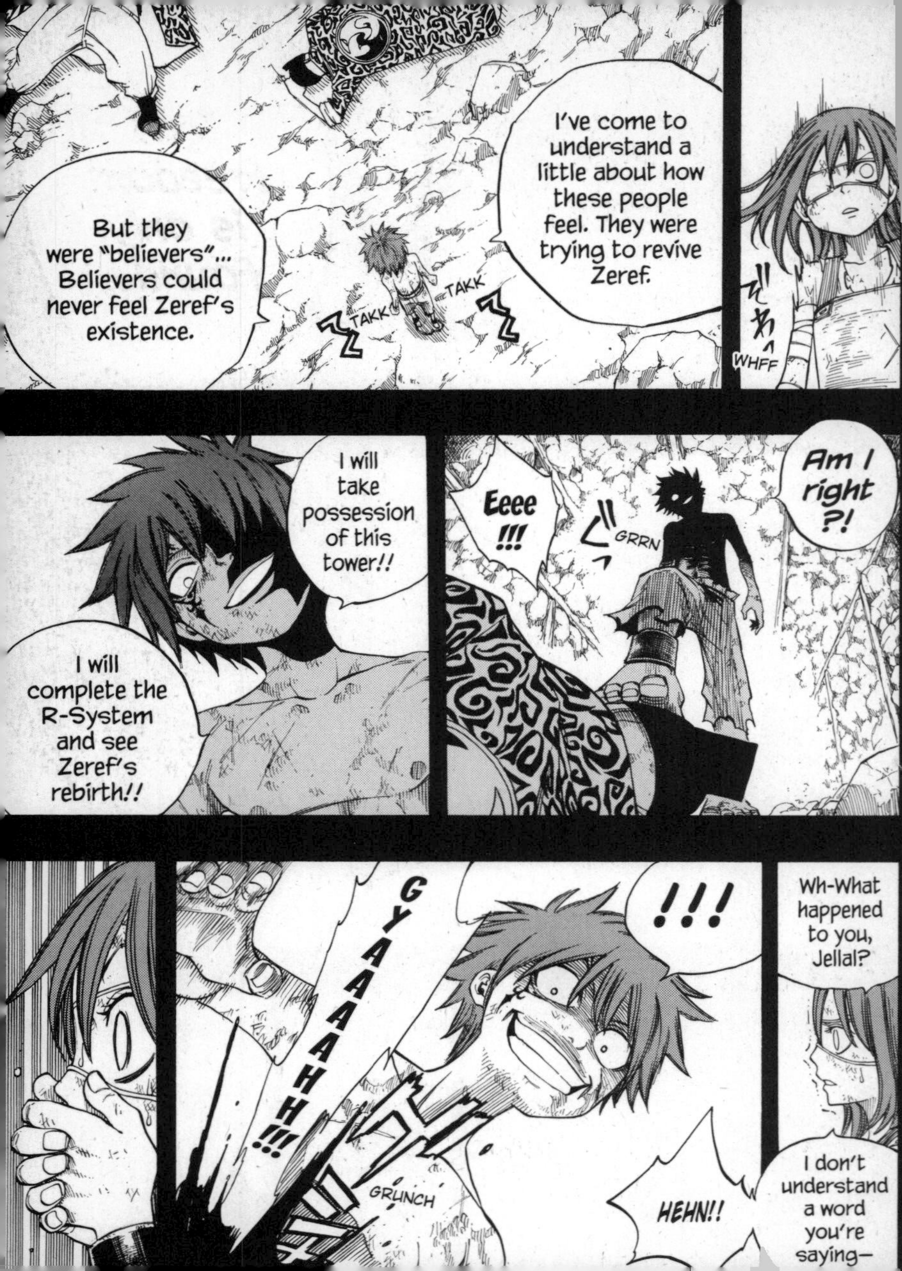
WHFF
I've come to understand a little about how these people feel. They were trying to revive Zeref.
TAKK
TAKK
But they were "believers"... Believers could never feel Zeref's existence.
Am I right?!
GRRN
Eeee!!!
I will take possession of this tower!!
I will complete the R-System and see Zeref's rebirth!!
Wh-What happened to you, Jellal?
I don't understand a word you're saying—
!!!
HEHN!!
GYAAAAAHH!!!
GRUNCH

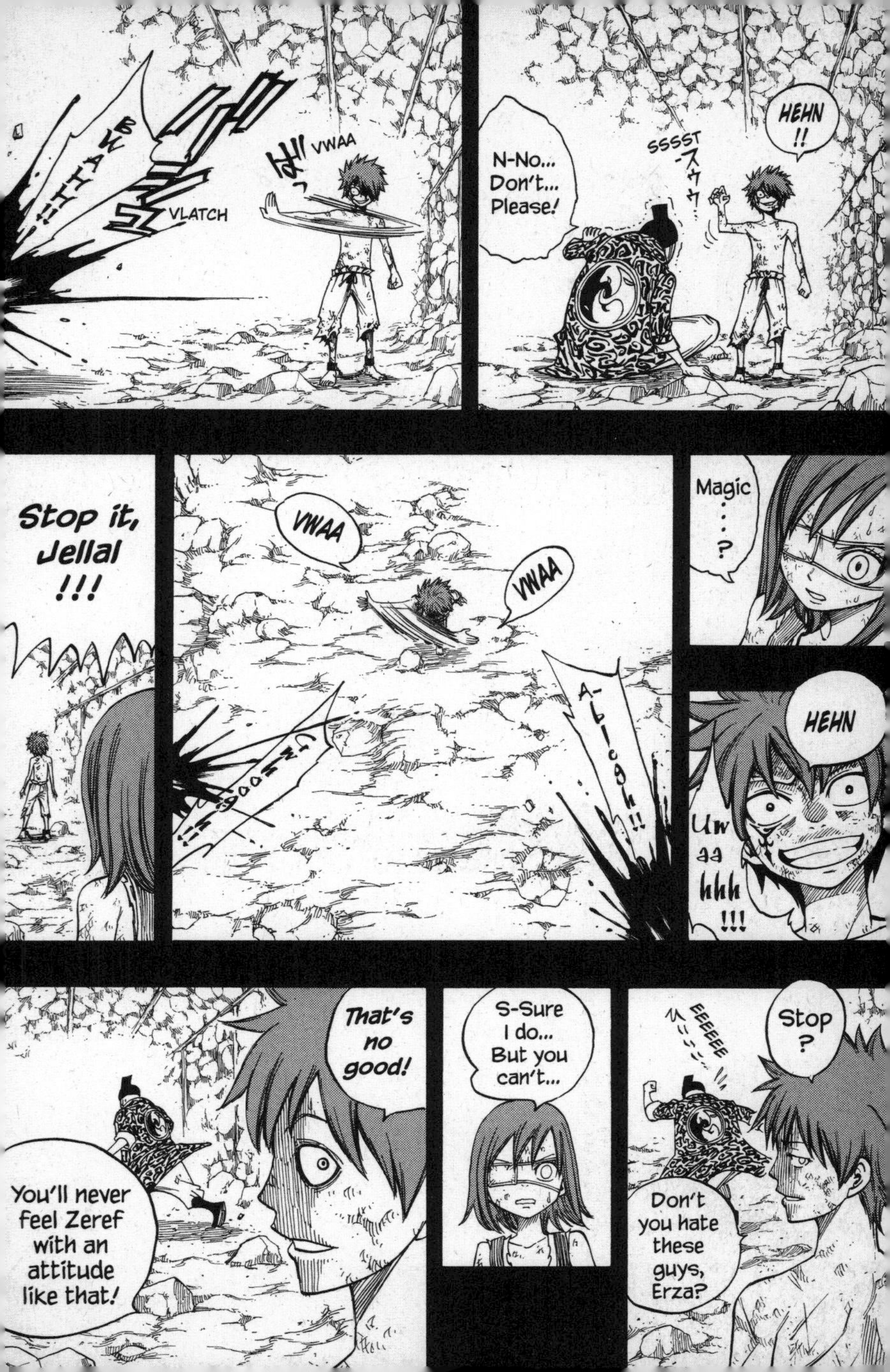
HEHN !!
SSSST
N-No... Don't... Please!
VWAA
VLATCH
BWAHH!!
Magic...?
HEHN
Uwaahhh!!!
VWAA
VWAA
A-blegh!!
Gwoogh!!!
Stop it, Jellal!!!
Stop?
EEEEEE
Don't you hate these guys, Erza?
S-Sure I do... But you can't...
That's no good!
You'll never feel Zeref with an attitude like that!

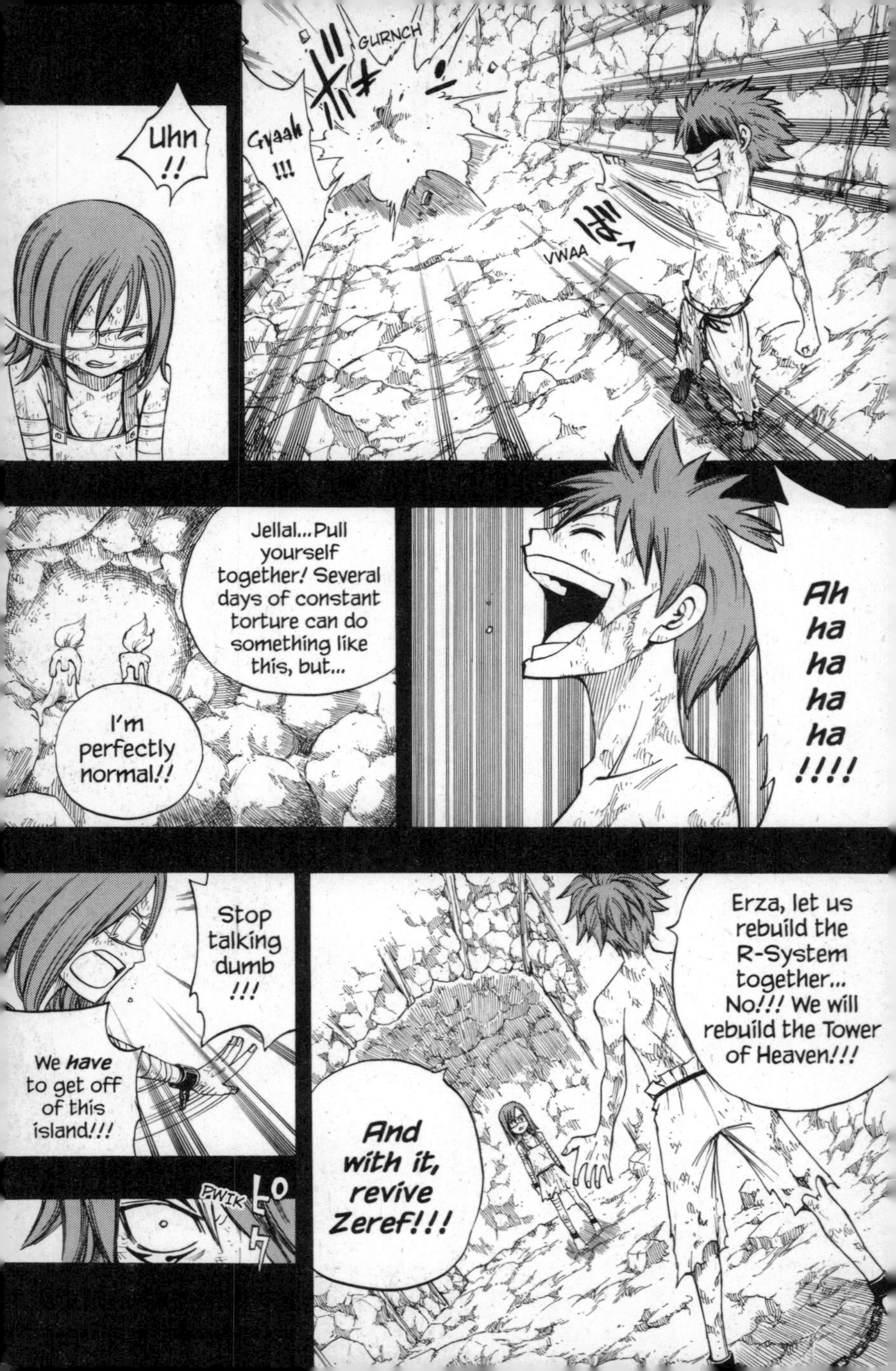
GURNCH
Gyaah!!!
VWAA
Uhn!!
Ah ha ha ha ha!!!!
Jellal...Pull yourself together! Several days of constant torture can do something like this, but...
I'm perfectly normal!!
Erza, let us rebuild the R-System together... No!!! We will rebuild the Tower of Heaven!!!
And with it, revive Zeref!!!
Stop talking dumb!!!
We *have* to get off of this island!!!
PWIK

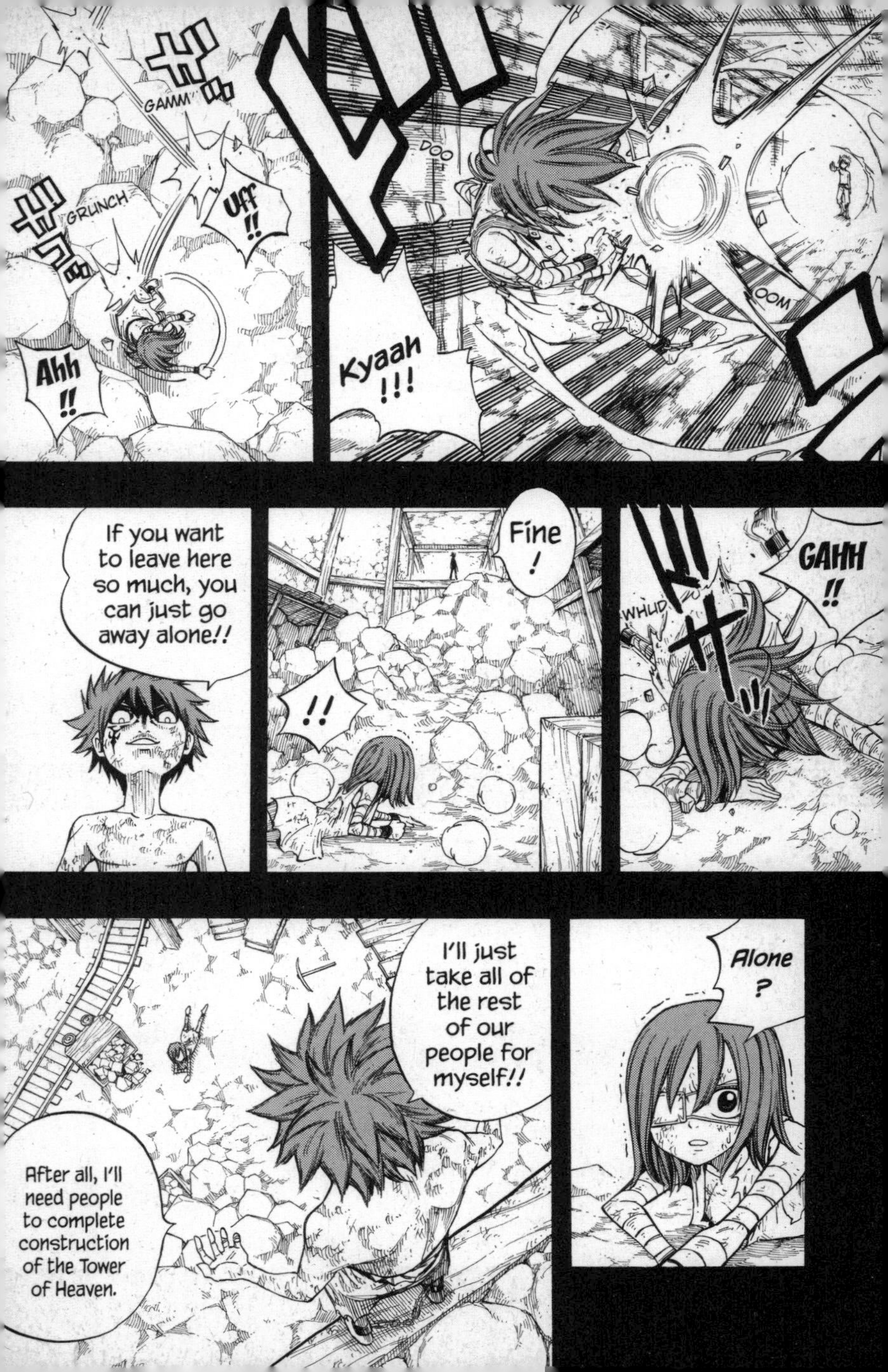
DOO
OOM
Kyaah !!!
GAMM
Uff !!
GRUNCH
Ahh !!
GAHH !!
WHUD
Fine !
!!
If you want to leave here so much, you can just go away alone!!
Alone ?
I'll just take all of the rest of our people for myself!!
After all, I'll need people to complete construction of the Tower of Heaven.

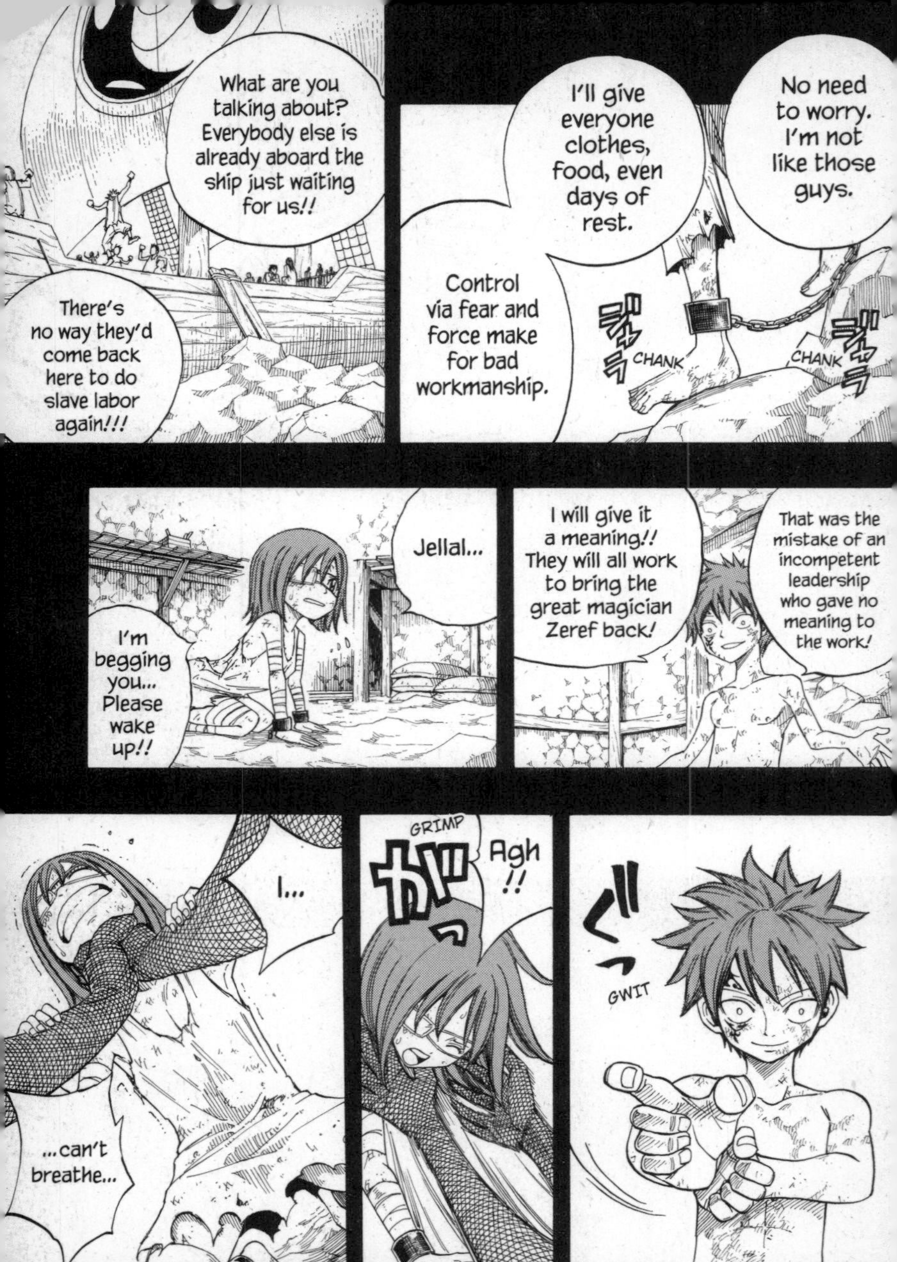
No need to worry. I'm not like those guys.
I'll give everyone clothes, food, even days of rest.
Control via fear and force make for bad workmanship.
ジャラ
CHANK
ジャラ
CHANK
What are you talking about? Everybody else is already aboard the ship just waiting for us!!
There's no way they'd come back here to do slave labor again!!!
That was the mistake of an incompetent leadership who gave no meaning to the work!
I will give it a meaning!! They will all work to bring the great magician Zeref back!
Jellal...
I'm begging you... Please wake up!!
ぐっ
GWIT
がっ
GRIMP
Agh!!
I...
...can't breathe...

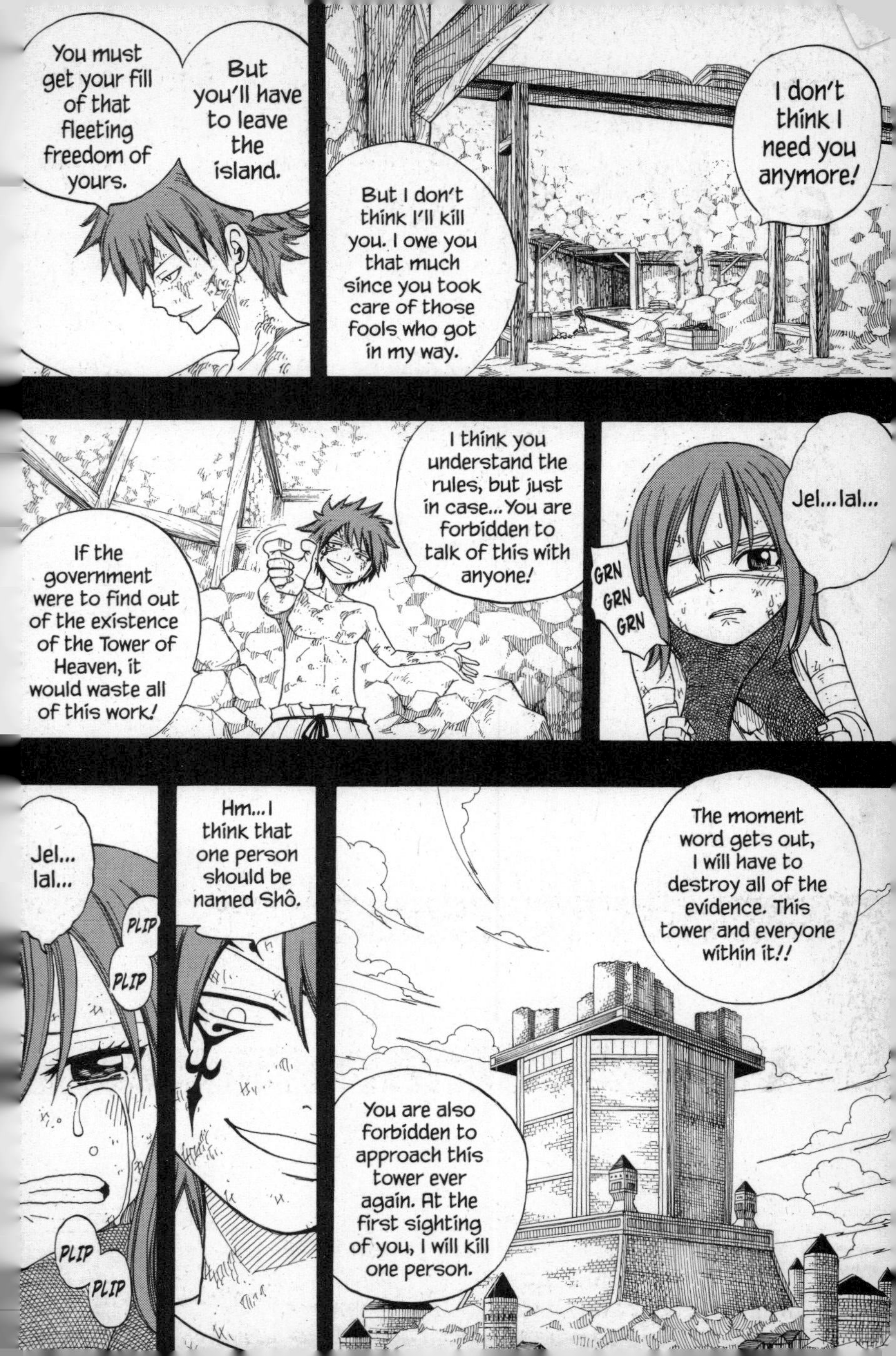
I don't think I need you anymore!
But I don't think I'll kill you. I owe you that much since you took care of those fools who got in my way.
But you'll have to leave the island.
You must get your fill of that fleeting freedom of yours.
Jel...lal...
GRN GRN GRN
I think you understand the rules, but just in case...You are forbidden to talk of this with anyone!
If the government were to find out of the existence of the Tower of Heaven, it would waste all of this work!
The moment word gets out, I will have to destroy all of the evidence. This tower and everyone within it!!
You are also forbidden to approach this tower ever again. At the first sighting of you, I will kill one person.
Hm...I think that one person should be named Shô.
Jel... lal...
PLIP
PLIP
PLIP
PLIP

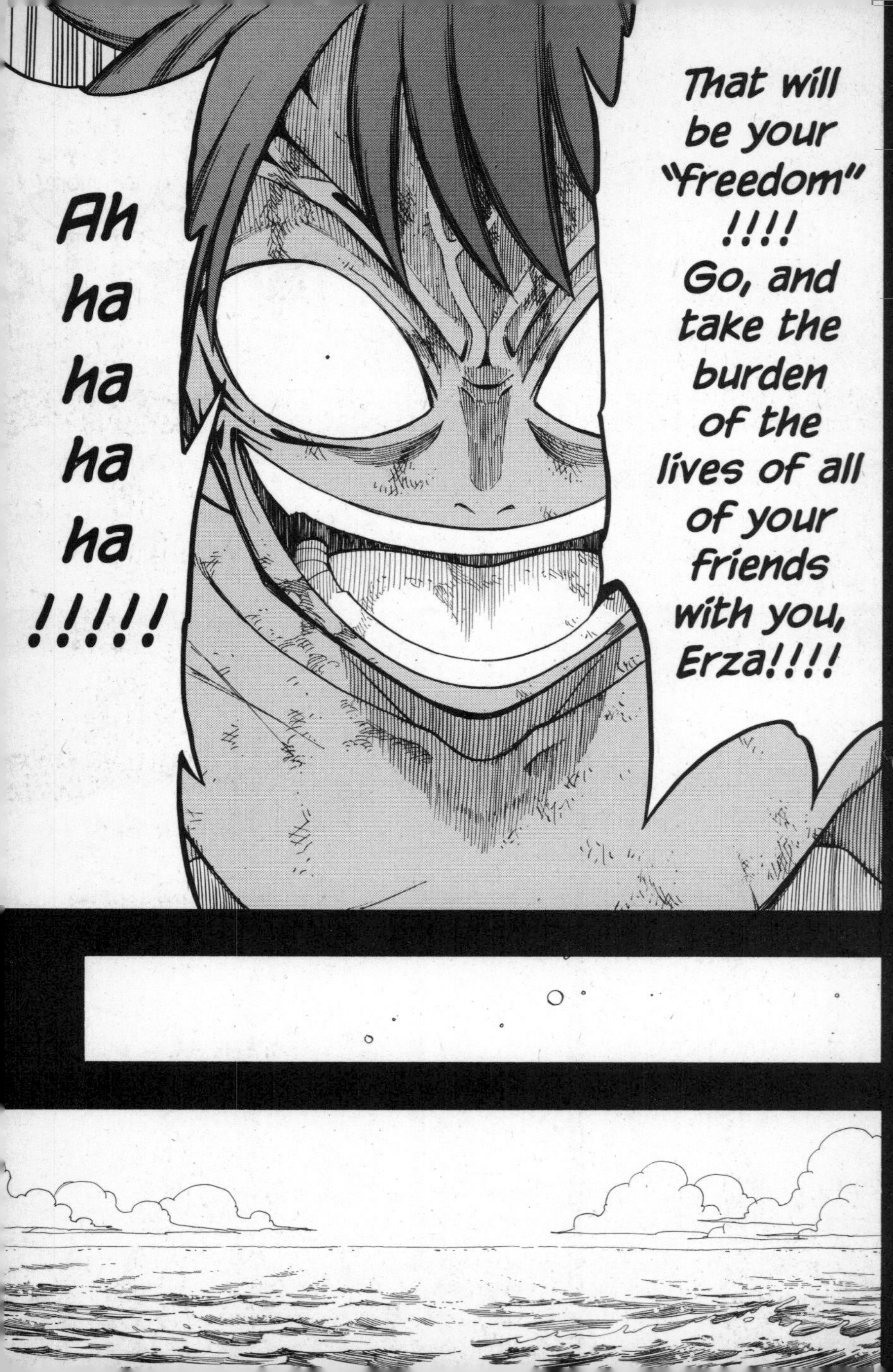
That will be your "freedom" !!!! Go, and take the burden of the lives of all of your friends with you, Erza!!!!
Ah ha ha ha ha !!!!!

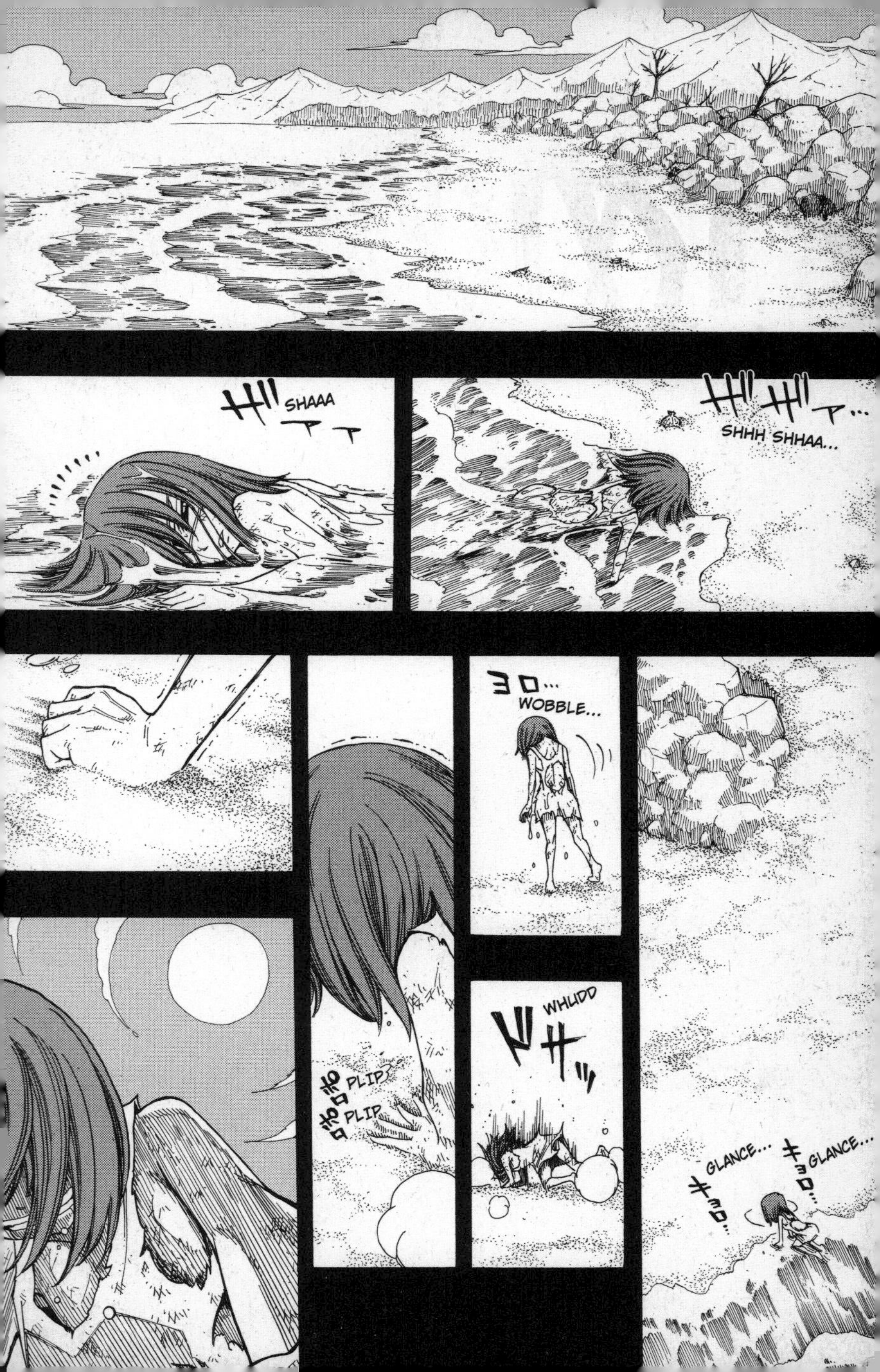
ザザァ...
SHHH SHHAA...
ザァァ
SHAAA
キョロ...
GLANCE...
キョロ...
GLANCE...
ヨロ...
WOBBLE...
ドサッ
WHUDD
ポロポロ
PLIP
PLIP

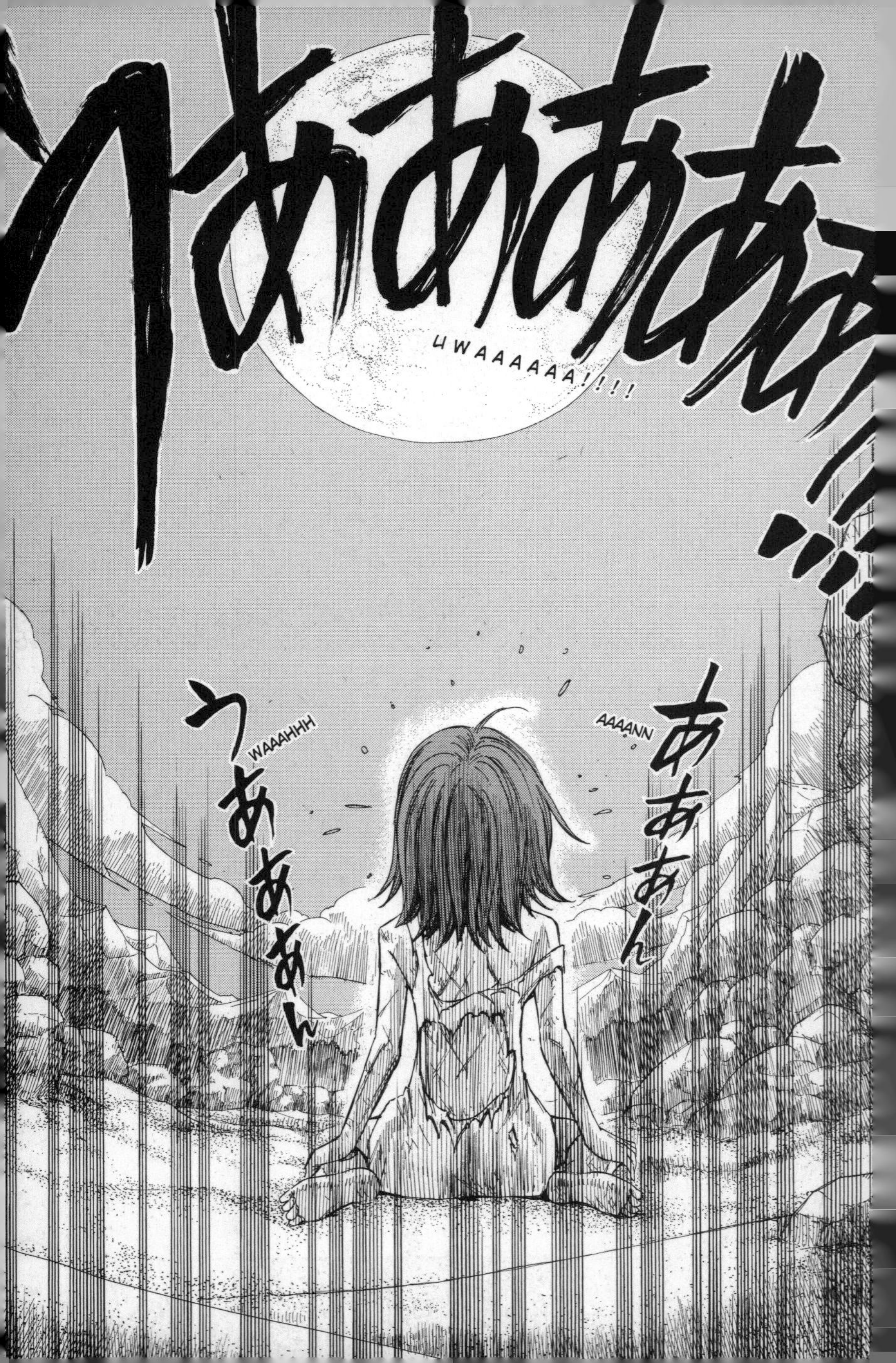
うあああああ!!!
UWAAAAAAA!!!!
あああん
AAAANN
うあああん
WAAAHHH

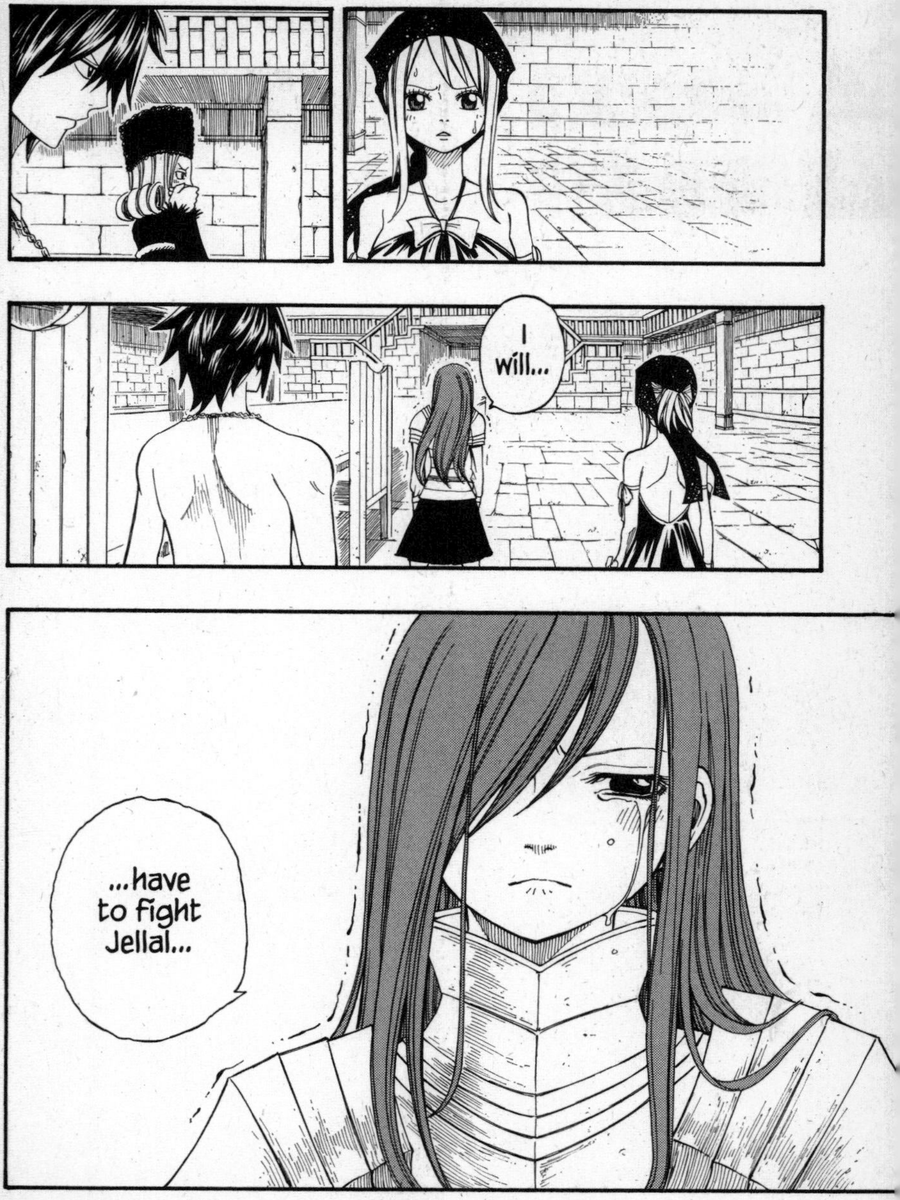
I will...
...have to fight Jellal...

TO BE CONTINUED

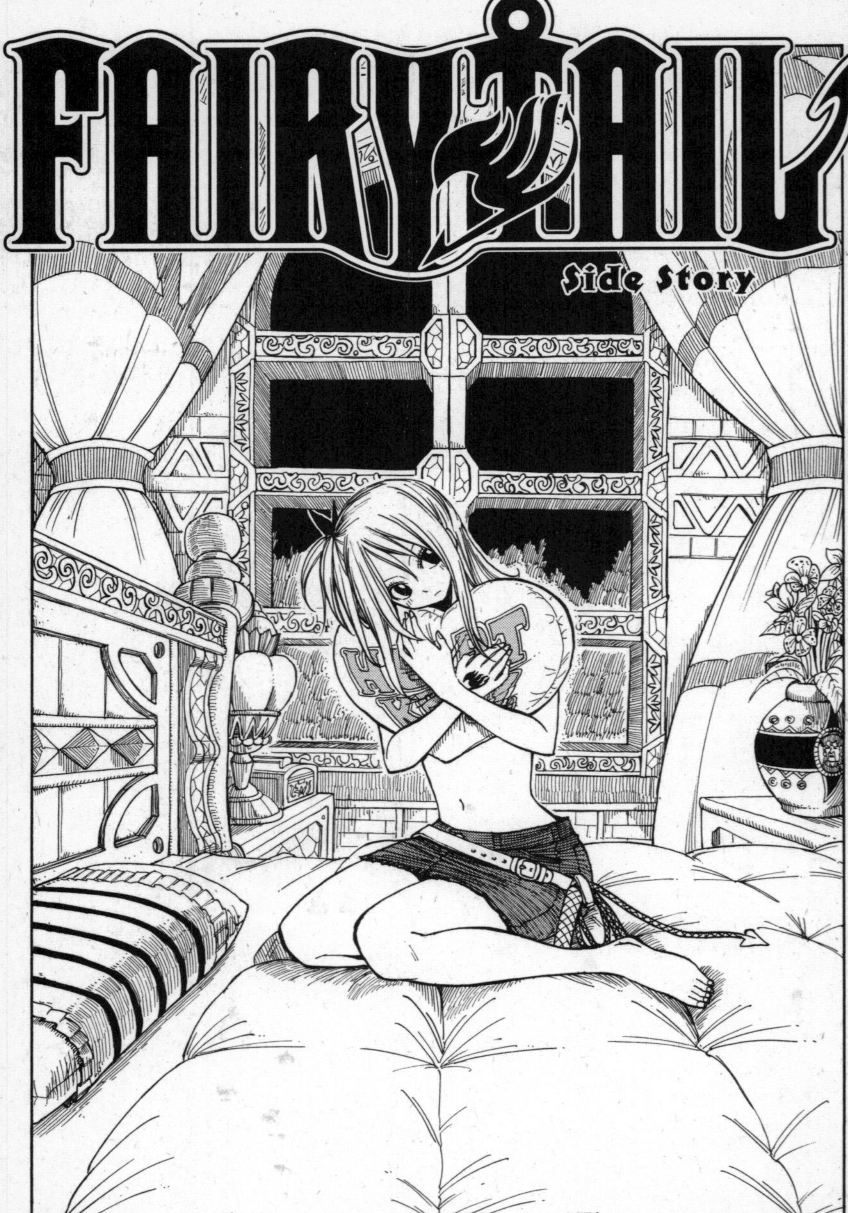
FAIRY TAIL
Side Story

Special Mission: Beware of Guys Who Show a Keen Interest

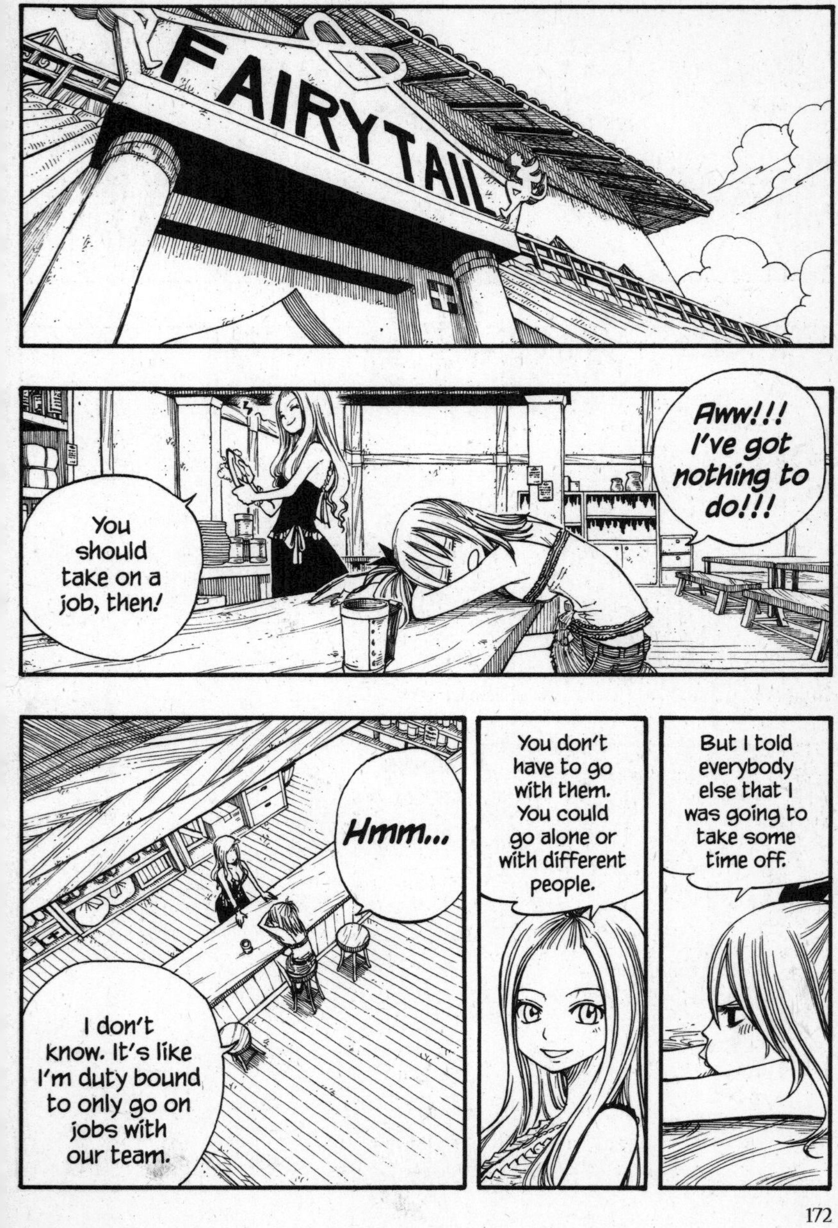
FAIRY TAIL
Aww!!! I've got nothing to do!!!
You should take on a job, then!
But I told everybody else that I was going to take some time off.
You don't have to go with them. You could go alone or with different people.
Hmm...
I don't know. It's like I'm duty bound to only go on jobs with our team.

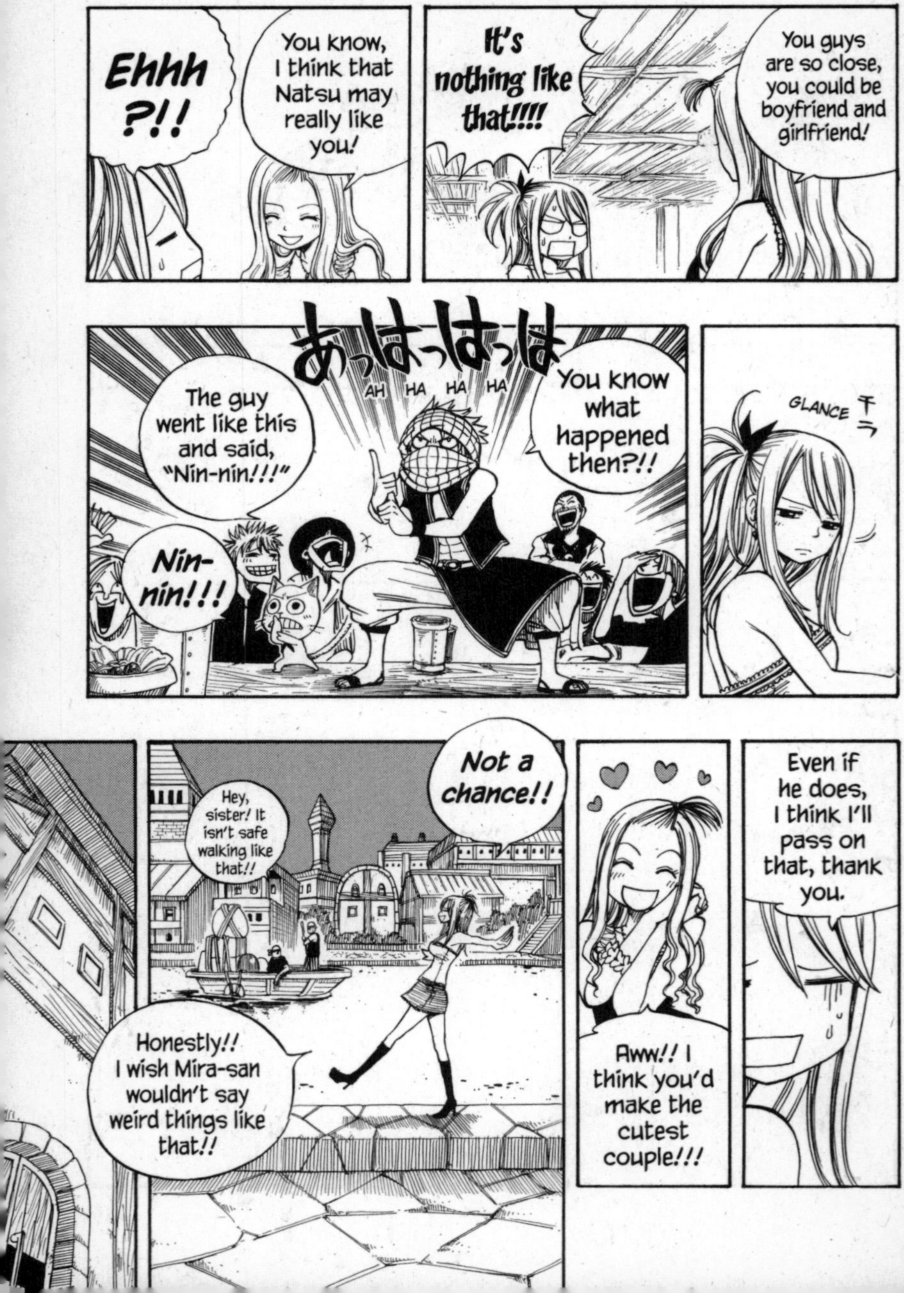
You guys are so close, you could be boyfriend and girlfriend!
It's nothing like that!!!!
You know, I think that Natsu may really like you!
Ehhh ?!!
GLANCE チラ
You know what happened then?!!
あっはっはっは
AH HA HA HA
The guy went like this and said, "Nin-nin!!!"
Nin-nin!!!
Even if he does, I think I'll pass on that, thank you.
Aww!! I think you'd make the cutest couple!!!
Not a chance!!
Hey, sister! It isn't safe walking like that!!
Honestly!! I wish Mira-san wouldn't say weird things like that!!

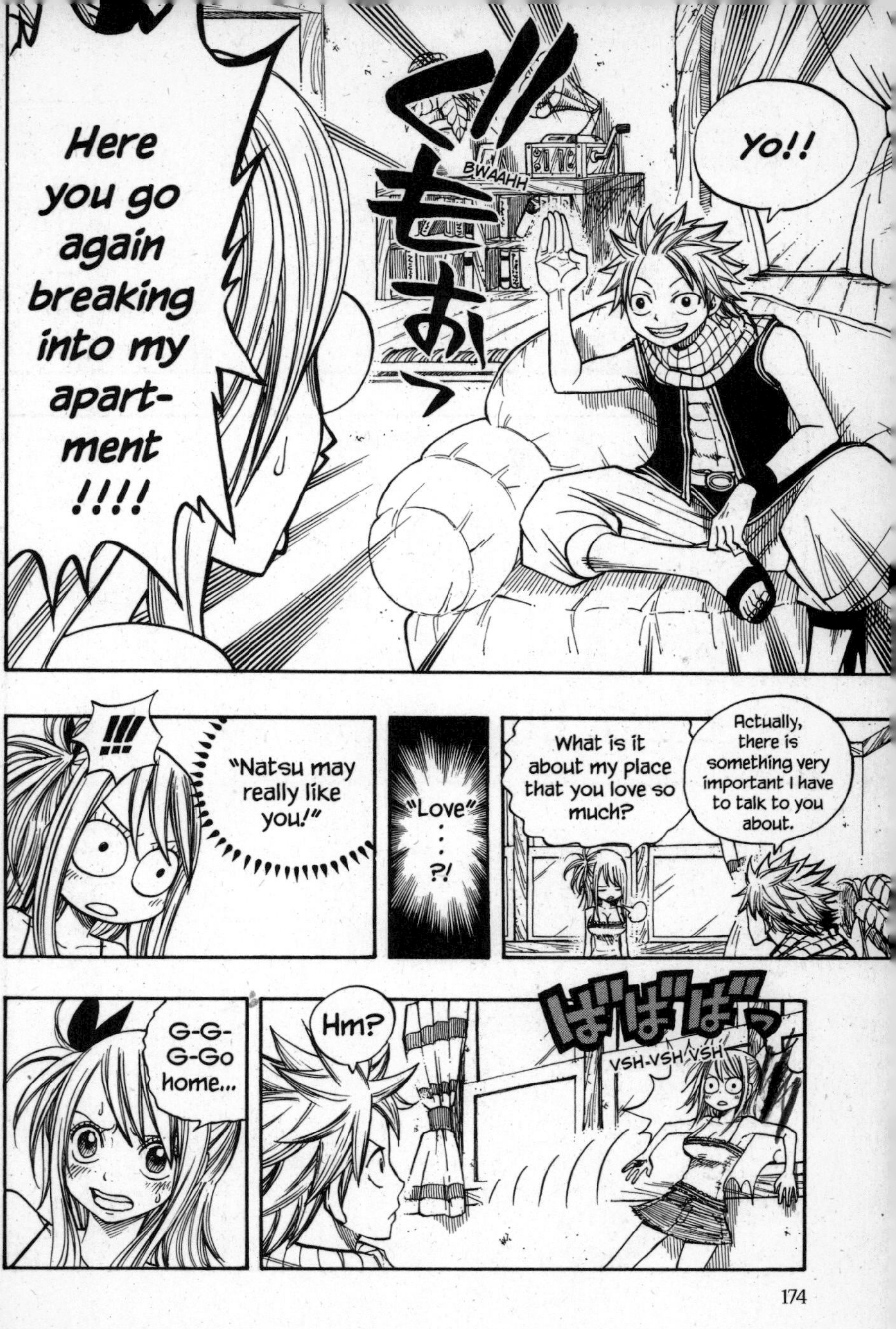
Yo!!
BWAAHH
Here you go again breaking into my apartment!!!!
Actually, there is something very important I have to talk to you about.
What is it about my place that you love so much?
"Love"...?!
"Natsu may really like you!"
!!!
ばばばっ
VSH-VSH VSH
Hm?
G-G-G-Go home...

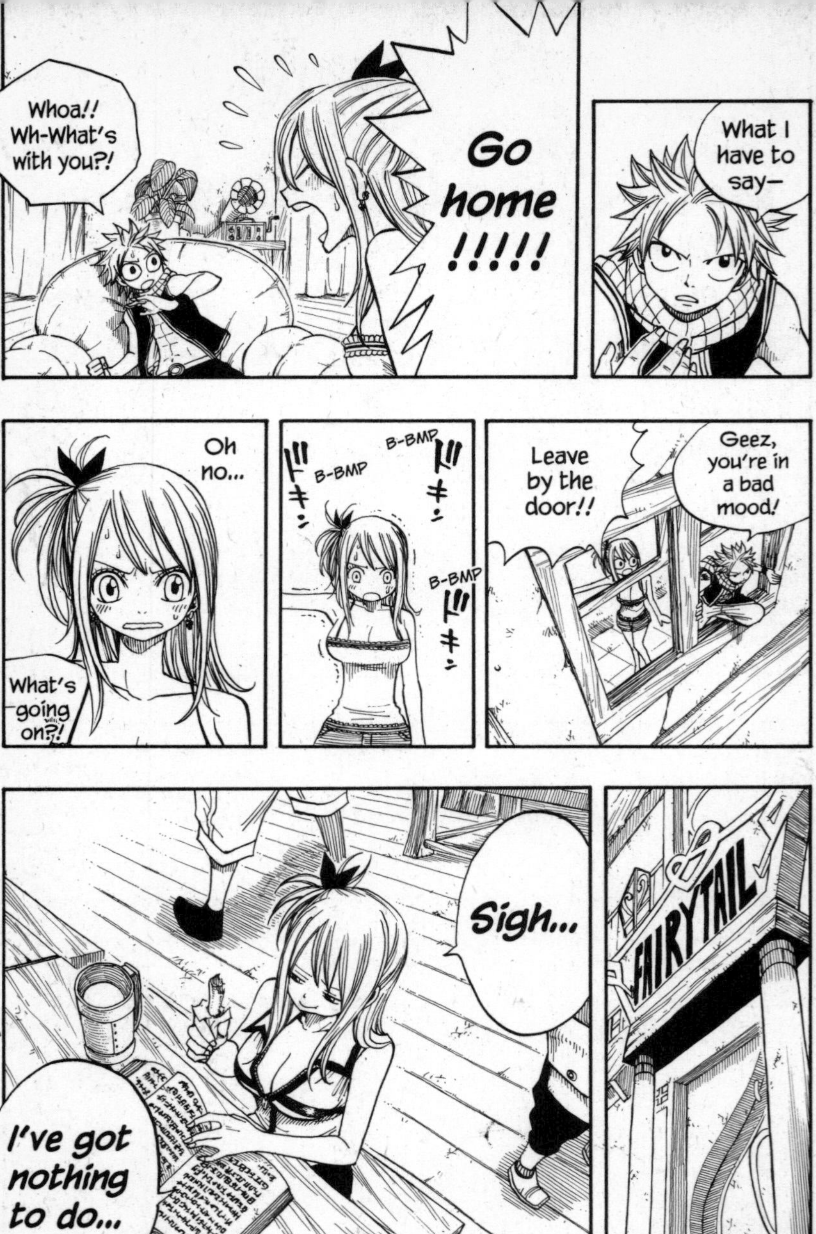
What I have to say—
Go home!!!!!
Whoa!! Wh-What's with you?!
Geez, you're in a bad mood!
Leave by the door!!
B-BMP
ドキン
B-BMP
ドキン
B-BMP
ドキン
Oh no...
What's going on?!
FAIRY TAIL
Sigh...
I've got nothing to do...

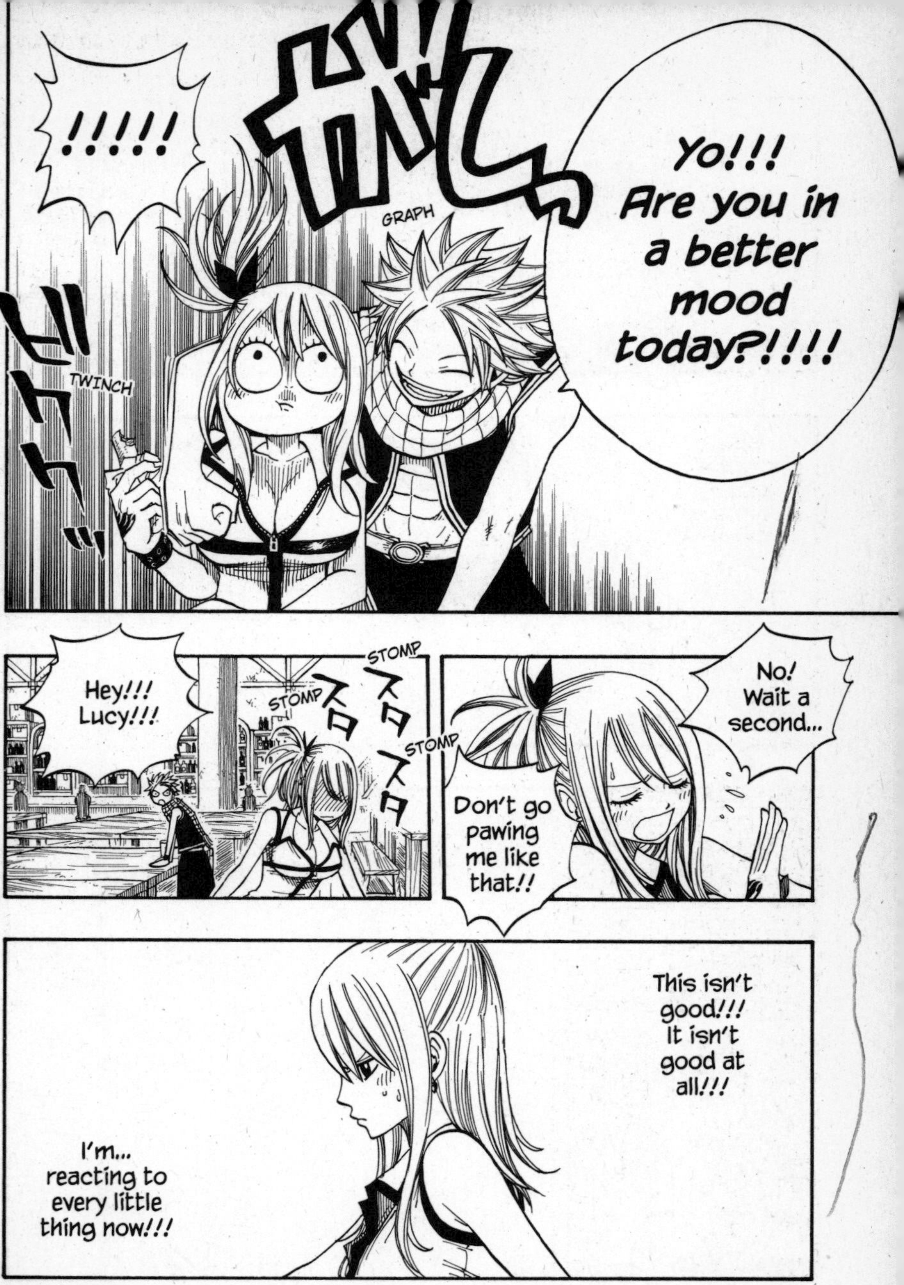
Yo!!! Are you in a better mood today?!!!!
GRAPH
!!!!!
TWINCH
No! Wait a second...
Don't go pawing me like that!!
STOMP
STOMP
STOMP
Hey!!! Lucy!!!
This isn't good!!! It isn't good at all!!!
I'm... reacting to every little thing now!!!

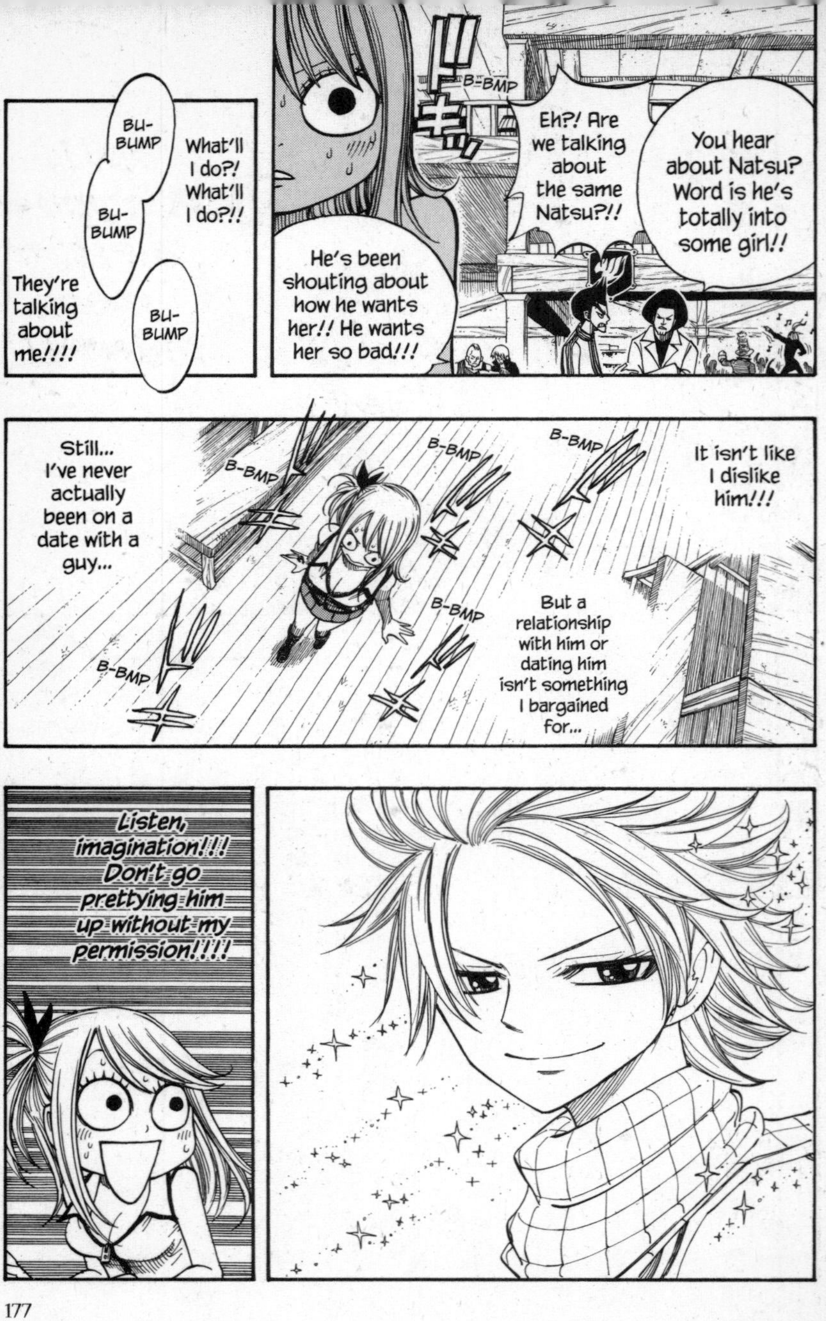
B-BMP
You hear about Natsu? Word is he's totally into some girl!!
Eh?! Are we talking about the same Natsu?!!
He's been shouting about how he wants her!! He wants her so bad!!!
What'll I do?! What'll I do?!!
BU-BUMP
BU-BUMP
BU-BUMP
They're talking about me!!!!
It isn't like I dislike him!!!
B-BMP
B-BMP
But a relationship with him or dating him isn't something I bargained for...
B-BMP
Still... I've never actually been on a date with a guy...
B-BMP
B-BMP
Listen, imagination!!! Don't go prettying him up without my permission!!!!

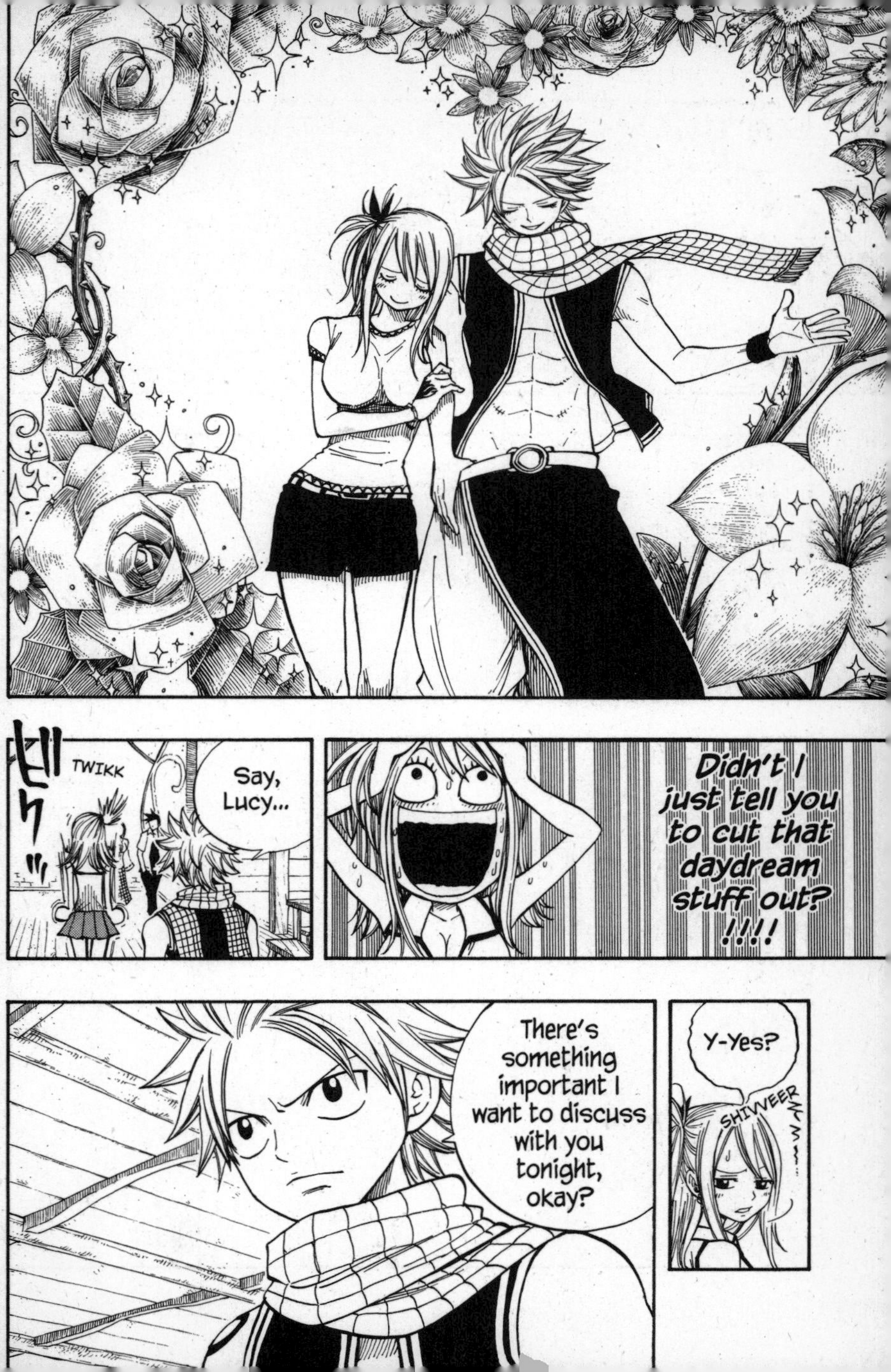

Didn't I just tell you to cut that daydream stuff out?!!!!
Say, Lucy...
TWIKK
Y-Yes?
SHIVVEER
There's something important I want to discuss with you tonight, okay?

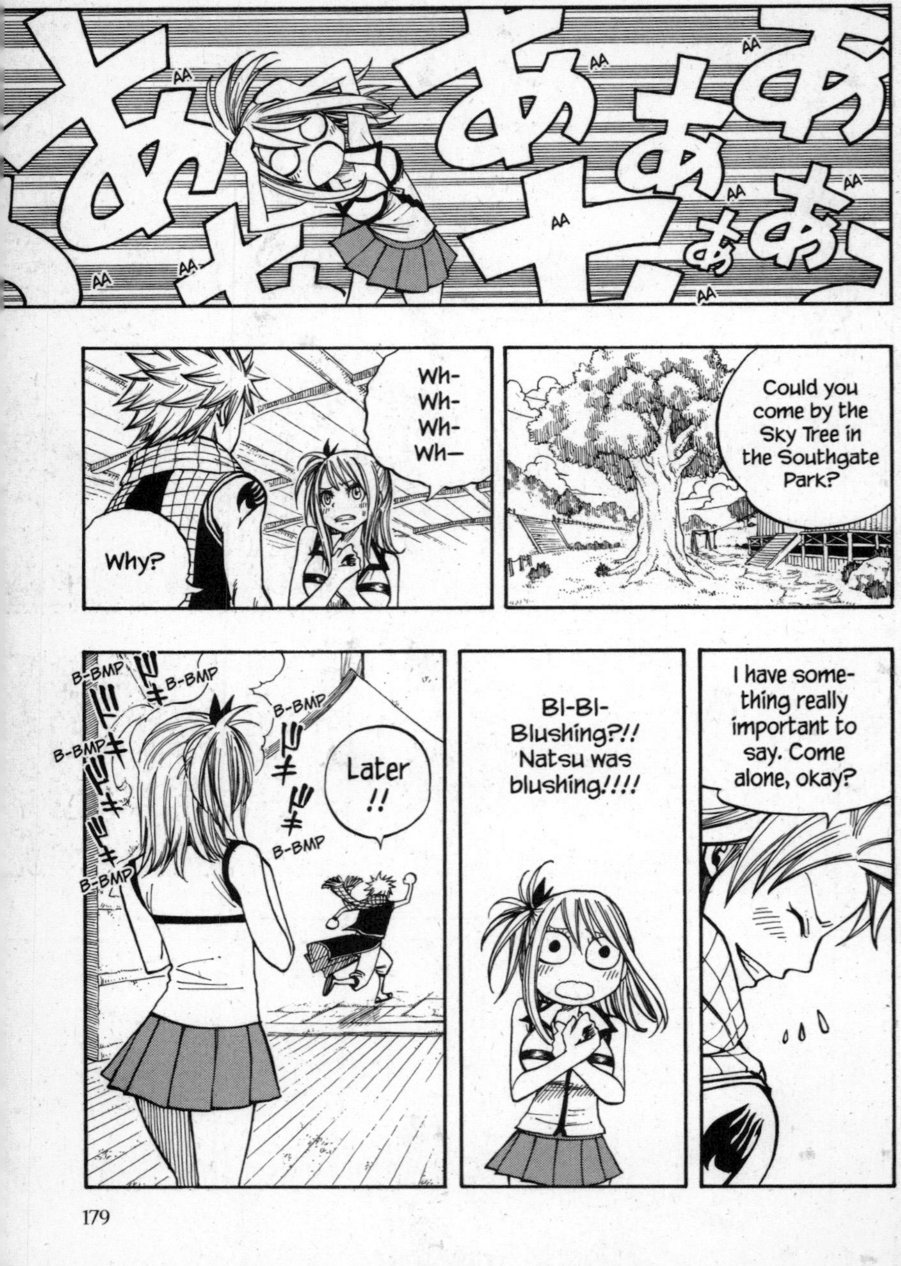
AA
AA
AA
AA
AA
AA
AA
AA
AA
Could you come by the Sky Tree in the Southgate Park?
Wh- Wh- Wh- Wh–
Why?
I have some-thing really important to say. Come alone, okay?
Bl-Bl-Blushing?!! Natsu was blushing!!!!
B-BMP
B-BMP
Later!!
B-BMP
B-BMP
B-BMP
B-BMP

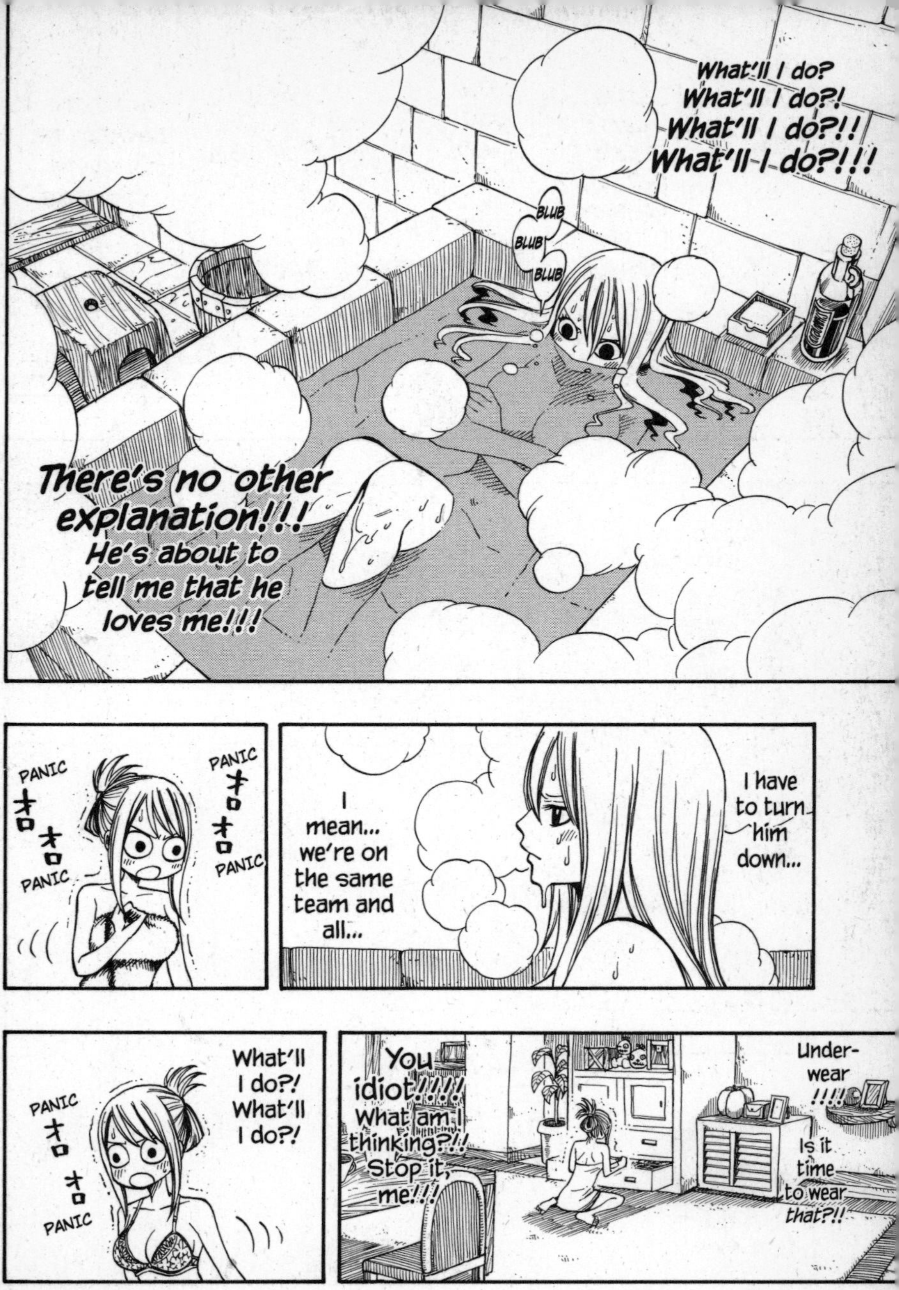
What'll I do?
What'll I do?!
What'll I do?!!
What'll I do?!!!
BLUB
BLUB
BLUB
There's no other explanation!!!
He's about to tell me that he loves me!!!
I have to turn him down...
I mean... we're on the same team and all...
PANIC
オロ
PANIC
オロ
PANIC
オロ
PANIC
オロ
Under-wear!!!!
Is it time to wear that?!!
You idiot!!!! What am I thinking?!! Stop it, me!!!
What'll I do?! What'll I do?!
PANIC
オロ
PANIC
オロ

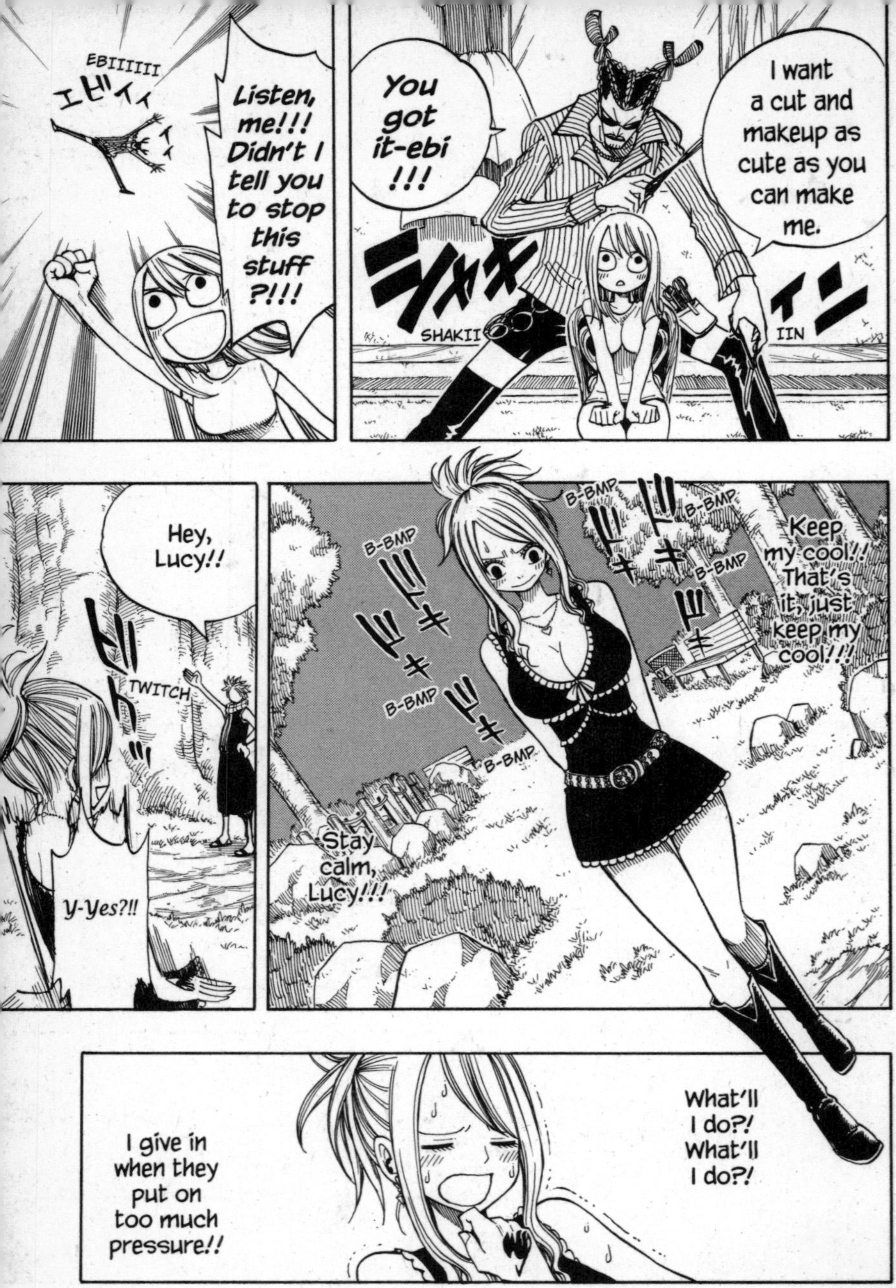
I want a cut and makeup as cute as you can make me.
You got it-ebi!!!
IIN
SHAKII
Listen, me!!! Didn't I tell you to stop this stuff?!!!
EBIIIIII
Keep my cool!! That's it, just keep my cool!!!
B-BMP
B-BMP
B-BMP
B-BMP
B-BMP
B-BMP
Stay calm, Lucy!!!
Hey, Lucy!!
TWITCH
Y-Yes?!!
What'll I do?! What'll I do?!
I give in when they put on too much pressure!!

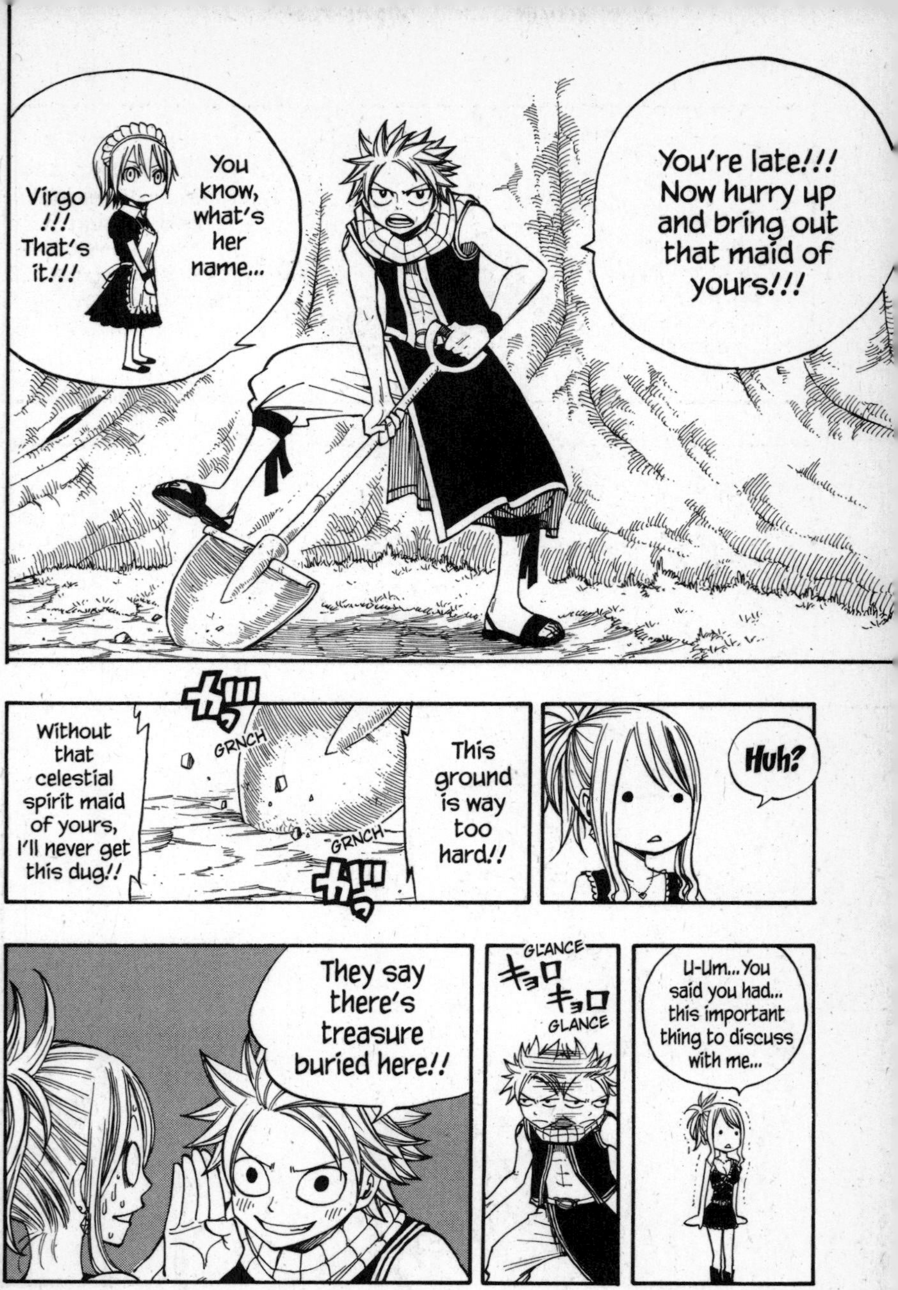
You're late!!! Now hurry up and bring out that maid of yours!!!
You know, what's her name...
Virgo!!! That's it!!!
Huh?
This ground is way too hard!!
GRNCH
GRNCH
Without that celestial spirit maid of yours, I'll never get this dug!!
U-Um...You said you had... this important thing to discuss with me...
GLANCE
キョロ
キョロ
GLANCE
They say there's treasure buried here!!

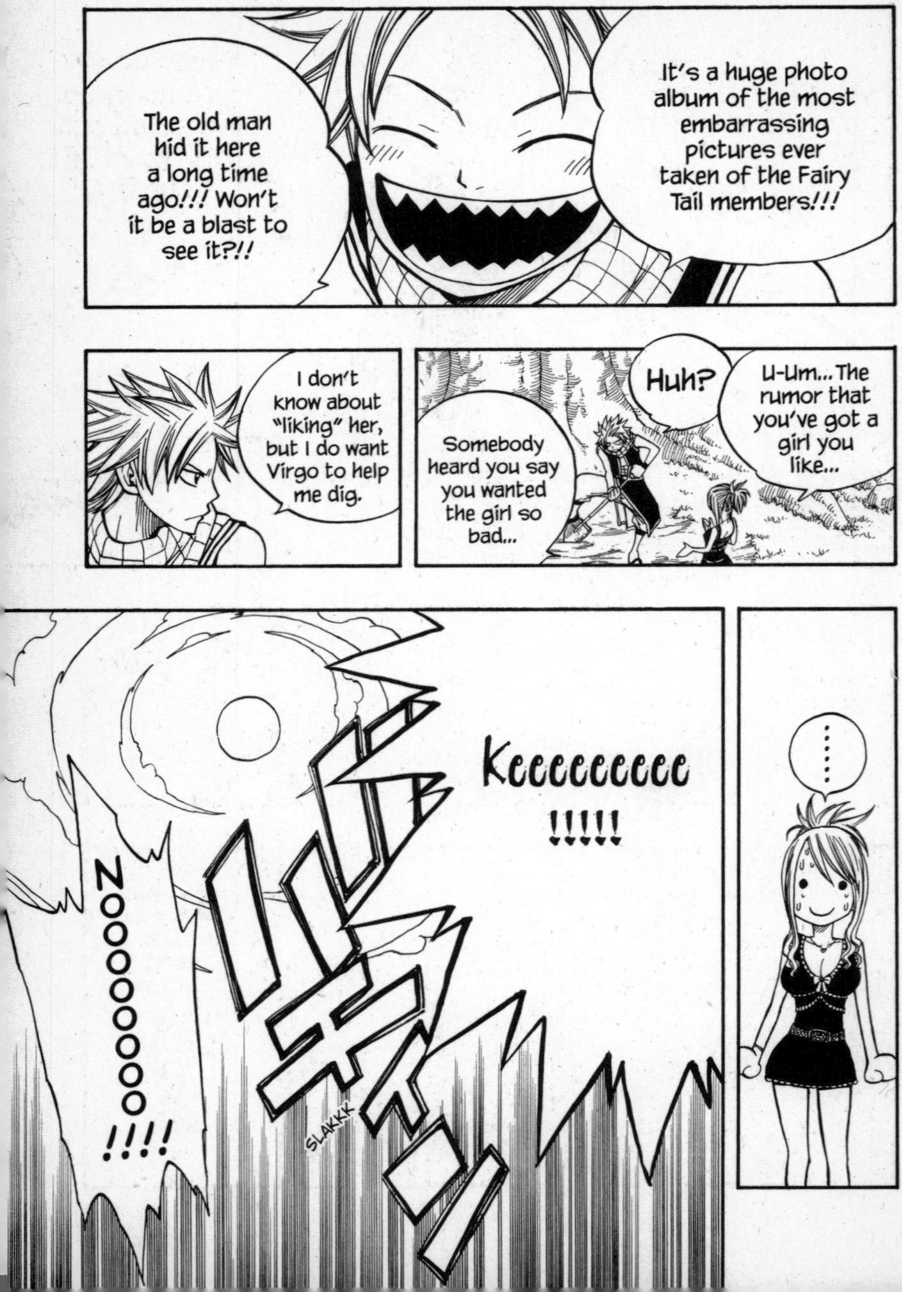
It's a huge photo album of the most embarrassing pictures ever taken of the Fairy Tail members!!!
The old man hid it here a long time ago!!! Won't it be a blast to see it?!!
U-Um... The rumor that you've got a girl you like...
Huh?
Somebody heard you say you wanted the girl so bad...
I don't know about "liking" her, but I do want Virgo to help me dig.
......
Keeeeeeeee !!!!!
SLAKKK
NOOOOOOOOO!!!!

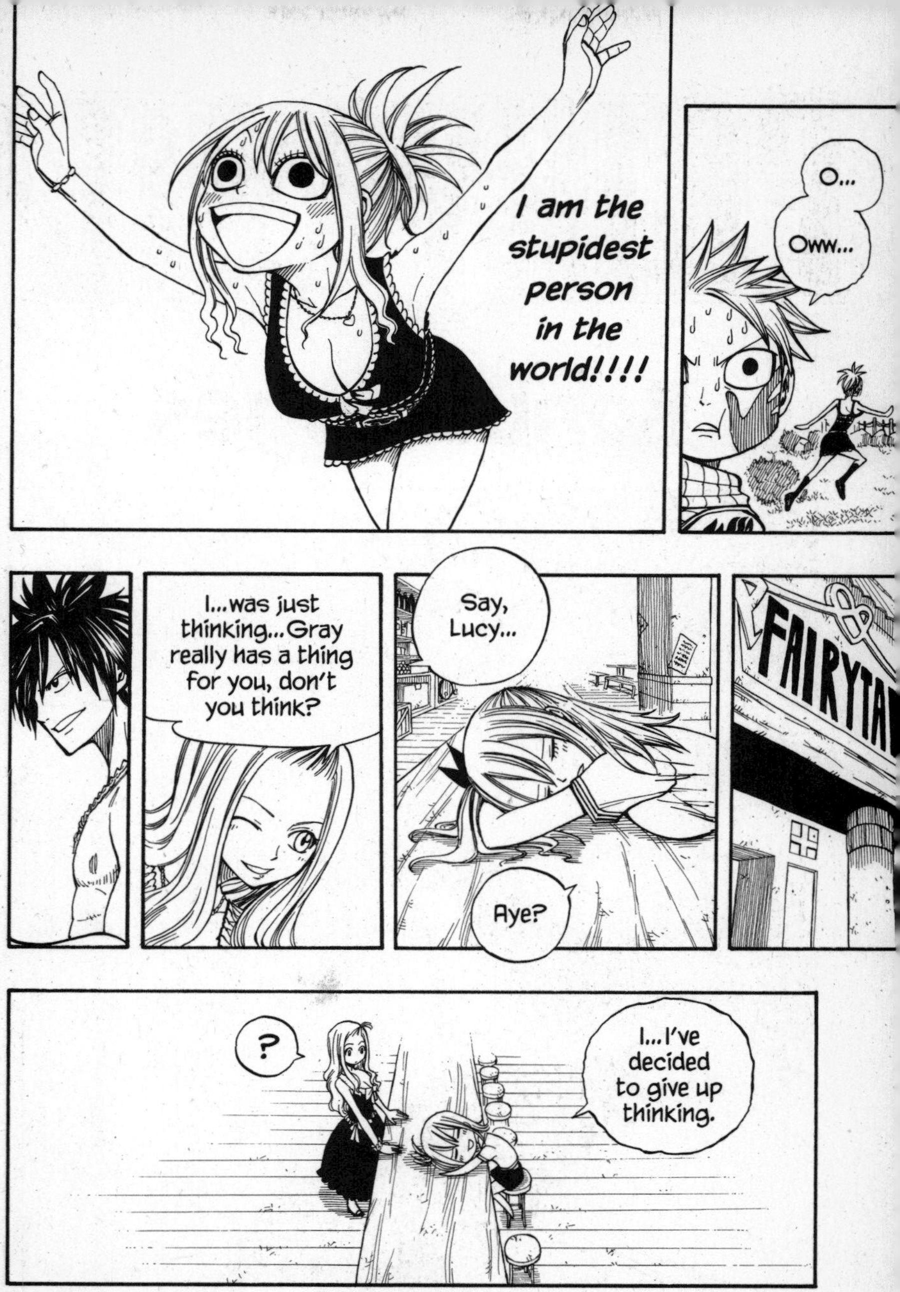
O...
Oww...
I am the stupidest person in the world!!!!
Say, Lucy...
Aye?
I...was just thinking...Gray really has a thing for you, don't you think?
I...I've decided to give up thinking.
?

The End

Bonus Pages

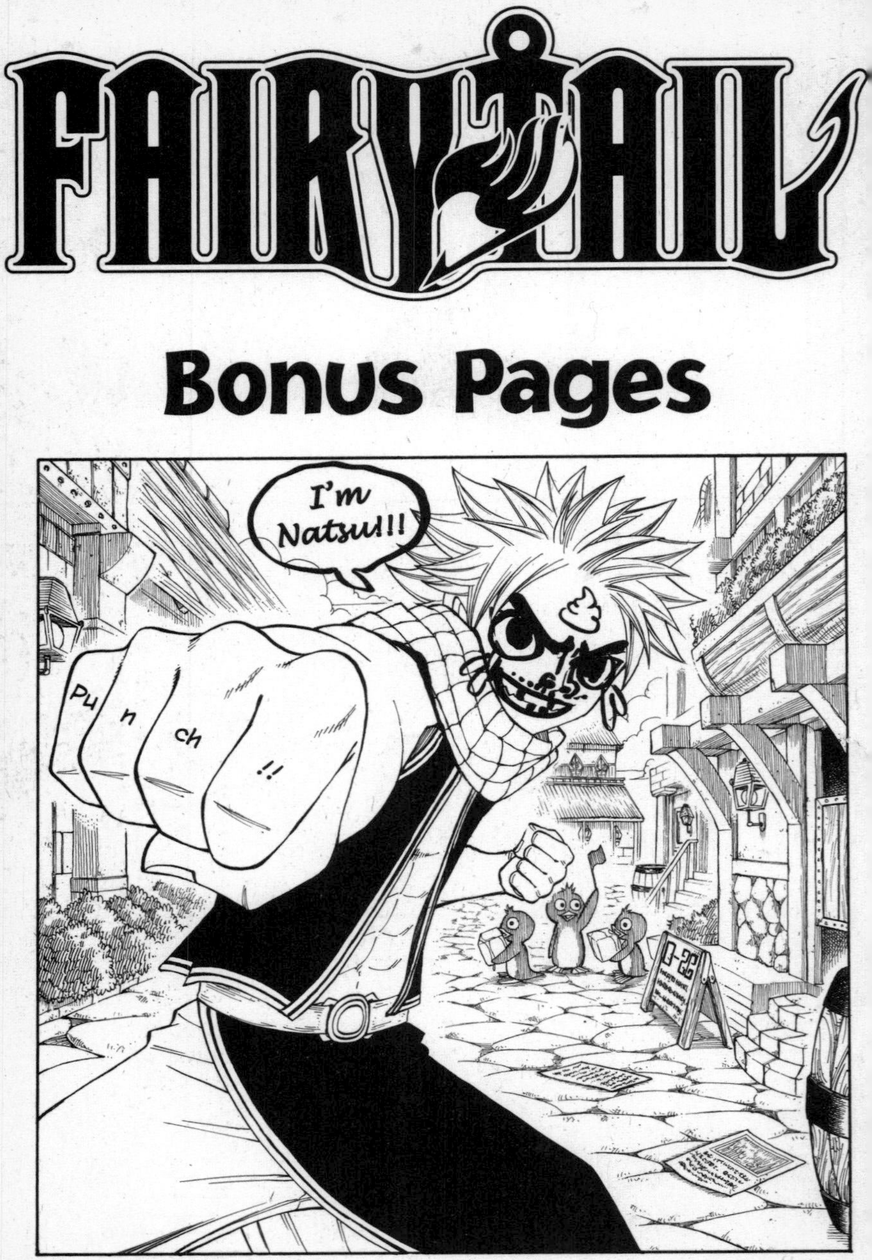
I'm Natsu!!
Pu n ch !!

Rejected Splash Page

The pose wasn't very natural. After I noticed that, I quickly placed it in the rejected pile.

TAIL D'ART

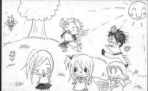

The *Fairy Tail* Guild d'Art is an explosion of fan art! Please send in your black-and-white art on large postcard stock!! Those chosen to be published will get a signed mini poster! ♪ Make sure you write your real name and address on the back of your postcard!

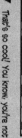

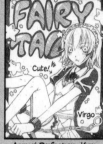

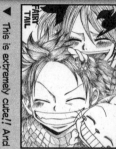

FAIRY TAIL

▼ What wonderful smiles!! One great piece of artwork!

Hiroshima Prefecture, MIE

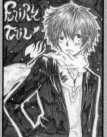

FAIRY TAI
Cute!
Virgo

▼ This is extremely cute!! And so well drawn!

Aomori Prefecture, Kuro

FAIRY TAIL

▼ That's so cool! You know, you're not supposed to draw better than I can!!

Niigata Prefecture, Ai

▼ Well done!! You've got drawing experience, don't you?

Niigata Prefecture, Reina

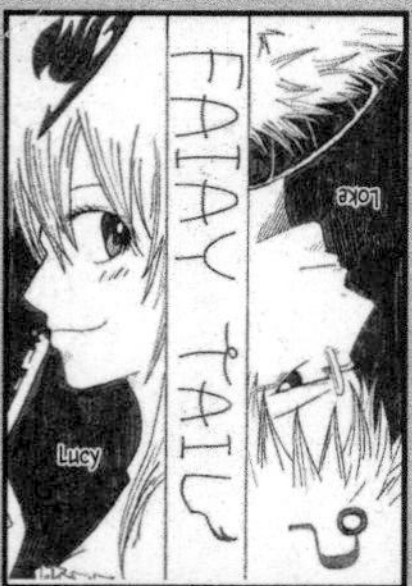

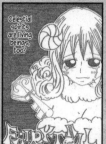

Celestial spirits are living beings, too!

▼ I get lots of letters asking what became of this girl!

Miyagi Prefecture, Ikkome-chan

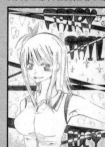

FAIRY TAIL
Loke
Lucy

▼ What did you think of the Loke story? Personally I liked it a lot.

Nagasaki Prefecture, Lemon-Sui

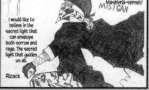

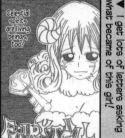

FAIRY TAIL

▼ This is so cute!! Oh no!! I'm feeling too content!!

Kanagawa Prefecture, Mei Shimizu

Fight! Mashima-sensei!
MISTGAN
I would like to believe in the sacred light that can envelope both sorrow and rage. The sacred light that guides us all.
Alzack

▼ I-I know his back-story!! R-Really! I've thought everything out!!

Yamagata Prefecture, Fuyu

Send to DEL REY MANGA, Hiro Mashima, 1745 Broadway, New York, NY 10019, delreymanga@randomhouse.com*

*Del Rey Manga will make every effort to send your letters to Mashima, but cannot guarantee a response.

FAIRY GUILD

Any letters and postcards you send with your personal information, such as your name, address, postal code, and other information, will be handed over, as is, to the author. When you send mail, please keep that in mind.

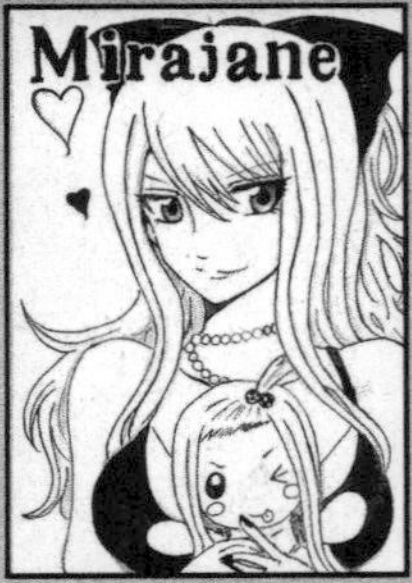
Mirajane
Miyagi Prefecture, Aoi

▼ It's Mira-chan from long ago! I'm getting the itch to tell that story.

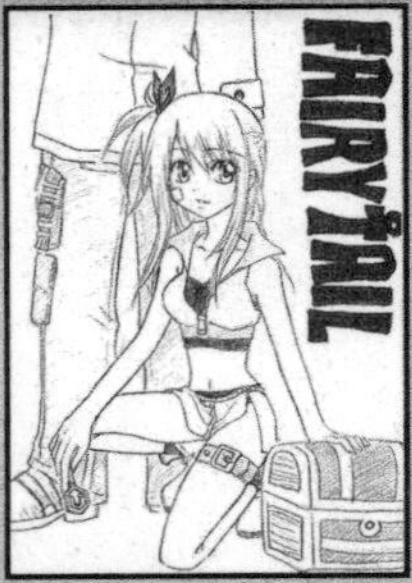
FAIRY TAIL
Gifu Prefecture, Yasuyo Hayasaka

▼ I like her expression and pose! Petite and sexy!

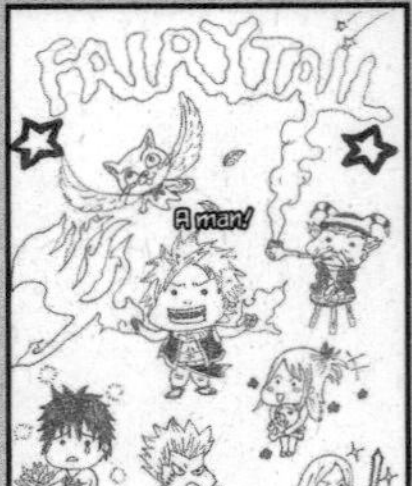
FAIRY TAIL
A man!
Wakayama Prefecture, Buguo

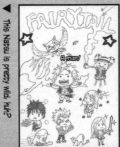

▼ This picture has an interesting flavor. What's that in the bottom left...?

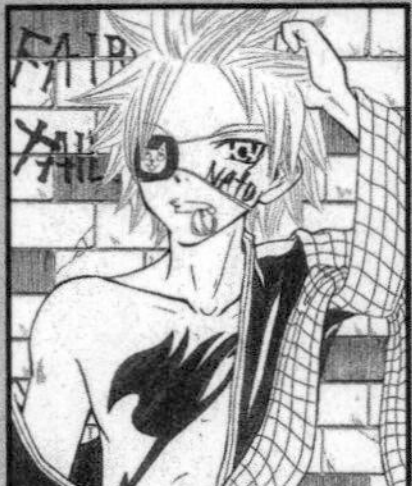
Hiroshima Prefecture, Tabinosuke

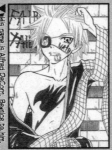

▼ This Natsu is pretty wild, huh?

Rejection Corner

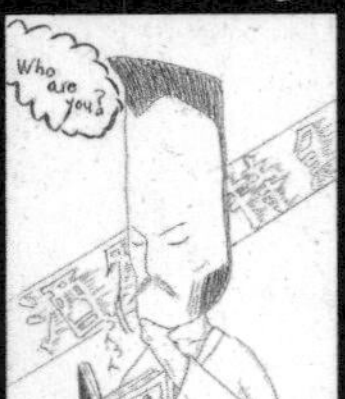
Who are you?
Osaka, Yûki Inoue

▼ This name is Alfred DeCorn. Be nice to him.

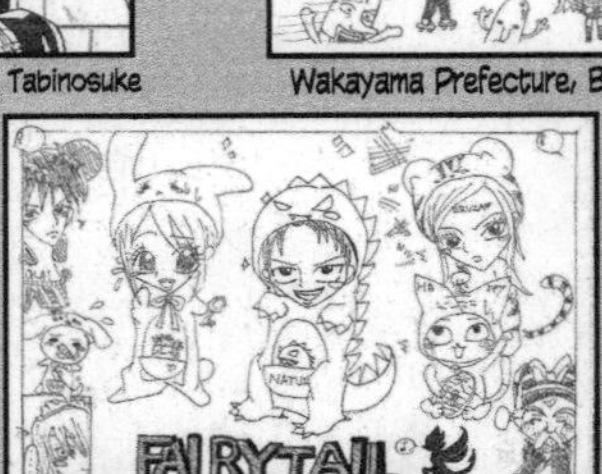
FAIRY TAIL
Shiga Prefecture, Ami Horii

▼ Everybody's in animal costumes!! But Happy doesn't need a costume!

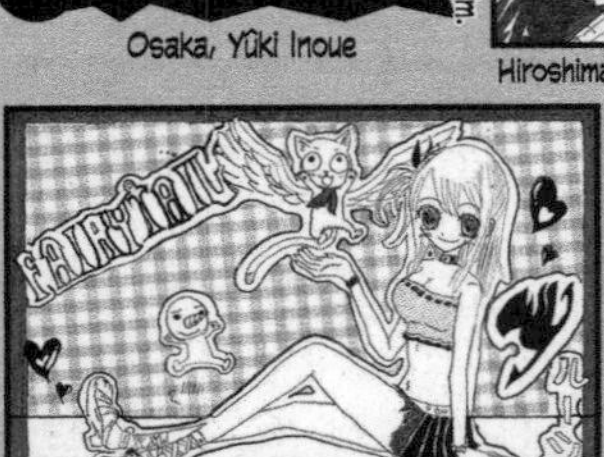
FAIRY TAIL
Okayama Prefecture, Arashi ♡

▼ That's amazingly cute!! I love this kind of picture!!

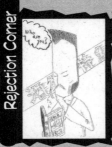

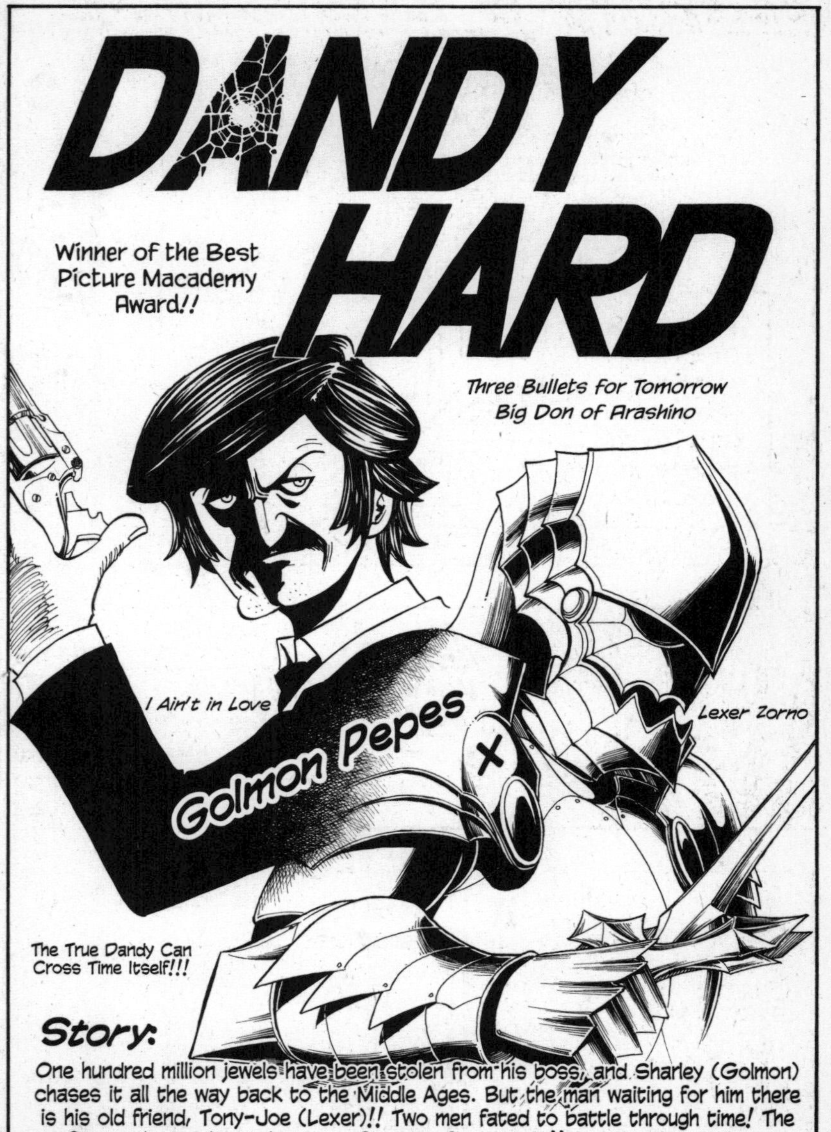
DANDY HARD
Winner of the Best Picture Macademy Award!!
Three Bullets for Tomorrow
Big Don of Arashino
I Ain't in Love
Golmon Pepes
Lexer Zorno
The True Dandy Can Cross Time Itself!!!

Story:

One hundred million jewels have been stolen from his boss, and Sharley (Golmon) chases it all the way back to the Middle Ages. But the man waiting for him there is his old friend, Tony-Joe (Lexer)!! Two men fated to battle through time! The mafia vs. the knight in this one-of-a-kind final battle!! At last, this Macademy Award—winning epic comes to a lacrima crystal near you!!!

Happy's Little Job

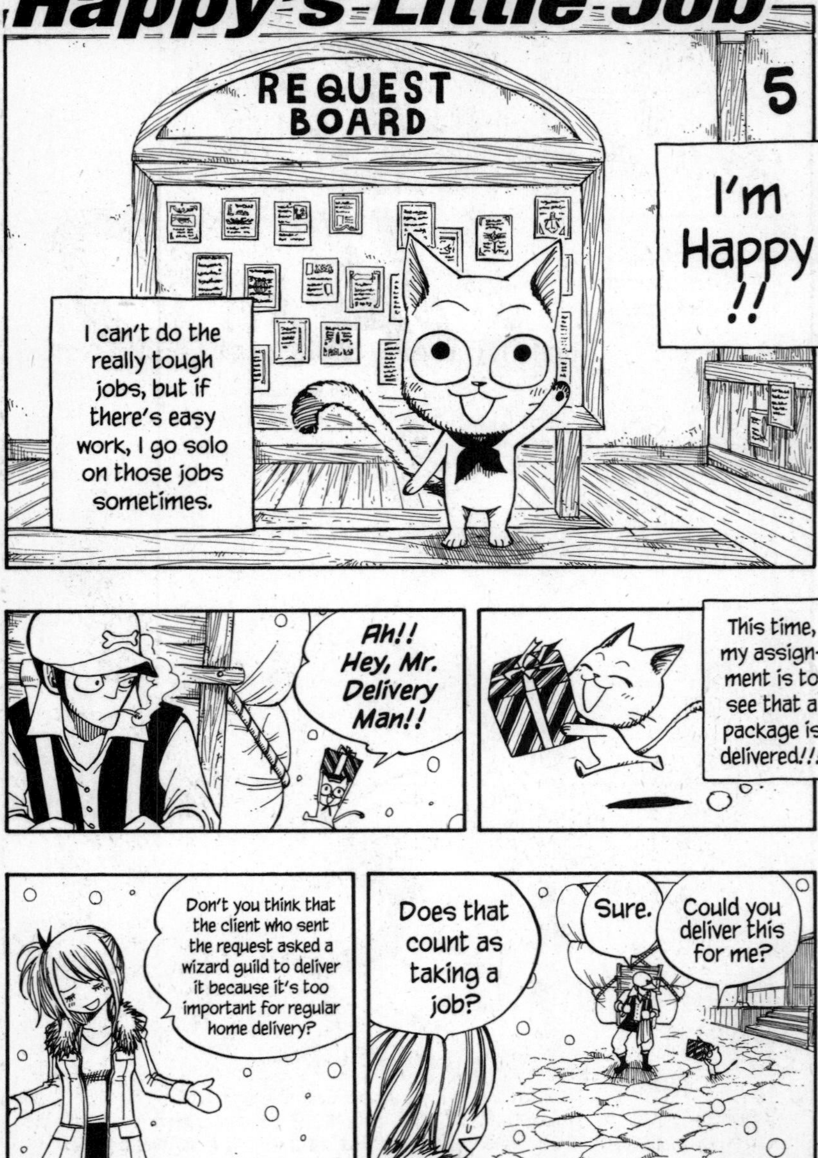
5
REQUEST BOARD
I'm Happy!!
I can't do the really tough jobs, but if there's easy work, I go solo on those jobs sometimes.
This time, my assignment is to see that a package is delivered!!!
Ah!! Hey, Mr. Delivery Man!!
Could you deliver this for me?
Sure.
Does that count as taking a job?
Don't you think that the client who sent the request asked a wizard guild to deliver it because it's too important for regular home delivery?

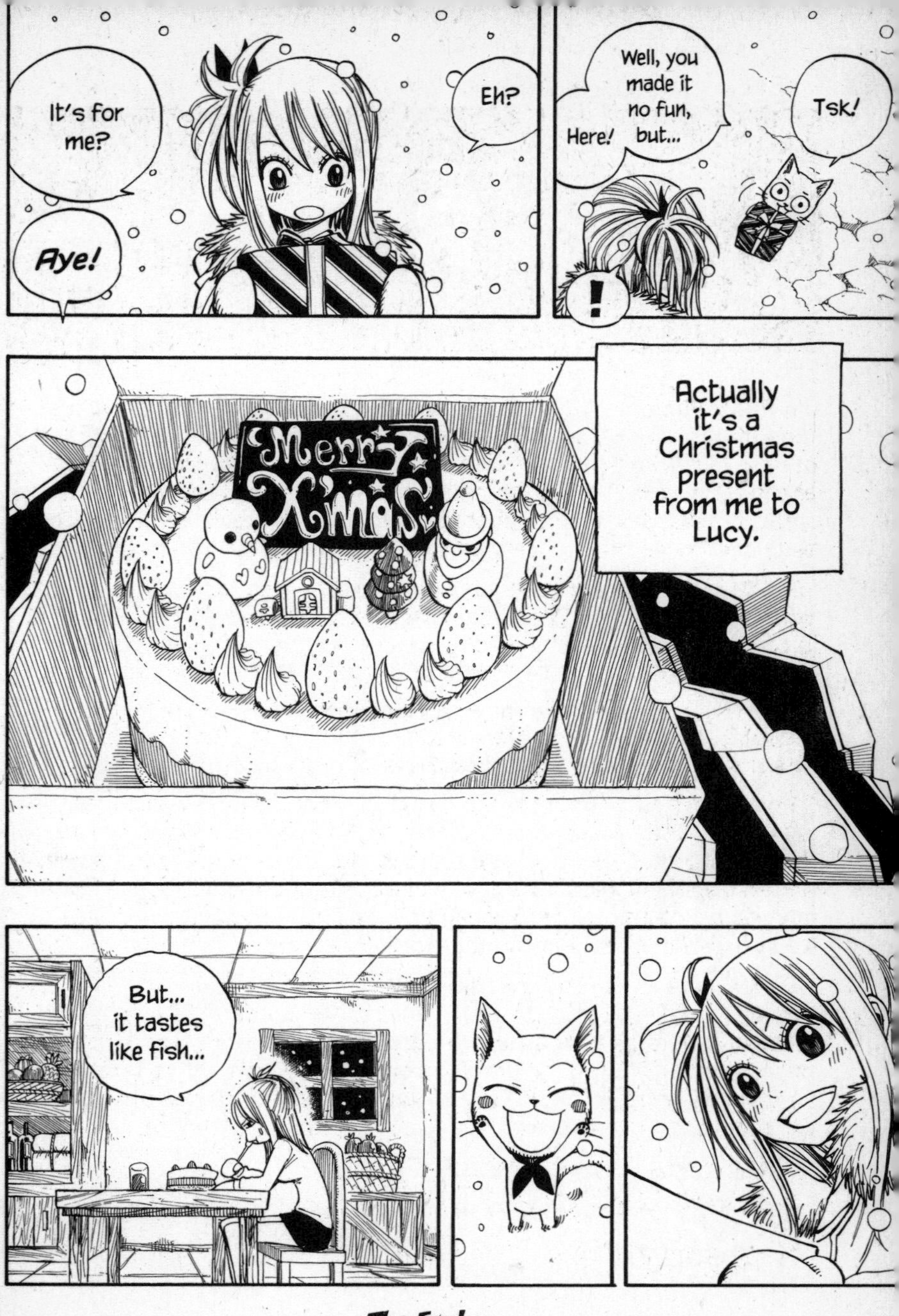
Tsk!
Well, you made it no fun, but...
Here!
!
Eh?
It's for me?
Aye!
Actually it's a Christmas present from me to Lucy.
Merry X'mas
But... it tastes like fish...

The End

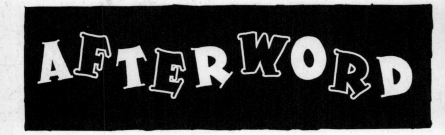

AFTERWORD

In this volume, we plunge right into the Erza story!! You know, it's kind of hard to get the balance between the heavy dramatic stuff and the fun stuff! I try to get even a small laugh at least once into every chapter, but really, these dramatic scenes truly get in the way! This series of episodes are extremely heavy, but upon second reading, there were a lot more fun scenes than I expected (sweat sweat)!

By the way, does anybody have any guesses why there are butterflies when we first go into Erza's flashback scenes? Actually this was a leftover from an idea that was rejected. Does anybody out there know of the Chinese story, "The Dream of the Butterfly"?

> One day, there was a man who dreamed that he was a butterfly. When he awakened, an odd thought struck him. Could it be that my life as a butterfly was real? That I am not a man dreaming that I am a butterfly, but...

I was thinking of using a plot like that. That the present Erza is actually just the young Erza's dream of the future. Or something to that effect. But if I were to use that idea for real, what would happen to Natsu and Lucy and everybody else?! And I thought about it for a few weeks, and now the idea can only be found in those remnants. Keeping it would have made the story very complicated!

Also, there is a one other secret that's part of this episode. It's a very mean-spirited, evil plot (ha ha)! Those in the know will know what I'm talking about! And those who don't will have the enjoyment of watching the whole thing unfold. It will all become clear in volume 11...or maybe volume 12? Any of you who were fooled should scream out the words as follows:

"Mashima, you meanie!!!"

And I'll give you my answer in advance,

"I'm sorry!!"

About the Creator

HIRO MASHIMA was born May 3, 1977, in the Nagano prefecture. His series *Rave Master* has made him one of the most popular manga artists in America. *Fairy Tail*, currently being serialized in *Weekly Shônen Magazine*, is his latest creation.

Translation Notes

Japanese is a tricky language for most Westerners, and translation is often more art than science. For your edification and reading pleasure, here are notes on some of the places where we could have gone in a different direction in our translation of the work, or where a Japanese cultural reference is used.

General Notes:
Wizard

In the original Japanese version of *Fairy Tail*, you'll find panels in which the English word "wizard" is part of the original illustration. So this translation has taken that as its inspiration and translated the word *madôshi* as "wizard." But *madôshi*'s meaning is similar to certain Japanese words that have been borrowed by the English language, such as judo (the soft way) and kendo (the way of the sword). *Madô* is the way of magic, and *madôshi* are those who follow the way of magic. So although the word "wizard" is used in the original dialogue, a Japanese reader would be likely to think not of traditional Western wizards such as Merlin or Gandalf, but of martial artists.

Names

Hiro Mashima has graciously agreed to provide official English spellings for just about all of the characters in *Fairy Tail*. Because this version of *Fairy Tail* is the first publication of most of these spellings, there will inevitably be differences between these spellings and some of the fan interpretations that may have spread throughout the Web or in other fan circles. Rest assured that the spellings contained in this book are the spellings that Mashima-sensei wanted for *Fairy Tail*.

Dream of a Butterfly, page 3

The story that Mashima-sensei notes in his Afterword is a retelling of a story told in a book by the ancient Chinese philosopher Zhuangzi (also known as Chuang Tzu, 369–286 BC), who is considered to be one of the two greatest philosophers of Daoism. While Confucianism was based on self-sacrifice and conformity, the Daoism of Zhuangzi was the opposite, based on individual freedoms and escape from society and its pressures. Zhuangzi encouraged spontaneous behavior and thought, since he believed that such was a reaction to reality as it truly is, rising above societal and linguistic limitations.

Smashing Watermelons on the Beach, page 10

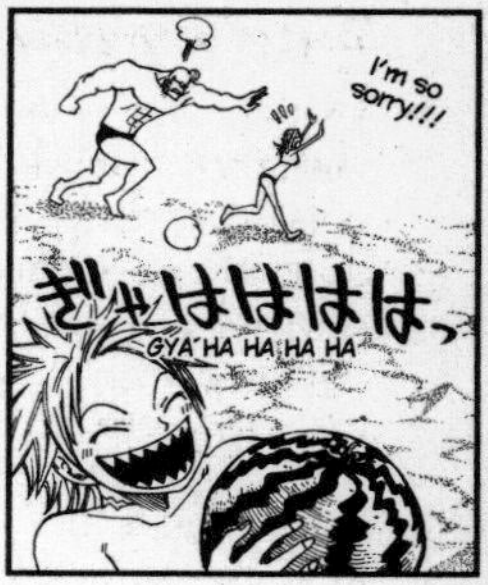
I'm so sorry!!!
ぎゃはははっ
GYA HA HA HA HA

This is a traditional summer game for children in Japan. Like piñata games, the player is blindfolded and given a stick. Unlike a piñata, the watermelon is left sitting on the sand (or on a blanket on the sand) so Natsu's direction of "up" would make no sense. Once the watermelon is smashed, all the children divide up the watermelon pieces and eat it.

Dandy, page 20

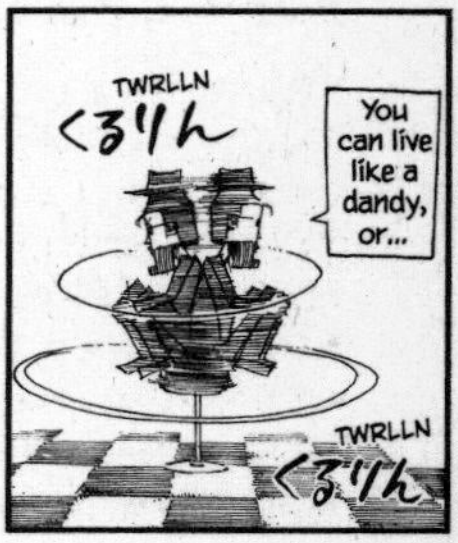
You can live like a dandy, or...
TWRLLN
くるりん
TWRLLN
くるりん

There are many words that make their way from English into Japanese and get their meanings changed along the way. The word "dandy" doesn't mean the same in Japanese as its present English definition of a fop or a shallow, fashion-obsessed man. One Japanese dictionary starts off its definition with "a real gentleman." That is probably what Mashima-sensei was thinking when he wrote Wally's character. Since Wally got the word from the lacrima crystal movie Dandy Hard, I couldn't use "gentleman" or any other English word that might more closely indicate the Japanese meaning.

Get it?, page 23

This is an approximation rather than a translation. In Japanese, Wally uses the sentence ending particle ze at the end of most of his sentences. The way Wally uses the particle is the same way men use it when they are trying to act tough — like in the yakuza or in a street gang. The "get it" in English sounds a little like the tough character that Wally wants to be.

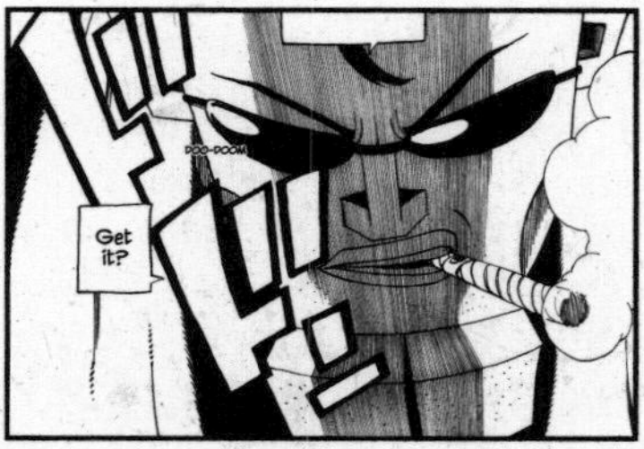
Get it?

Big Sis, page 26

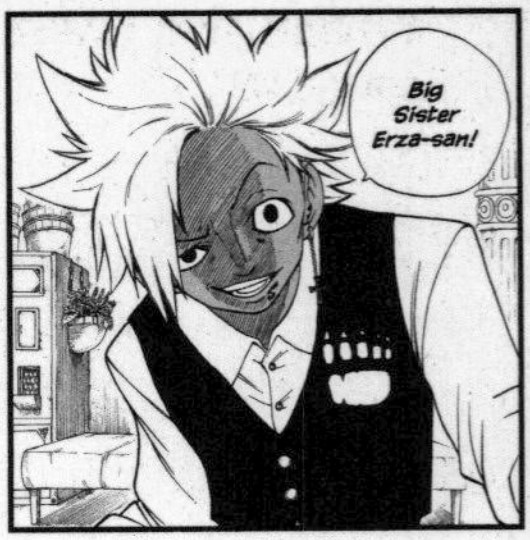
Big Sister Erza-san!

Readers of the manga *School Rumble* will be familiar with the Japanese honorific *nee-san* (or *Onee-san*), which is used by younger siblings when referring to their older sister. However, this honorific can also be used by people who are unrelated to the "big sister," such as children talking to an older girl or shop clerks who want to address a young lady but don't know her name. In *School Rumble*, the honorific appears all of the time. But here, only Shô uses it, so I decided to translate it rather than leave the honorific in Japanese.

Are you pumped up?, page 36

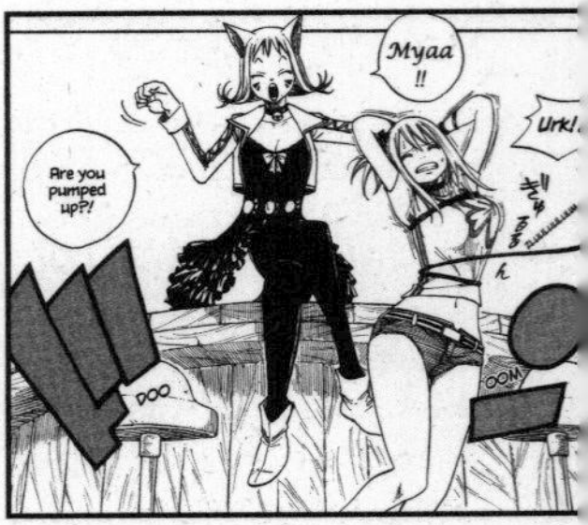
Urk!
Myaa !!
Are you pumped up?!
DOO...
OOM

This was kind of difficult to translate. This is a slightly unusual phrase in Japanese that Millianna used that means about the same thing as "Are you at top energy?" But it's also similar to the standard Japanese question, *O-genki desu ka*, which basically means, "How are you?" I had to come up with a distinctive phrase that could be Millianna's catchphrase without losing the meaning of the original. "Are you pumped up?" seemed like a good compromise.

-ebi, page 102

As explained in the notes for volume 2, some manga and anime characters end their sentences with small, meaningless syllables that are distinctive to the character. In Japanese children's stories, crabs usually end their sentences with *-kani* (*kani* means "crab" in Japanese). But although Cancer is a crab, he ends his sentences with *-ebi* (*ebi* means "shrimp" in Japanese). It was a little joke in volume 2, but it has also become a part of Cancer's character.

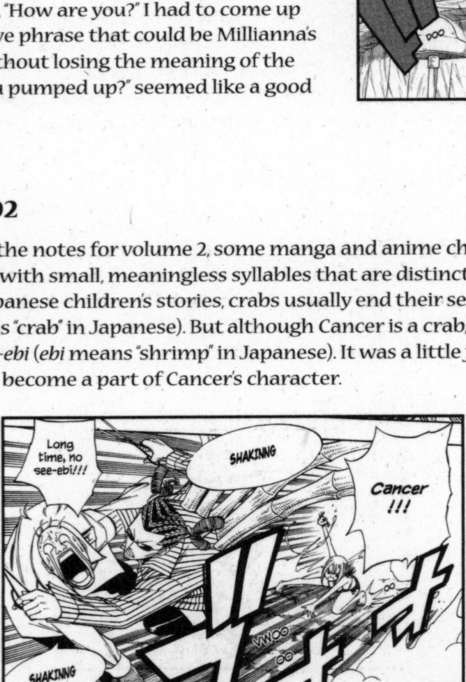
Cancer !!!
SHAKINNG
Long time, no see-ebi!!!
VWOO
OO
SHAKINNG

Preview of Volume 11

We're pleased to present you with a preview from volume 11. Please check our website (www.delreymanga.com) to see when this volume will be available in English. For now you'll have to make do with Japanese!

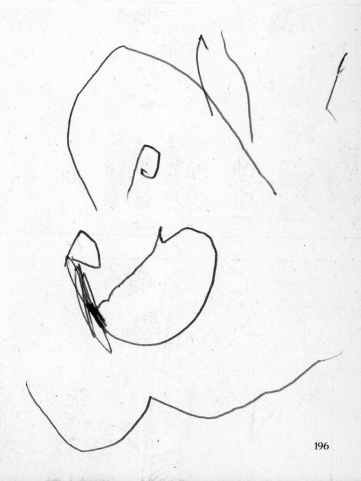

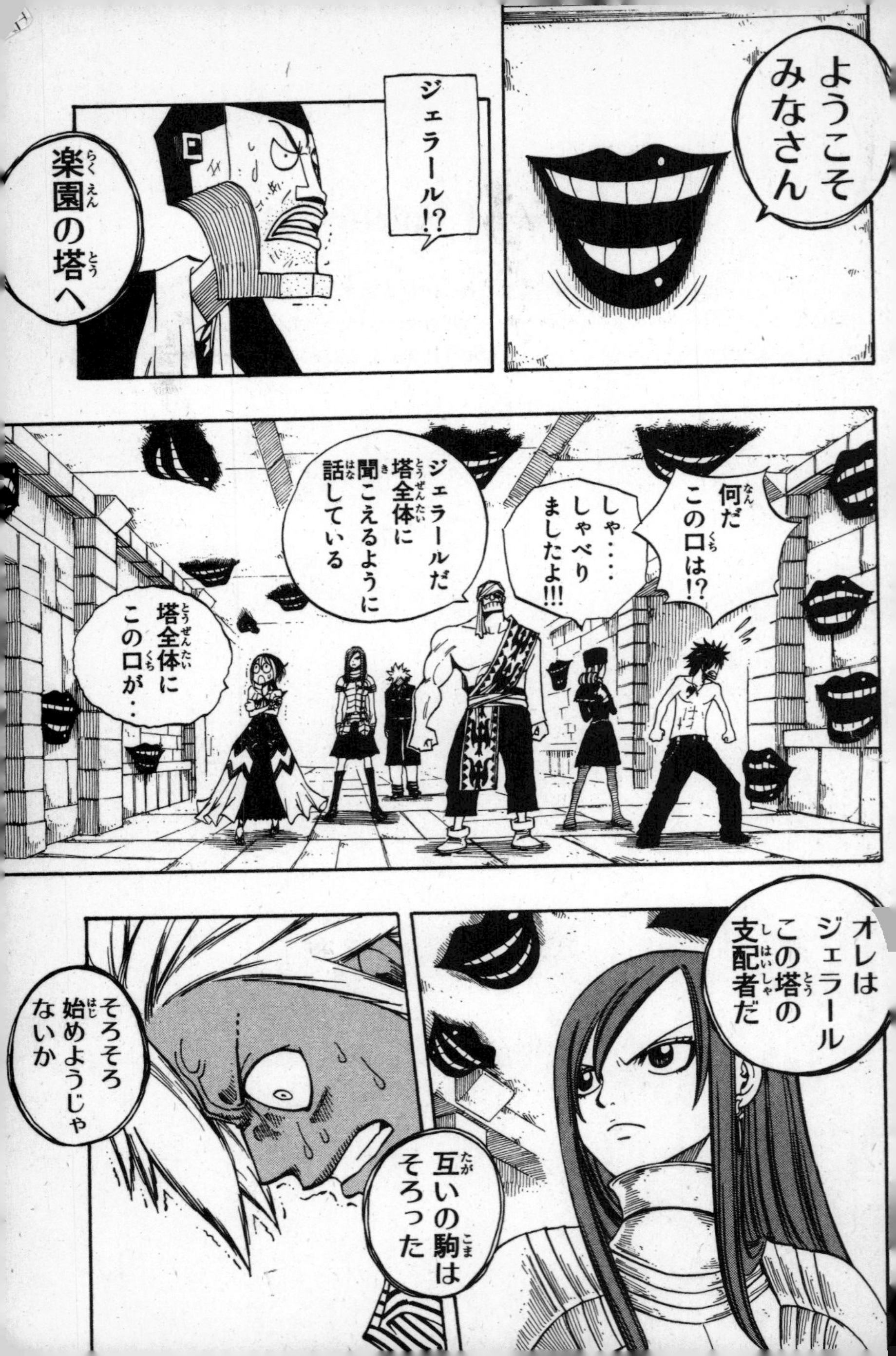
ようこそみなさん
ジェラール!?
楽園の塔へ
何だこの口は!?
しゃ…しゃべりましたよ!!!
ジェラールだ塔全体に聞こえるように話している
塔全体にこの口が…
オレはジェラールこの塔の支配者だ
互いの駒はそろった
そろそろ始めようじゃないか

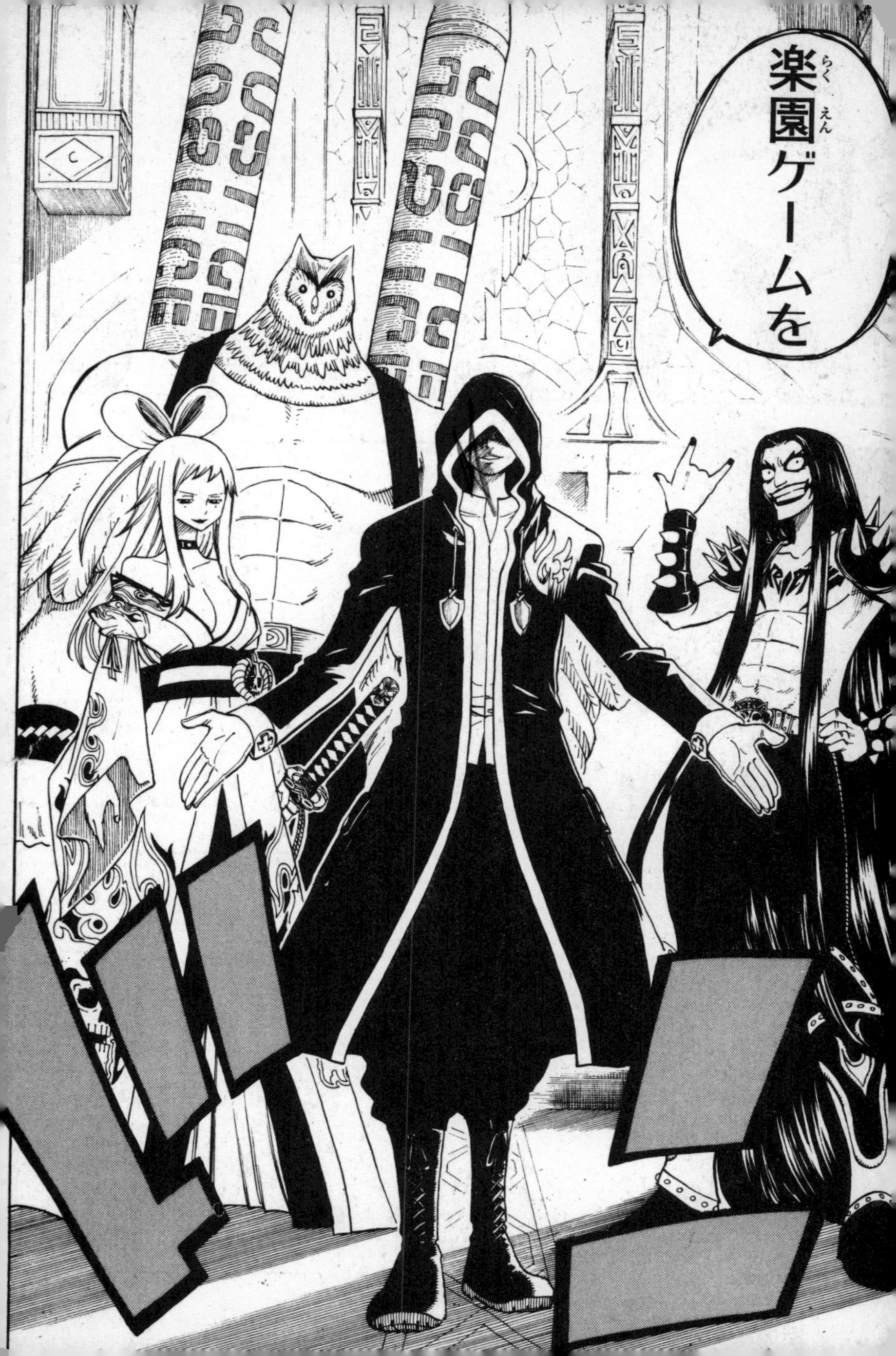
楽園ゲームを

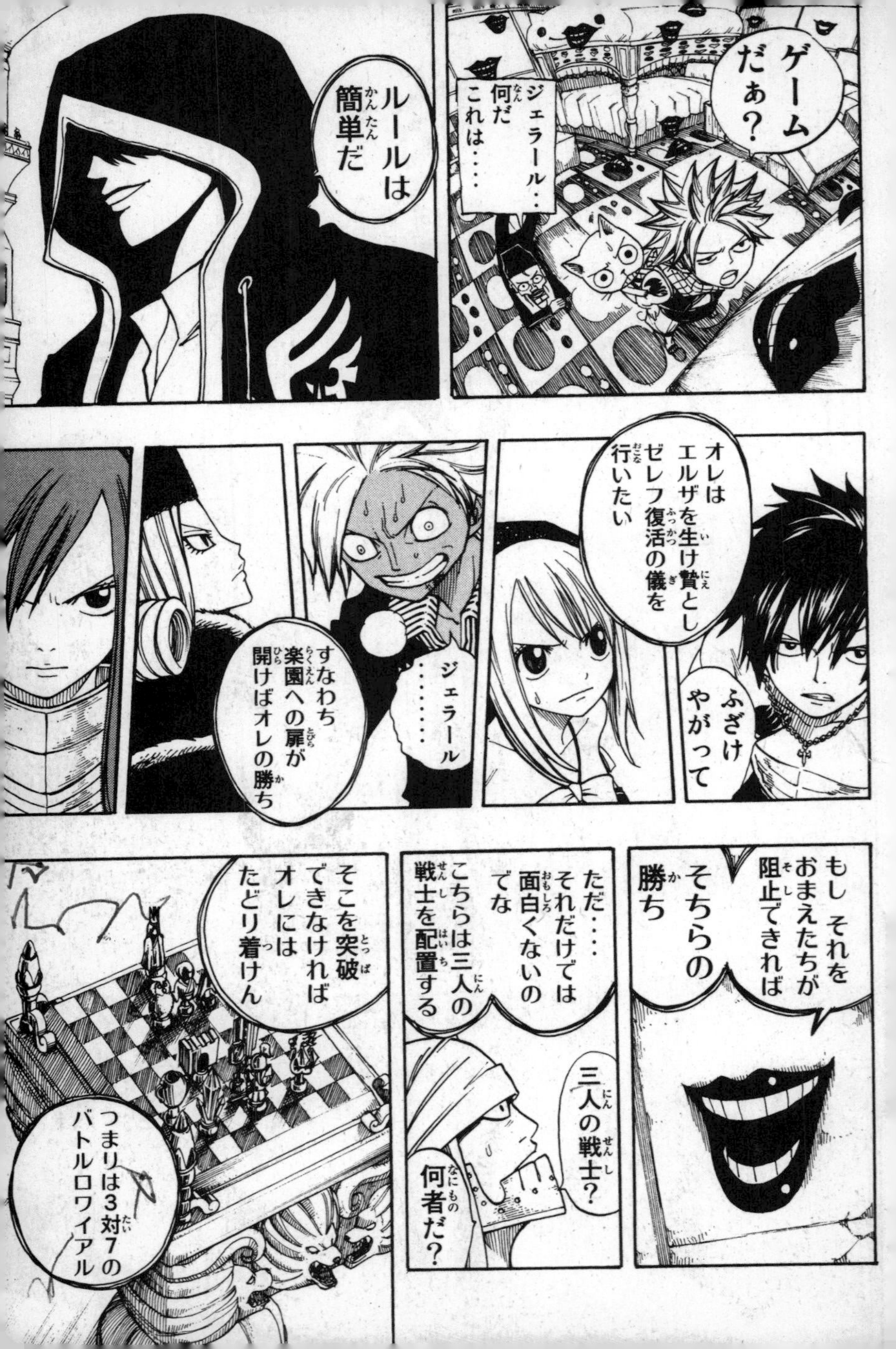
ゲームだぁ？
ジェラール・・・何だこれは・・・・
ルールは簡単だ
オレはエルザを生け贄としゼレフ復活の儀を行いたい
ふざけやがって
ジェラール・・・・・・・
すなわち楽園への扉が開けばオレの勝ち
もし それをおまえたちが阻止できれば
そちらの勝ち
ただ・・・・それだけでは面白くないのでな
こちらは三人の戦士を配置する
三人の戦士？
何者だ？
そこを突破できなければオレにはたどり着けん
つまりは3対7のバトルロワイアル

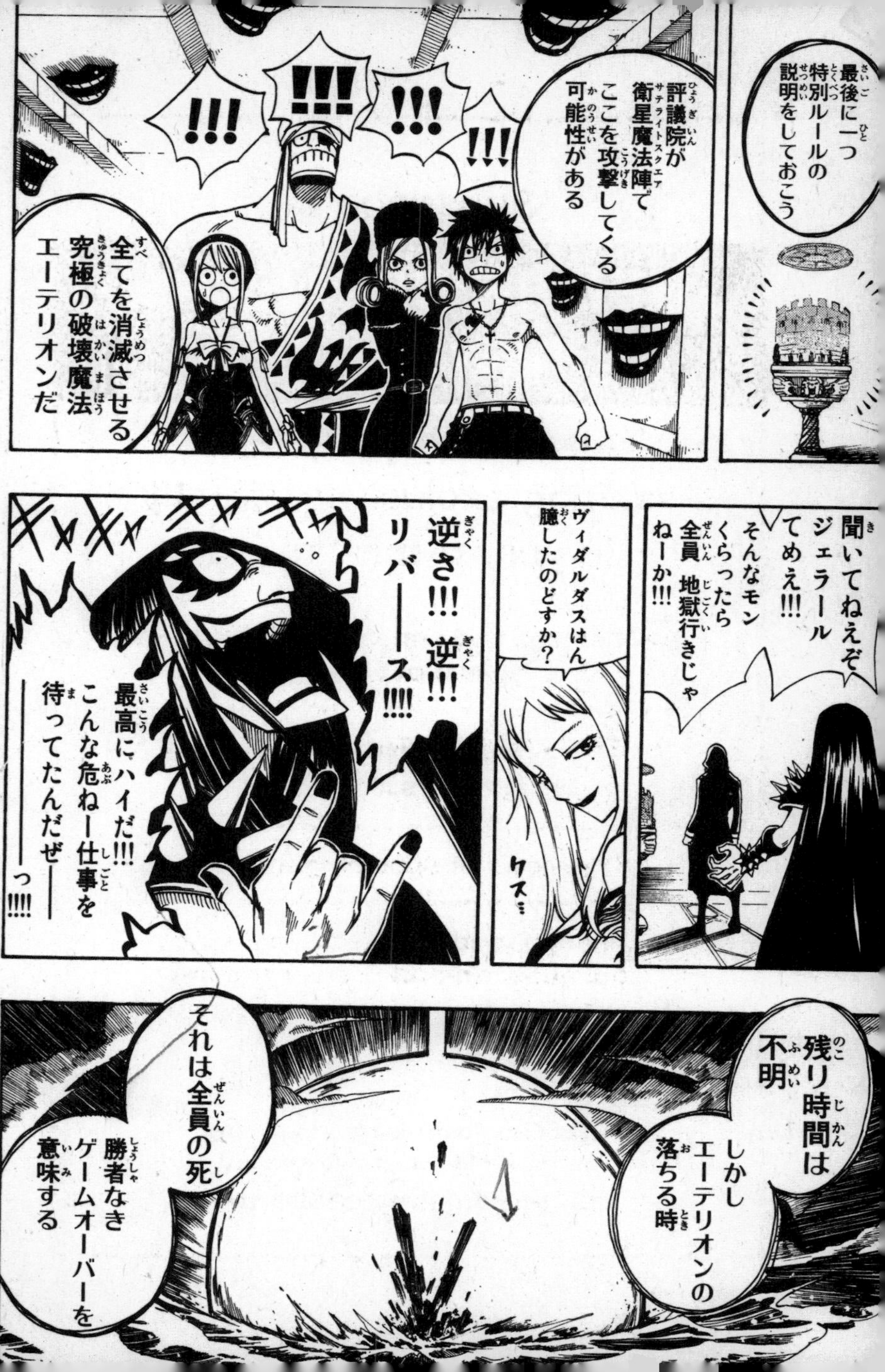

最後に一つ特別ルールの説明をしておこう
評議院が衛星魔法陣でここを攻撃してくる可能性がある
!!!
!!!
!!!
!!!
全てを消滅させる究極の破壊魔法エーテリオンだ
聞いてねえぞジェラールてめえ!!!
そんなモンくらったら全員地獄行きじゃねーか!!!
ヴィダルダスはん臆したのどすか?
クス…
逆さ!!! 逆!!! リバーース!!!!
最高にハイだ!!! こんな危ねー仕事を待ってたんだぜーーっ!!!!
残り時間は不明
しかしエーテリオンの落ちる時
それは全員の死
勝者なきゲームオーバーを意味する

TOMARE!

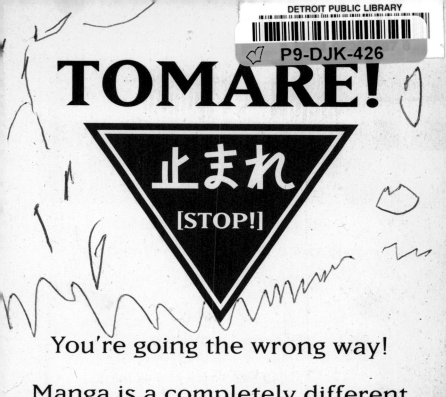

止まれ

[STOP!]

You're going the wrong way!

Manga is a completely different type of reading experience.

To start at the *beginning*, go to the *end*!

That's right! Authentic manga is read the traditional Japanese way—from right to left, exactly the *opposite* of how American books are read. It's easy to follow: Just go to the other end of the book and read each page—and each panel—from right side to left side, starting at the top right. Now you're experiencing manga as it was meant to be!